# Professional Practice for Interior Designers

# Professional Practice for Interior Designers

Christine M. Piotrowski, ASID, IBD

VNR VAN NOSTRAND REINHOLD
New York

Library of Congress Catalog Card Number 88-17389
ISBN 0-442-27519-6

*Part Opening Photo Credits*

| | |
|---|---|
| Part One: | Photo, Gene Balzer |
| Part Two: | Photo, Gene Balzer |
| Part Three: | Photo, Gene Balzer |
| Part Four: | Graphic design and permission to reproduce, Phoenix Design One, Phoenix, Arizona; photo, Gene Balzer |
| Part Five: | Drawing, Tina Swan; photo, Gene Balzer |
| Part Six: | Photo, Gene Balzer |

Printed in the United States of America

Designed by The Total Book

Van Nostrand Reinhold
115 Fifth Avenue
New York, New York 10003

Chapman & Hall
2-6 Boundary Row
London SE1 8HN, England

Thomas Nelson Australia
102 Dodds Street
South Melbourne, Victoria 3205, Australia

Nelson Canada
1120 Birchmount Road
Scarborough, Ontario M1K 5G4, Canada

16  15  14  13  12  11  10  9  8  7  6  5  4

**Library of Congress Cataloging-in-Publication Data**
Piotrowski, Christine M., 1947–
    Professional practice for interior designers / Christine M.
Piotrowski.
        p.     cm.
    Bibliography: p.
    Includes index.
    ISBN 0-442-27519-6
    1. Interior decoration—Vocational guidance—United States.
2. Design services—United States—Marketing.     I. Title.
NK2116.P5 1989
747'.068—dc19                                      88-17389
                                                        CIP

*For my parents, **Martha** and **Casmer:***
*I am sorry you are not here to share this with me.*

# CONTENTS

# PREFACE

Operating an interior design practice is no longer a matter of setting up an office in an unused room and relying on the contacts of friends and relatives for clients. It is a competitive, dynamic, and demanding profession. To be successful today, the interior designer must combine good business practices with aesthetic ability.

With so many design skills to acquire, designers often fail to become familiar with basic business practices. These are often learned on the job—the hard way. Mistakes are made in the preparation of purchase orders, resulting in the receipt of the wrong merchandise. Work is started or orders are placed without signed contracts, which leaves the firm without legal recourse for collections. The company runs out of money to pay its bills and possibly closes because of insufficient projects to generate revenues. Law suits occur related to specification errors, breach of contract, and professional liability. Problems such as these do not discriminate. They affect big firms and small firms equally.

I feel it is important for all professionals and students to have a working knowledge of business practices. Such knowledge is vital for the professional whether he or she works for someone else or owns his or her own business. The professional must constantly search for ways to become more efficient and effective in the profession. The firm's manager or owner must be sensitive to human resources management and efficient business management concepts. And the student must have a basic understanding of business practices in order to be a more effective professional in the future.

This book began after several years of research into design office management and general business practices. The research revealed a lack of information concerning the complete range of business practices specifically for the professional interior designer. Moreover, the texts available to teach a course in professional practice were unsatisfactory. Consequently, I decided to prepare a reference that would be of assistance to the professional and the student in understanding the range of concerns in the establishment and management of an interior design practice.

You will find that this book explores many areas that heretofore have been ignored or given cursory attention in current references on interior design professional practice. Among these are legal responsibilities, personnel management, legal requirements of contracts, the sale of merchandise, general accounting, financial management, marketing, and the search for employment. To be a complete reference on the interior design practice, the book also presents a review of basic principles common in the literature. Among these are the history of the profession, considerations required when organizing a practice, and general project management. This book can help provide important insights into and information on the interior design professional practice for the practicing professional, the owner or manager, and the student searching for an understanding of interior design business.

It is hoped that *Professional Practice for Interior Designers* unravels, in a clear, simple manner, some of the complexities of managing an interior design practice. I hope you will find the information helpful, applicable to your business practice, and thought-provoking.

Readers should note that, when first mentioned in the text, terms included in the glossary are italicized.

## *Acknowledgments*

A project of this scope can never be accomplished truly alone. I would like to acknowledge the many people who played important roles in the completion of the manuscript.

I would like to gratefully acknowledge the following individuals for reviewing portions of the manuscript and providing many excellent suggestions: Jean Wilder; Ken Walters; Kristen Swanson; Lori Cutler, ASID, IBD; David Petroff, IBD; Judith C. Everett; John W. Schabow; Dr. John Durham; and Marena Bennett.

Sincere thanks to the individuals and business organizations that provided much information and the use of their documents: Office Designs; Larry Sneed, Walsh Bros. Office Equipment; Murray Goodman and Barbara Schneider, Goodmans Design-Interiors; Fred Messner, IBD, Phoenix Design One; Betty Upton, Cunninghams Interiors; Jain Malkin, Jain Malkin, Inc.; Tom Williams, AIA, and Karen Payne, Howard Needles Tammen and Bergendoff; Jack Gabus, IBD, Environetics International, Inc.; Elizabeth J. Schroeder and Melanie A. Matus, Perkins and Will; Jan Wynn, ASID, Ball Stalker Co.; Tina Swan, Ambiance; Nancy Green, Herman Miller, Inc.; Robert Bauler, Steelcase, Inc.; and James Chisholm, Transcon Lines.

I would also like to thank the Institute of Business Designers, the American Society of Interior Designers, the National Council for Interior Design Qualification, the American Institute of Architects, and the many publishers who granted permission to reprint information and documents.

Thank you to Christopher C. Everett and Eugene Balzer for photography, Clayton E. Peterson for drawings, and Peter Stephens for production assistance.

Special thanks to Judith C. Everett, Kristen Swanson, Erin Dean, and Dale Hoskins for being able to work willingly under pressure.

Jan Hancock of Knoll International not only went above and beyond the call of duty to obtain important illustrations but also gave continued encouragement throughout the completion of the manuscript.

To my good friend Barbara Munson for adding her special touch early in the development of the final manuscript—a special thank you.

And finally, special thanks for their help to the staff at Van Nostrand Reinhold: Lilly Kaufman, editor; Cynthia A. Zigmund, associate editor; Joy Aquilino, editorial supervisor; and to Kate Scheinman of The Total Book.

# Professional Practice for Interior Designers

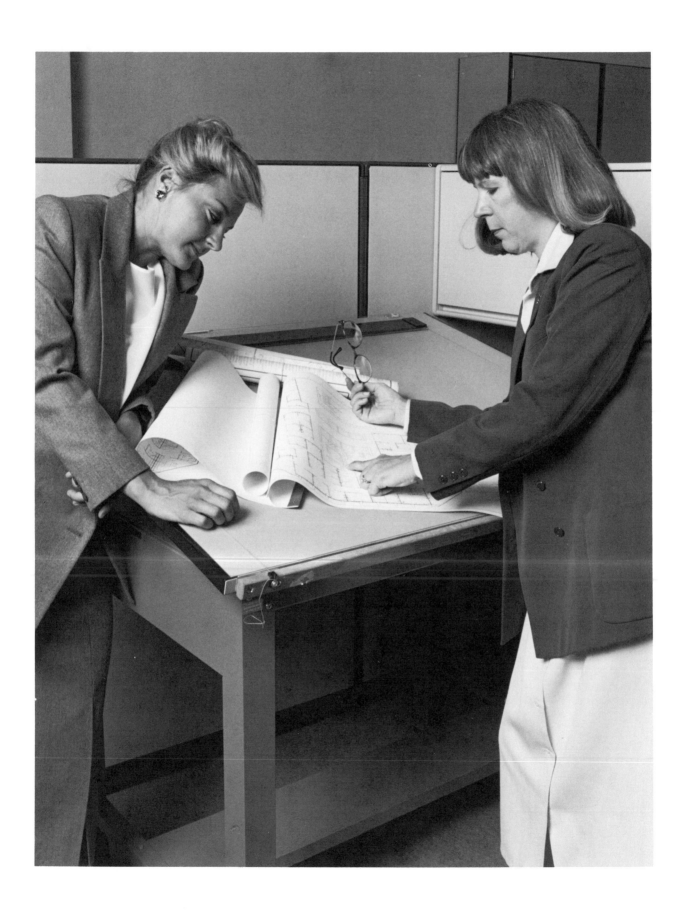

# Part 1

## An Introduction to the Profession of Interior Design

# Chapter 1

## THE PROFESSION

*T*o discuss the broad range of topics involved in the professional practice of interior design without discussing the profession itself would be an injustice. But first, we should ask, What is a profession? Sociologists define a profession as existing when a specific set of characteristics can be associated with it. According to Abercrombie, they are the following:

1. the use of skills based on theoretical knowledge;
2. education and training in these skills;
3. the competence of professionals ensured by examinations;
4. a code of conduct to ensure professional integrity;
5. performance of a service that is for the public good;
6. a professional association that organizes members.[1]

The profession of interior design, as we know it today, is guided by all these points. But the profession itself, and the professionals associated with it, did not evolve overnight. In many ways, it is still evolving.

A professional does not emerge merely from learning the technical principles needed in the profession. To become a professional also requires an attitude of dedicated commitment to the work one does and the advancement of the profession. So must he or she have some understanding of the history of the profession and the issues important to maintaining the vitality of the profession. Understanding what it takes to organize and maintain an interior design practice follows understanding the roots and contemporary concerns of the profession.

To this end, Chapter 1 will present a short history of the profession and the professional organizations as well as the membership requirements of ASID and IBD. It will also review the qualifying examination established as the benchmark for professional membership and licensing as well as examine licensing and title registration issues and professional ethics. It must be noted that each of these topics in itself could constitute a book. However, the purpose of presenting this information in this book is to offer a brief introduction of these topics to serve as a reference about the growth of the interior design profession.

---

[1]*The Penguin Dictionary of Sociology,* by Nicholas Abercrombie, Stephen Hill and Bryan S. Turner (Penguin Books, 1984), copyright © Nicholas Abercrombie, Stephen Hill and Bryan S. Turner, 1984, p. 168. Reproduced by permission of Penguin Books Ltd.

## *History*

Interior design is a young profession. The first use of the term *interior design* did not appear in general usage until after World War II. Prior to that, the profession was known as *interior decoration,* and even that term was not used in relation to a profession until the turn of the twentieth century.

Before the twentieth century, interior decoration was the responsibility of architects and artisans such as the Adam brothers, Antonio Gaudi, William Morris, and Michelangelo. No matter what their "profession" in the arts, they clearly served the function of interior decorators. These architects, painters, sculptors, and other artisans were considered artists or craftsmen. Those who designed and produced the fabrics, carpets, and furniture items were considered shopkeepers. Called *ensembliers* or *ateliers* in Europe, the shopkeepers also did not deal with interior decoration as a profession but as suppliers.

It was Elsie deWolfe (1865–1950) who brought the concept of professionalism to interior decoration. Born in New York City and a member of the upper class, deWolfe began her career as a professional interior decorator in 1904, when she was 39. Her first commission, in 1905, was for the design of the Colony Club in New York City. Her use of white and pastels was a decided change from the dark colors popular during the Victorian period. Among deWolfe's clients were such notable figures as Henry C. Frick and Anne Pierpont Morgan. Because of their often wealthy clientele, the term *society decorator* was often associated with the early decorators. DeWolfe also wrote one of the first true books about interior decoration. *The House in Good Taste* (1913) related her philosophy about decorations for homes.

DeWolfe's success inspired other women to enter the profession. However, formal training was difficult for them to obtain. It was not until 1904 that courses in interior decoration became available. The New York School of Applied and Fine Arts—now known as Parsons School of Design—in New York City was one of the first to offer such courses. Those who could not afford or were unable to avail themselves of formal courses would learn from magazines of the time like *House Beautiful* or *House and Garden*.

After World War I, postwar prosperity began to trickle down to the middle class, allowing an increased interest in and employment of the interior decoration professional. Department stores, with their displays of home furnishings, flourished as women had more time to shop. Manufacturing centers, especially for furniture, arose in places such as Grand Rapids, Michigan, and High Point, North Carolina. Most of these manufacturers produced inexpensive imitations of period pieces which remained popular in the United States. Design education strengthened in many parts of the country.

In the 1920s, the Art Deco style had an important impact on the interior design of houses and offices. Department stores such as Macy's, Wanamaker's, and Marshall Fields constructed vignettes[2] to display the new style. These efforts did much to popularize the Art Deco style in the United States. Art Deco also revolutionized the interior and exterior design of office buildings and other commercial structures. Most interior design in commercial structures was done by men. Dorothy Draper (1889–1969) is credited as being the first woman interior decorator who specialized in commercial interiors.[3]

By the late 1920s, many local Decorators' Clubs had been started in various parts

---

[2]*Vignette*, as used in the interior design profession, means a display of furniture and furnishings that is done to simulate an actual room.
[3]Tate and Smith 1986; 322.

of the country. It was the economic depression of the 1930s that spurred the formation of the first nationwide professional organization for interior decoration.

The Great Depression had a disastrous effect on the ability of the middle class to purchase furniture produced in the United States and Europe. Many furniture manufacturing centers were on the brink of closing. The leaders of the Grand Rapids manufacturing center conceived an idea to bring the decorators to Grand Rapids. Together with William R. Moore of Chicago, they put together a conference to organize a national professional organization. The conference was held during July 1931, in Grand Rapids, and speakers such as Frank Lloyd Wright were scheduled to entice the decorators to the conference. The manufacturers provided the money—and furnishings—for the decorators to design model room displays. And, of course, the decorators were invited to the various manufacturing plants to see the furniture firsthand.

By the end of the conference, the American Institute of Interior Decorators (AIID) had been founded, with William R. Moore as its first national president. In 1936, the organization moved its headquarters from Chicago to New York and changed its name to the American Institute of Decorators (AID).

The early organization established membership requirements based on education and work experience. Over the years, these requirements changed and became more stringent. However, there was still no formal testing for competency.

The profession itself was changing, which complicated membership qualifications and certification of competency. After World War II, nonresidential design was becoming an increasingly important aspect of the profession. The role of the decorators, as established prior to World War II, was especially challenged by those involved in commercial design. New design concepts related to space planning and the design of office and commercial space created tension and arguments over admission and educational requirements. A debate even ensued over the terms *decorator* versus *designer*.

In 1957, a group belonging to the New York branch of AID broke off and formed the National Society for Interior Designers (NSID). Disagreements over qualifications, testing, and terminology continued for many years between the two organizations. In 1961, the American Institute of Decorators became the American Institute of Interior Designers (AID). Finally, in 1975, the American Institute of Interior Designers and the National Society for Interior Designers overcame their differences and merged into one national organization, the American Society of Interior Designers (ASID), which is today's major professional organization with over 28,000 members.

All through the 1960s, discussions regarding educational training and a testing procedure for qualification existed. The NSID favored licensing to restrict practice to qualified professionals; AID favored creation of a qualifying examination. An examination was devised, and in the 1960s and early 1970s, prospective members of AID had to pass the examination for membership. Because of philosophical differences, NSID designed and utilized its own qualifying exam. It was not until 1974 that the National Council for Interior Design Qualification (NCIDQ) was formed to develop a common examination.

As interest in the profession grew, the numbers of programs in colleges, universities, and professional schools increased, as did the number of faculty involved in education. Since most of these educators considered academics as their full-time occupation, many limited their practice of interior design. Needing an organization to keep abreast of the profession as well as advances in educational goals, the Interior Design Educators Council (IDEC) was formed in 1968. Today, IDEC publishes the only scholarly journal of the profession, the *Journal of Interior Design Education and Research*.

As concerns about educational programs evolved, AID, NSID, and IDEC worked together to encourage the creation of the Foundation for Interior Design Education Research (FIDER) in 1973 to deal with the accreditation of educational programs. Today FIDER is the agency charged with evaluating interior design education programs and determining those that meet the standards established for formal accreditation. This organization yearly publishes a list of the schools providing accredited undergraduate and graduate interior design programs in the United States.

In the late 1960s, a new professional organization, the Institute of Business Designers (IBD), was incorporated to meet the needs of the commercial/contract designer. The IBD was conceived in 1963 by members of the National Office Furnishings Association (NOFA) who were concerned about the importance of the interior design service in office furnishings dealerships. Later in 1963, NOFA-d (NOFA designers) was formed as a branch of NOFA. Membership was open to interior designers working for office furnishings dealers, although membership was basically limited to those designers working in Chicago and New York. In 1967, NOFA was renamed NOPA (the National Office Products Association) after merging with stationery and office supply dealers. Meetings began at this time concerning the status of NOPA-d. After discussions and a pledge of assistance from NOPA, NOPA-d became an independent organization in 1969 and was renamed the Institute of Business Designers (IBD). Charles Gelber was elected the first president in 1970. Today, there are over 3000 members of IBD nationwide. The membership remains open to those who work primarily in commercial design. Figure 1-1 summarizes the chronological development of the profession.

All through the evolution of the professional organizations, the furniture and furnishings industry itself was changing. The modernism of the Bauhaus had a great effect on the design of buildings and interiors in the United States from the 1930s on. The industrialism of post–World War II also lead to new manufacturing techniques which changed furniture and design styles.

Trade shows at markets like the Merchandise Mart in Chicago became a popular way for manufacturers to present their new products to the decorators, designers, and other tradespeople. Today, the Neocon Show held in Chicago in June is the largest market show in the country, attracting over 20,000 professionals.

Changes in the philosophy of the workplace created new furniture concepts, such as office landscape. Office landscape was first introduced in Germany in the early 1950s. Office landscape, as practiced in Germany, produced offices laid out without walls, utilizing plants, bookcases, and file cabinets as "screens" while creating wide-open floor plans. As companies embraced this planning philosophy, new specialists in space planning, lighting design, acoustics, and so forth, became part of the profession.

The profession has seen many changes in its brief history and will continue to see changes as efforts in the areas of licensing and certification increase. In 1931, AID prepared the following definition of a decorator: "A decorator is one who, by training and experience, is qualified to plan, design, and execute interiors and their furnishings and to supervise the various arts and crafts essential to their completion."[4]

Today, ASID and IBD endorse the definition of a professional interior designer prepared by NCIDQ. It states:

> The professional interior designer is a person qualified by education, experience, and examination, who

---

[4]Gueft, Olga, 1980, 8. Reprinted with permission, ASID, Copyright 1988, American Society of Interior Designers.

**Chronology**

| | |
|---|---|
| 1904 | First real use of term *interior decoration.* |
| | First courses in interior decoration are offered at the New York School of Applied and Fine Arts. |
| 1905 | Elsie deWolfe obtains her first commission as an interior decorator. (She is credited as being the first interior decorator.) |
| 1913 | Elsie deWolfe publishes the first true book on interior decoration, *The House in Good Taste.* |
| 1920s | Larger marketing effort of home furnishings by department stores. |
| | Manufacturing centers of home furnishings begin to develop. |
| | Art Deco period creates greater interest in interior decoration of homes and offices. |
| | Dorothy Draper is credited as being the first woman interior decorator to specialize in commercial interiors. |
| | Decorator clubs begin forming in larger cities. |
| 1931 | Grand Rapids furniture show. Meeting to create a national professional organization. |
| | American Institute of Interior Decorators (AIID) is founded (July). |
| | William R. Moore is elected first national president of AIID. |
| 1936 | AIID's name changes to American Institute of Decorators (AID). |
| 1957 | National Society for Interior Designers (NSID) is founded from a splinter group of the New York AID chapter. |
| 1961 | AID changes its name to the American Institute of Interior Designers (AID). |
| 1963 | National Office Furnishings Association (NOFA) creates NOFA-d (NOFA-designers), a professional group for interior designers working for office furnishings dealers. |
| 1967 | NOFA and NOFA-d change to NOPA and NOPA-d, respectively, when NOFA merges with stationery and supplies dealers to form National Office Products Association. |
| 1968 | Interior Design Educators Council (IDEC) is founded to advance the needs of educators of interior design. |
| 1969 | Institute of Business Designers (IBD) is incorporated. NOPA-d is the parent organization. |
| 1970 | Charles Gelber is elected the first national president of IBD. |
| 1973 | Foundation for Interior Design Education Research (FIDER) is founded. Responsible for reviewing and accrediting undergraduate and graduate interior design programs. |
| 1974 | National Council for Interior Design Qualification (NCIDQ) is incorporated. Charged with the development and administration of a common qualification examination. |
| 1975 | American Society of Interior Designers (ASID) is formed from the merger of AID and NSID. |

FIGURE 1-1
A chronology of the interior design profession.

1. identifies, researches, and creatively solves problems pertaining to the function and quality of the interior environment
2. performs services relative to interior spaces, including programming, design analysis, space planning, and aesthetics, using specialized knowledge of interior construction, building systems and components, building codes, equipment, materials, and furnishings; and
3. prepares drawings and documents relative to the design of interior spaces

in order to enhance and protect the health, safety, and welfare of the public.[5]

---

[5]The definition of a professional interior designer was formulated by the National Council for Interior Design Qualification (NCIDQ). It has been accepted and adopted by all national interior design organizations in the United States and all national or provincial ones in Canada, by the International Federation of Interior Architects/Interior Designers (IFI), by the Foundation for Interior Design Education Research (FIDER), and by those states in the United States and provinces in Canada with licensing or certification statutes.

Today's interior design professionals and students are faced with continuing changes in the profession. As members work on projects restricted by legal constraints, licensing issues, educational and qualification concerns, public opinion, and better business practices, the profession will continue to grow and evolve.

## Divisions of the Profession

An in-depth discussion of the divisions of the profession and the many career choices within the profession is presented in Chapter 25. However, at this time it would be beneficial to point out that there are two universally accepted divisions of the profession. They are residential interior design and commercial interior design. *Residential design* is concerned with the planning and/or specifying of interior materials and products used in private residences. A private residence could be a free-standing home, a condominium, town house, mobile home, or apartment. *Commercial interior design,* sometimes called contract interior design because of the predominant use of a contract for services, is concerned with the planning and specifying of interior materials and products used in public and private spaces such as offices, stores, hotels, restaurants, schools, airports, and hospitals.

## Membership Qualification

Approximately 30,000 residential and commercial interior designers have become members of ASID or IBD. While many fine interior designers choose not to belong to either professional organization, association with one or the other of these organizations affords the member a network for continued professional growth. The professional organizations provide local chapter meetings, national conferences, professional seminars and workshops, continuing education classes, public relations, business and legal support, promotion of design excellence through nationwide competitions, and public prestige.

In the summer of 1987, ASID consolidated its membership categories into three groupings: Professional, Allied, and Students. The membership categories for IBD consist of Professional, Affiliate, and Allied. A discussion of the qualifications of each membership category follows.

### PROFESSIONAL MEMBERSHIP

Professional membership is the highest category of membership in either ASID or IBD. It is reserved for those members whose work experience, educational background, and successful completion of the NCIDQ examination permits them to apply for this membership category. Only professional members hold voting privileges and may use the appellation *ASID* or *IBD* after their names.

At this writing, the minimal requirements for professional membership are very similar for the two organizations: (1) graduation from a recognized four- or five-year design school or college with a major in interior design or a related field, (2) a minimum of two years full-time employment in interior design (for membership in IBD, this work experience must be with a firm engaged in at least 80 percent contract interior design), and (3) successful completion of NCIDQ examination. This examination will be discussed later in this chapter. Those without these basic professional membership requirements may still apply. To obtain specific membership requirements for those without the basic four- or five-year interior design major, contact the membership chairperson at the local chapter level or request information from national offices.

## ALLIED MEMBERSHIP (ASID)

For ASID, the allied membership category combines Practitioners (working interior designers, formerly called Associates), Affiliates (those in allied professions, such as architecture), Educators, and Press Members into one level. The most significant impact of the change in membership classifications affects the working interior designer. Current Associate members are required to have all the same membership requirements as the Professional member, with the exception of not as yet completing the NCIDQ examination. Moreover, an ASID Associate member must advance to professional membership within five years or face associate membership termination. The new Allied Practitioner category (in effect as of December 31, 1987) allows anyone who has completed a two- to five-year program in interior design or architecture to become an Allied Practitioner member. This program must include a minimum of 48 semester hours in interior design. Prospective Allied members without formal training may apply after achieving a minimum of six years verifiable work experience. This new level sets no time limit for taking and/or completing the NCIDQ examination to rise to professional membership. All members of this new Allied group will be able to use the appellation *Allied Member ASID* after their names.

## AFFILIATE MEMBERSHIP (IBD)

General membership requirements for affiliate membership is the same as for professional membership except, of course, for not yet completing the NCIDQ examination requirement. This membership category is usually utilized by those individuals who have just completed their design education or who have been actively engaged in the profession for some years and wish to become involved in the professional organization.

Affiliate members must apply for and advance to professional membership within three years of eligibility. This includes successfully passing the NCIDQ examination. Those IBD Affiliate members who do not advance to professional membership within three years face termination of their affiliate membership. Those Affiliate members who take but fail the NCIDQ exam sometime during their membership may be granted an extension of an additional two years.

Affiliate members have no voting privileges and may only use the appellation *Affiliate IBD* after their name.

## STUDENT MEMBERSHIP

Both organizations have student memberships available to individuals enrolled in a recognized design school or college program. The ASID has a national Student Chapter Organization with student chapters at approximately 170 colleges, universities, and schools of interior design. Beginning in 1988, students who are part of an interior design program that does not have an ASID student chapter may apply for membership as a Student Corresponding Member. Student members of IBD become members of the local chapter rather than a national student organization.

In both cases, students who maintain their student membership in good standing through graduation may apply for affiliate/allied membership immediately upon graduation. If a student applies within 90 days of graduation, he or she would automatically advance to affiliate/associate membership.

Student members may use the membership appellation *Student Member, ASID* (or *IBD*).

### OTHER MEMBERSHIP CATEGORIES

In addition, each organization has specialized membership categories for those who do not practice interior design. Allied (IBD) membership exists for allied professionals—those engaged as architects, industrial designers, facility managers, graphic artists, photographers, and so on. Education membership is reserved for those who head or teach full-time in a postsecondary interior design program. Trade members (IBD) and Industry Foundation members (ASID) are the membership categories for manufacturing firms and the sales representatives who work for those firms. Press affiliate membership exists for those individuals who work as editors, publishers, and reporters associated with magazines, advertising agencies, or other kinds of media involved with the interior design profession. The ASID's new Allied category includes those working in allied professions, educators, and press members.

None of these membership categories have voting privileges, and none may use the appellation ASID or IBD without using their qualifying classification.

### OTHER PROFESSIONAL ORGANIZATIONS

A few words should be said about other professional organizations with which the interior designer may wish to affiliate. Members of the National Home Fashions League (NHFL) are those mostly involved with the merchandising of furniture and furnishings. Many of the membership work primarily as salespeople, managers, or owners of retail specialty shops.

Some interior designers may be eligible for affiliated membership in the American Institute of Architects (AIA). The AIA is, of course, the professional organization for the professional architect. Complete information regarding qualification and application procedures can be obtained from chapter offices. The end-of-book Appendix lists the addresses of the national offices of the professional organizations mentioned in this chapter as well as others in the United States with which interior designers become affiliated or otherwise involved.

## *NCIDQ Examination*

The NCIDQ, or the National Council for Interior Design Qualification, is the recognized qualifying examination for professional membership in ASID or IBD. The NCIDQ is an independent corporation concerned with maintaining standards of practice through the testing of members of the profession and assisting in the establishment of requirements for legal qualification for licensing and title registration.

The NCIDQ examination is given twice during the year—in April and October. When the membership committee of either ASID or IBD feels a candidate is qualified to sit for the examination, his or her name is submitted to NCIDQ. The organization then contacts the member to advise him or her of the next available examination date.

If the interior designer's application to sit for the examination is accepted, he or she is sent a packet of information containing a study guide. The study guide provides sample questions, a sample design problem, a completed sample problem, and examples of the jurying sheets. It also contains a suggested reading list to help prepare for the written part of the examination.

The examination is a two-part test given on two consecutive days. The first part is a three-and-a-half-hour written examination consisting of 170 multiple-choice questions. This exam covers seven subject areas: programming and planning, theory, communication skills and contract documents, building construction and support systems, materials, business and professional practice, and history. The candidate must answer at least 70 percent of the questions correctly. Many who have taken the exam liken it to a three-and-a-half-hour comprehensive examination on their four or five years of college.

The second part of the exam is a design problem. The 10-hour, juried problem given on the second day tests practical design skills in program planning, space planning, furniture and furnishings, basic building and barrier-free codes, architecture, mechanical systems, presentation skills, and cabinet detailing. These design problems are based on actual projects one might encounter and are devised so as to allow the designer who has been working in either commercial or residential design an equal chance of succeeding.

As of 1987, it is required that applicants take both parts of the examination at the same testing time only the first time they attempt the exam. If an applicant fails both parts at the first try, he or she may choose which section of the exam to attempt at the next exam time. If an applicant takes both parts of the examination at the same time and passes one part, but fails the other, the applicant need only take the part failed. Once the applicant has passed both parts of the exam and continues uninterrupted professional membership in ASID or IBD, he or she would not be required to take the exam again to retain these professional memberships. However, reexamination may be required by state licensing, registration, or certification regulations. Upon eligibility to sit for the NCIDQ, applicants have three years to pass the exam.

### THE STEP PROGRAM

The ASID has devised special study programs to help candidates prepare for the NCIDQ. Although sponsored by ASID, any candidate for the exam may participate. The STEP (Self-Testing Exercises for Pre-Professionals) program assists applicants with study and design skills needed to pass the exams. STEP program leaders point out that the STEP program is not a crash course in design. Rather, it is a means to help preprofessionals learn to study.

STEP I is the study program for the design portion of the exam. The workshop, led by professionals and educators, takes the participant through the design process by means of a concept statement, bubble diagrams, floor plans, equipment plans, preparation of elevations, schedules, cabinet drawings, and perspectives.

STEP II focuses on the written part of the exam. It is also based on a workshop situation; STEP II helps participants relearn how to study and discusses exam-taking techniques. An interim period between workshops requires intensive self-study.

Both STEP programs require substantial fees. However, those who have taken part in either of the programs report them to be useful and worth the expense.

## *Licensing and Title Acts*

Licensing, title acts, legal recognition, certification—all are important topics to the interior design professional and student in the 1980s. Although a "hot" topic today, licensing efforts have been a part of the profession's activities since 1951, when the Southern California Chapter of AID attempted to get a bill passed in the state legislature. They failed. Today, the ASID and IBD national organizations, as well as chapter organizations in many states, continue to fight for licensing. As of this writing, both ASID and IBD seek licensing and/or title registration on a state-by-state basis; IBD also seeks to achieve uniform legal recognition through certification on a national basis.

Licensing and title acts are related since they both require legislation and state control. Title acts are, in fact, a type of licensing. *Title acts* are concerned with limiting the use of certain titles to individuals who meet agreed-on qualifications and who have registered with a state board. Licensing, or *practice acts,* establish guidelines as to what one can or cannot do in the practice of a profession. Individuals who wish to engage in a profession guided by a licensing or practice act must also register with a state board.

Both licensing and title acts, to differing degrees, serve to limit who can practice the profession. A title act does very little to limit who can practice the "activities of interior design," whereas the practice acts do a great deal. The intent of both, however, is to indicate to the consumer which individuals meet the specific criteria related to education and work experience indicating professional competence in the field.

Title acts only restrict the use of the title *interior designer* to those who meet the qualifications of the state title act. Interior designers who meet these qualifications must also register with a state agency or board. An individual who does not meet the qualifications of the title act may not use the title of *interior designer* in any of his or her business dealings. With title registration, the title *interior designer* connotes to the public that the individual meets the highest standards of the profession and can thereby provide the most competent service to the consumer. These standards are related to education, experience, abidance to a code of conduct, and the passing of a qualifying examination.

Practice acts are commonly legislated for those professions that deal with the "health and safety" of the public employing those professions. Lawyers, doctors, architects, and engineers have had to meet state practice act regulations for many years. Practice acts definitely limit who may practice the profession since they usually require very stringent qualification criteria. When a person enters into a contractual relationship with an unlicensed professional, the contract may or may not be enforceable, depending on the statutes in the individual states.

In recent years, some of the emphasis on licensing has been a result of increasing pressure to limit the practice of interior design. Architects, building contractors, and taxing authorities have, in various states, sought to limit the interior design practice by trying to legislate certain activities more common to the interior designer than to other more "traditional" professions.[6] And there are, at this writing, legislative efforts in several states either in effect or under consideration aimed at limiting what the interior designer can do.

An argument used by legislators opposed to licensing and title acts for interior designers is the belief that, since this legislation would limit who may practice the profession, competition would be limited. This limiting of competition might have a direct effect on the size of fees that can be charged. And, of course, high fees not only limit who can afford the service, but can, in time, affect the practice of the profession itself.

Legal recognition based on certification, on the other hand, is not meant to keep people out of practice, but rather to inform and protect the public through the certification of professionals. The IBD has been working toward a system of certifying professional contract interior designers for several years. In 1987, the orga-

---

[6]ASID March 1985.

nization approved the recommendations of the Certification Action Committee. The report recommended that a private corporation, separate from any state agencies, be formed to administer the certification program. The name of the corporation responsible for nationwide certification of professional contract designers is the Governing Board for Contract Interior Design Standards.

The certification program has definable standards, and is based on 39 core competencies. Educational requirements mirror those of FIDER. A minimum of four years of full-time professional experience in commercial design is also required. In addition, the candidate must have successfully passed the NCIDQ examination. He or she must also show continued commitment to his or her own professional growth and the growth of the profession by active participation in one of the professional organizations. Finally, certification requires recertification every three years. Recertification, in part, is based on professional development as marked by obtaining approved continuing education units (CEUs) or university credits related to the field.

Application for certification as a professional contract designer is in two parts. Part One requires the candidate to provide complete education and work experience history. A portion of the application requires the candidate to provide detailed information as to how the designer's responsibilities on six projects relate to 36 core competencies identified by the Governing Board. If the candidate's qualifications meet the minimum standards, the candidate is sent Part Two of the application materials. This consists of four essay questions related to 12 key competencies. The responses are evaluated by independent readers and recommendations are made as to granting certification. The number of those seeking certification is growing with many designers obtaining this new status.

In 1984, IBD and ASID conferees were able to agree that four basic criteria be a part of any title act, licensing or certification proposal and agreed to support only those licensing and title act efforts that at least initially included these four elements. Those four criteria are

Minimum requirements for education and experience.

An examination of minimum competency qualifications.

A Code of Practice Guidelines (Code of Ethics).

A requirement for continuing education.[7]

The organizations also agreed that NCIDQ be responsible for monitoring minimum requirements for education and experience through its testing program.

In 1985, ASID modified its requirements of minimal standards within title act legislation by adopting the following:

First, all bills must contain the NCIDQ definition of interior design. Second, they must require qualifications to take the state exam that are equal to those required to take the NCIDQ exam. Third, the "NCIDQ exam or equal" must be specified as the qualifying exam. Fourth, the bill must include a grandfather clause that states as a minimum: "If one has used the title interior designer for the one year immediately preceding the effective date of the act and meets all the education and/or experience required to take the NCIDQ examination, the exam will be waived, and a license issued if application is received within one year of enactment." Finally, there must be a reciprocity clause permitting designers in other licensed states to secure a license.[8]

---

[7]*Perspective*, Fall, 1984, p. 1. Reprinted with permission from the Institute of Business Designers.
[8]*Report*, January–March, 1985, p. 4. Reprinted with permission, ASID, Copyright 1988, American Society of Interior Designers.

With all this in mind, the reader is no doubt wondering if any states have succeeded in obtaining licensing or title acts. As of the this writing, no state has passed a practice act licensing the interior design profession. However, in 1986, Washington, D.C. did pass the first practice act for interior design. Puerto Rico also successfully passed a practice act. Four U.S. states and one province of Canada have succeeded in passing title acts. In 1982, Alabama became the first state to pass a title registration act. As of July, 1988, Connecticut, Louisiana, Florida, and Ontario, Canada, have passed similar title registration acts. Many other states are working on legislation for either title registration or practice acts.

Whether one works toward licensing, title registration, or legal recognition through national certification, the interior design professional and student must be prepared to accept the legal and ethical responsibilities such recognition brings. The next section discusses the codes of conduct of both professional organizations and Chapter 7 covers the legal responsibilities one must face.

## *Ethics*

One of the characteristics of a true profession is that an organization's members are guided by a set of *ethical standards*. These ethical standards define what is right and wrong in relation to the professional behavior of the members and even the practice of the profession. While a code of ethics does provide definable and enforceable standards, it cannot, by itself, produce ethical behavior. Ethical behavior must come from within the individual designer in his or her dealings with clients, peers, the public, and allied professionals.

The codes of ethics of both ASID and IBD deal with enforceable ethical standards of practice and provide philosophical comments concerning the professional conduct of members. The ASID Code of Ethics (Figure 1-2), revised in 1988, contains standards related to four areas of responsibility: (1) to the public, (2) to the client, (3) to other designers, and (4) to the Society and the profession. The IBD Code of Ethics (Figure 1-3), was adopted in 1980. It consists of three sections: (1) Rules of Conduct, (2) Concepts of Professional Ethics, and (3) Interpretations of Rules of Conduct.

The reader is urged to become familiar with both codes of conduct before completing this chapter. The following summary relates the most important issues of the codes: The designer must not knowingly misrepresent himself or herself or allow other members of the firm to misrepresent themselves or the firm to clients and others. He or she must fully inform the client as to the means of compensation to the designer. The codes prohibit the designer from requesting or accepting any kind of fee or other compensation from suppliers for goods specified. Members are also prohibited from disclosing any confidential information about the client without the permission of the client. The designer may not make any comments about another designer which may result in damaging the reputation of that designer. A member of either professional organization may not interfere with the contractual relationship that is in existence between a client and another designer.

These rules of conduct exist for members of the organization and address their dealings with other designers, whether or not the other designers are members of one of the organizations.

Both ASID and IBD have judicial councils and ethics committees that review ethical charges brought against members. Recently, ASID began to publish in the national newsletter the names of those members whose memberships have been revoked by the national ethics committee. Although this may be personally em-

## CODE OF ETHICS

### American Society of Interior Designers

**Preface**

A member of the American Society of Interior Designers is required to conduct his or her professional practice in a manner that will command the respect of clients, suppliers of goods and services to the profession, and fellow professional designers, as well as the general public. It is the individual responsibility of every member of the Society, both Professional and Associate, to observe and uphold this code and to maintain standards of professional and personal conduct that will reflect in a responsible manner on the Society and the profession.

**Responsibility to the Public**

The designer shall conform to existing laws, regulations, and codes governing business procedures and the practice of interior design as established by the State or Community in which he or she practices.

The designer shall at all times consider the health, safety, and welfare of the public in spaces that he or she designs. The member agrees, whenever possible, to notify property managers, landlords, and/or public officials of conditions within a built environment that endanger the health, safety, and/or welfare of occupants.

The designer shall not engage in any form of false or misleading advertising or promotional activities and shall not imply through advertising or other means that staff members or employees of the firm are qualified interior designers unless such be the fact.

**Responsibility to the Client**

The designer will, before entering into a contract, verbal or written, clearly determine the scope and nature of the project and the method or methods of compensation.

The designer may offer professional services to the client as a consultant, specifier and/or supplier on the basis of a fee, percentage or mark-up.

The designer shall have the responsibility of fully disclosing to the client the manner in which all compensation is to be paid. Unless the client knows and agrees, the designer is forbidden, under this code, to accept any form of compensation from a supplier of goods and services in cash or in kind.

The designer shall perform services for the client in a manner consistent with the client's best interests, wishes, and preferences, so long as those interests, wishes, and preferences do not violate laws, regulations, and codes or the designer's aesthetic judgment, or the health, safety or welfare of the occupants.

The designer shall not divulge any privileged information about the client or the client's project, or utilize photographs or specifications of the project, without the express permission of the client, with an exception for those specifications or drawings over which the designer retains proprietary rights.

The designer shall not present design work to the client which has not been prepared by a professional designer or prepared under the supervision of a professional designer.

**Responsibility to Other Designers**

The designer shall not initiate any discussion or activity which might result in an unjust injury to another professional designer's reputation or business relationships.

The designer, when asked, may render a second opinion to a client, or may serve as an expert witness in a judicial proceeding.

The designer shall not interfere with the performance of another designer's contractual arrangement with a client.

The designer may enter into the design work on a project upon being personally satisfied that the client has severed contractual relationships with a previous designer.

The designer shall only take credit for work that has actually been created by the designer or under the designer's direction.

**FIGURE 1-2**
**ASID Code of Ethics.**
*(Reproduced with permission, American Society of Interior Designers, copyright, American Society of Interior Designers)*

**Responsibility to the Society and the Profession**

In accepting membership in the Society, the member agrees, whenever possible and within the scope of his or her interests and abilities, to encourage and contribute to the sharing of ideas and information between interior designers and other allied professional disciplines as well as the industry that supplies goods and services to the profession, and to offer support and encouragement to students of interior design and to those interested in the study of interior design as well as those entering the profession and to become involved in those community projects which enhance and improve the quality of life for all people.

Any deviation from this code, or from subsequent revisions of it by the Board of Directors of the American Society of Interior Designers, or any action detrimental to the Society and the profession as a whole shall be deemed unprofessional conduct subject to discipline by the Society's Board of Directors.

**FIGURE 1-2**
**ASID Code of Ethics.**
*(Continued)*

# CODE OF ETHICS

## Institute of Business Designers

This Code of Ethics serves not only as a guide to professional interior designers in dealing with complex business relationships, but also as an assurance for our clients. It is also intended to illustrate to young persons entering our profession that contract interior design provides an opportunity to achieve personal growth and to earn the respect of the public.

**Applicability of Rules:**

The Institute's Code of Ethics derives its authority from the Bylaws of the Institute, which provide that the Judicial Council may, after a hearing, admonish, suspend, or expel a Member who has been found guilty of infringing on any of the Bylaws or any provisions of the Rules of Conduct.

The Rules of Conduct that follow apply to all Members involved in the practice of interior design.

A Member may be held responsible for compliance with the Rules of Conduct by all persons associated with the Member in the practice of interior design.

A Member shall not permit others to carry out on his behalf, either with or without compensation, acts which if carried out by the Member would place him in violation of the Rules of Conduct.

**100. Integrity, Objectivity, and Competence**

100.1 A Member shall not make misleading, deceptive, or false statements or claims about professional qualifications, experience, or performance.

100.2 A Member shall not knowingly misrepresent facts and shall not subordinate judgement to others.

100.3 A Member shall not permit his name to be used in conjunction with a design or project in which he was not directly or indirectly involved.

100.4 A Member will participate only in projects that are ethically sound in conformance with pertinent legal regulations.

100.5 A Member shall be required to divulge to his client the complete method of compensation being received for design services.

100.6 Members are specifically prohibited from requesting a fee from a manufacturer or his agent for the specification and/or purchasing of the manufacturer's product on a design project.

100.7 Members are specifically prohibited from accepting a fee offered by a manufacturer or his agent for the specification and/or purchasing of the manufacturer's product on a design project.

100.8 A Member shall conform to all laws relating to his profession and shall not engage in any conduct involving fraud, deceit, misrepresentation, or dishonesty in professional or business activity.

**FIGURE 1-3**
**Excerpts from the IBD**
**Code of Ethics.** *(Reprinted with permission from the Institute of Business Designers)*

### 200. Responsibilities to Clients and Colleagues

200.1 A Member shall not disclose any confidential information obtained in the course of a professional engagement except with the consent of the client.

200.2 Members of the Judicial Council of the Institute shall not disclose any confidential client information that comes to their attention in disciplinary proceedings or otherwise in carrying out their official responsibilities. However, this prohibition shall not restrict the exchange of information within a duly constituted investigative or disciplinary body.

200.3 Members shall not discriminate against any business associate, employee, employer, or applicant because of race, religion, sex, national origin, age, handicap or sexual orientation.

200.4 Members shall recognize and respect the professional contributions of their employees and business associates.

### 300. Other

300.1 A Member may identify himself as a member of IBD in the appropriate category on business cards and stationery, temporary job signs at construction sites, building plaques, professional documents, office identification signs, building directories, and similar professional notices.

300.2 Members may purchase dignified advertisements and listings in newspapers, periodicals, directories, or other publications, indicating firm name, address, telephone number, staff, descriptions of field of practice in which qualified, availability, and cost of basic services.

### Summation:

Members who violate the Rules of Conduct contained in this Code shall be subject to discipline by the Institute in proportion to the seriousness of the violation. The Judicial Council shall have the sole power to interpret these Rules of Conduct. Its decisions shall be final.

Any suspected transgressions of these Rules of Conduct are to be reported to the local IBD Chapter Board, which shall refer the matter to the Judicial Council for review. The Judicial Council is responsible for completely investigating the violation and recommending appropriate action.

Reports may be made directly to the chairperson of the Judicial Council accompanied by a statement as to the necessity for bypassing the Chapter Board.

## 2. CONCEPTS OF PROFESSIONAL ETHICS

To be a professional involves the acceptance of responsibility to the public. The Institute's Rules of Conduct as set forth in Section I are minimum levels of acceptable conduct and, are mandatory and enforceable. It is in our best interests, however, to strive for conduct beyond that merely indicated by prohibitions. Ethical conduct is more than merely abiding by the letter of explicit prohibitions. Rather, it requires unswerving commitment to honorable behavior, even at the sacrifice of personal advantage. The conduct toward which interior designers should strive is embodied in three broad concepts:

### Integrity, Objectivity, and Competence:

A Designer should maintain, at all costs, integrity and objectivity. A Designer should observe the profession's technical standards and strive to continually improve competence and the quality of services.

### Responsibilities to Clients and Colleagues:

A Designer should be fair and candid with his clients and serve them to the best of his ability with professional concern for their best interests, consistent with his responsibility to the public. A Designer should conduct himself in a manner which will promote cooperation and good relations among members of the profession.

### Other Responsibilities:

A Designer should conduct himself in a manner which will enhance the stature of the profession and its ability to serve the public.

The above principles are intended as broad guidelines, as distinguished from the Rules of Conduct. Even though they do not provide a basis for disciplinary action, they constitute the philosophical foundation upon which the Rules of Conduct are based. The following is meant to expand on the above principles. Members are to be cautioned that

**FIGURE 1-3**
**Excerpts from the IBD Code of Ethics.** *(Continued)*

the public is generally unaware of the qualifications required for professional interior designers. To a great extent, we enjoy a privileged trust not available to many other professions. For this reason, we must treat this sacred trust with reverence. Once destroyed, this trust shall not be easily replaced.

Competition is the hallmark of our profession; however, it can be easily abused. Members should be cautioned to maintain their professionalism when competing against IBD Members or other designers.

It must be remembered that our goal is to provide our clients with professional interior design services. Free design sketches, office layouts, or other design services, except through recognized design competitions, may provide a premature design solution, which may deceive the client in evaluating the capabilities of the Designer.

Members should strive to make clear to the client that the primary considerations in selection of a Designer should be ability and competence to provide the services required. Members should not compromise the quality or adequacy of services to be provided in establishing compensation.

As professionals, Members should not undertake any engagement which they cannot reasonably expect to complete with professional competence.

Members should also be cautioned as to the type of representatives engaged to solicit design work from clients. As professionals, we are responsible to the client for those who speak for us.

When a Designer is in the position of being responsible for providing some or all of the furnishings and finishes specified, the Designer must take extra care to ensure that the sales transaction is handled in an ethical manner and that the client is aware that a portion of the compensation does derive from the profit on the sales.

In the performance of professional services, Members shall not allow their own financial or other interests to affect the exercise of independent, professional judgement on behalf of their clients.

Members should conduct themselves in a professional manner to inspire the confidence, respect, and trust of their clients and of the public.

If a Member becomes involved in a project that is deemed unsafe or economically unfeasible, or about which the Member has serious moral reservations, he should notify the client.

Members should strive to maintain and improve their professional knowledge through participation in continuing education and other professional development programs.

Members should refrain from illegal and immoral conduct and should reveal voluntarily to the Chapter officers all knowledge of Members' conduct that they believe to be in violation of the Code of Ethics.

Members should provide their associates and employees with a suitable working environment, compensate them fairly, and facilitate their professional development.

**FIGURE 1-3**
**Excerpts from the IBD Code of Ethics.** *(Continued)*

barrassing to the member whose name appears in print, it also may serve to advise all members that the code of ethics will be enforced by the organization.

The IBD Code of Ethics, in the section "Concepts of Professional Ethics," provides a fitting ending to this discussion.

To be a professional involves the acceptance of responsibility to the public. The Institute's Rules of Conduct . . . are minimum levels of acceptable conduct and are mandatory and enforceable. It is in our best interests, however, to strive for conduct beyond that merely indicated by prohibitions. Ethical conduct is more than merely abiding by the letter of explicit prohibitions. Rather, it requires unswerving commitment to honorable behavior, even at the sacrifice of personal advantage.[9]

---

[9]"Code of Ethics." Reprinted with permission from the Institute of Business Designers, 1980, p. 3.

# *Summary*

Having an understanding of the roots and issues of a profession is an important part of being a member of that profession. Knowing what it is all about is crucial to making the time spent in the career a meaningful commitment of time and effort rather than an ordinary "job." Society tends to grant professionals higher status, money, and respect. Yet these do not come only with accomplishing the educational criteria of the profession. They come to the individual with the attitude of service, commitment, and knowledge expected of the professional.

In this chapter we have looked at the issues surrounding the profession of interior design: professional membership, qualification, licensing, and ethics. In the next chapter we will briefly look at personal goal-setting.

# Chapter 2

## PERSONAL GOAL-SETTING

*O*pening a studio is the dream for almost everyone who has entered the career of interior design. If not one's own studio, then the professional involvement as a design director for a major design office. Perhaps the career dream is to work for a major manufacturer. Maybe having a project published. Or to be a chapter or national officer in one of the professional organizations. It may, of course, be any number of other career and professional titles and achievements. Yet for many, these goals are never reached.

Family, friends, children—all these obligations and others can enter the picture and hold one back from reaching personal goals. But in most cases, the inability to achieve a goal or a dream is not due to other individuals or job responsibilities. Rather, it is more a case of a lack of planning, a lack of goals. Or maybe, setting the wrong goals.

Although businesses spend a lot of time and energy determining and setting goals for the coming year, individuals often ignore their own needs for the future. In this chapter we will look at personal goal-setting.

## *Goals*

*If You Don't Know Where You're Going, You'll Probably End Up Somewhere Else*[1] is the title of a wonderful book. To know where you are going can sometimes be very difficult. But without some kind of direction, your personal and professional life can be very frustrating and unfulfilling.

Most people have dreams, but many have no goals. Dreams are imaginary hopes, whereas to many, goals are concrete ideas representing some kind of end that a person tries to achieve. Philosophically, goals are brief stops along the way of life that mark achievement in an individual's personal and professional life. Finally owning your own studio one day is not an end even though it may have been the goal. Now you must be ready to create new goals related to the success and growth of the studio. Goals are concrete ideas requiring effort and commitment for their achievement.

---

[1]Campbell 1974.

## Risks in Goal-Setting

Many people have difficulty setting goals or don't consciously bother once they have achieved some immediate goal like getting a job in the interior design field. To set a goal requires commitment of time, energy, mental processes, and so on. Some do not wish to really make a commitment of any kind much beyond their immediate physiological needs. Setting goals also runs the risk of failure—that is, not achieving the goal. But not achieving the goal does not automatically mean failure. The goal may have been unattainable at the present time for one reason or another.

Because there are risks in setting goals, goals must be set with certain considerations in mind. First, set goals that satisfy you—not a husband, a wife, a boyfriend, a girlfriend, parents, or peers. If you are setting a goal to please someone else, you will probably never achieve it. And should it be achieved, it may never bring you satisfaction.

Second, some goals are unattainable without proper experience. To own your own studio or to be a design director does not happen overnight. It takes time to gain the experience to have these opportunities. For a student just ready to be graduated from college to set a goal of being a design director in two years would be to invite disappointment. The attainment of such a goal would happen in only the most extraordinary situation.

Third, don't be afraid to change goals or change directions. Life is not perfect, and reality usually does not match fantasy. Be flexible in goal-setting. If you desire to open your own studio by the time you are 30, but unexpected circumstances make reaching that goal impossible within that time frame, you may have to wait until you are 35 or even 40.

There is one undisputable fact about life: Life will change. For most, change means growth. So don't be afraid to grow. Mary had a goal to be a design director with a major dealer. One day she was offered a two-year position as a designer in Hawaii. Not looking at the possibilities that opportunity would provide in the future, she refused the position and stayed working in a medium-sized city in the northwest. Several years later, still not in a position to be a design director, she looks back longingly at that lost opportunity. Do not be afraid to take different paths of opportunity.

## Setting Goals

The best way to set goals is to try to look at yourself in the future. An instructor this writer had in college had the class write their own obituaries. A rather jarring thought at age 21. But the idea was to focus on long-range goal-setting—what each student wanted to be remembered for, what each hoped would be accomplished by the time he or she passed away some time in the future.

Understandably, writing your own obituary is difficult to do. It may be easier to start thinking of what you want to accomplish by the time you are 30 and 40 and 50 and at retirement age. And if you find *that* too hard to do, try to figure out where you want to be in your professional and personal life during the next five years.

Once you have some idea where you want to be, you can start looking at that goal in terms of the concrete things that need to be accomplished in order to get there. "I want to own my own studio by the time I am 35." What kinds of work experience will be needed to meet that goal? Where do you want that studio to be located? Where will you get the finances to open the doors? Do you want to work alone or with someone else? Being your own boss sounds goods, but are you going to be willing to sacrifice family and personal time to keep the studio in operation? These are some of the questions related to that goal.

Some of the mini-goals related to achieving the preceding goal might be

- Work with a residential firm for five years to gain experience in residential practice.
- Work with a commercial firm for five years to gain experience with general commercial clients.
- Become a senior designer or design manager with either a residential or commercial firm in order to gain business and management experience.
- If necessary, take additional business classes at a community college or an MBA program to gain the business knowledge to own your own studio.

These are all concrete mini-goals needed to accomplish the larger goal of owning your own studio. Once the opportunity of opening that studio occurs, new goals must be decided related to the business and the next "stop" on the road.

## Summary

It is important for all of us to make goals in order to provide direction to our lives. Setting goals is risky and they take commitment, but if the goals we set are goals that interest us, they will likely be fulfilled.

Achieving a goal may or may not be within our control. It must be remembered that some goals take a certain kind of expertise or maybe a credential like an M.B.A. Without the expertise or credential, accomplishment of the goal may be unlikely. Goals take time. Just as Rome was not built in a day, becoming the owner

---

**GOALS**

The purpose of this exercise is to analyze skills, interests, and abilities in relation to the kind of job opportunities you will be seeking in interior design. Completing this exercise will make you more aware of what you have to offer your present or future employers as well as discover some goals to work on in the next year or so. Answer the following questions in as many or as few words as necessary.
  1. What kind of skills in interior design do you have?
  2. What special skill(s) do you have to offer your present employer or another employer?
  3. If you were going to a job interview tomorrow, what specific career goal would you share with the interviewer?
  4. List three of your biggest successes.
  5. List three of your biggest "failures."
  6. List five goals you wish to accomplish during the next calendar year.
  7. List three goals you hope to accomplish by the time you are thirty.
  8. List three goals you hope to accomplish by the time you are fifty.
  9. Assuming it were possible for you to achieve any goal in interior design, what would it be?
  10. List ten mini-goals needed to support that ultimate goal.

FIGURE 2-1
Personal goals exercise.

of the biggest dollar-volume interior design firm in the country does not come overnight. And life changes. Do not be afraid of making changes if the opportunity looks interesting.

Figure 2-1 may help in setting goals related to a career in interior design. Those who have difficulty in setting goals may also wish to read one of the books listed in the bibliography or find others on goal-setting and self-direction.

# Part 2

## How to Establish an Interior Design Practice

Chapter 3

---

# THE BUSINESS PLAN

*A*nyone who might consider starting his or her own business should prepare a business plan. "Fundamentally, a business plan (also referred to as a proposal, a prospectus, or a brochure) is the primary vehicle for giving credibility to an idea."[1] If the interior design practice will involve the resale of goods, the business plan may well be the key to obtaining necessary funding from banks or venture capitalists. An interior design practice which obtains revenue from selling services requires less initial funding. In this case, the business plan is prepared more to provide substantive thought as to what the business is all about and how it is going to operate.

In this chapter we will look at the business plan—or business planning—with the latter considerations more in mind. Just as we saw in Chapter 2 that personal goal-setting helps the individual know where he or she is going, business planning helps the firm know where it is going.

## *The Business Plan*

There is no sure-fire way to prepare a *business plan*. One should not look for a perfect "template" plan which requires the prospective owner to only fill in the blanks. Nor should one look to his or her attorney, accountant, or banker to provide all the answers. The business plan is a personal expression of what the owner feels the firm is all about and how he or she hopes it will grow. Although preparing a business plan will not guarantee success, the process of thinking the business through will help the prospective owner face the realities of starting the business. The plan, if thoroughly done, also provides the opportunity to anticipate problems and avoid them, if possible—or at least to know how to cope with them as they arise.

The business plan is not something that can be done overnight. If a designer is anticipating opening a practice, the prospective owner should allow time to develop the business plan. It may take weeks or even months for this to be prepared, depending on how much time can be devoted to the research and writing of the

---

[1]Dible, Donald M., *Up Your Own Organization.* Reprinted by permission of the publisher, Reston Publishing Company, Prentice-Hall, Inc., © 1974, p. 118.

plan. At times, outside consultants may be required to help, especially if a formal plan is being prepared to obtain substantial financial backing.

If the owner finds himself or herself preparing the plan after opening for business, an even greater time may be required since the owner must keep the business going at the same time. An outside business consultant familiar with the interior design profession may be helpful in this case.

The plan, once completed, helps the prospective owner in many ways toward the goal of having his or her own practice. The plan helps the designer to see if the idea is realistic and feasible. Financial backing will be easier with a well-prepared plan. The business plan also sets initial goals and objectives for the firm, which can be measured by the performance of the firm. Later, if performance does not meet these initial objectives, the plan and the ongoing analysis of the plan help the owner determine what to do to get back on track—assuming the plan was feasible in the first place.

# *Research*

An important ingredient of all business plans is research. A very thorough period of research should be undertaken before the business plan is written. Certain kinds of information are always expected to appear in the plan. It will be necessary to complete research in areas of skills and abilities, the marketplace, operational considerations such as pricing, expected capital required, and projected financial planning. For all prospective interior design practices, items one through seven in the following list must be thoroughly investigated and considered. Depending on the actual business idea and use of the plan, the next three items and more research must be prepared to culminate in item eleven, production of the plan.

The following steps outline the kind of research that the interior design practice owner must develop in order to prepare the business plan. The outline presented is the suggested sequence in which the research should be conducted.

### *Business Plan Research*

1. Analyze personal abilities and interests related to owning an interior design business. If additional employees are anticipated or are already hired, analyze their abilities.
2. Analyze the potential market for the firm's services including the existing competition.
3. Prepare a marketing plan which includes what aspect of the market the firm will address. Determine pricing policies, what services the firm will offer, and considerations for advertising and/or promotional activities.
4. Determine which business formation will be used: a sole proprietorship, a corporation, or a partnership.
5. Determine legal responsibilities and tax obligations. Consult with an attorney concerning contracts and liabilities, an accountant concerning record-keeping, and an insurance representative on insurance obligations.
6. Estimate how much capital will be required to "open the doors." Estimate the first year's expenses. Determine sources of initial capital.
7. Develop a financial plan and income projections. Include projected balance sheets, income statements, and cash-flow forecasts.
8. If the firm will engage in retail selling of inventoried goods, develop an inventory plan of what will be purchased, where it will be stored, and when it will be purchased.

 9. Prepare an organizational plan including job descriptions, employee benefits, projected personnel needs, and purchasing procedures.
10. Develop a concept of the firm's image: appearance of letterhead, business cards, exteriors of delivery trucks, title blocks for drawing paper, and so on.
11. Produce the business plan.

The most important parts of the research for the business plan will be steps two and seven. One must clearly determine if the services the interior designer wishes to provide are needed in the community and if one can obtain the capital to start and maintain the business. If the research concerning either of these concerns is in doubt, the business venture should be reconsidered or possibly rejected.

## *Writing a Business Plan*

After the research has been done, the actual writing can be prepared. In most cases an overview of the company should come first, with the financial material second. The books in the bibliography provide several outlines of business plans. The following outline is but one suggestion.

I. Business summary
   A. Name of owner or board of directors.
   B. Location of business.
   C. Type of business formation (legal structure).
   D. Description of business, including types of services to be performed.
   E. A summary of the owner's and/or manager's expertise in running the business might be desirable.
II. Market research
   A. Describe how the information concerning the business was obtained.
   B. Describe the need for the firm's service in the community. Include numbers of potential clients for your service.
   C. Describe as much as possible about the known competition.
   D. Detail existing sales for this kind of firm in the community. This might be available from the chamber of commerce.
   E. Describe any industry or local trends that might affect the success of the projected firm.
III. Marketing plan
   A. Detail what portions of the market the firm will address.
   B. Describe what services will be offered. This may be detailed enough to explain how boards will be done.
   C. Determine how services and/or products will be priced.
   D. If a warehouse/delivery service is used, determine how these charges will be passed on to the client.
   E. Outline what kinds of advertising and promotional activities will support the business.
   F. Describe any problems concerning expected seasonal business, if this appears applicable.
IV. Operational plan
   A. Organizational structure.
   B. Hiring of personnel and job descriptions.
   C. Recordkeeping and control.
   D. Employee benefits.

E.  Dealings with suppliers, delivery people, and subcontractors.
F.  Customer relations.
G.  Projected personnel needs.
V.  Financial information
    A.  Projections of initial capital and first-year estimates to keep the business operating. Detail how the money will be expended.
    B.  Estimates of additional revenue (monthly) beyond break-even points.[2]
    C.  Month-by-month projected profit-and-loss statements.
    D.  Accounting practices to be used—especially those related to depreciation, leasing, and inventories.
    E.  A beginning balance sheet.
    F.  An explanation of how projections were made.
    G.  Any additional information required of a corporation form of business.

Remember that starting a business should involve serious thought and time, or failure may result. If the prospective owner is not willing to devote the time and effort to producing a well-written business plan, he or she may not be ready to expend the energy to keep it going either.

## *Control and Evaluation*

Planning the design business is very important. But it is equally important to evaluate the progress of the practice. Many portions of the business plan will establish some of the control mechanisms that can be used to evaluate the financial and organizational success. For example, financial projections prepared in the business plan can easily be compared to actual performance. Project pricing developed in the marketing plan section can be compared to actual performance. Additional control reports might well be suggested by the firm's accountant, attorney, or from the experience of the owner/manager. These reports should address issues of asset management, productivity, and profitability. Many of these control and evaluation reports are discussed in Chapter 12 on financial management control.

## *Summary*

Knowing you want to open an interior design practice and having the skills and experience are not enough. It is important to analyze the abilities of all the individuals as well as the goals and policies of the proposed practice. Through this research and analysis, the best possible decisions about the configuration, direction, and future of the practice can be made. If the prospective owner or the current owner/manager is not willing to put in the effort to develop a well-thought-out business plan, he or she may not be ready to own or operate a practice. The business plan could very well be the most important piece of "design" work the owner/manager does in his or her career.

In this chapter, we have discussed the need for and definition of the business

---

[2]The *break-even point* is the point at which revenues equal expenses. At this point, the firm is neither making nor losing money.

plan. This chapter also describes the steps in developing the research material required to prepare a business plan and provides a general outline for the plan. The prospective owner or current owner/manager who is interested in preparing a business plan for an interior design practice should refer to one of the suggested books in the bibliography. Other sources may be found at the public library, in bookstores, or from the Small Business Administration.

# Chapter 4

## ADVICE AND COUNSEL

*A*ll potential business owners need certain professional advisers and counselors. Since very few people have expertise in all areas of business, the potential interior design practice owner should find the best advisers possible to help establish and maintain the practice.

In this chapter we will discuss the most important advisers one should consider engaging when starting or operating an interior design practice. Those advisers are accountants, who provide information concerning financial matters; attorneys, who render assistance in many legal areas; bankers, who may help obtain the financing the firm needs to operate; insurance advisers to help obtain proper insurance protection; and technical consultants, who are the many allied professionals who help the interior designer with specialized design problems.

## *Accountants*

One of the most important sources of advice and counsel will be from the firm's accountant. The new firm will probably retain an accountant rather than hire one as an employee. A large existing firm may have one or more bookkeepers or accountants on their staff and retain an outside accounting firm to do special reports. The accountant's job is to help the business owner decide what kinds of operational reports are going to be needed, to provide guidance in how to prepare them, to assist the owners in interpreting these reports, and to prepare the needed financial accounting reports such as the profit and loss statement,[1] balance sheet, and income statement. The accountant or accounting firm may also be needed for other important financial reporting activities, discussed below.

Day-to-day operational accounting—commonly called bookkeeping—may be done by the owner or an experienced bookkeeper. Daily bookkeeping reports are the means for the firm to keep track of income and expenses. From daily opera-

---

[1] A profit and loss statement is a clearing account that summarizes the net income or loss for the accounting period. In most cases, the profit and loss statement looks very much like a formal income statement.

tional bookkeeping records, formal financial reports such as the balance sheet can be prepared. These records, along with any other reports suggested by advisers or required by the owners, provide the quantitative financial and managerial picture of the operation of the firm. More specific concepts of accounting are discussed in Chapters 11 and 12.

The first thing the accountant will do for the firm is set up a list of bookkeeping records. He or she may also provide training to the owner or employees in how to do the bookkeeping. Another responsibility of the accountant will be to help the owner organize the office procedures for the bookkeeping functions. Included in this is the selection and/or design of forms needed for recordkeeping.

Another important initial job of the accountant will be to prepare local, state, and federal tax applications. If there are employees in the firm other than the owners, he or she will also need to file additional records with the state and federal governments. The credentials needed for such filings will be discussed more fully in Chapter 6.

The accountant, having knowledge of the owner's financial condition, will be able to provide counsel on the financial requirements of the business and the financial commitment of the owners to the business. Many business ideas fail as a result of the inability of the owners to meet the initial financial obligations of starting an interior design practice. Many others fail when the firm cannot bring in enough revenue to pay the expenses of the practice. The accountant can help the interior designer determine whether or not the designer has enough money to begin the type of practice desired, and if there is enough potential revenue available to keep it going.

As the months go by, the accountant will be retained to prepare formal financial statements. The balance sheet, income statement, and changes in financial condition will help the owner see where he or she stands at given points in time. These reports will also be required by lending institutions, investors, and perhaps creditors in order to obtain operating funds or credit to purchase needed supplies and products. All these reports are detailed in Chapter 11.

The accountant may be called upon to help the owner prepare nonfinancial reports related to financial and operational functions, called managerial reports. These managerial reports provide important information to the owner on the way the business is operating rather than on the dollars of revenue and expense the business generates. These reports are discussed in Chapter 12.

The accountant not only will help the firm file the necessary taxing credentials, but will also prepare the periodic tax returns required by the state and federal government. How often these returns are filed and what information is required will vary slightly depending on the type of business formation selected.

There are two other important responsibilities of the business for which the accountant can be of help. One is to advise the firm on the sales tax liabilities it will have. Sales tax is imposed by cities, states, and the federal government whenever tangible property is exchanged from a seller to a consumer. Even though the consumer is liable to pay the tax, the seller must actually collect and return this money to the appropriate tax agency. Each taxing authority has different regulations on what items or services must be taxed. The accountant should advise the interior designer in this important issue.

The other area of counsel where an accountant helps involves preparing credit reports needed for the firm to obtain a credit listing. Credit listing agencies serve as clearinghouses on the credit soundness of businesses. Other businesses, like manufacturers, will look for these credit listings before extending credit to the interior design firm. The design firm should strive for a credit listing with one of these agencies. A very important general agency is Dun and Bradstreet (D & B). D & B is a national credit agency that lists all kinds and sizes of businesses. The Allied Board of Trade is one of many specialized agencies. It provides credit information on interior designers. Another specialized agency is the Lyon Furniture Mercantile Agency. This agency is important for those designers who wish to provide retail sales of goods along with design services.

## Attorneys

The firm's attorney will be as important as the accountant. The attorney will be needed to help with the formalities of setting up the business. If the firm is starting as a corporation, it is extremely important to retain an attorney to set up the legal forms of the corporation. A partnership form does not require an attorney, but it is highly advisable to have the aid of an attorney to set up the partnership agreements. The sole proprietorship form does not require an attorney to aid in the business formation, but one should be consulted about the legal ramifications of starting a business.

The attorney should be involved in the development of design contracts. This does not mean that the attorney must review each contract the interior designer prepares. Rather, he or she must work with the designer in developing a standardized or typical contract. The firm may decide to utilize one of the ASID, IBD, or AIA standardized contracts. The attorney can help decide if any of these are appropriate to the firm's needs or if something else is more appropriate.

With the escalating number of liability suits, the attorney can provide counsel on how to avoid a potential suit. The professional designer must be aware of what kinds of actions can get him or her into legal trouble. Awareness should help the designer avoid legal consequences. An attorney will, of course, be needed to represent the design firm if any suits are brought by other parties.

## Bankers

Any new business needs to have a banker on its "team" of advisers and counselors. First of all, banking facilities that will handle the firm's account need to be located. The business will need a commercial account. Commercial accounts, especially for the sole proprietorship, show the business community that the firm is a serious business.

In addition to a location for the firm's commercial accounts, banks and bankers can help the interior design practice in many ways. The bank can provide the designer with help in checking credit references of clients. Just as potential creditors of the firm will check with the bank on the firm's financial situation, the designer should be checking on potential clients' creditworthiness.

When the business needs to borrow money, whether for initial capitalizing funds or other needs, banks would be the first source of funds. In addition, banks have information on investors who may wish to invest in or loan money to the firm.

Once the firm is financially healthy, some banks can provide services concerning investments. This advice may concern general investment information for the firm or assistance in setting up profit-sharing plans for the employees.

# *Insurance Advisers*

The interior design practice, whether providing only specifications and drawings or also providing goods to clients through the resale process, will have some insurance requirements. The firm with part-time or full-time employees will also be required by law to have certain kinds of insurance. A qualified insurance agent who handles commercial businesses will be another adviser the firm will need.

The exact combination of insurance a firm requires will depend on the actual practice. A firm should definitely consider malpractice insurance. Malpractice insurance, called professional liability insurance, protects the designer in the event an action causes bodily injury or property damage as a result of the professional negligence of the designer. This is the same kind of insurance physicians obtain for malpractice. The ASID does sponsor a policy for this kind of protection.

The firm will probably require general insurance to cover property damage, liability, and personal injury. This is often sold as a grouping of insurance coverage. Any practice that owns its facility would consider this group of insurance coverage a must. Where the practice rents space, insurance covering the same situations would be required. Property damage insurance protects the building and any improvements made to the interior of the building. It also covers damage or loss to studio furniture, office equipment, and inventory.

Liability policies provide protection for acts of negligence by the designer/owner as well as other employees or individuals that the owner hires. For example, the bodily injury/property damage part of the insurance would pay for damage to the other party if a delivery person had an accident on the way to the client's house. Another liability insurance the practice may wish to have would provide product liability insurance. Product liability insurance provides protection when the products and/or installation of products causes some injury to the client. Finally, depending on the nature of the interior design practice, the firm may require insurance to protect the designer if the subcontractors and contractors the designer hires do not have insurance.

Personal injury insurance provides protection should the designer be sued for libel, slander, or defamation as well as other torts against a person, such as invasion of privacy. These torts are explained in more detail in Chapter 7.

Additional insurance will be required for vehicles owned and operated by the firm and the firm's employees. This might include insurance for personal cars used for the firm's business.

When the firm adds employees, additional insurance coverage may be either required or desirable. The government requires the employer to provide workers' compensation insurance to protect the employee in case of work-related injuries. The firm may also wish to provide health and possibly life insurance to employees as a benefit of working for the company.

# *Technical Consultants*

Almost every interior design firm—especially the newly organized firm—will require the advice and counsel of allied professionals. Architects, electrical engineers, lighting designers, other mechanical systems consultants, and contractors are some of the allied technical counselors that a firm will occasionally consult.

These allied professionals may not be full-time employees of the firm. More likely, the interior design firm will establish a working relationship with these professionals and hire them on a per-job basis, just as a client would hire an interior designer. The interior design firm should not be afraid to admit the need for these professionals. Interior designers preparing documents without the proper license and expertise can easily be sued by the client.

## *Summary*

It is easy to see that there are many very important advisers that the interior design firm owner should consult. No one designer, or even group of design professionals, will have the education or job experience to have all the answers. Business advisers such as accountants, attorneys, bankers, and insurance advisers will help with specialized business questions that may arise for any interior design practice. Allied professionals can offer the firm advice on technical matters that the staff of the design firm may not be familiar with or legally qualified to handle. These advisers are engaged to help the firm remain professionally competent, to stay out of legal problems, and most important, to remain a viable business.

Chapter 5

# BUSINESS FORMATIONS

*T*here are several kinds of business formations for an interior design practice. All have their advantages and disadvantages for the small business owner. It is important for the designer wishing to start his or her own business to understand the differences between these formations as they relate to financial liability, taxes, and other issues so that he or she may choose the business formation most suitable to the designer's business plan. An appreciation for the various forms is necessary for understanding the responsibilities of the owner.

This brief discussion will not provide all the answers concerning the selection of a business formation. It does, however, emphasize how important it is for the interior designer to consult with an attorney and an accountant to be sure he or she is making the right choice. In some cases, it is absolutely necessary to consult with an attorney to help set up the necessary legal papers. However, it is now even more important for the designer to seek the advice of a tax accountant prior to establishing a form of business. In 1987, major changes in the tax laws went into effect. This chapter will briefly discuss these changes in relation to each form of business.

We will discuss the sole proprietorship, general and limited partnerships, the corporation, and some specialized forms and the advantages of each in some situations. These specialized forms are the subchapter S corporation, the private corporation, and the joint venture. Chapter 6 will discuss the various legal filings of each form of business.

## *Sole Proprietorships*

The *sole proprietorship* is the simplest and least expensive form of business. In this form of business ownership, the company and individual owner are one and the same. Business is most commonly conducted under the owner's name, such as Mary Jane Smith, but may also be done under a company trade name, such as Creative Interior Designs. Since the owner and the company are the same, the company has no existence if the owner quits operating the business. In other words, if Mary Jane Smith decides to leave the interior design business, "Mary Jane Smith" company no longer exists.

To start a sole proprietorship in most states, all that is necessary is to establish a location, open a bank account in the firm's name, prepare the appropriate business stationery, and begin to establish credit with trade sources. If the company plans to sell merchandise to clients, most states and many cities will require the firm to have a resale license. This resale license is required in order for the firm to pass on state and city sales taxes to the end user. Additional requirements exist when employees are hired. These are covered in Chapter 6.

There is also a tax advantage for the sole proprietor. The costs of doing business and the income losses from the business are deducted from the gross receipts of the company. If the company suffers a loss, the loss is deductible from any other income the owner may have.

Many interior design businesses have started as sole proprietorships because of ease and low cost. There are disadvantages to a sole proprietorship, however, that must be considered. First, the owner has unlimited liability, which means that the owner and his or her estate are personally responsible for all losses and debts of the company. If the firm cannot pay a bill owed to a creditor, the creditor may seek payment from the owner's personal savings or property. In many states this includes the co-owned assets of spouses. If a suit by a client results in damages which must be paid by the defendant, the plaintiff can collect from the firm's assets and, if necessary, from the personal assets of the owner.

Although all profits go to the sole proprietor, these profits are considered ordinary income and are taxable for the year along with any other personal income. The income of the company is reported on a Schedule C attachment to the owner's federal and state income tax forms.

Another disadvantage of the sole proprietorship is that of raising capital or establishing credit. If the design firm intends to sell merchandise as well as provide design services, the firm will need to establish credit with manufacturers and suppliers. Many of these will only sell to sole proprietorships with substantial down payments or payments in full prior to shipping. This large volume of money may be difficult for a sole proprietor to obtain from a bank, unless he or she has an excellent personal credit rating or substantial personal assets. To many banks, even substantial personal assets or excellent personal credit does not, in itself, mean that the business will be successful, and therefore banks may not want to risk supporting the business through loans.

# *Partnerships*

There are two types of partnerships that can be used by the interior design practice: the general partnership and the limited partnership.

### GENERAL PARTNERSHIP

When two or more people join for the purpose of forming a business, and these people alone share in the profits and risks of the business, a partnership is formed. The name of the firm may be a trade name like Creative Interior Designs, ID Associates, or it may be the partners' names, such as Brown and Williams Associates. Two or more interior designers often start a business as a partnership because the partnership brings (1) more design talent (perhaps some skill or experience that the other partner lacks) to the company, (2) the assets and credit of the partners, and (3) shared responsibilities of the company.

Although many states do not legally require the writing of a formal partnership agreement, it is a very good idea to do so. The partnership agreement should spell out the responsibilities of each of the partners. These include how much capital will be contributed by each, how the profits will be divided, and how the drawing accounts (checking and savings) will be used. In addition, the partnership agreement should detail the method of dissolving the partnership in case of death, retirement, or other reasons at the request of the partners. In the absence of written agreements, the Uniform Partnership Act governs the operation of the partnership.

Those items mentioned for the sole proprietorship plus the preparation of a partnership agreement will legally create the partnership. The relative ease of formation and the benefit of one or more people involved in the affairs of the business are advantages of this form of business ownership.

The disadvantages are similar to those of a sole proprietorship. First, when employees are hired, some additional paperwork will be required. Second, the partnership has unlimited financial liability for any losses or debts of the partnership. In many instances, however, the creditors of the partnership cannot attach the personal assets of the partners until the personal creditors' claims are first met. The following serves to explain this concept. Jones, Smith, and Brown (a general partnership) dissolved their company, which has assets of $100,000 but liabilities of $125,000. This, of course, meant that the company had liabilities of $25,000 when all company assets were used to absolve debts. If Jones and Smith had no personal assets remaining but Brown did have personal assets of $25,000 remaining, the creditors of the company could seize the personal assets of Brown *only* if Brown had no personal liabilities. Thus, unlimited financial liability also means that if one partner is unscrupulous, the others can lose their share of the partnership assets and possibly their personal assets as well.

Profits are split as determined by the partnership agreement (or equally if no written agreement has been prepared). This income is considered personal income and is taxed as such on each individual partner's federal and state income tax forms in the same way as the income from a sole proprietorship.

There are some other disadvantages of the partnership form of business. The firm and each partner of the firm is responsible for the actions of all the other partners. This means that any wrong-doing of one partner, or any promises made by one partner, are the responsibility and obligation of the other partners also. If John Jones, one of the partners of Jones, Smith, and Brown, contracts with Knoll International for $50,000 of Bertoia chairs, the assets of Jones, Smith, and Brown and the personal assets of Mr. Jones, Ms. Smith, and Mr. Brown might be needed to pay for the order if the company's assets are insufficient.

Any change in the relationship of the partnership dissolves the partnership. If any of the partners wishes to withdraw from the partnership, the original partnership is dissolved. If the remaining partners (assuming there were more than two to start) or others wish to continue the business, a new partnership must be formed. If, at some time, a new partner wishes to join the firm, the original partnership is again dissolved and a new one is formed. Should one of the partners die or become physically incapacitated so as to be unable to perform agreed-upon duties, the partnership is likewise dissolved.

In addition to the advantages and disadvantages noted, there are two other important factors to consider in selecting the general partnership form for an interior design business. The first is that each partner is usually involved with the management of the firm. In most cases, this is a good idea since two heads may lead to better ideas. However, many partnerships dissolve because of the disagreements of partners in the management of the business. The other factor is that it is generally easier for the partnership than it is for the sole proprietorship to obtain capital since there are two or more individuals' credit rating and personal assets available to pledge for loans.

### LIMITED PARTNERSHIP

A *limited partnership* is formed according to statutory requirements, with a limited partnership agreement on file with the state in which it was formed. If the limited partnership operates in other states, it may be necessary that an agreement be on file in those other states. A limited partnership is formed with at least one general partner and other partners designated as limited partners. The general partner(s) have responsibility for the management of the firm. They also assume the same kind of personal financial responsibility that is true for members of a regular partnership. The role of the limited partner(s) is limited to that of investor.

The limited partner(s) contribute assets toward the operation of the partnership and receive a portion of the profits, but they cannot make any management decisions regarding the operation of the firm. The limited partner(s) are financially responsible for the losses and debts of the partnership only to the amount of each partner's investment in the design firm. The general partner(s) have the same legal responsibilities as members of a normal general partnership. Should any of the limited partner(s) become involved in the management of the design firm, he or she is no longer a limited partner but a general partner. When this happens, the partner now shares in the liability of the firm as do the general partners.

A limited partnership might be a good form of business for designers who are looking for people to invest in their company. A disadvantage for investors would be that the profits of the limited partnership are taxed as personal income. Personal income is taxed at a higher rate than many kinds of investment opportunities.

## *Corporations*

A *corporation* is an association of individuals created by statutory requirements and, as such, is a legal entity. The corporation exists independently of its originators or any other member. It can sue and be sued by others, it can enter into contracts, and it can commit crimes and be punished. A corporation also has powers and duties distinct from any of its members, and survives even after the death of any or all of its stockholders. Simply stated, a corporation is like a person—legally and financially separate and distinct from any of its members (called stockholders) yet legally and financially responsible, like any individual person. A stockholder's liability extends only to the ownership and value of his or her stock. Individual stockholders of a corporation cannot be sued, enter into contracts, and so on.

### HOW A CORPORATION IS FORMED

The rules governing the right to form corporations are held by the individual states. The states establish regulations concerning chartering a corporation and its general organization and operational limitations. If a firm engages in interstate commerce, it will also be regulated by the federal government.

Corporations that might be formed for the interior design profession are called *private corporations*. This means that the corporation has been formed for private interests. Public corporations are those formed by some government agency for the benefit of the public. The U.S. Postal Service is an example of a public corporation.

When all the shares of stock of a corporation are privately held by a few individuals, and the stock is not traded on any of the public markets, the corporation is called a close corporation. Other names for a close corporation are family corporations or closely held corporations. If a corporation sells its stock on any of the exchanges (New York Stock Exchange, American Stock Exchange, Over-the-Counter Market), it is commonly called a public corporation, although, by the definition given, the term is technically misleading. In this case, the sale of the stock would be regulated by the Securities Exchange Commission.

Firms generally incorporate in the state in which they do business if they engage only in intrastate commerce. A corporation formed in one state and doing business in that state only is called a domestic corporation. When firms engage in interstate commerce, they may find it advantageous to incorporate in some other state as well. In this case, the corporation must obtain permission to operate in the second state from the second state. A corporation formed in one state and doing business in another state is referred to by the second state as a foreign corporation. A foreign corporation does not have an automatic right to operate in the second state.

A corporation may be formed by one or more persons, depending on the state of origination. The organizers of the corporation must prepare a document called the articles of incorporation. This document must be prepared by an attorney and submitted to the proper authority in the state. The following information is generally required in the articles:

1. The name of the corporation.
2. The purpose and nature of the business in which the corporation will engage.
3. The initial capital structure.
4. The place the corporation will do business.
5. The names of the initial board of directors.
6. The names of the incorporators.
7. Other information as might be required by the state for that type of business.

When the articles of incorporation are completed, they are sent to the state, usually the secretary of state, along with a filing fee. Generally, after approval, a certificate of incorporation is returned, along with the articles, by the secretary of state.

The first organizational meeting, the date of which is stated in the articles of incorporation, is then held. During this meeting, the board of directors are elected, the bylaws are prepared, discussions or actions concerning the sale of stock take place, and so on. When this is completed, the corporation may formally begin operation.

It is possible for anyone to start his or her design business as a corporation. The many advantages of the corporate form influence interior designers to begin their business in this manner. There are also some disadvantages for the small firm owner or the designer who will be working alone while the business is getting established. But let's look at the advantages first.

## ADVANTAGES OF CORPORATION FORM

An important advantage of the corporate form of business is the limited liability of originators and stockholders. Financial liability of the originators (or principals) and stockholders is limited to the amount of money each invests in the corporation. The personal assets of the principals and stockholders cannot be touched to pay any operational costs or to satisfy legal judgments resulting from the operations of the business or initiated by any individual employee of the business. This is an important consideration for the interior design firm since lawsuits for many kinds of problems—especially breach of contract—have been on the increase in the design profession.

There can be considerable tax savings to the principals and stockholders of the corporate form. The corporation must pay taxes on its profits. Generally, that tax rate is lower than on the same amount of income if it were reported as personal income. The 1987 changes in the tax law eliminated the five tax brackets and established three graduated brackets. This change may affect the net income level of many design corporations.

Corporations generally have an easier time of deducting business expenses for such things as equipment, automobile usage, entertainment, and so on, than do partnerships and sole proprietorships. Although the new tax laws have also affected these kinds of deductions, the ease of taking these deductions for a corporation still exists. Since it is beyond the scope of this book to detail all the changes in the new tax laws, the reader is referred to his or her accountant to obtain information related to his or her specific situation.

Another advantage of the corporate form is that the corporation has continuity even if the originators and stockholders change or cease to be involved with the corporation. The originators may sell their interests in the firm to other stockholders or to outside parties at any time, and the corporation goes on. Stockholders may also sell their stock back to the principals or to outsiders, and the firm goes on without major change. If the principals or any of the stockholders die or otherwise withdraw from the operation of the business, the corporation still remains intact.

Corporations can cease to exist, however. The corporation would cease when the expiration time of the corporation (as stated in the articles of incorporation) is reached or as a result of unanimous action by all the shareholders. The board of directors and shareholders may vote to dissolve the corporation. The corporation may be dissolved by an act of law passed in the state of its origin. Or the attorney general in the state of origin may ask the court to decree for a dissolution because the corporation acted in opposition to, or did not act according to, the regulations of corporations in the state.[1]

The relative ease in raising capital is another advantage of the corporate form. The primary way a corporation raises capital is to sell stock. When the corporation is formed, the initial board of directors determines how many shares of stock will be issued and how much of this first issue will be sold. Later, the corporation may sell additional stock to raise more capital. How stock amounts are determined, including par value[2] and methods of selling the stock are beyond the scope of this book. The reader is recommended to seek the advice of financial consultants, accountants, and attorneys. Books on finance, business law, and accounting and in-depth studies of how to incorporate may also be reviewed.

A firm may also raise capital by going to lending institutions and pledging future assets as collateral to secure loans. Although this method is open to partnerships and sole proprietorships also, it is much easier for a corporation to obtain loans than it is for these other forms of business.

## DISADVANTAGES OF CORPORATION FORM

What can be viewed as an advantage or disadvantage of the corporation form is the management structure. In very large corporations, the stockholders have little to say about how the corporation is managed. Their only opportunity to influence

---

[1]Clarkson 1983.

[2]When the board of directors decides to offer a new issue of stock, a par or legal value of the stock is determined. The par value is often far below the market value of the stock.

management or have a say in how the firm is managed is at the annual stockholders' meeting. Here each stockholder has one vote for each share of stock and can possibly use his or her vote(s) to change the management of the firm. Stockholders working individually usually have little effect on the decisions of the board of directors. However, most design firms are very small, and although each stockholder still has one vote per share of stock, the influence on the management of the corporation is greater. Stockholders with large numbers of stock can influence the direction of the corporation and can even change the leadership of the board of directors by voting for their removal.

The main disadvantage of the corporate form is the cost and paperwork necessary. Initial costs of incorporation include lawyer's fees and filing fees for the articles of incorporation. It is very important to hire an accountant to set up the bookkeeping procedures for the corporation. City, state, and federal regulations will involve the filing of monthly reports of various kinds. These will include unemployment insurance, taxes, funds for the employer's share of social security, and payment of city and/or state sales taxes on merchandise sold to clients. Also, most corporations must file quarterly income tax statements rather than annual statements. All these activities result in increased time spent by the interior design principals on paperwork or the additional costs of hiring additional professionals to take care of these requirements.

Other considerations relate to the responsibilities of the corporation to stockholders. Whether the firm is a publicly traded or closely held corporation, annual stockholders' meetings must be held. Here the corporate officers are required to inform the stockholders of the financial condition of the corporation and conduct other such business as might be dictated by the board of directors or stockholders. An annual financial report must be prepared by an accounting firm and provided to the stockholders. If additional stock or a new stock issue is to be made to raise capital, the corporation may incur costs related to these sales. The board of directors generally does not need stockholder approval to sell additional stock, but may need approval to sell a new issue of stock.

## *Subchapter S Corporations*

*Subchapter S corporations* enjoy many of the advantages of the corporation but pay taxes as a partnership. Many interior designers use the subchapter S corporation as their form of business, when they begin their practice, in order to have the liability protection of the corporation. Later, they change to the corporate form when the firm no longer meets the eligibility requirements of subchapter S. The eligibility requirements include: (1) that the firm be engaged only in domestic business, (2) that shareholders can only be individuals—not other corporations, (3) that there are no more than thirty-five shareholders, (4) that all shareholders be American citizens, (5) that the corporation has only one class of stock, and (6) that the firm obtains no more than 20 percent of its revenues from investments.

Corporate earnings and losses are paid or deducted by the shareholders on their personal federal and state income tax forms, in proportion to the share of stock they hold in the corporation. The S corporation can choose to use the lowest tax bracket of its shareholders whether or not income is distributed.[3]

---

[3]Jentz 1987.

## *Professional Corporations* _____

A relatively new form of business—a professional corporation—is a corporation formed by persons in professions such as law, medicine, dentistry, accounting, architecture, and interior design. The letters *P.C.* (professional corporation), *P.A.* (professional association), or *S.C.* (service corporation) follow the name of the firm to identify it as a professional corporation. The rules governing the right to form this kind of corporation are held by the individual states. Not all states allow all professions to utilize this formation; some have very limiting restrictions related to the professional corporation.

This kind of business is formed in the same manner as an ordinary corporation. Tax benefits are the same as for any other corporation. And in most instances, the professional corporation must act like a normal corporation in order to receive those tax benefits.

However, liability of the members is a little different. If one of the members commits an act that is malpractice, the other members are generally not liable. Yet, some courts governed by statutory regulations may rule that all members of the corporations are liable for the actions of the others.[4] Shareholders would not be liable for torts unrelated to malpractice. For example, if a delivery person working for the professional corporation has an accident while on the way to a client's home, the corporation and the delivery person would be liable, but the stockholders of the corporation would not be personally liable. Like corporations, any shareholder of a professional corporation who is guilty of a negligent act is personally liable for the injury and damages.

Strict laws enacted in 1981 have limited the formation of professional service corporations. These were passed because many felt that professional service businesses were taking too great a tax advantage from the business form. The newer rules do not allow many of the tax loopholes formerly permitted.

## *Joint Ventures* _____

A *joint venture* is a temporary contractual association of two or more persons or firms which agree to share in the responsibilities, losses, and profits of a particular project or business venture. The key to the joint venture is its temporary status. It is treated much like a partnership, but it is for a limited time period or certain activity. Not being a legal entity, it cannot be sued, but the individual members of the joint venture can be sued. The profits and losses of the venture are usually taxed as they would be for a partnership.

The firms agreeing to enter into a joint venture should prepare a formal agreement clearly explaining the responsibilities of each party, the conditions of the arrangement, the manner in which the profits and losses will be divided, the method for paying employees, and so on. A joint venture is like beginning a brand new business; thus, the joint venture companies often select a new name for the temporary partnership for the duration of the project. When this happens, neither firm loses its original identity, and both generally go on with other projects that are separate from the joint venture project. When the project is completed, the temporary partnership ends, and each firm goes back to working on a completely individual basis.

---

[4]Clarkson 1983.

This kind of business relationship is most often entered into by architectural offices for very large projects, but it is something that can also be used by interior design firms. Architectural and interior design firms enter into joint ventures for several reasons. The most common reason is because a project is so large that no single firm would have the time and support team to do it alone. Devoting the entire work force to one project, especially commercial projects that often take a substantial amount of time, would leave any design firm without a steady source of income. Depending on the income from that one project might leave the design firm in financial straits until the project is completed.

Joint ventures also give firms an opportunity to gain experience in a kind of project for which they have little or no experience. One firm may have the staff to do the drafting and documentation needed for a hospital project but no experience with the interview and design development stages of hospital design. A second firm may not have enough draftspersons to handle the increased work load but has the interview and design development experience to plan the hospital. If these two firms create a joint venture, both will gain from the project.

The joint venture also provides a very strong design team for the client. Using the expertise from two firms can mean better design and follow-through for the client than when only one firm is employed, which may not have the support staff or expertise to complete the project in a timely fashion.

Combining the staffs of two or more firms increases the speed inherent in a large staff. If one firm were to obtain the contract, it might be necessary to hire additional designers, either to work on the new project or other existing projects. This learning time cost can be a problem in completing any of the projects the firm has under contract and could be too costly for the design firm to even undertake. The temporary partnership brings the staffs of both firms into use and may negate any further need to hire additional employees on a short-term basis.

Through the joint venture, both firms continue with their own individual identities and with projects other than the joint venture project. If the firms did not create a temporary partnership in this way, but wished to join together, one firm would have to merge with the other. This, of course, means that one firm would no longer exist.

Finally, a joint venture gives the two firms an opportunity to learn from each other in areas other than design. The relationship of the two firms may bring about exchanges of information on how to make presentations, ideas on general business practices, marketing strategies, and so on. Although competing firms do not willingly give away their design and business secrets, some ideas and concepts can be shared while respecting the integrity of both firms.

## *Summary*

Determining which business formation to use is one of the many important decisions that must be made as an interior designer plans for his or her own business. It is important to understand the many differences in the formations so as to appreciate the obligations of the owner.

This chapter has briefly outlined the advantages and disadvantages of the many legal forms of business that can be used by the interior design practice. This chapter has covered the advantages and disadvantages of the sole proprietorship, partnership, corporation, subchapter S corporation, professional corporation, and joint venture. In our next chapter, we will discuss the legal filings necessary to form a business using one of the major forms.

# Chapter 6

## LEGAL FILINGS

*D*epending on the exact nature of the practice, even without employees, some legal forms are required to begin most types of businesses. This chapter discusses some of the various legal papers or applications, other than partnership agreements and articles of incorporation, which must be processed in order to start an interior design business. Some of the filings are only necessary once employees are hired. And a few specialized filings that do not necessarily relate to starting a practice but that may be required or needed are also covered in this chapter. This will include title registration and copyright protection.

## *Federal Forms*

The federal government requires one form to be completed by any business formation. That form is the Application for Employer Identification Number. Additional forms are required of all businesses that have employees. And, of course, different income tax forms are required depending on the form of business. This section will briefly describe the different federal forms required to begin and maintain a business.

### SS-4: APPLICATION FOR EMPLOYER IDENTIFICATION NUMBER

The employer identification number (EIN), issued by the Internal Revenue Service (IRS), identifies the interior design firm to the federal government as a business. It is required of all businesses that have been formed as corporations or partnerships or any formation with employees. A sole proprietorship formation with no employees would not be required to apply for an EIN. However, since the EIN is required on Schedule C, obtaining an EIN is recommended for the sole proprietorship form.

Remember, when the practice has been formed as a corporation, anyone working for a corporation is an employee. This means that even if only one individual actually *generates income* for the corporation and this one individual is one of the board of directors/stockholders for the corporation, that individual is an employee.

A subchapter S corporation must file a Form 2553 within seventy-five days of the date operations of the corporation commence. This form must be signed by all the shareholders electing to be taxed as a subchapter S corporation.

## FORMATIONS WITH EMPLOYEES

When the firm has employees, additional federal forms must be completed.

### Form 940: Employer's Annual Unemployment Tax Return

Form 940 is used to report and pay the Federal Unemployment Compensation Tax. It must be filed and paid on an annual basis in January. The liability is calculated quarterly and must be deposited when it reaches or exceeds $100.

### Form 941: Employer's Quarterly Federal Tax Return

Form 941 reports the amount of income tax and social security tax withheld from all the employees' wages. It also reports the amount of social security tax matched by the employer for all employees. The amount of social security tax must be calculated on a monthly basis and paid to the depository bank by the fifteenth of the next month.

### Form W-4: Employee's Withholding Allowance Certificate

Each employee is required by law to fill out a Form W-4. The employer is required to keep this form on file and must send a copy of the W-4 to the IRS if the employee claims nine or more exemptions. This form indicates how many deductions to which the employees is entitled, which determines how much income tax is withheld from wages. With the 1987 Tax Reform Act, it is even more important for employees to fill out this form correctly as they may face penalties if too much or too little tax is withheld. Employees who paid no income tax in the previous year and expect not to have any tax liability in the coming year may file the W-4 on an "exempt" status. Employers and employees should consult with an accountant to be sure they are fulfilling their legal responsibilities related to Form W-4.

### Form W-2: Employer's Wage and Tax Statement

By January 31 of each calendar year, the employer must give each employee two copies of the Wage and Tax Statement. States with a state income tax require three copies so that a copy is available for filing with the state tax return. Form W-2 shows all wages paid; federal, state, and city taxes withheld; and social security taxes (shown as FICA) withheld. Other information may also be reported on this form depending on the structure of benefits and wages for the interior design firm.

### Form W-3: Transmittal of Income and Tax Statements

Copy A of all W-2s and a completed Form W-3 are filed with the Social Security Administration by the employer. Form W-3 totals all the information on the W-2 and provides income information to the Social Security Administration.

### Forms 1099: Information Returns

In certain circumstances, the employer will have to file one or more copies of Form 1099. There are many different 1099s to report specific information. These forms report taxable income that does not fall under the normal wages category. Special types of income include dividends on stock and nonemployee compensation, such as compensation paid to contract labor. Other 1099s may have to be filed, depending on the exact nature of the business and benefits program.

## FEDERAL INCOME TAX FORMS

Each business formation must file federal income tax forms. The exact form differs for each business formation. The following is a brief description of the most common federal tax forms filed for each business formation.

## SOLE PROPRIETORSHIP

### Schedule C, Form 1040 and Schedule SE, Form 1040

The proprietorship, as such, does not pay income taxes. Taxes are the responsibility of the sole proprietor. Income and deductions from this business form are filed on Schedule C, Form 1040. A self-employment tax is required of any net earnings totaling at least $400 (in 1987) in the taxable year.[1] This tax is figured and reported on the Schedule SE, Form 1040. The self-employment tax is the same as the social security tax paid by employees. The government acts as an agent to collect this tax for the Social Security Administration. Both schedules are filed with the normal 1040 and are due at the same time as the 1040.

## PARTNERSHIP

The partnership as an entity does not pay income taxes. Each partner, however, is responsible for paying income taxes on his or her share of the earnings of the partnership as part of his or her own personal income tax. The partnership must prepare and file a Form 1065. This is an informational return that must be signed by one of the partners.

### Schedule K, Form 1065 and Schedule K-1, Form 1065

Schedule K and Schedule K-1 of Form 1065 are used to show each partner's share of income, deductions, credits, and so on.

### Schedule E, Form 1040

Each partner's share of the income or loss is reported on Schedule E of Form 1040. This schedule is filed along with the remainder of the individual Form 1040 filed by each partner.

A limited partnership, depending on the partnership agreement, may require federal tax forms other than those listed. If the interior design practice has been formed as a limited partnership, the partners should consult with an accountant to be sure they are filing the correct forms.

## CORPORATION

Interior design practices formed as corporations are entities in and of themselves and as such the business entity must file income tax forms. In addition, each employee and stockholder of the corporation must provide appropriate information on his or her individual Form 1040.

Corporations pay taxes based on graduated rates. For the most part, the corporation determines the gross income and taxable income of the firm in a fashion similar to that of an individual. However, the corporation has certain limitations as to exclusions of income and certain advantages as to deductions from income. Exactly what factors constitute income and what factors constitute allowable deductions for a corporation should be determined in consultation with an accountant.

### Form 1120

Form 1120 calculates and reports the total actual income tax for the previous year. It is due by March 15 if the corporation is on a calendar year accounting basis. The filing time for corporations on a fiscal year accounting basis would be different. Each quarter (April 15, June 15, September 15, and December 15), the corporation must prepare an estimated income tax for the current year using a Form 1120ES

---

[1] Prentice-Hall 1987.

and deposit the quarterly amount with a Federal Tax Deposit (FTD) Coupon Form. The deposit must be made in a federal reserve or authorized commercial bank.

## SUBCHAPTER S CORPORATIONS

The subchapter S corporation basically pays no income tax, although it may have to pay income tax on such items as capital gains, and it may have to pay the minimum tax. Net income (or loss) of the S form is passed on to the shareholders. The shareholders are responsible for paying taxes on their share of the income of the S form of corporation. The subchapter S form retains its privilege not to pay federal taxes as long as the S corporation does not lose its eligibility to be an S corporation.

### Form 1120S

The subchapter S corporation must file a copy of Form 1120S each tax year. This is a calender-year report that informs the IRS of gross income and allowable deductions, distributions to stockholders, and information on the stockholders related to the stockholders' share of income and loss.

## PRIVATE CORPORATIONS

The private corporation, in order to receive the tax benefits of this formation, must behave as a normal corporation. Therefore, it must file the same tax forms with the federal government that the normal corporation must file.

## JOINT VENTURES

Since joint ventures are special forms of partnerships, as far as the federal government is concerned, the joint venture must file annual partnership returns. Each member of the joint venture must also report his or her share of the gains and losses of the venture on his or her personal income tax return. This is done until the joint venture is terminated.

# State Forms

It is not possible in the space allotted to fully discuss all the specific requirements of the various states. The following is a rather general discussion of the legal filings that would be common to all the states. The interior design practice owner must check with the proper counsel to be sure he or she is fulfilling the requirements of the state in which the firm will be located.

## EMPLOYER'S IDENTIFICATION NUMBER

Many states will require that the business obtain a state employer's identification number in addition to the federal identification number. This number, issued by the state revenue service, helps to determine what rate of tax the business must pay. It also helps to determine withholding and unemployment taxes for which the business may be responsible. In the states where an employer's identification number is required, it is most often required whether or not the business has employees.

## STATE TRANSACTION PRIVILEGE (SALES) TAX LICENSE

Most states will require all businesses to obtain the Transaction Privilege Tax License whether or not the business will be selling goods. It is imperative for businesses that intend to resell goods to the end user. The sales tax license allows the interior designer to pass on the state sales tax to the consumer. It must be remembered that if the business fails to collect and pay this tax to the state and/or city, the taxing authority will hold the business responsible for the tax monies. Generally, the amount collected must be reported and paid on a quarterly basis.

## USE TAX REGISTRATION CERTIFICATE

If the business will be purchasing goods from out of state, and these goods are taxable in the state in which the interior design firm is doing business, the business will be required to obtain a Use Tax Certificate. This ensures that sales taxes or use taxes are collected by either the state selling the goods to the interior design firm or by the firm to the state where the goods are used.

## CORPORATION IDENTIFICATION NUMBERS

Since the privilege of operating a corporation rests with the states, the states require that all businesses formed as corporations be registered by the state before operations may begin. In most cases, corporation identification numbers are obtained from the state department of revenue. In many states, the corporation may also be regulated by either the state attorney general's office or some other state office.

## EMPLOYEE WITHHOLDING REPORTINGS

For businesses with employees, the firm must file income tax withholding, unemployment, and workers' compensation reports with the state revenue department. The manner in which these are collected, amounts, and reporting methods vary from state to state. The interior design firm must check with the proper agency to be sure it meets the legal obligations of its particular state.

## PERSONAL PROPERTY

In states where personal property of the business is taxed, the value of the personal property of the business will have to be reported. In most cases, this information will be given to the county attorney or county assessor of the county in which the business resides rather than the state revenue department.

## INCOME TAXES

All forms of business will have to report income and losses of the business on a yearly basis. Since most states model their income tax reporting on the federal laws, the reporting methods will be similar. Forms and actual reporting methods are, of course, different for each state. In addition, at the time of this writing, most states had not adjusted their income tax laws to reflect the changes of the 1987 Federal Income Tax Reform Act. It is expected that the states will generally adopt many of the federal laws into their own income tax laws.

## OTHER FORMS

### Doing Business under a Fictitious Name

If the business is operating under a name other than that of the owner(s), the state will require the business to file a Fictitious Business Name Statement. This filing will be required of all forms of business except corporations and is usually filed with the county clerk. Its purpose is to identify to the state and the general public the owner(s) responsible for any business formed within the state. In some states, it may also be necessary for the new business to publish a statement of ownership. It is relatively common for corporations to print a copy of the corporation papers in the business section of the local newspaper.

## Local Forms

Each city and county may have particular licenses, property taxes, or tax requirements that the business must obtain and file. The interior design business owner should be checking with local city and county authorities to be sure these are satisfied.

### CITY TRANSACTION PRIVILEGE (SALES) TAX LICENSE

Many cities also require transaction privilege (sales) tax licenses. In some states, it is possible to obtain this form at the same time the business applies for the state license. If it is not available from the state, it can be obtained from the offices of the city in which the business is residing. The city license serves the same function as the state license.

### ZONING RESTRICTIONS

Cities have certain zoning restrictions as to where businesses may operate. Many interior design businesses begin operation out of a private home. If the interior design firm is selling merchandise to clients, this business may very well be operating illegally. Should neighbors complain to the city that the designer is operating a business in a residentially zoned area, the designer may be liable for a fine.

It is best to check with the local zoning office before applying for a city business license. If the business does not have employees, does not have deliveries arriving at the residence, keeps visits of clients to a minimum, or conducts no direct sales, it may be legal for the interior designer to operate a business out of his or her home even if the area is residentially zoned. In some cases, it may be necessary to apply for a zoning variance. The zoning variance allows the business to operate legally in the residentially zoned area. A request for a zoning variance usually requires notification of neighbors and a hearing before the zoning commission.

## Specialized Filings

### CONTRACTORS' LICENSES

In many states, the supervision of construction work and the installation of architectural finishes that an interior designer might specify for a client need to be done by a licensed contractor. Such items as structural work, carpet laying, wall coverings installation, and other items that are attachments to the building may often be done only by a licensed contractor. Although it is rare that interior designers be required to obtain a general or one of the several specialized contractors' licenses, some firms obtain these documents as a means to expand the potential of the practice. More likely, the interior designer hires contractors and subcontractors who hold these licenses to do the work.

The requirements related to the use of licensed contractors for construction work and installation of architectural interior finishes or attachments vary from state to state. Most states require that work done for private residences be performed only by licensed contractors. Some states do not have restrictions on who may work on commercial facilities. If the designer hires unlicensed contractors to perform work when a licensed contractor is required, the client may not have any legal obligation to pay the designer. It may also be a criminal offense for the interior designer to use the unlicensed contractor.

States have various provisions regarding the definition of a contractor as it is being discussed here. The owner of the interior design firm should be familiar with the statutes of the state in which it is located, and *any* state in which it may be doing business. Questions should be directed to the state registrar of contractors.

### INTERIOR DESIGN TITLE REGISTRATION OR LICENSURE

Interior designers working in states where title registration or licensing has already been passed must now meet certain regulations to maintain their practice under the title of *interior designer.* As of the writing, Connecticut, Alabama, Louisiana, and Florida have obtained title registration acts. The first interior designer's licensure act was passed in Washington, D.C., in 1986.

Title registration/licensing regulations vary slightly among each of the regulated states. Basically, the applicant would have to show that he or she has the acceptable level of education and experience, has passed the NCIDQ or an equal examination, is involved in continuing education within the professional area, and meets any other specific regulations of the state. Students and professionals must keep abreast of how these laws are becoming formulated in their state and be prepared to meet the specific requirements of the statutes.

### WORK AUTHORIZATION VERIFICATION

With the passage of the Immigration Reform and Control Act of 1986, it is now unlawful for individuals and businesses to hire aliens who do not have proper authorization to work. Since it is also unlawful for the company to discriminate in its hiring practices, companies are required to have all applicants hired after November 6, 1986, submit acceptable identification and work authorization information.

Not only must the applicant be asked and provide acceptable documents, but the individual or business doing the hiring must keep a record of the request and verification on file. Figure 6-1 is a form available from the U.S. Department of Justice, Immigration and Naturalization Service.

## *Copyrights and Patents*

The work of the interior designer usually results in a great deal of intangible design work in the creation of floor plans, sketches, and sample boards. Often, it is hoped, these intangible items result in a tangible completed interior, or possibly a custom-designed product. There will be some instances when the designer will wish to legally protect these design ideas so that they cannot be duplicated or copied without permission and fair compensation. In some cases, the client may also wish that these designs not be duplicated.

The method of legally protecting written and graphic designs is by a *copyright.* The legal protection of custom product design which results in a tangible object is by a patent.

In a very broad sense, the Federal Copyright Act of 1976 protects works of authorship and pictorial or graphic works. Design specifications would fall under the authorship category, whereas drawings and plans would fall under the latter category. The design idea itself is not copyrightable or patentable, but a drawing of a

# EMPLOYMENT ELIGIBILITY VERIFICATION (Form I-9)

**1** **EMPLOYEE INFORMATION AND VERIFICATION:** (To be completed and signed by employee.)

| Name: (Print or Type)   Last | First | Middle | Birth Name |
|---|---|---|---|
| Address: Street Name and Number | City | State | ZIP Code |

| Date of Birth (Month/Day/Year) | Social Security Number |
|---|---|

**I attest, under penalty of perjury, that I am (check a box):**

☐ 1. A citizen or national of the United States.

☐ 2. An alien lawfully admitted for permanent residence (Alien Number A _____ ) .

☐ 3. An alien authorized by the Immigration and Naturalization Service to work in the United States (Alien Number A _____ ,

or Admission Number _____ ,   expiration of employment authorization, if any _____ ) .

**I attest, under penalty of perjury, the documents that I have presented as evidence of identity and employment eligibility are genuine and relate to me. I am aware that federal law provides for imprisonment and/or fine for any false statements or use of false documents in connection with this certificate.**

| Signature | Date (Month/Day/Year) |
|---|---|

PREPARER/TRANSLATOR CERTIFICATION (To be completed if prepared by person other than the employee). I attest, under penalty of perjury, that the above was prepared by me at the request of the named individual and is based on all information of which I have any knowledge.

| Signature | Name (Print or Type) | | |
|---|---|---|---|
| Address (Street Name and Number) | City | State | Zip Code |

**2** **EMPLOYER REVIEW AND VERIFICATION:** (To be completed and signed by employer.)

Instructions:

Examine one document from List A and check the appropriate box, **OR** examine one document from List B **and** one from List C and check the appropriate boxes. Provide the *Document Identification Number* and *Expiration Date* for the document checked.

| List A Documents that Establish Identity and Employment Eligibility | List B Documents that Establish Identity | **and** | List C Documents that Establish Employment Eligibility |
|---|---|---|---|
| ☐ 1. United States Passport | ☐ 1. A State-issued driver's license or a State-issued I.D. card with a photograph, or information, including name, sex, date of birth, height, weight, and color of eyes. (Specify State)_____ ) | | ☐ 1. Original Social Security Number Card (other than a card stating it is not valid for employment) |
| ☐ 2. Certificate of United States Citizenship | | | ☐ 2. A birth certificate issued by State, county, or municipal authority bearing a seal or other certification |
| ☐ 3. Certificate of Naturalization | ☐ 2. U.S. Military Card | | |
| ☐ 4. Unexpired foreign passport with attached Employment Authorization | ☐ 3. Other (Specify document and issuing authority) | | ☐ 3. Unexpired INS Employment Authorization Specify form |
| ☐ 5. Alien Registration Card with photograph | _____ | | # _____ |
| *Document Identification* | *Document Identification* | | *Document Identification* |
| # _____ | # _____ | | # _____ |
| *Expiration Date (if any)* | *Expiration Date (if any)* | | *Expiration Date (if any)* |
| _____ | _____ | | _____ |

**CERTIFICATION: I attest, under penalty of perjury, that I have examined the documents presented by the above individual, that they appear to be genuine and to relate to the individual named, and that the individual, to the best of my knowledge, is eligible to work in the United States.**

| Signature | Name (Print or Type) | Title |
|---|---|---|
| Employer Name | Address | Date |

Form I-9 (05/07/87)
OMB No. 1115-0136

U.S. Department of Justice
Immigration and Naturalization Service

## FIGURE 6-1
**Employment eligibility verification.** *(U. S. Department of Justice, Immigration and Naturalization Service)*

custom-designed product would be copyrightable. And the object itself, if it is substantially different from any other product design, must be patented to receive legal protection from unauthorized duplication.

It has been upheld in court that work commissioned by a client and done by the designer still belongs to the designer even when there are no clauses in the design contract giving ownership to the designer. This protection is afforded only when the work contains the proper notification and meets registration and publication requirements.

Any written or graphic work created after January 1, 1978, is protected by copyright for the life of the author/designer plus fifty years. The creator of a patentable product is given exclusive right to make, use, and sell the product for seventeen years.

Since most of what the interior designer might wish to protect legally would be written or graphic materials, we will continue the rest of this discussion with regard to copyrights only. The copyright begins at the moment the interior designer begins the act to complete the work. This means that the moment the interior designer begins the working drawings, sketch, or specifications, the right to legally protect the work begins. However, the work must bear a copyright notification prior to its being "published" in order to receive full legal protection.

"Publication" occurs when the creator has somehow distributed the work to others for review without restriction of use. It does not mean that the work is printed and published by a publishing house. For example, if the interior designer gives a floor plan to the client for his or her review, the plan has been published. Providing to the client or to others copies of the work for the purpose of display constitutes publication.

*Copyright notification* must contain the following elements:

1. The word *Copyright,* the abbreviation *COPR,* or the copyright symbol, ©.
2. Year of publication.
3. The name of the copyright claimant for the copyright.

Notice of the above three elements does not begin the copyright. Notice serves to protect what the claimant publishes. Copyright begins at the moment of creation.

Copyright notification itself, however, does not provide complete legal protection. The proposed copyrighted materials must be registered with the federal government in order for the interior designer to file suit in federal district court for infringement. In order to register a copyrightable item, the creator must obtain the proper forms from the copyright office. The V-A form is used for graphic works, and the T-X form is used for books, articles, and other general written works. As of this writing, these forms may be obtained by calling the copyright hotline: (202) 287-9100. After dialing this number, the caller will hear a recording telling him or her that the only messages acted upon will be for the ordering of forms. Any other message will be ignored. The recording will provide a second number that the caller may use to obtain general information regarding copyrighting. As of this writing, that number is (202) 479-4700.

An original form, not a photocopy of the form, must be accompanied by one copy of the work if the work is unpublished and two copies of the work if it has already been published. The copy of the work must be a "best edition" copy. Since originals cannot be readily submitted, properly prepared photocopies, photographs of the work, or diazo prints of floor plans may suffice. What constitutes a best edition copy, however, is up to the copyright office. A fee to process the copyright will also be required.

It is not necessary to send each project under a separate copyright form. A bulk of work, called a collection, may be submitted at one time. A collection can constitute any work created within the same year as long as all the work is of the same basic type and falls under the same form.

Registration, in order for full statutory and actual damages to be awarded, must occur either prior to the work being published or under specific circumstances. If the work is registered within three months of first publication, the copyright holder would still be able to claim statutory and actual damages. If the work is registered up to five years of first publication, there is a presumption of a valid copyright. After five years, the claimant will have to prove that he or she is the original author. In both of these cases, the copyright claimant may receive actual damages but not statutory damages or attorney's fees and costs.

Statutory damages refer to set amounts determined by the court for each infringement. Actual damages relate to damages the copyright holder suffers as a result of the infringement. Actual damages may mean payment of design fees, profits the designer might have lost, and profits the infringer may have made by the infringement.

Infringement is any unauthorized use of copyrighted materials. This can best be explained with a few examples. Assume in the examples that the designs have been properly copyrighted. The designer prepares the custom design of a cabinet, and the cabinetmaker not only produces the cabinet for the client, but begins to produce the design for other clients of his or her own. Since the plans were provided to the cabinetmaker for the exclusive purpose of producing one set of the cabinets, the cabinetmaker has infringed on the designer's copyright by producing additional copies of the cabinet. In a second example, the designer has prepared a set of working drawings for the interior of a small fast-food restaurant in a specific location. If the owner of the fast-food restaurant later duplicates the plans in another location, the restaurant owner has infringed on the copyright.

Copyrights of any design work created by individuals who are employees of an interior design firm belong to the employer, not the employee. This is true as long as the work was done as part of the normal responsibility of the employee. However, an independent contractor (contract laborer) performing interior design work for a firm owns the copyright, not the firm hiring the individual.

Although it may not always be necessary for the interior designer to be concerned with the copyrighting of design documents, there may be certain projects or parts of projects that require this protection. Knowing how to prepare the documents for legal protection is very important. Including a clause in the design contract related to "design ownership" or "copyright permission" would also aid in legally protecting the designer.

## *Summary*

An individual or group of designers may have the skill, experience, and finances to open a design practice. Once the partnership agreement or articles of incorporation have been prepared, there are several other legal filings required by the federal, state, and local governments. This chapter has attempted to briefly describe those legal forms and documents.

Some states require specialized filings or documents. Those discussed here are contractor's licenses, interior design title registration or practice acts, and copyright protections. One or more of these specialized filings affect almost all interior design practices in some way.

The reader, whether a professional considering opening his or her own practice or a student, should now be able to see that there is much work involved beyond design skill and ability in establishing a practice. The next three chapters will conclude the topics related to organizing and establishing a practice. Chapter 7 will provide an overview of the legal responsibilities of the designer, and Chapters 8 and 9 will explore office organization and personnel concerns.

# Chapter 7

## LEGAL RESPONSIBILITIES

$A$s professional licensing and increased recognition become a reality, interior designers must face their increasing legal responsibilities. Interior designers are legally liable for the work they or members of their staff do, and as such can be sued. Commercial designers have added responsibilities toward fire and barrier-free codes.

Interior designers must be aware of how the law can help protect them in responsibilities related to performance of contracts and the Uniform Commercial Code for selling regulations. They must also be aware of the law as it might be used against them for such activities as malpractice and negligence.

This chapter will briefly introduce the differences between criminal and tort law and discuss issues of tort law which are important to the designer. Chapter 15 will have a discussion of contracts and Chapter 22 will cover legal responsibilities related to the selling practices of designers as defined by the Uniform Commercial Code.

## Criminal versus Tort Law

When a person (or business, in the case of a corporation) perpetrates a wrong against society, a *crime* has been committed. If the alleged wrongdoer commits an offense that is regulated by statute—which is considered an offense against all people in society—the offense is a criminal offense. The punishment for the criminal act is imprisonment and/or a fine.

Although most people think of a crime as an offense against another person, there are some crimes affecting business. Embezzlement, or the fraudulent taking of another person's property or money by the one entrusted with it, is a well-known crime affecting business. Falsifying public records and altering legal documents are forms of forgery. These are but a few of the areas where crimes are committed against businesses or even by businesses. If a corporation is involved, the corporation officers can be held responsible for their acts or neglectful acts of employees on behalf of the corporation.

Most legal problems interior designers experience do not involve criminal acts, but rather they involve torts. A *tort* is "alleged wrongful conduct by one person that causes injury to another."[1] This injury may be to the person or to the person's property. When one person causes injury to another person or his or her property, the injured person may seek various remedies for the damages caused. Since the act is against one person by another, a tort is a civil action where the person harmed sues, in a civil court, the person who has done the harm. Some torts, such as assault and battery, are also criminal acts if there are statutes that describe them as such.

By far, the most common kinds of tort cases that might involve interior designers are related to negligence and breach of contract. Negligence liability, often referred to as professional negligence, legally means that the designer failed to use due care in the performance of his or her design responsibilities. Breach of contract liability refers to the failure to complete the requirements of a contract. Other torts that can affect the interior design practice, although these are less likely to occur, are torts for false imprisonment, defamation, and misrepresentation. Strict liability, a tort related to product liability, is another tort liability that can entangle the design practice.

## *Negligence*

One of the kinds of torts most commonly involving interior design practice is *negligence*. "Negligence is the failure to use due care to avoid foreseeable injury which might be caused to another person or property as a result of the failure to exercise due care."[2] The person accused of negligence created a risk. This risk must be such that a reasonable person could anticipate it and prevent it. If there is no creation of risk, there cannot be negligence. Because of this factor, it is more a way of committing a tort rather than a kind of tort.

To prove negligence, the harmed party must prove several things; first, that the defendant owed a duty—most commonly "reasonable care"—to the plaintiff; second, that there was a breach of that duty either intentionally or unintentionally; third, that the act caused damages and that the act caused the harm; and fourth, that there were damages or harm to persons or property. Inadvertently switching numbers on a purchase order which results in the wrong wallpaper being hung at the client's home is negligence. Selling and installing a carpet that the designer knows does not meet fire codes is negligence.

Some other examples, commonly referred to as professional negligence, pointed out in Justin Sweet's *Legal Aspects of Architecture, Engineering, and the Construction Process* are worth repeating here.

Specifying material that did not comply with building codes

Failing to inform client of potential risks of using certain materials

Drafting ambiguous sketches causing extra work

Designing closets not large enough for the clothing to be contained in them

Designing a project that greatly exceeded the client's budget

Failing to engage and check with a consultant[3]

### DUTY OF CARE

Interior designers owe a duty of care to their clients in many ways. This duty relates to the care in selection of materials and products that are proper and adequate to

---

[1]Clarkson 1983, 35. Copyright West Publishing Company.
[2]Barnes, A. James, *A Guide to Business Law,* Richard Irwin, © 1981, p. 11.
[3]Sweet 1985, 329–330. Copyright West Publishing Company.

meet the functional and legal (if codes are binding) needs of the project. Specifying residential grade carpet in most commercial interiors would give inadequate performance and would be negligent. A designer owes a duty to the client not to allow defective work to be done on the job site. A designer visiting a job site sees that the carpet installer is using a nonquick-release glue to affix carpet tiles when a quick-release glue was specified; the designer has a duty to the client to stop the work and have it corrected. The designer also has a duty not to expose others to risks created by defective designs. The designer must be sure that the structure of the building will support any wall-hung units that are specified.

## BREACH OF DUTY

A breach of duty of reasonable care results when the designer fails to act in a way that is considered reasonable for the professional designer. The breach may be an act such as knowingly specifying the wrong carpet for the client (intentional) or an omission such as not stopping the work when the designer sees that the carpet being installed is incorrect (carelessness).

## CAUSATION

A person may have a duty to another, and he or she may in some way breach that duty, but the act (the breach of duty) must cause some injury or harm for a tort to have been committed. If the injury occurs only because of the designer's act, then there is a causation in fact. An example will help to explain this. A designer knows that the manufacturer requires 5/8-inch drywall to support its wall strips and knows the client has already installed 1/2-inch drywall; if the designer has the wall strips hung anyway, there is a causation in fact. Often the "but for" test is used to determine causation in fact: "But for the wrongful act, the injury would not have occurred."

How far a person's responsibility goes in performance of a wrongful act is covered by proximate cause. "The question is whether the connection between an act and an injury is strong enough to justify imposing liability."[4] If the consequences of the act that does harm are unforeseeable, there is no proximate cause. For example, if the wall strips pull out from the wall and the falling books hit a lamp, which shatters and starts a fire that burns down the house, there would probably be proximate cause if it were reasonable that the lamp would create a fire when broken in such a manner. How foreseeable one act is on another is determined by the courts and is not easy to establish.

## INJURY

A tort of negligence has not occurred unless there has been some legally recognizable loss, harm, wrong, or invasion to a plaintiff. Injury must occur in order for the plaintiff to recover compensation. Remember, plaintiffs in tort cases seek compensation for damages from the defendant; they do not usually seek punishment. More often courts find in favor of the plaintiff when personal injury, rather than property or economic damage, occurs.

## PRINCIPAL DEFENSES FOR NEGLIGENCE

The principal defenses for negligence are assumption of risk and contributory negligence. In assumption of risk, the plaintiff who knowingly and willingly enters

---

[4]Clarkson 1983, 53. Copyright West Publishing Company.

into a risky situation will not be able to recover damages if injury occurs. If a client agrees to purchase a residential grade carpet, knowing it will not provide the wear required in his or her commercial installation, the designer would be absolved of the negligence.

In using contributory negligence as a defense, it must be shown that both sides were negligent and that injury resulted. This comes from the idea that everyone should look out for his or her own interests and safety. Where contributory negligence is successfully used as a defense, the plaintiff will not be able to recover damages no matter how great the injury or how slight the contributory negligence.

## *Intentional Torts against the Person*

Intentional torts against the person must show intent; that is, the person consciously performed the act knowing or was substantially certain that the act would harm another. Assault, battery, false imprisonment, defamation, invasion of privacy, and misrepresentation are some of the torts included in this area.

Assault occurs when a person intentionally performs an act so that another has a feeling of apprehension or fear of harm or physical injury. Actual contact or physical harm is not necessary for an assault to occur; causing another to be apprehensive is enough. A battery occurs when there is intentional touching or other physical contact by one upon another without consent or justification.

False imprisonment (or false arrest) is the intentional confinement of a person for an appreciable duration of time. This is of particular importance to designers who are engaged in retail selling. A business owner must be reasonably certain that someone has shoplifted in order to detain the customer, or the customer can sue for false imprisonment.

Defamation is the wrongful harming of a person's good reputation. If the defamation is in writing it is called libel; if it is oral, it is slander. To be defamatory, statements must be made to or read or heard by a third party. It is not necessary for the defamed party to hear or read the defamation. It is for this reason that interior designers must be careful about what they say or write concerning their competitors or competitors' products. Telling a client that Jones Interiors "did a lousy job" on their last three residential commissions would be defamation by slander. Jones Interiors could sue the offending designer.

Invasion of privacy is a tort against a person's right to freedom from others' prying eyes. For this reason it is important to obtain written permission to photograph an installation (and any people who may be seen in the photograph) if it is used for publication. Care must also be taken in obtaining information concerning a person's or business's affairs—such as obtaining credit information without permission.

To misrepresent is to alter facts to deceive or use fraud in order to receive personal gain. Misrepresentation would begin by a misstatement of facts—not opinions, unless the person expressing the opinion is considered an expert in the subject matter—that the speaker knows to be false. These "untrue facts" must be made with the intent that the client will rely on them. The deceived party must have justifiably relied upon the information, and the reliance must have caused damages to occur.

Sellers' talk or "puffing" is not usually considered misrepresentation, unless the seller represents as fact something that he or she knows is not true. To say that your design firm is the "best interior design office in town" is not fraud since the word *best* is subjective, not objective. To say "we are the only firm in town that can do this work" when it is not true would be misrepresentation.

# *Intentional Torts against Property*

The three torts against property are trespass to land and personal property, conversion, and nuisance. Although each may be a problem to the interior designer, the torts of trespass to personal property and conversion are potentially the most damaging.

Trespass to land means entering land that does not belong to us. Trespass to personal property occurs when a defendant either injures the personal property of another or interferes with the owner's right to exclusive possession or use of the personal property. The most common form of trespass of personal property is conversion. Conversion occurs when the rightful property of one person is taken by another. In criminal law this is commonly called stealing or theft.

When an employee takes merchandise or supplies that belong to the employer and uses those items for his or her own use rather than for company-related use, conversion has occurred. Although most employers do not prosecute or sue (remember, both are valid here) when employees take home pens and paper paid for by the employer, they have a legal right to do so. Another instance of the tort of trespass to personal property is illustrated in the following example: Jane is at the client's office to measure for new draperies. While she is measuring the window, she knocks over a lamp and breaks it. Jane has trespassed upon the personal property of her client and is liable to replace the lamp—even if it no longer worked prior to Jane's breaking it.

A suit for nuisance can also be brought against an interior designer. "A nuisance is an improper activity that interferes with another's enjoyment or use of his or her property."[5] For the designer this could mean that the designer and the client can be sued by a neighbor because the noise and dust from a remodeling project has interfered with the neighbor's enjoyment of his or her home.

# *Strict Liability*

*Strict liability* is a tort "whereby a person is held liable for the consequences of that person's acts regardless of whether the person exercised all possible due care."[6] Strict liability is generally applied to activities that are abnormally dangerous. It is also very important in the area of product liability.

Strict liability, as it applies to product liability, must be a concern of interior designers. The interior designer specifies a product; if the product fails, causing injury, the designer is almost always named in the suit along with the manufacturer. It should be remembered that product liability will usually be concerned only with reasonable, normal use of the product. If the client uses a product in a way for which it was not designed, the interior designer would not be responsible. We shall discuss product liability in more detail in Chapter 22.

Strict liability is sometimes called liability without fault. Generally considered a negligence tort, liability without fault involves some act that has departed from the use of reasonable care. For the designer, this may result from incorrect information in drawings, documents, and/or specifications that causes injury. For example, if the designer incorrectly labels a material in a construction drawing, and the structure later fails, causing injury, the designer would be responsible based on this premise.

---

[5]Jentz 1987, 55. Copyright West Publishing Company.
[6]Barnes 1981, 12.

## Codes Compliance

An area of professional responsibility that is very important—especially to the commercial interior designer—is compliance with various codes. *Codes* are systematic bodies of law created by federal, state, and local jurisdictions to ensure safety. During the course of a project, the interior designer's work may need to be judged against building codes, life-safety or fire codes, and handicapped-access codes. Other codes the project may have to meet include electrical codes, health department codes, and zoning laws.

Although many federal agencies, states, counties, and cities have adopted one or more of the model codes, such as the Uniform Building Code (UBC) related to the laws regulating construction or the Life Safety Code related to fire safety, these government agencies may modify the model codes to their specific needs. Interior designers must be sure they understand which codes apply in the locations they are designing. This information can be obtained from local fire marshals, planning and building departments, and state and federal agencies responsible for specific types of structures. Noncompliance with codes can result in work being stopped, torn out, and/or redone—generally at the expense of the interior designer.

An excellent brief introduction to codes is presented in S. C. Reznikoff's *Specifications for Commercial Interiors*. Peter S. Hopf's *Access for the Handicapped* is an excellent source of information on handicap-access regulations for all 50 states.

## Summary

As interior designers seek professional recognition, they must also accept the professional responsibilities and liabilities. Students beginning their pursuit of a career as well as those already actively engaged in the profession must realize that their design efforts—whether in residential or commercial design, whether in the specification of products or the drafting of floor plans—place them in a position of responsibility to their clients that goes beyond designing an aesthetic environment.

This chapter briefly discusses the differences between criminal and tort law. It also discusses many of the common tort classifications that can result in a civil suit against the interior designer. Professional responsibilities related to contracts, the selling of products, and employee-employer relationships will be discussed in other chapters.

# Chapter 8

## BUSINESS ORGANIZATION AND PERSONNEL MANAGEMENT

*T*he business organization of a small interior design practice is not very complicated, nor should it be. However, once the firm begins to grow in finances, number of clients, and employees, organizational structure becomes necessary. The purpose of this organizational structure is to aid all employees to understand the various activities of the firm and to show who is responsible for those activities. The larger the firm grows, the more complex the organizational structure will become. As long as the firm continues to plan for changes in the organization rather than reacting to them, the firm will continue to grow and prosper.

Personnel issues are important to the business organization. Articles in trade magazines report high turnover rates and basically low salaries. How much of this is due to the lack of good personnel management is difficult to say, but the articles do indicate that job satisfaction is an important issue for interior designers. The areas of personnel management discussed in this chapter will be job descriptions, performance evaluation, compensation, and benefits. Other legal considerations of personnel management including the concept of employment at will and employee contracts will be discussed in Chapter 9.

## *Office Organization*

Many interior design practices begin as one-person studios located in the owner's home. In this smallest of situations, the owner is the president, business manager, marketing director, designer, salesperson, draftsperson, order entry clerk, expediter, complaint department, bookkeeper, secretary, librarian, installer, and any other title required to get the job done. Eventually, the practice becomes prosperous enough to add one or two support people. Usually the first areas where full- or part-time employees are hired are the secretarial and bookkeeping areas.

It is possible that another designer may join the practice as an employee, but more likely the single-designer practice finds a compatible partner, and the practice changes to a partnership or corporation. Now decisions must be made as to which of the two partners (for simplicity) will be responsible for which business functions: marketing, financial management, operational management, and employee supervision. It must be decided if employees will be hired and given responsibility for certain activities such as office management, bookkeeping, and day-to-day accounting, or if one of the partners will take on these responsibilities. Decisions must also be made as to what the business card will look like, what the boards will look like, as well as all the specific issues of operating the practice. The partners need to sit down and honestly evaluate their strengths and weaknesses in order to determine who will do what. Egos must be put aside. The failure of the partner in charge of marketing to really be able to market can very well mean the failure of the business.

In time, the practice will start adding additional employees. As the firm grows the chain of command[1] becomes increasingly important. The small, personal, "family" business of the early days eventually gets into communications trouble. The open doors to the owners' offices never seem to close; thus, these important senior members have trouble getting their work done. New secretaries go to the owners with their complaints rather than to senior secretaries who are supervising them. Delivery personnel come straight to the owners' office rather than to the warehouse supervisor. As is often the case in many fast-growing companies, good yearly planning has not been going on so that many times everyone seems to be spending more time "stamping out fires" than getting really productive work done. It is time for some organizational planning.

Everyone knows that the designers are one group of workers, that the secretaries and clerks constitute another work group, and bookkeepers and warehouse/delivery people form others. So the start of organizational planning is obvious. Authority must be delegated within these work groups in order to manage each staff group. If the group is large enough, the staff will require titles that differentiate seniority and responsibility. If decisions as to who will manage each work group have not already been established, the owners will need to evaluate each of the existing employees to see if any of them can take on the management responsibility. If not, they will need to determine what to do until external individuals can be interviewed and hired.

Job descriptions need to be worked out for each distinctly different job or job level in the work groups. An employee handbook describing specific personnel policies also needs to be prepared. In addition, policies regarding work activities for each group need to be established. And with the assumption that this was not done in the past, a procedure for developing yearly marketing plans, financial plans, budgets, and the annual business plan will have to be prepared—overwhelming tasks for many business owners. Yet, these are things that must be done to assist the practice in continuing to achieve healthy, profitable growth.

How projects are managed administratively is an important part of the firm's organization. When the single owner obtained a client, it was very obvious who was responsible for all the design activities. When a partner joined the firm, each partner was most likely responsible for his or her own design project work. As design employees were added as assistants, some project responsibility was delegated to these less experienced individuals. But what starts to happen when the company grows to about six or eight designer/salespeople plus the owners? Who brings in the new work? What happens to it once the client signs the contract? Who is responsible for all the design work? Who writes the specifications?

---

[1]From the military; *chain of command* refers to the formal reporting links from one level of employee to another.

# *Business Organizations*

The following covers the primary business organizations that are found in the interior design profession. The purpose is to describe the different ways that a practice can be organized. Of course, these brief descriptions are very generalized and should not be considered the only way to organize an interior design business.

## RESIDENTIAL RETAIL STORES

Retail stores involved in interior design furniture sales and services often have one group of individuals who are strictly floor salespeople. These individuals remain in the store and sell merchandise to clients who do not really need an interior designer's services. These clients are often just looking for one or two items to supplement or replace something in their homes or offices. If the company is large enough, these "in-house" salespeople may specialize in areas such as furniture, wall coverings, and floor treatments. In-house salespeople may or may not be trained interior designers.

A second group in the retail store would be the interior designers. When the client requires the services of an interior designer, they are referred to one of the people in this group. The interior designer is responsible for finding out what the client needs in the way of products and services, discusses contracts (if the company charges a fee for design service), and is responsible for all the design work needing to be done. In some situations, the designer may have an assistant (an entry-level interior designer) to help him or her gather information, find appropriate products, and prepare necessary documents. However, the experienced interior designer is the primary person dealing with the client.

## OFFICE FURNISHINGS DEALERS

Office furnishings dealers, generally considered retail establishments, will have outside salespeople and a group of designers. The salespeople are responsible for selling products, but their efforts also often bring in a major portion of the interior design work done by the company. When they find a client who also needs interior design services, they will alert the appropriate department.

For smaller dealers, interior designers work out of the "interiors department." In this situation, it is common that any one of the designers, with the time and experience to handle a client, will meet with the client and be responsible for the project. In larger companies, there might be an interiors department or even a separate affiliated interior design company. In either of these cases, the interiors group is headed by a manager, and the salesperson would contact the design director concerning the project. The design director would either visit with the client himself or herself or assign one of the senior designers to that task. Whoever then meets with the client must get the complete picture of the project, determine if and what amount of fees will be charged, and determine who would be responsible for preparing all the design work.

In a small firm, a contract would be prepared by the designer who visited with the client. In larger firms, the contract is likely to be prepared by the design director or, with approval of the design director, by the project designer who interviewed the client.

### INDEPENDENT INTERIOR DESIGN FIRMS

Independent interior design practices may or may not sell furnishings or have a retail showroom. Client contact, contract development, design responsibility, and project management responsibility in a small firm are all part of what each designer in the firm would be expected to do. The owner, most likely, will also be doing a lot of project work in addition to management duties.

The larger firms will have various management and staff levels. In some firms, there will also be individuals with many specialized job functions, such as specification writers and renderers, that free the project designers from these activities.

## *Job Classifications*

Organization and project responsibility become more critical when the design department has several interior designers with varying amounts of experience and expertise. In these situations a more formally organized structure becomes important.

The chain of command or, more formally, the organizational structure, helps everyone in the organization understand what are the formal communication patterns. A graphic representation of the chain of command is the organizational chart. Even though it is commonly found that the real chain of command does not exactly reflect the organizational chart, larger organizations find it useful to chart the company in order to show the formal flows of official communication. Figure 8-1 shows an organizational chart that defines the job classifications to be reviewed. This discussion of typical job classifications does not include the owner since that job has many unique activities based on the organization and size of the firm. The descending order of responsibility reflects no specific organization and merely describes the most common levels.

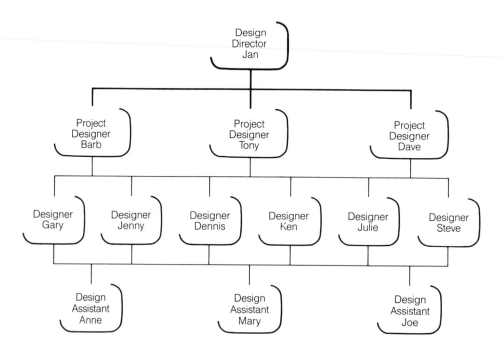

**FIGURE 8-1**
Design office
organizational chart.

## DESIGN DIRECTOR

At the top of the organizational chart is the manager. The job title might be design director, vice president–design, design manager, or perhaps some other title indicating leadership. This person can have many different job responsibilities depending on the actual size of the firm, but usually the job responsibilities will include (1) administration, (2) marketing, and (3) design.

Administrative duties include all the management functions. Planning, hiring and firing, assignment of work, and preparing contracts are some of these. In addition, the design director is responsible for preparing various management control reports, establishing policies, and attending management meetings. The training and development of the design staff is an important part of the design director's responsibilities.

The most important marketing duties of the design director are making contacts and subsequent presentations to prospective clients. Design managers are often involved in the development of marketing tools like brochures. In many firms, the director is also the public liaison for the company related to design activities. And, of course, he or she is involved in planning and participating in the development of marketing plans.

Design responsibility of the manager may be minimal in large, very active design firms, or it may be an important part of the manager's responsibility in a small firm. By design responsibility we first mean that the manager is in charge of design projects in which he or she plays the role of the project designer. In this situation, the design director is making client contacts, preparing design documents (or supervising others in their preparation), preparing and reviewing purchase orders, and making himself or herself available for installation supervision.

The design director also sets the minimum standards for all design work that leaves the office by reviewing projects during their progress and before they are presented to clients. In this second role, the design director remains involved with project activities without actually doing them.

In very large design firms, the design department leadership may be broken down into two or more areas—design administration and marketing and design production—with different individuals responsible for each group of activities.

## PROJECT MANAGER

The second common level in larger firms comes under such titles as project manager, senior designer, and senior project designer. In large firms where the design director is primarily involved in administration, this becomes the key design and client-contact level. Project managers commonly have five or more years of professional experience and have substantially developed the technical design skills needed by the hiring firm. Often, they are also required to have good communication skills in dealing with clients and other designers.

The project manager is the lead designer and may supervise other designers. As the lead designer, he or she meets with clients to determine needs, substantially designs the interior, prepares or directs others in the completion of design documents, and is responsible for order entry supervision and installation supervision. In some firms, the product manager is required to market the firm's design services to obtain new projects and may even be required to negotiate the design contract.

## STAFF DESIGNER

The next level of designers are given titles such as staff designer or designer. Staff designers commonly are required to have one or more years of professional experience and well-developed technical design skills as needed by the particular firm. On large projects, these individuals would work under the supervision of the project designers. They may be involved with client interviewing and information gathering conducted by the project designer; they may be asked to prepare preliminary drafting and other documentation and preliminary product specification, in addition to other tasks assigned by the project designers. On smaller projects, they may be responsible for all phases of the project—from obtaining needed information from the client to being responsible for installation supervision. Administrative responsibility is limited to personal time and recordkeeping.

## DESIGN ASSISTANT

The entry-level position for most firms is commonly called design assistant or junior designer. Entry level means that these individuals have little professional experience other than perhaps an internship. They work under the direction of a more experienced designer for one or more years. The kinds of work performed are most commonly drafting, preparation of sample boards, preparation of specifications lists for furniture and furnishings, perhaps installation supervision, maintenance of the library, and other tasks assigned by the design director or project designer. After several months, it is not uncommon for the design assistant to be given full responsibility for small-sized projects. As in the case of the designer, administrative responsibility for the design assistant would only require time and recordkeeping for his or her individual efforts.

## OTHER JOB CLASSIFICATIONS

Depending on the actual interior design practice and size of the firm, there may be some additional specialized job classifications. In large office furnishings dealers, commercial interior design firms, and architectural firms, a job classification called space planner might exist. Space planners are responsible for the overall space plan or for tenant improvement work, but not the specification of furniture and furnishings. The documents they prepare are working drawings and the needed specifications for construction.

Another specialized job classification would be specification writer or estimator. As the title implies, these individuals are responsible only for the preparation of finished specification documents. This job classification is most commonly found in very large interior design firms or architectural firms.

A job classification that can be a specialization or an expected responsibility of any designer is a renderer or graphics designer. Renderers and graphic designers have as their major responsibility the production of perspectives and colored renderings of the interiors designed by the interiors staff. Graphics designers are also responsible for the design of graphics, such as business cards and brochures, presentations, and presentation graphics for clients, as well as similar graphics for the interior design firm. Only the larger firms might have specialized renderers and graphics designers.

A relatively new job classification is CADD (computer-aided design and drafting) operator. A CADD operator has experience in the use of some kind of computer-aided design equipment and software. Depending on how this job is used in the firm, the workers may have been trained as interior designers or as computer operators. They may serve as a separate function of the firm or they may be a part of the interior design department. CADD job classifications are still rather uncommon in small sized interior design firms. See Chapter 10 for a fuller discussion of CADD.

## *Job Descriptions*

When the firm begins to hire employees, job descriptions should be prepared for the expected positions. The *job description* communicates the qualifications, skills, and responsibilities of each job classification within the firm. Job descriptions should be provided to individuals at the point that they are seriously being considered for a position or upon hiring. Job descriptions should also be available to existing employees so that they may see what qualifications and skills are required of higher-level positions.

Job descriptions are usually prepared in outline form. They should contain statements that are specific enough to differentiate between individuals yet broad enough to allow the manager some flexibility in hiring. The content of the job description must be kept current and complete. It also must accurately reflect the desired skills required to perform the responsibilities of the position. As much as possible, the descriptions of responsibilities should be stated in measurable terms to aid in performance evaluation.

Job descriptions should have statements related to qualifications, skills required, and responsibilities, and they may have statements related to the job. Figures 8-2 and 8-3 provide examples of job descriptions for few typical interior design positions.

---

### SENIOR DESIGNER

**Principal Responsibilities**
1.  Responsible for seeking out prospective clients; determine the scope of the project; the work to be done; select the appropriate design contract from our Master Contract; present the contract; get credit approval, signature, and deposit *before* work begins.
2.  Responsible for entire project which may include layout drawings, color coordination, furniture selection, design concept, merchandising, installation, and sign-off. Function as the Project Designer on assigned projects.
3.  Compile comprehensive schedules of equipment and colors; coordinate color schemes for the offices and entire building when applicable.
4.  Collaborate with the Associate Director in establishing schedule of production effort, design reviews, presentation meetings, and/or periodic progress checks as dictated by the nature and scope of the project. Responsible for coordinating the work load of Staff Designers with Associate Director.
5.  Responsible for dealer/client conferences and presentations regarding design project.
6.  Recommend type of equipment required to facilitate the job function of each of the customer's areas and occupants; review work and communication flow for client; recommend work flow improvements.
7.  Suggest methods of control for acoustics; suggest lighting improvements; direct clients to proper source of supply for their accessories required to furnish office when applicable.
8.  Participate in periodic project reviews to evaluate standard of design and the appropriateness to client needs, requests, and exception. Develop a "team effort" on each project.
9.  Develop and maintain client work file containing records of all written correspondence, notes on all pertinent verbal discussions, design sketches, schedules, contracts; develop a diary of job from inception to completion.
10. Allocate time in design contract to give on-site consultation or supervision of installation.
11. Provide technical supervision for Staff Designers in performing their assigned tasks.
12. Maintain client confidence and good relations. Develop effective communications and keep client informed of project status.

**FIGURE 8-2**
**Job description for a senior designer.** *(Reproduced with permission, Walsh Bros. Office Equipment, Phoenix, Az.)*

13. Approve all staff design work before it leaves Office Design. Make certain Staff Designers are *not* sent out on *initial* design projects alone. They should *always* be accompanied by a Senior Designer, Interior Architect, or Project Coordinator. (EXCEPTION—smaller projects and after Associate Director's approval.)
14. Responsible for the successful completion of project so that we can collect our total design contract fee.
15. Keep a ledger sheet on each job with a breakdown of hours billed and time (dollars) remaining on contracts and coordinate status with Staff Designers.
16. Review Staff Designers' time sheets to better evaluate the time needed by different Staff Designers to do different types of contract jobs.
17. Assist sales personnel, through design, in securing profitable project sales.
18. Perform any of the following job functions to support sales representatives as directed.
    (a) Information gathering.
    (b) Space planning and layout.
    (c) Selection of style, type, and color of furniture, upholstery, wallcoverings, finishes, carpet, and accessories.
19. Merchandise products necessary to create proper environment.
20. Inform Associate Director of any prospective design contracts.
21. Assist in developing goals and objectives of Office Designs.
22. Coordinate work load of Staff Designers with Associate Director and other Senior Designers.
23. Help each Staff Designer evolve into a Senior Designer with continuing responsibility for their professional development.
24. Attend weekly sales meeting for product and company knowledge.
25. Attend Office Design meetings and participate in Office Design projects when requested.
26. Continue personal education through seminars, professional organizations, and other training experiences.
27. Report competitive practices or products for evaluation by management or design staff.
28. Participate in growth of firm as a cooperative member of the team and accept other responsibilities assigned by supervisors.

**Special Responsibilities**
1. Aid in layout and product selection for floor display, when requested.
2. Aid in layout and design of department within the company as requested by management.

**Position Qualifications**

| | |
|---|---|
| *Education:* | College degree in interior architecture or design, or associate degree with actual experience and knowledge may substitute in some cases—desired. |
| *Experience:* | Four to six years experience with actual design firm in a sales support role or design contract marketing—desired. |

**FIGURE 8-2**
**Job description for a senior designer.** *(Continued)*

The qualifications section will outline the minimal educational requirements. This section would also specify the minimum amount of work experience in years. Statements such as "graduation from at least a four-year college or university with a major in interior design" would set one of the minimum criteria for an interior design position.

In the section concerning skills required, statements related to any specific technical abilities along with any skills or abilities of a general nature would be outlined. Although this section often comes second in a job description, it is often easier to finish writing this section after the responsibilities section is completed. In any case, it is important for the skills required to correlate with the responsibilities expected and the qualifications demanded. These skills and general abilities should be listed in the order of importance to the job. For a firm involved in commercial interior design, drafting skill may be of primary importance for an entry-level design assistant, and therefore should be listed first. For a residential firm, color coordination may be primary for an entry-level person.

---

### STAFF DESIGNER

**Principal Responsibilities**
1. Assist senior designer/designer in design and layout of floor plans for customers, showing location and arrangement of furniture, using drafting skills.
2. Assist senior designer/designer in devising and coordinating harmonious furniture color schemes to interior building colors, using professional judgment and knowledge.
3. Assist senior designer/designer in selecting wall and floor coverings and assist installer and supervise the installation.
4. Assist senior designer/designer in preparing schedule of furniture used in layout, providing necessary model identification information.
5. Assist senior designer/designer in preparing presentation boards for use in showing scheduled furniture to client.
6. Assist senior designer/designer in maintaining records of time spent on all projects.
7. Assist senior designer/designer by participating in periodic project review to evaluate design standards and appropriateness to client needs, requests, and expectations . . . become a project team member.
8. Assist senior designer/designer in dealer/client conferences regarding floor plan layout and color selections as requested.
9. Participate in the organization, arrangements, maintenance, and updating of reference library and sample materials.
10. Responsible for getting senior designer's/designer's approval on all work before presenting to client.
11. Assist all sales personnel, through design, in securing profitable product sales.
12. Assist in the merchandising of products necessary to create a proper environment.
13. Attend Office Design monthly meetings and participate in Office Design's projects when requested.
14. Continue personal education through seminars and other training experiences.
15. Participate in the firm's growth as a cooperative member of the team, and accept other responsibilities as assigned by supervisor.
16. Report competitive practices or products for evaluation by management or design staff.
17. Keep senior designer/designer informed of job progress on a daily/weekly basis.

**Special Responsibilities**
1. Aid in layout and product selection for floor display when requested.
2. Aid in layout and design of departments within company as requested by management.

**Position Qualifications**

*Education:*   College degree in design-related or interior architecture, or associate degree with actual experience and knowledge may substitute in some cases.

*Experience:*   Two to four years experience with actual design firm in sales support role and/or design function desired.

*Knowledge and Skills:*
    (a) Excellent drafting skills.
    (b) Good sense of color and coordination.
    (c) Wide range of product knowledge.
    (d) Knowledge and/or experience of open office planning.

**FIGURE 8-3**
**Job description for a staff designer.** *(Reproduced with permission, Office Designs, Phoenix, Az.)*

The responsibilities section must be detailed enough so that the individual in the position knows what is expected of him or her. Government agencies and large corporations, which have a great deal of experience in the preparation of job descriptions, often have very detailed outlines of responsibilities. Interior design firms, which have limited experience in this area, often have vague, unclear descriptions (if they have them at all).

A reference as to whom the person reports, either as a separate section or within the responsibilities section, should be noted. This helps clarify the chain of command and also aids new employees in knowing who will be his or her supervisor.

Since people leave their positions, reference is best made by job title rather than by name.

## *Performance Evaluations*

For almost every owner or manager of a design firm, preparation of *performance evaluations* of employees is an unpleasant task. In part, the evaluation is difficult for design managers since few have training or experience with the performance evaluation process. In far too many practices, the performance evaluation is an informal mental review of each employee's work contribution. This informal review is almost always based on the manager's subjective opinions rather than any objective evaluation of work performance based on the responsibilities of the job.

Managers also dislike evaluation time because preparing evaluations can take so much time. Even with an informal review process, it is not uncommon for the manager to spend many hours during the year considering each employee's past performance and discussing these impressions with the employee. To many managers, a formal process will mean even more time spent on this activity.

Employees also find the review process an anxiety-producing, negative time period. Far too many employers conduct performance evaluations as a time for negative criticism rather than an evaluation of progress and direction toward development of the employees. It is no wonder that employees dislike the evaluation process.

In this section, we will discuss the performance evaluation and suggest some ways to make it more useful to the employee and the employer, and perhaps less difficult for the employer.

### PURPOSE

The purpose of the performance evaluation is to appraise the positive and negative work efforts of an employee. Its primary goal should be the development of the employee for the future, not the punishment of the employee for past performance (see Figure 8-4). These evaluations must be based on the responsibilities that the employee understands to be within his or her control during the period of the evaluation. Evaluations must primarily be made objectively and based, as much as possible, on measurable criteria related back to responsibilities (see Figure 8-5).

Performance evaluation should be designed to

1. *Encourage the development of employees.* Companies that continually hire designers straight out of college, train them for a year or two, and then see them leave for a job with more responsibility at another company apparently enjoy being part of the educational processes of the interior design profession. However, this kind of hire/train/gone/rehire circle costs the firm more in the long run than the savings obtained by continually hiring inexperienced designers at low salaries. The training, development, and keeping of quality employees costs the company less and helps the company grow by showing clients that the firm is stable.

2. *Aid the employer/employee supervisory relationship.* Individuals in management positions in interior design offices should have as clearly defined aspects of their job the supervision and training of design staff employees. Even though the design director is often expected to "wear many hats" in the office, the management of design personnel should not be the least important. Managers must take the time to observe the design staff as to how they do the work

assigned. When necessary, they must be ready to train employees in aspects of the firm's design processes. And, they must be ready to recognize when employees are in need of training from outside sources.

3. *Determine compensation increases, promotions, and dismissals.* Too many companies and employees view the performance evaluation as a means to the end for an increase in salary or a promotion. When this is the primary goal, individuals who do not get the expected increase or promotion often become frustrated and leave the design firm. This occurs most often when the reason for not receiving the increase or promotion is never clarified or when the employee suddenly finds out that he or she was not doing what was expected in order to receive the adjustment. However, a well-thought-out review process can be counted on as a means to determine these adjustments as well as to help in the motivation of employees toward agreed-on responsibilities and work performance.

4. *Aid human resource planning.* The evaluation process helps determine which areas of expertise existing employees have and which areas of expertise are

---

**SUBJECT:    YOUR PERFORMANCE REVIEW**

Date:        _____

To:          _____

From:        _____


The firm has implemented a Performance Review Program for all employees. The main purpose of the program is to provide the opportunity for regular, two-way communication between employee and supervisor, which should result in improved job performance and productivity. Please be reminded that your performance review does not directly affect your compensation review, and we ask that you respond to this review as openly as possible.

Your Performance Review meeting is scheduled on _____ at __ A.M./P.M. Please allow at least one hour for this meeting. You will need a copy of your current job description for this review and copies of each of these attached forms: Employee Performance Review Summary and Employee Performance Review Worksheets.

Since each employee is to share the responsibility of the review with his or her supervisor, you are asked to do a self-review prior to our meeting. Please use your job description, which lists your major responsibilities, and the attached Review Worksheet, which will review the level of performance for each of the responsibilities. Number each item to correspond with the numbering on your job description. Write in any comments you care to make.

Also please complete the Performance Review Summary, and spend a few minutes thinking about item 4—your goals for the next performance review.

As your supervisor, I will also prepare for your review in the same way. Then at our scheduled meeting, we will review both Worksheets and the Summary, and reach agreement on the level of performance expected.

Again, the main purpose of this program is to improve communications, thus resulting in improved job performance and productivity. This is not just an exercise in filling out forms! Our goal is to *talk* about and *improve* performance. Think of the program as an ongoing "process," and not a one-time "grade." Remember that your comments and suggestions about your job performance are welcome, and you are encouraged to play an active role in this process.

This performance review program will be a continuous process, and I will provide you regular feedback on an ongoing basis as to your performance throughout the year.

Thank you for your cooperation in this very important program!

_____

**FIGURE 8-4**
**Sample notice for the employee's performance review.** *(Reproduced with permission, Office Designs, Phoenix, Az.)*

**EMPLOYEE PERFORMANCE REVIEW SUMMARY**

Name _____ Position _____
Dept./Div. _____ Supervisor _____

1. What is the basic purpose or objective of this position?
   _____
   _____

2. How well have the basic objectives been accomplished?
   _____
   _____
   _____

3. What changes in approach to the job would help improve the overall job performance?
   _____
   _____
   _____

4. List specific goals for the next performance review and when they should be completed.

   GOAL                                    TARGET DATE

   _____          _____
   _____          _____
   _____          _____
   _____          _____
   _____          _____

5. How well have the goals from the past performance review been accomplished?
   _____
   _____
   _____

6. Additional comments:
   _____
   (use reverse side for additional comments)

Supervisor's Signature _____ Date _____
Employee's Signature _____ Date _____

**FIGURE 8-5**
**A performance review summary sheet.**
*(Reproduced with permission, Walsh Bros. Office Equipment, Phoenix, Az.)*

needed either through training or the hiring of new employees. For instance, if the design firm decides to pursue health care facilities planning, performance evaluations will help the manager decide whether or not someone within the firm can do the work. Understanding this, the manager can then recruit someone experienced in health care work or someone to take over the current staff member's ongoing responsibility as he or she shifts to the new area.

For the employee, the performance appraisal must tell each how he or she is doing. It should also tell the employee where he or she can likely progress in the future and how to advance there. For new employees, this means that the manager must indicate clearly what the responsibilities of the position are and what kind of performance level will be expected. A well-written job description will define responsibilities. If, however, the individual's actual job responsibilities deviate from the job description in some way, these should be written down and clearly understood by both parties. Performance levels also need to be discussed and agreed on. Interim evaluations should focus on the achievement of goals and, where satisfactory progress does not exist, constructive criticism and direction toward the development of success should be addressed.

For the continuing employee, the evaluation must be based on responsibilities and performance levels agreed to at the last review. Since the performance evaluation is for development of the individual, deficiencies must be in terms of correction and future achievement, not punishment. Discussion should also occur regarding new goals and how current and expected responsibilities and performance levels fit into these goals. This becomes the performance criteria for the next review.

### TIMING

Although informal evaluation situations may occur at any time for any level of employee, most companies find that a formal evaluation should take place yearly. It is a very good idea, however, for new employees to be evaluated more frequently during the first year. A common time schedule has the first evaluation take place at the end of the probationary period, which is usually ninety days. Many firms find it advantageous to have reviews at thirty-, sixty-, and possibly seventy-five–day intervals for new employees during the ninety-day probationary period. Subsequent evaluations would occur after the first six months and then after one year. The one-year date can be either at the anniversary date of hiring or on a day set when all evaluations are done.

New employees, especially those just out of college, are going to be looking for more constant evaluations of their progress. This is due in part to the uncertainty of being in a new situation as well as to the familiar constant evaluations received in college. However, if employees know what their responsibilities are and what level of performance is expected, constant evaluation and "pats on the back" will not be necessary or expected.

### THE EVALUATOR

The performance evaluation is most commonly performed by the employee's immediate supervisor. In design offices where people often work in teams to complete projects, individuals who are not truly an employee's supervisor may be asked to evaluate an employee's performance. If this occurs, the employee should be made aware of who is making the evaluations and why he or she was involved if he or she is not, in fact, the employee's supervisor.

Often individual evaluations are supplemented by self- or peer evaluations. Self-evaluations can be helpful, but it is not uncommon for employees to either be too hard or too easy on themselves as compared to a superior's evaluation. Peer evaluations, where employees rate co-workers, only seem to work when employees trust each other, when they are truly in a position to be very familiar with each others work, and when they are not competing with each other for raises or promotions. Experience has shown that peers will be either too easy on each other so as not to get co-workers angry or too hard on individuals they do not like.

### THE INSTRUMENT AND EVALUATION

For the performance evaluation process to be effective and meaningful, the instrument used must produce reliable and valid measurements of the criteria. An instrument is reliable if it produces consistent data. This would mean that if two different supervisors were to evaluate the same individual, the results should be the same. For the instrument to be valid, it must deal with only those factors that are relevant to an individual's performance. For example, a design assistant may be told that drafting is a primary responsibility of the position. If the quantity of work produced is not relevant, but the quality of work is, then only the quality of work should be evaluated. Projects themselves cannot be easily evaluated under the constraints of validity. What can be evaluated more easily is how things were done, such as error-free drafting and specification writing, proper completion of necessary correspondence, the meeting of schedules with clients and others, and so on.

The rating scale must be as objective as possible. Dealing with specific skills and skill levels as they relate to job responsibilities is one way to maintain objectivity. Being sure the rating instrument does not contain a lot of questions related to either the personality, attitude, or appearance of the employee also maintains objectivity. The instrument should also not evaluate based solely on the employer's personal opinion—especially if that personal opinion has not been satisfactorily communicated to the employees. The right kind of evaluation method will help obtain objectivity in the evaluation, which is necessary to make it fair for all employees.

The most commonly used evaluation method is the rating scale (see Figure 8-6). Rating scales consist of four or five valuations such as outstanding, very good, satisfactory, fair, and poor. If valuations such as these are used, then each is given some kind of numeric scale also. The evaluator is asked to assign one of these values to a series of job traits. These traits may be stated as questions or as short one-or-more-word statements.

These ratings are then "totaled." If certain traits are to receive more value than others, then the traits or grouping of traits have to be weighted. Then a total is given. In the simplest form, the person with the highest ranking gets the highest salary increase (or first shot at promotion, and so on). This does not mean that the person with the lowest ranking gets fired, but it does mean that he or she definitely requires the most counseling for improvement. In almost all cases, employers should be required to provide a written sentence or two related to each trait evaluation. Some firms, however, only require comments when very high or very low ratings are given.

Since rating scales are prone to subjective judgment, the ratings are also affected by such things as the evaluator's being overly strict or overly lenient. The ratings can also be affected by central tendency mistakes and halo effects. Sometimes managers, in a mistaken belief that employees will do better work when coerced, will have exceedingly harsh standards of performance. They feel that negative motivation will somehow inspire the employee to work harder. On the other side is the employer who tries too hard to give the employee a good rating, thereby never giving an honest assessment. Being too harsh will frustrate employees, whereas being too lenient will allow less than satisfactory work to be considered acceptable. Lenient evaluations eventually catch up with employees, surprising them with the knowledge that their work is below par and their services are no longer required. Other employees, seeing someone "getting away with it," will wonder why they are working so hard.

Central tendency mistakes refer to a manager's rating of all employees in the average or satisfactory range. In this case, no one is judged as being outstanding, or poor, or even above average or below average. When no distinction is made, there is no motivation for the outstanding employee to continue to work hard and no motivation for the poor employee to improve. In fact, very little motivation exists for anyone when this occurs.

The halo effect appears when the evaluation of one set of traits colors the other traits. If someone is given low ratings on traits related to the quality of the work he or she does, that person may also be given low ratings on other traits, such as initiative, even if he or she really has high levels of initiative.

To overcome these problems, evaluators could use a method of "forced distribution." Forced distribution is like grading on a curve in school. The evaluator is

## EMPLOYEE PERFORMANCE REVIEW WORKSHEET

Name _____    Position _____

Date of Review _____    Date of Job Description _____

CODE:        PR—Principal Responsibilities        DR—Department Responsibilities
             GR—General Responsibilities          CR—Company Responsibilities
             SR—Special Responsibilities

| CODE | JOB DESC. LINE # | BRIEF DESCRIPTION OF THE TASK | COMMENTS REGARDING PERFORMANCE OF TASK | EXCELLENT | ABOVE STANDARD | STANDARD | IMPROVEMENT NEEDED | UNACCEPTABLE |
|---|---|---|---|---|---|---|---|---|
| | | | | | | | | |
| | | | | | | | | |
| | | | | | | | | |
| | | | | | | | | |
| | | | | | | | | |
| | | | | | | | | |
| | | | | | | | | |
| | | | | | | | | |
| | | | | | | | | |
| | Both the employee and supervisor are to fill out as many worksheets as needed. | Please use the back of this sheet for any additional comments. | | | | | |

FIGURE 8-6
**Sample performance rating sheet.** *(Reproduced with permission, Walsh Bros. Office Equipment, Phoenix, Az.)*

forced to place a certain percentage of employees in each of the categories. Knowing that only certain percentages of individuals will be ranked in the highest category encourages the evaluator to make a more conscious effort at objective evaluations. However, there are some problems with forced distributions. First, some individuals do not make it into the highest categories because one aspect of their performance always holds them back. This is akin to the student who never seems to be able to study for multiple choice tests and always does poorly in classes with exams but is outstanding in studio classes. Another problem with forced distribution is that with everyone knowing that only a few individuals will be ranked very high, the average employee might not see any reason to try to improve. Finally, the wrong kind of competitive atmosphere may be created in the office where people believe it necessary to undermine co-workers in order to advance.

There are some other methods of evaluation that can be used. One is a checklist where the evaluator checks off the items that best (or least) describe the employees performance. The items on the checklist are very specific statements related to job behavior.

Another method is a comparison of one employee to another. One way of doing this is by the paired comparison method. Employees are first paired. "In a four-person department, for example, employee A would be compared with B, A with C, A with D, B with C, and so on. Then for each trait, analyze who is the most effective employee of the pair. After all the traits are compared, add up the number of times the employee was rated highest. The employee chosen most often for traits of equal value receives the highest rating."[2] Other methods of ranking can be found in some of the references listed in the bibliography and in other books on performance appraisal.

### INTERVIEW

The interview should be scheduled sufficiently in advance for the manager and employee to be adequately prepared to discuss the employee's past performance with respect to previously agreed-on goals. Notice to the employee should also indicate what will occur during the interview. The interview should be private, and only the employee and manager should be present.

Sufficient time must be scheduled so that the interview can progress uninterrupted by telephone calls, clients, or anything else. A minimum of one hour is generally required if the interview does not include a discussion of next year's goals, but two or more hours may be needed to fully discuss both issues. The employer should allow approximately half the time for his or her comments and the other half for the employee's comments.

It is important for the employer to put the employee at ease at the beginning of the interview and to explain to the employee how the interview will proceed. The employer must also be clear that the purpose of the evaluation is for the continued development of the employee as well as a review of current performance. The employer should understand that the interview is not a disciplinary session.

The employer should start his or her review comments with a positive statement. This helps put the employee at ease and prevents him or her from being immediately on the defensive. Criticism should be constructive in nature. It often helps to place comments on negative performance between positive comments. The employer should seek to be as descriptive as possible in positive and negative com-

---

[2]Block, Judy R., *Performance Appraisal on the Job: Making It Work.* Reprinted by permission of the publisher, Executive Enterprises Publications Co., Inc., New York, N.Y., © 1981, pp. 35–36.

ments, and these comments should be based on performance criteria, not personal feelings. This helps the employee understand more precisely what he or she is doing right or wrong.

The employee should be asked to evaluate his or her own progress for the year. Some evaluators start with the employee's comments so that the employee does not become unnecessarily defensive about the negative comments of the employer. It is necessary for the employee to comment about his or her own performance to allow the employer to understand how the employee views his or her own work role.

The interview should focus on strong points if the evaluation received a high mark. This reinforces positive future activity and motivates the employee to make further progress. If the evaluation received particularly low marks, the employer must be prepared before the interview for potential hostility and disbelief, and should have a course of action in mind if the employee gives no indication of improvement being possible.

The last portion of the interview should focus on the future, with discussions concerning what the employee can do to resolve performance deficiencies. Discussion and negotiation must occur so that the course of action becomes an agreed-on plan, not one dictated by the employer. Most successes come from focusing on two or three of the more important negative areas rather than a longer list. This is a more satisfactory method, since it is difficult for people to try to improve on many things and at the same time maintain positive aspects. A realistic timetable for the improvement should also be agreed to as an aid in future evaluation.

The interview should be concluded with a summary of the satisfactory and unsatisfactory areas as well as the action plan for the resolution of agreed-on unsatisfactory areas. The interview should end on a positive note with the employee clearly understanding how his or her performance is viewed by the employer and what the future will bring for that employee.

After the interview, the employer should prepare some notes related to what occurred during the interview. This is also a good idea for the employee. The agreed-on goals and timetable should be prepared as soon as possible. Whoever is responsible for preparing this must quickly provide a copy to the other party. It should then be reviewed individually, and any discrepancies should be discussed and agreed on immediately.

The employer should follow up the evaluation through observations and other monitoring of the employee's progress toward the goals. Some areas may need special monitoring, and the manager must be ready to spend the time training or working with the individual. Remember that performance evaluations fail when the employer only considers evaluation and development as important issues during the formal evaluation time period.

## *Compensation and Benefits*

What the salary for working at an interior design office is and how it is arrived at are very important considerations for both the employee and the employer. There is more than one way for interior design employees to be compensated. *Compensation* in the form of the weekly or biweekly paycheck is only part of payments made to the designer. Benefits, such as paid vacations and health insurance, also make a significant contribution to the total compensation package. The most common methods will be briefly discussed in this section.

## COMPENSATION

The most common methods of compensating design employees are hourly wage, straight salary, and commission. A bonus plan is sometimes tied to any of these.

In the hourly wage, the interior designer is paid some rate for every hour he or she works. The weekly salary would then be computed by figuring the average work day (e.g., eight hours) and the average work week (e.g., forty hours). If a design assistant is paid six dollars an hour, his or her weekly salary would be $240 per week for a forty-hour week. Some firms, however, have slightly shorter work weeks. It is possible for a company's work week to be thirty-five or thirty-seven hours. It is up to the individual company to determine the length of its normal work week. Since the federal wage and hour laws apply to interior design firms, the firm has to pay hourly wage employees overtime for any hours worked beyond the normal work week. This amounts to time and a half for weekday overtime work and double time for Sundays and holidays.

From an employee's standpoint, an hourly wage is a good compensation method since it pays employees for every hour (and portion of an hour) they work. The employee, however, will have to show the manager that he or she is being very productive during the workday to be sure that overtime worked is really necessary. Overtime hourly wages for interior designers can be very costly to the firm if the overtime is not expected when estimating design fees or when it occurs because the employees have not been productive during the workday.

Because of the nature of interior design work, the hourly wage is used less often as a method of compensation, except where the monitoring of the employees' productivity and work responsibilities is relatively easy. It is more commonly used to compensate entry-level employees and "production"-type employees like secretaries, bookkeepers, and delivery people.

The straight salary method of compensation provides a fixed amount of salary to the employee no matter how many hours in the week he or she works. Of course, the firm still requires the employee on salary to work a normal work week of thirty-five to forty hours. The employee's weekly pay would be determined by dividing the yearly salary by fifty-two weeks.

An employee compensated on a straight salary method would not be eligible for any overtime pay. When overtime is worked, the employee usually is expected to, at some convenient time, utilize "compensatory time." Compensatory time is time off during the normal work week to make up for the overtime hours worked. In all cases, the utilization of compensatory time must be approved by the manager so that the absence of the employee will not be detrimental to the regular office work. Firms generally have an additional policy that compensatory time cannot be "saved up" for an extended period nor added at the beginning or end of a vacation period.

Interior designers whose work responsibilities are more involved with the selling of products or services rather than in design work may be paid *commission*. When commission is used as the compensation method, the designer is paid some percentage of the gross, net sale, or gross margin of the merchandise sold or the amount of the contract.

Commission on the gross sale means that the commission percentage is paid on the amount for which the client is billed. For example, if the designer is paid 10 percent of the gross sale, and the client was billed $5000, the commission to be paid would be $500.

When commission is based on the net sale, the percentage is calculated after certain items are deducted. Deductions could include special discounts, freight charges, delivery charges, and returns. For example, assume a gross sale of $5000 has a commission on the net sale of 10 percent and a $250 deduction for delivery and freight charges. The commission paid to the designer would be $475.

In the gross margin method of paying commission, the commission percentage is paid based on the gross margin of the sale. *Gross margin* (also called *gross profit*) is the difference between the selling price and the cost price of the goods or services being sold. Designers are motivated to sell merchandise and services for the highest gross margin possible in order to receive the most commission possible. In the preceding example of a $5000 sale with a 10 percent commission, assume the cost price of the sale to be $2500. The amount of commission to be paid in this case would be $250.

Some firms utilizing the gross margin commission method also incorporate a sliding scale of commission. In this situation, different percentages are paid, depending on the amount of the gross margin percentage. For instance, if the gross margin was 90 percent (nearly retail price), the commission percentage might be 50 percent. If the gross margin was only 5 percent (nearly cost price), the commission percentage might only be 2 percent.

Bonus plans are methods of paying extra compensation based on the employee's producing more than a specific personal quota. Bonuses are most commonly paid to design employees who sell merchandise. If they meet or exceed their sales quotas, the employees would be paid some kind of bonus. Since designers responsible for creative and "on the boards" design work cannot easily establish a quota of design work, bonuses are less often paid to these individuals. However, some interior design firms do have a bonus method that rewards the "on the boards" designers. These are usually based on meeting or exceeding the amount of contracts budgeted or for exceeding a budgeted amount of specifications on a certain kind of furniture or furnishings.

## BENEFITS

Compensation only represents part of the payments from the employer to the employee. Approximately 20 to 60 percent of payments to the individual is from *fringe benefits*. These fringe benefits represent approximately 32.5 percent of the overall payroll.[3]

Fringe benefits take many forms and will not be consistently offered from one interior design firm to another. The most common fringe benefits given or paid directly to the employee are group health insurance, paid vacations, paid holidays, and employee discounts on purchases. Other benefits offered to the employee might include group life insurance, supplemental health insurance such as dental programs, paid sick leave, profit-sharing plans, and professional-growth benefits. Professional-growth benefits would include such things as paid educational benefits, partial or full payment of professional association dues, and partial or full payment of NCIDQ testing fees.

Other benefits that would not directly be paid to the employee but must be paid by the employer include social security tax contributions, workers' compensation taxes, and unemployment compensation taxes. These are benefits that the employee may or may not draw from for some time. Social security would not be payable until the employee retires (or is physically disabled and can no longer work). Workers' compensation covers on-the-job injuries, and unemployment compensation would only be paid, under certain circumstances, when the employee is laid off from the design firm.

---

[3]Beam 1985, 5.

When an individual is applying for a job, considering a promotion, or weighing the merits of staying with the present employer, the complete benefits package must be looked at carefully. A position with one firm with a slightly lower salary but a good employer-paid health insurance program may be better than another position where the salary is a bit higher, but there is no health insurance program available to employees.

## *Summary*

As interior design firms grow, it becomes increasingly important for the owners and managers to review and define the organizational structure. Job responsibilities become more specialized and roles must be defined.

To keep good employees, research has shown that more must be done for employees than occasional raises. Performance evaluations keyed to job descriptions help employees understand how they are doing. These also show employees where they can advance in the firm. Fair compensation and benefits are also needed to keep turnover low.

In this chapter we have looked in depth at the issues of organization, job classifications, job descriptions, and performance evaluations as well as some of the different kinds of compensation methods. The next chapter will cover legal issues of employment, such as the agency relationship and employment contracts.

## Chapter 9

# LEGAL ISSUES OF EMPLOYMENT

"*I*t is becoming much harder to be an employer than to be an employee!" commented a design director one day. Interpretations of older laws and the enactment of new laws to protect the employee have made it difficult for the employer to hire or fire individuals when they do not perform as expected. New strategies are being used to protect the employer. Many employers are finding it necessary to protect themselves with employment contracts. Firms never before finding it necessary to have job descriptions and performance evaluations are busy developing these important documents to clarify the responsibilities of the employees. Even small design studios with just a few employees are looking into the development of employee handbooks to explain how things are to be done within the studio.

Employees generally do not want to sue their employers over personnel issues, and many do not. However, more and more employees are utilizing the courts to satisfy their grievances. In the interior design profession, suits might occur as a result of misunderstandings with employment contracts or layoffs for which there is seemingly little reason. Although employers of larger firms are quickly learning their rights and obligations, far too many interior design employees only find out about legal rights and obligations after some unpleasant experience.

In this chapter we will look at many issues related to legal regulation of employment and issues that are related to legal regulation. We will briefly discuss federal laws regulating employment, the concept of employment at will, the agency relationship, employment contracts, and the employee handbook.

## *Federal Laws Regulating Employment*

Many of the laws written to protect employees have more impact on firms that are unionized. Since it is almost unheard of for an interior design firm to be unionized, there will be no attempt to discuss those laws. However, several federal laws do affect the nonunion professional office in relation to the hiring and firing of employees.

### HIRING

One of the most important federal laws passed to protect employees from job discrimination is Title VII of the Civil Rights Act of 1964. This law, as well as the Equal Employment Opportunity Act passed in 1972, prohibits the employer from discriminating on the basis of sex, race, color, religion, or national origin. These laws and their subsequent amendments reinforce these prohibitions as well as prohibitions related to educational opportunity and other public issues of discrimination.

Equal employment laws make it illegal for employers to ask verbally or on a job application such things as (1) age, (2) date of birth, (3) maiden name, (4) marital status, (5) sex (male or female), (6) or any other directly stated question related to age, sex, religion, national origin, color, or marital status.

It is possible for the employer to obtain this information in less direct ways if the information has significance as to whether the interviewee is capable of performing the job responsibilities. For example, it is legal for the employer to ask something like, "Are you between the ages of 23 and 50?" or "Are you a citizen of this country?" The key, of course, is whether the questions and the way the questions are asked are used to discriminate against potential employees.

Interior design practices involved in work with the federal government would need to comply with some additional federal laws. Executive Order 11246 requires firms that do more than $10,000 of business with the federal government to have nondiscrimination clauses in their contracts. If an interior design firm does more than $2500 of work for the federal government, the Rehabilitation Act of 1973 and 1974 would require the design firm to be sure that handicapped employees are accommodated. Other requirements may be enforceable depending on the exact nature of the design firm's work with the federal government.

### FIRING

A few issues related to firing and the law were addressed in Chapter 8 in the section on performance evaluations and will be discussed in the following section on employment at will. One concern here for the employer is the issue of firing based on discrimination. If an employee has been fired as a result of discrimination related to age, sex, and so on, the employer will be held legally liable. Large settlements that could bankrupt many interior design firms could result from firing based on discrimination. The best advice is for employers to document performance and warnings related to problems on the job. Well-designed performance evaluations and a consistent procedure of written warnings will aid the employer in legally firing an employee without the worry of later lawsuits.

The National Labor Relations Act protects the employee from being fired or otherwise discriminated against as a result of the employee's filing any kind of charges or giving testimony against the employer. An example might be an employee who is fired after filing a complaint related to a wage discrimination claim with the Federal Wage and Hour Board. Depending, of course, on the exact nature of the complaint and the manner in which the firing took place, the employer would be liable for illegally firing this employee.

### OTHER ISSUES

The Equal Pay Act of 1963 requires employers to pay all employees with the same basic work responsibilities and work experience the same amount of salary or wages. In this case, if two employees with the same job title and job responsibilities were hired at the same time and started with approximately the same work experience, each must be paid the same starting wage. If future proven performance or responsibility issues became different for the two individuals, then each could be paid a different amount.

The Occupational Safety and Health Act (OSHA) of 1970 requires all employees to be given a safe place to work. OSHA inspectors, although primarily found in production facilities, do make inspections in the office environment. In the interior design studio, an OSHA inspector may look for properly located and functioning fire extinguishers, first-aid kits, and the proper reporting of employee injuries.

## Employment at Will

The concept of *employment at will* relates to the doctrine that an employee who is not bound by a written contract and who has no written terms of his or her employment spelled out can be fired by the employer at any time with no explanation. The courts have ruled, since the employee may quit at any time without reason, that the employer has the right to fire the employee at any time without reason, as long as the firing does not violate any federal or state employment laws.

The vast majority of employees in the interior design profession are subject to the employment-at-will doctrine. Most design employees are put to work and continue in specified duties without ever signing an employment contract. Since there is no contract, the employer is not bound by law to give the employee any reason for termination. Likewise, the employee has the right to give notice and leave the firm at any time without any reason.

There are some restrictions on the employer's right to terminate an employee under the employment-at-will doctrine. An employee cannot be fired merely because of his or her sex, race, religion, age, or handicap. An employer cannot fire an employee because of malice or retaliation or bad faith. In addition, an employee may not be fired because he or she reported company violations of health or safety laws. All of these restrictions relate to the various federal and state laws enacted to protect employees.

Of course, to be protected from firing for these reasons, the designer must be able to prove in court that the firing was a result of one of these illegal reasons. This can be very difficult for the employee to prove. The designer can protect himself or herself by requesting written information regarding expectations and performance evaluations on a regular basis. It is also important for the designer to document any events that might relate to the reasons listed for possible termination.

Unfortunately, sexual harassment can be a problem in the office. If a designer feels that she[1] is being harassed by a supervisor, she should document for her files any details about the episode. Should the harassment continue and the designer find that she is fired, these notes would be needed to prove that harassment rather than work deficiencies was the reason for termination.

Large firms have attempted to protect themselves from potential charges by changing management practices. Regular performance evaluations of all employees hired "at will" is one way to ensure that a terminated employee has been fired for inadequate work performance. Documented meetings during which the manager

---

[1]Although the author understands that either sex can be sexually harassed, the vast majority of cases still affects females.

discusses and warns employees not meeting expectations is another method the employer can use to protect his or her right to fire noncontract employees.

For the most part, the states are basically upholding the concept of employment at will. Few employees have been able to win court cases against the employer in these issues.[2] The main reason for this seems to be that the courts still support the idea that the employer must retain the right to fire employees who are incompetent, unqualified, unwilling, and so on. However, as more and more court cases related to improper termination occur, it is important that both employers and employees take the hiring, evaluation, and termination sequence more seriously.

Both employers and employees should be aware of each other's rights in terms of employment and termination. Employers may no longer terminate an employee capriciously if the employee is fulfilling his or her duties in accordance to satisfactory levels of performance. And employees do have the right to retain employment without fear of retaliation, sexual harassment, and discrimination.

## *The Agency Relationship*

In common law, an *agency relationship* occurs when one person or entity agrees to represent or do business for another person or entity. The first person is called the agent and the second the principal. The agency relationship also gives the principal the right to control the conduct of the agent in the matters entrusted to the agent. In today's law, the employer-employee relationship is a reflection of the agency relationship. The principal in the interior design office is the owner (or controlling board members), whereas the agents are all the employees, whether they are in management positions or staff positions.

"An employee is an agent (other than an independent contractor) who has an appointment or contract for hire with authority to represent the employer."[3] According to the law, the key is that the employer has some right to control the actions of the employee. An independent contractor, someone who works for himself or herself and usually has a specific short-term work relationship with the firm, has individual rights, is not considered an employee of the company, and thus cannot be an agent.

The agency relationship, in some manner, will spell out the specific extent of the relationship between the employer and employee. Unlike most contractual relationships, the conditions of the agency relationship do not have to be in writing. There does have to be affirmative agreement to the effect that the employee is willing to be an agent for the employer. Accepting a position and knowing what the responsibilities of the position cover would imply agreement. Since all positions in the firm have different responsibilities and different levels of trust within the employer-employee relationship, it is important for employees to fully understand what they are responsible for. For example, not all employees will have the right to sign purchase orders to buy supplies for the office. Carefully prepared job descriptions, as discussed in Chapter 8, explain most of these responsibilities. Employee handbooks should outline other, more detailed responsibilities.

---

[2]Harragan 1986, 43.
[3]Clarkson 1983, 605. Copyright West Publishing Company.

Because of the agency relationship, each party is obligated to certain duties with respect to the other party. Each party has a primary duty to the other to act in good faith toward the other party. There are specific legal duties of each party in an agency relationship. Let us look first at the duties of the employer to the employee.

## EMPLOYER TO EMPLOYEE

The employer is obligated to provide the employee with a reasonable amount or kind of compensation for the completion of the agreed-on services. What this reasonable amount would be is not defined by law except that it must conform to what would be customary compensation for the services performed.

The employer also has a duty to assist and/or cooperate with the employee so that he or she may be able to perform the agreed-on services. It could be construed as a violation of the employer-employee agreement if the employer prevents or inhibits the employee from performing his or her duties. For example, if it is understood that the employer provides all the necessary tools and materials for the employee to do drafting work and later requires the employee to pay for those tools, the employer is inhibiting the employee from performing his or her duties.

Common law, as well as federal and state regulations, require that the employer provide safe working conditions for employees. Should an employee feel that his or her working environment was unsafe, the employer cannot dismiss the employee for reporting unsafe conditions.

The preceding relate to general duties of the employer to the employee. Other duties may also be required of the employer, depending on the exact nature of the agreement.

## EMPLOYEE TO EMPLOYER

The employee has several basic duties to the employer and may have additional ones as outlined by any formal agreement or written contract. The employee has an obligation to perform his or her duties with reasonable diligence and skill. At what level the diligence and skill must be is related to what would be considered common for the services required and experience level expected. For example, if an employee is hired as a renderer on the basis of a high-quality portfolio, the employer has a right to expect that all the rendering work performed would be of that same quality.

A second duty of the employee is loyalty. An employee is expected to act in the interests of the employer, not for the benefit of any outside party or even of the employee. This means, for example, that a designer preparing the design work for a major company cannot be hired by the client to design an additional area of the company "on the side." Should the designer moonlight in this way, the employer would have the right to terminate the employee for breach of the agency relationship.

Another fundamental duty of the employee to the employer is a duty to keep the employer informed of anything related to the relationship. "What the agent actually tells the principal is not relevant; what the agent *should have told* the principal is crucial."[4] The following provides an example: One day MaryAnne men-

---

[4]Jentz 1987, 479. Copyright West Publishing Company.

tions to her boss that company A appears to be ready to order 100 chairs from a certain manufacturer. The boss, thinking that it is a good opportunity to order an additional amount of the same chair for inventory, orders another 100. After the order is placed, MaryAnne learns, but neglects to tell her boss, that the client has changed his mind and will not order that chair after all. The furniture store, now responsible for paying for all the chairs, could consider MaryAnne in breach of the agency relationship.

A fourth duty of the employee is that of obedience. By this it is meant that the employee is required to follow all legal and clearly stated instructions or policies of the employer. Only certain emergency situations allow the employee to deviate from these obligations. For example, if the company has a policy that warehouse workers may not use the company vehicle for personal business, it would be a violation of this duty if one of the drivers used a company truck on the weekend without getting permission from the proper supervisor.

Finally, for the employee who has access to company funds or property, the employee has a duty to keep a proper accounting of the inflows and outflows of funds or use of property. A designer who has authorization to sign purchase orders for supplies would be breaching this duty if he or she used one of the purchase orders to obtain supplies for his or her own needs. In this case, the breach is also a criminal act, and the employer could press charges.

A doctrine that is part of the agency relationship that should be discussed briefly is the doctrine of shop right. The shop-right doctrine says that any creation or invention of tangible or intangible products that is not the result of the employee's normal working duties belongs to the employee, not the employer. If an employee creates or invents something on company time, the employer has a shop-right interest in the invention, but the employee has ownership rights. For example, if the employee has not been hired to write articles on business practices but uses company time to write articles, the employer has a shop right to use the articles without paying the employee any kind of royalty.

Remember that any creative works, tangible or intangible, produced on the job and as part of normal work responsibilities belong to the employer, not the employee. A custom-designed coffee table prepared for a client belongs to the employer if it is reasonable for the design of custom furniture to be a regular part of the employee's duties.

## *Employment Contracts*

Employment contracts are becoming a part of the interior design profession, although not yet a widespread practice. Employment contracts are more prevalent for various sales and management positions. Traditional "on the boards" design positions are more often considered employment at will.

An employment contract does not have to be in writing. An oral employment contract technically would be formed when the employer and employee have agreed to such things as responsibilities, compensation, and terms of the employment. Written contracts are prepared to clarify more complex issues that may be of interest to the employer or the employee. An interior designer responsible for sale of goods may want a written contract to spell out commission structure, sales quotas, bonuses, seasonal layoffs, and so on. Many employers seek written contracts to limit the employee from taking clients to competing firms if the employee quits.

In general, the written employment contract should cover

1. *Compensation.* Will the employee be paid hourly, salary, or commission? If commission will be paid, the method of payment should also be spelled out.
2. *Employment responsibilities.* This should indicate, in sufficient detail, what the employee has been hired to do.
3. *Termination.* Even with an employment contract, termination must be allowed by either party. Statements to that effect and the manner in which either party must give notice should be in the contract. For the protection of the employee, statements should also outline how any outstanding commission (if commission is part of the compensation method) is to be paid.
4. *Termination for cause.* Such a clause protects the employee from being terminated for some capricious reason. Reasons for termination for cause include negligence, incompetence, dishonesty, disloyalty, and nonadherence to company policies.
5. *Territory rights.* Sales personnel especially are limited to working with clients only in certain territories. This territory might be only certain cities, or states, or even certain clients. If the employee is limited to his or her territory, this should be defined in the contract.

There may be other clauses in the contract to protect one or the other party. A clause regarding return of company property may be in the contract. Although most employment contracts in the interior design profession would not have an ending date, the employer or the employee may wish to have a duration clause that specifies a fixed date when the contract would expire. It is understood that the contract remains in force as long both parties agree to continued employment.

Some employers put restrictive covenants in employment contracts. "Restrictive covenants are provisions in contracts that do not allow the [salesperson] to directly compete or work for a competitor after leaving [his or her] old company."[5] These restrictive covenants can effectively prevent the employee from working for a competitor of the employer or starting his or her own business and limit the territory in which the employee may seek new employment. Restrictive covenants in employment contracts are enforceable by the courts as long as they do not last for an unreasonable length of time or unfairly restrict the individual from making a living in the same location as the former employer. What that length of time is and what area is considered reasonable would be up to the courts in the area.

Employment contracts can protect both the employee and the employer. If the employer requests that a written contract be signed, the prospective employee should be certain that he or she understands all the terms of the contract. If an oral agreement is made, the same advice is suggested. It is far more pleasant for both the employer and employee to be in agreement concerning the terms of employment, compensation, and other conditions of the employment relationship rather than at odds about those conditions in a court.

## *The Employee Handbook*

The purpose of an employee handbook is to provide managers and employees a concise reference to company policies. In small design firms, the employee handbook might include both general operating policies, such as the policies related to

---

[5]Sack 1981, 46.

special ordering merchandise for clients, as well as personnel policies. In larger firms, it is likely that there is one handbook for personnel issues and one or more additional handbooks to explain operational policies by department.

A well-designed handbook will help to clarify policies in order to prevent complaints, grievances, and morale problems before they occur. The policy handbook will also help the company prevent complaints or lawsuits related to equal employment opportunity laws. These well-defined policies also assist managers and owners in the decision-making and control process by providing consistent treatment of the defined issues.

### HOW TO PREPARE A HANDBOOK

It is important that the individual charged with preparing the handbook be given full authority and responsibility—and time—to accomplish the task. In relatively small firms, the owner will most likely attempt to prepare the handbook himself or herself. In departmentalized firms, managers may be asked to submit policies related to their areas. Then either through committee meetings or through the efforts of one manager, a composite handbook would be produced.

The ground rules should be set by the interior design practice owner or primary manager. Those ground rules would include

1. Who will write it.
2. What will be covered.
3. From where the information will come.
4. What will be the time frame for completion.
5. Who will accept final responsibility for content and format (usually the owner/primary manager).

After it is determined who will be responsible for the preparation of the handbook and what will be covered, discovery of the information to be included must be started. Many policies may already be in writing or are well known even though they are not written down. These become the starting point for the handbook. Some information may have to be obtained from company records. For example, paid holidays may have varied over the years. Company records will show which holidays were considered paid each year. Vacation and sick-time-allowance history may also only be obtained from company records.

Many companies have "unwritten rules" that have sprung up over the years, but which have dubious authority. These unwritten rules should be discovered and decisions made as to their current validity. An example of an unwritten rule might be that "no employee may make client appointments outside the office from 8 to 9:00 A.M." This unwritten rule may have addressed an earlier need to be sure someone was in the studio to answer the phone until the bookkeeper came in at 9:00. Now that there is a secretary who comes in at 8:00, the unwritten policy probably has no validity.

If the handbook is combining operational and personnel policies, they should be grouped separately. An example of an operating policy might be that "no products will be ordered by telephone without prior approval of Mary Jones, owner."

Many statements of policy that come up in initial information gathering probably should not appear in the final handbook. Things like "employees will be courteous in dealing with clients" does not belong in a handbook since professionals do not need to be reminded of this and may even be insulted by such comments.

Policies should then be grouped by those applicable to all departments and those of specific departments. Most personnel policies will apply to all departments. However, some policies may be different for various departments. For example, vacation allotment may vary depending on compensation method. Hourly and salaried employees may be entitled to specific numbers of weeks of vacation per years of continuous employment. Commissioned employees, on the other hand, may have much more freedom and flexibility. These differences must be clearly stated in either the overall handbook or in the department addenda.

What the format of the final draft becomes is less important than organization and clear, concise content. The organization should be logical for the company. The following are a few examples of general organization. First, one could use a logical sequence of events as the organization. In this case, issues related to hiring would be first; perhaps hours of work, absenteeism, and such next; employee benefits in the middle; and termination at the end.

A second method would be by grouping the topics alphabetically. In this case each general policy category strictly comes in order of the alphabet. So *absenteeism* might come first, *hiring policies* somewhere in the middle, and *training* near the end.

Another method would be by the use of numerical codes. Code numbers would be assigned to each general topic with subnumbers for policies related to that topic. A general topic such as training might be organized in the following manner.

21. Training

    21.1  Company indoctrination

    21.2  Eligibility for out-of-town training at factories

    21.3  Eligibility for educational reimbursement (CEU)

    21.4  Eligibility for educational reimbursement (university or community college)

Whatever organizational structure is used, it is helpful if it is explained at the beginning of the handbook.

As much as possible, clear, concise wording is important. The use of a simple outline format within the organizational structure and wording of the actual policies works very well. Terminology that everyone understands or is in common usage should be adopted. Instead of "The studio, workrooms, warehouse, and bookkeeping areas will be open and maintained by appropriate personnel on a daily basis Monday through Friday from 8:30 A.M. to 5:30 P.M.," use "Scheduled work hours all departments: Monday–Friday, 8:30 A.M. to 5:30 P.M."

Remember that the employee handbook and the included policy statements are to inform, not to impress with flowery prose. Also remember that some employees are not interior designers and may not be familiar with some of the jargon of the interior design profession.

The new handbook, when completed and approved by management and owners, should not just be handed to employees. Especially when a design firm has never had a handbook, it is important for upper management and the department managers to meet with employees to explain why the handbook was prepared, to define the purpose of the handbook, and to go over the contents. Even if employees have not been a part of the process, at least they will feel less threatened by a new set of rules if they are explained before the rules are put into effect.

## WHAT TO INCLUDE

Precisely what depth of information should go into a policy handbook is up to the interior design firm. The complexity of written policies should match the management style and philosophy of the owners/managers while providing the policies needed to aid management in control and decision-making. Many people begin a career in interior design because they seek freedom of expression and a certain freedom of time. A studio composed of primarily self-motivated, self-directed individuals will rebel or even quit if a great number of strictly enforced "rules" are suddenly thrust upon them. A new handbook should begin with a statement related to the purpose of the manual and the reason for its development and implementation. Figure 9-1 gives an example of a short introductory statement.

Broad categories of personnel policies include

1. Hiring policies.
2. Performance evaluation.
3. Promotion.
4. Employee benefits.
5. Hours of work.
6. Salary policies.
7. Training.
8. Termination.

Each of these broad categories would include one or more specific policies related to that topic. Figure 9-2 provides an example of policies related to hours of work.

Operational policies relate more to the function of the department or areas of the firm. The design department might have written policies related to presentation boards. The sales area would have policies related to the ordering of merchandise

---

**FOREWORD**

The purpose of the Burns Interiors Employee Handbook is to provide each employee with a complete source of the policies and procedures of the firm. Our experience has shown that providing each employee with a handbook of this information helps to promote consistency in the operations of the firm. This consistency results in a more efficient, productive and, therefore, more profitable association for the employees and the firm.

As you flip through the pages, you will see that the handbook is broken down into four parts: Introduction, Personnel Policies, Operating Policies, and Department Policies and Procedures. The Introduction provides you with the philosophy and mission statement of Burns Interiors, a brief history of the firm, and a presentation on the organizational structure of the firm. In the section on Personnel Policies, there is an explanation of hiring, performance evaluation, termination policies, and employee benefits. Section three on Operating Policies explains general business policies such as the business hours, holidays and sick leave, overtime, and so forth. The final section contains policies and procedures specific to your department. The material in this section may be supplemented by additional information provided to you by your supervisor. These, of course, should be inserted in this section.

The policies and procedures of this firm have evolved over many years. As the firm changes, so may some of its policies. As policies and/or procedures change, these will be completely presented and discussed with employees.

We are happy to have you as an employee at Burns Interiors and look forward to working with you for many years. The management wishes you great success as you grow with us.

MaryLee Burns, President

**FIGURE 9-1**
**Example of an opening statement for an employee handbook.**

5. Hours of Work

A. Business Hours
Monday through Friday, 8:30 a.m. to 5:30 p.m.

Both hourly and salaried employees are expected to be at work during normal business hours.

B. The Work Week
The normal work week for hourly and salaried employees is forty (40) hours.

C. Lunch Hours
Hourly employees are entitled to one hour for lunch. It must be taken between 11:30 a.m. and 2:00 p.m. Salaried employees are expected to take one hour for lunch. It should be taken between 11:30 a.m. and 2:00 p.m.

D. Breaks
Hourly employees are entitled to two 15-minute breaks. One should be taken in the morning and one in the afternoon.

E. Overtime
Hourly employees must have the approval of their supervisor to work overtime. Overtime pay begins after a minimum of forty (40) hours of work in a normal work week. The pay rate for overtime will be 1½ times the normal hourly rate.

Hourly employees may taken compensatory time in place of overtime pay. One hour of compensatory time may be taken in place of the 1½ times overtime pay rate. Approval and arrangements must be made with the employee's supervisor.

Salaried employees are not entitled to overtime pay.

F. Absences
You must keep your supervisor informed of absences you know of in advance.

If you must be unexpectedly absent for illness or some other reason, you must telephone your supervisor as soon as possible. If you must be absent for more than one day, telephone your supervisor daily.

G. Lateness
You should contact your supervisor if you find that you will be unavoidably late.

**FIGURE 9-2**
**A page of policies from an employee handbook.**

for clients. Bookkeeping/accounting departments would likely have written policies related to the handling of paperwork and procedures for when invoices would be written, payments made, advance deposits processed, and so on.

After the handbook is prepared, it must be remembered that it is not ever really finished. Contents should be reviewed periodically by management and owners to keep it as up to date as possible. As the business continues to change, policies need to be reviewed and possibly modified.

Whatever the size of the firm or the type of practice, written policies related to operational and personnel issues aid the owners and management of the firm in running the interior design practice in a professional manner. Written policies also help clarify how things are done and where employees stand in their relationship with the firm. Policies that are clear and functional for the type of practice will be adhered to by all employees. Those that are counter to what is happening in the firm or seem to be constantly ignored by some in the firm cannot be enforced and also tend to undermine the management.

# *Summary*

Part of the organization and continued growth and development of interior design practices involves employees. There are many laws regulating the hiring and firing of employees that apply to the interior design profession. Employers and employees should be familiar with these laws to alleviate government intervention or lawsuits.

The employer-employee relationship itself also involves specific legal obligations on the part of both parties. High turnover resulting from employee job dissatisfaction can be eliminated in part by the development of job descriptions and performance evaluations. Other obligations and expectations can be explained by the development and use of employee handbooks.

All these legal issues are not meant to handcuff the employer or employee. Rather, both sides must realize that hiring employees and accepting positions with companies must be done in good faith as well as within legal restraints. It is too expensive for companies to hire, train, and fire or watch employees leave design firms. It is too emotionally draining for the employee to have to sue or even threaten to sue over employment misunderstandings or mistreatment. As the profession continues to grow and change, it must accept the responsibilities related to employees as well as it accepts responsibilities related to the client.

## Chapter 10

# COMPUTERS IN THE INTERIOR DESIGN OFFICE

*C*omputer technology has made a significant impact on the interior design profession. Few practices get by without some computer assistance. With the ever-increasing ease of operation coupled with the growing sophistication of small desktop personal computers, it is becoming more difficult for designers to ignore the labor-saving tools of the computer. Students increasingly seek interior design programs in which they will gain experience with computers for general business functions as well as computer-aided design and drafting (CADD).

In this chapter we will briefly discuss the kinds of software that can be used by the interior design practice. We will also look at many of the considerations related to purchasing computer systems. However, with so many different kinds of computer systems available, it is difficult to discuss specific hardware and software trade names in the confines of this book.

## *Accounting and Financial Management*

Probably the most used of the computer software in the design office is for accounting and/or financial management. Accounting packages allow for all the financial data of the firm, such as general ledgers, accounts payable, and accounts receivable, to be inputted into computer memory. Retrieval of information is faster, and a significantly greater number of reports can be generated. These reports aid in the management decision-making processes described in Chapter 12. Computer-supported accounting and financial data allow the business owner, and especially the small business owner, faster access to financial data.

It is important that the firm's manual accounting and financial management system be working effectively before purchasing any computerized system. First, computer accounting packages are costly. It is easy to spend $1000 or more for this software alone. Second, if the manual system is not in good working order, a computer system may lead to total financial disorganization.

## *Spreadsheets*

Spreadsheet programs use a grid of rows and columns made up of individual cells to present various configurations of data. Data is entered into each cell in different formats to produce meaningful reports. Spreadsheets permit the introduction of formulas into the grid so that the data within the cells can be converted to usable values. Prewritten accounting packages are based on spreadsheet programs.

Other than developing your own accounting software, spreadsheets also allow for "what if" analysis of data. What-if analysis allows the user to introduce a factor that manipulates known values. It then measures and reports the effect of the change. For example, designers can use what-if analyses to see how changing the markup on individual items of a specification will change the gross margin for the entire project. These calculations, done manually by many designers, become fast and accurate when done on the computer. Spreadsheet programs also permit the interaction of data in order to produce several kinds of charts, such as pie charts and bar charts. This charting capability provides an additional important reporting tool for use by management as an aid to decision-making.

There are also various programs that supplement the basic spreadsheet programs. Software producers have developed many templates that can be used for specific reports, such as income tax forms, budgeting reports, amortization schedules, sales forecasts, and so on.

## Word Processing

Word processing is the most popular use of the computer in today's general business office and is often used in the interior design office. A word processing system utilizes for hardware a keyboard and a CRT screen. Entering data in a computer word processor is just like typing on a regular typewriter. A word processor, however, provides the user with the capability to make changes easily before the final copy is printed. Adding, deleting, and modifying text by utilizing a word processor is simple and fast.

Designers utilize word processing systems for writing letters, preparing specifications, preparing reports to clients on project progress, and any other documentation where production and manipulation of words is the primary activity.

There are many kinds of software which are compatible with basic word processing packages that allow for additional uses of the basic system. Spell checkers make excellent spellers of us all. Communication packages permit "mail" to be left electronically on each workstation's desktop computer. Mail-merge programs permit easy production of form letters that automatically add the "personalized touch." And outliners facilitate the writing and decision-making processes via a "coached" system of organizing thoughts.

Desktop publishing software, a relatively new entry in the business computer catalog of software, allows almost anyone to produce high-quality newsletters, advertisements, press releases, and reports—anything for which the firm may have previously needed outside typesetting help. Desktop publishing consists of combining graphics and text on the same page. However, reproduction of the documents can still be done more inexpensively by traditional printing methods, such as offset printing. This revolution in business computer software has permitted many design companies the opportunity to utilize what are now relatively inexpensive marketing tools.

## Databases

Database software manipulates groups of data or information in almost any way the user chooses. Some databases are relational, which means that they can report the interrelationships of data. An address book is a good example for a database. The complete address for an individual or company is called a record. Each portion of the record (name, street address, ZIP code, city, and so on) are called fields. Databases allow the user to create reports (or files) based on any of the fields. The relational database allows the user to create files based on more than one field.

Interior designers would use databases primarily for client mailing and for information lists and vendor lists. Depending on the format and content of each record, other kinds of tracking and reports can be achieved. For example, if the square footage and dollar value of all projects are included in the client record, a file could be created reporting all those projects of a certain amount of square footage and dollar value. These files would assist in such management functions as marketing, estimation of fees, and budgeting.

Most database software is complex. It is very important for the design firm to understand what it wants to be able to do with the information that commonly is incorporated into a database before purchasing any software product.

# CADD

CADD, or computer-aided design and drafting, has been receiving a lot of attention in the trade magazines and at the trade markets. CADD, which is an excellent design tool for repetitive work, allows the designer to quickly manipulate spaces and furniture pieces. Computer graphic images, such as furniture pieces, need only be drawn once. Then the computer quickly duplicates the images as many times and in as many places as the designer wishes.

Today, CADD is more likely to be found in the larger-sized design firms. Loebelson reported in its January and July 1987 reports that of the top 100 and second 100 design firms, almost 75 percent utilize CADD of the top 100 firms as compared to 58 percent of the second 100 design firms.[1]

The larger firms have used CADD before the average-sized and smaller firms in part because of the expense of the hardware and software. CADD hardware and software packages, even for the least complicated of minicomputers, can cost several thousand dollars. Small firms have a difficult time justifying the expense of a CADD system. This software also takes a significant amount of time to learn. Smaller firms have fewer employees to assign responsibility for learning CADD systems. The introduction of lower-cost minicomputer CADD systems in the later part of the 1980s will undoubtedly begin to have an effect on the number of CADD systems purchased by smaller interior design offices.

# How to Buy

Before the individual designer or the design firm runs out and gets on the computer bandwagon, there are a few things necessary to consider. First, and most important, the firm should determine what functions the computer must perform. Although computer hardware and software have become less expensive with the introduction of personal computers, a good computer system is still a major investment. Purchasing the wrong computer, a computer system that cannot be upgraded, or a system that will not receive a variety of peripherals will become outdated far sooner than it should. Before even going to talk to computer sales

---

[1]Loebelson, *Interior Design*, January and July 1987.

representatives, prepare a list of what business functions the computer system should be able to perform for the company. These functions should be the ones that can speed the work of the firm, whether in word processing, data management, financial management, or computer-aided design.

This list of suitable functions should be developed with as much input as possible from the various users. All management levels and consultants to the firm should be involved in developing the list of desired functions. The decisions related to what computer functions are needed and which system to buy should not be left to only one person, except, of course, for the final decision to be made by the owner/manager.

Second, realize early in the research on computer systems that computers do not solve problems in and of themselves. A firm with a cumbersome manual system will not have its system corrected automatically with the introduction of a computer. Moreover, additional problems can occur as a result of the ease with which computers can produce reports. The capability of the computer to produce a large quantity of simple and complex reports very quickly can lead to a paper explosion in the office. Managers and owners can easily be consumed with all kinds of new paperwork, not knowing what the reports mean or understanding which are useful. Any manual system that produces confusing or misleading reports will compound its problem when converted to the computer.

Third, understand that computers rarely displace or eliminate personnel. In fact, in most cases, computers add to the number of employees needed. This results from increased productivity related to the uses of the computer, thereby allowing the firm to handle more work. As people become familiar with computers in the office and at home, they become less fearful of having to use computers. Students in the classroom eagerly await an opportunity to use computers. Anyone becoming reasonably familiar with word processing software is very reluctant to go back to a typewriter.

The fourth consideration in purchasing a computer system is to buy as much computer—meaning the best system—the firm can possibly afford based on the requirements determined within the firm. In addition, it is important that the system can be upgraded. Computer systems are becoming more powerful and smaller, with increasingly sophisticated software programs. It is important for the firm to buy the very best system it can afford at the outset and to be assured that the system can be upgraded as technology advances. Many have invested in a computer system that was "bargain basement," just to have a computer. No sooner did the owner or operator figure out how to work it than the hardware and available software could no longer satisfy the needs of the firm. Although buying an inexpensive or nonupgradable computer will save money initially, in the long run it will cost the firm much more.

Finally, work with reputable vendors and dealers who are knowledgeable about the hardware and software they sell. Too many computer salespeople are just that—salespeople—who know the jargon but cannot really help with hardware or software problems. Be sure the vendor includes a training program as part of the cost and can provide additional training or help after installation. Buying a computer for an interior design office is like a client coming to you to buy some furniture.

It is sometimes fun to be a pioneer, but not when it comes to computers. Although no one company's hardware or software for the interior designer is advocated here, many quality hardware and software products are available for the interior design practice. Discussing any particular products would go against the first suggestion offered in this section—that the firm's management team evaluate the firm's needs before purchasing any computer system product. It is recommended that the design firm only purchase hardware and software that have a track record. Many small computer companies have already gone out of business. "Vaporware," software that is advertised but never makes it to the market, is a constant problem. Dealers go out of business, leaving the purchaser without training, help, or even warranties. When considering a particular item, ask how long the particular version of hardware or software has been on the market. Find out if firms like yours are using the same system so that you could talk to them about satisfaction. Care in determining needs, finding the right vendors, and choosing proper products will lead to a happy experience with computers.

## *Summary*

Once the interior design firm decides to purchase a computer system, it will see how the computer and the hundreds of software products on the market can be used to assist the firm. The computer can speed repetitive tasks; perform many mathematical functions related to pricing and accounting quickly and accurately; produce graphic documents such as floor plans, perspectives, working drawings, and newsletter graphics; help prepare high-quality professional business correspondence quickly and easily; and help the design manager and/or owner in many ways related to budgeting, financing, and decision-making.

The computer will continue to make significant changes in how the interior designer performs his or her tasks related to business practices and design activities. At one time it was possible for a design firm to ignore the computer as a tool and continue to run its practice using manual systems. The future will discourage this attitude. Computers, whether used for word processing, accounting and financial management, or CADD, will continue to be accepted by design professionals for one or all of the functions described in this chapter. The speed and efficiency of the computer can only help the designer become more proficient and productive in a highly competitive profession.

Work In Progress/Age Analysis
As of July 1987

Accounts Receivables

| | Total ($) | Work In Progress ($) | Current ($) | 30 Days | 60 Days | 90 days | 120 days and Over |
|---|---|---|---|---|---|---|---|
| | | | | $800 | | | |
| ...rporation | $1,567 | $767 | 1,500 | | 3,500 | | 2,0... |
| ...te Co. | 3,000 | 1,500 | 2,000 | | | | |
| ...ess Park | 8,500 | 3,000 | 2,750 | 4,500 | 3,200 | | |
| ...s | 10,500 | 7,750 | | 250 | | 700 | 1... |
| ...ration | 16,500 | 6,800 | 2,750 | | 1,500 | | |
| ...d Trust | 7,500 | 4,500 | 3,700 | | | 1,250 | |
| ...t Co. | 11,500 | 5,600 | 9,500 | 6,500 | | | |
| ...ductor Inc. | 35,000 | 17,500 | 1,500 | 1,250 | | | $... |
| ...ster, P.C. | 7,500 | 3,500 | | | $8,200 | $1,950 | |
| | | | $23,700 | $13,300 | | | |
| | $101,567 | $50,917 | | | | | |

# Part 3

## Managing the Business Finances

# Chapter 11

## FINANCIAL ACCOUNTING

*Financial accounting* is concerned with the day-to-day and periodic measurement and reporting of a firm's resources. This measurement and reporting would be of interest to external individuals such as bankers, government agencies, stockholders, and auditors. All the various accounts, journals, and ledgers that are kept by the firm and used to prepare balance sheets, income statements, and statements of cash flows are part of financial accounting. Although financial accounting is prepared for use by external individuals, the firm's members—especially its owners and management—should be familiar with the information and able to read, interpret, and analyze the results.

The three reports most commonly prepared by businesses are (1) the balance sheet, (2) the income statement, and (3) the statement of cash flow (formerly the funds flow statement). These reports, prepared by a professional accountant, show anyone inside or outside the firm the financial condition of the design firm. It is these three forms that we shall deal with in this chapter.

## Accounting Methods: Accrual versus Cash Accounting

Before discussing financial accounting reports, it is important to look at the accounting bases used by businesses. The two most common accounting bases are the accrual method and the cash accounting method. Central to the difference between the two methods is the time when revenue is recognized[1] and expenses are recognized (recorded). *Revenue* is the amount of inflows from the sale of goods or the rendering of services during an accounting period. *Expenses* are outflows of resources as a consequence of the efforts made by the firm to earn revenues. Rent, monthly utility bills, salaries, and advertising costs are examples of expenses.

In *accrual accounting,* revenue and expenses are recognized at the time they are earned (in the case of revenue) or incurred (in the case of expenses), whether the revenue has actually been collected or the expense actually paid. For example, Jane Doe Interiors has revenues of $5250 for January. Of that, $3250 is from cash sales and $2000 from invoices to clients that have not yet been received. In the same month, expenses of $4000 were incurred for the period—$3500 has already been

---

[1]Revenue is recognized during the period when goods are delivered or services are performed.

| | *Accrual Method* | *Cash Method* |
|---|---|---|
| Revenue | $ 5,250 | $ 3,250 |
| Expenses | (4,000) | (3,500) |
| Gross Income | $ 1,250 | $ − 250 |

**FIGURE 11-1**
Comparing accrual and cash accounting methods for the realization of revenue.

paid and $500 is still due. With the accrual method, there would be a $1250 profit for the month. In this case, the profit is a "paper profit" since $2000 has not been collected yet (see Figure 11-1).

In *cash accounting,* revenue and expenses are recognized in the period the firm actually receives the cash or actually pays the bills. In the preceding example, only $3250 of revenue and $3500 of expenses would be recognized for the month since that was all that was actually received or paid out. Using the cash accounting method, Jane Doe Interiors would show a $250 loss for the month.

Although there are benefits to design firms that only deal in services to use the cash accounting method, generally accepted accounting principles (GAAP)[2] utilizes the accrual method. It should also be pointed out that the Internal Revenue Service expects businesses to pay income taxes based on the accrual method.

It is recommended that all firms use the accrual method for an additional reason. Even though the accrual method may require extra accounting time, it provides a more comprehensive picture of profit and loss for the firm at any period. Having a more accurate financial picture of the firm at all times helps the owner/manager make more intelligent management decisions.

This chapter discusses accounting principles based on the accrual method.

## *The Balance Sheet*

A *balance sheet* shows the financial position of a firm as of a particular moment in time with a statement of its assets (resources) and equities (claims against total resources) of that moment. The balance sheet is composed of two parts that must equal each other. These two parts are called *Assets* and *Equities.* The reader may wish to refer to Figure 11-2 during this discussion.

### ASSETS

*Assets* are any kind of resource—tangible or intangible—that the firm owns or controls and which can be measured in monetary terms. Note that employees, though useful to the firm, are not accounting assets, since the firm cannot own the employees.

Assets are of three general kinds: current assets, which are resources the firm would normally convert to cash in less than one year; fixed assets, also called property, plant, and equipment, are long-lived items used by the firm; and other assets, which are assets such as patents, copyrights, and investment securities of another firm.

Current Assets typically include the following accounts: Cash, Accounts Receivable, Inventory, Prepaid Expenses, Supplies, and Marketable Securities. Cash is the cash on hand in the firm's bank accounts, checking accounts, cash registers, or

---

[2]GAAP is a set of principles established by the Financial Accounting Standards Board. This board studies accounting problems and establishes a standard way of handling many topics in accounting. Although companies are not required to follow the standards, many government agencies pressure companies to follow them.

**Balance Sheet**
**Arizona Interior Designs**
**As of January 31, 19X8**

*Assets*

| | | |
|---|---|---|
| Current Assets: | | |
| Cash | $ 5,200 | |
| Accounts Receivable | 15,350 | |
| Inventory | 5,713 | |
| Supplies | 750 | |
| Prepaid Expenses | 1,250 | |
| Total Current Assets | | $28,263 |
| Fixed Assets: | | |
| Plant and Equipment: | | |
| Office Furniture at Cost | $23,500 | |
| Less: Accumulated Depreciation | (1,200) | |
| Automobile at Cost | 12,500 | |
| Less: Accumulated Depreciation | (5,600) | |
| Net Plant and Equipment | | 29,200 |
| Total Assets | | $57,463 |

*Equities*

| | | |
|---|---|---|
| Current Liabilities: | | |
| Accounts Payable | $   750 | |
| Notes Payable | 1,550 | |
| Accrued Expenses | 1,010 | |
| Deferred Revenues | 2,325 | |
| Total Current Liabilities | | $ 5,635 |
| Other Liabilities: | | |
| Long-term Debt | | 17,500 |
| Total Liabilities | | $23,135 |

*Owner's Equity*

| | | |
|---|---|---|
| Common Stock | $25,000 | |
| Retained Earnings | 9,328 | |
| Total Owner's Equities | | 34,328 |
| Total Equities | | $57,463 |

**FIGURE 11-2**
Typical balance sheet.

petty cash boxes. *Accounts Receivable* is the account that shows what others owe to the firm as a result of sales or billings for services. Inventory shows those items purchased by the firm for resale to the firm's customers. For an interior designer, a chair purchased to be sold to the firm's clients is inventory; a chair purchased and used by the bookkeeper in the office is equipment—the value of which is recorded in the Fixed Assets account. Marketable Securities are investments expected to be sold within the year for cash. Prepaid Expenses are prepayments of expenses, such as insurance policies paid on the equipment the firm owns and rent that may have to be paid in advance. Supplies represents the value of normal office supplies.

The Fixed Assets or Property, Plant, and Equipment account include the following categories: building and equipment, which is represented by the building, if owned by the firm, and any capital equipment—furniture used by office staff, blueprint machines, copy machines, typewriters, delivery trucks, and so on. The accumulated depreciation on these items is also shown on the balance sheet. Property or land is shown as a separate entry since it is not depreciated—land does not "wear out." Note that in Figure 11-2, the company does not own its building, so it is not listed as an asset.

*Depreciation* results from the concept that capital equipment has a limited useful life. It is intended to express the usage of a fixed asset in the firm's pursuit of revenue. Although many think of depreciation as a way to express the "wearing out" of an object, it more accurately relates to the usage of the object, not the wear and tear. Accountants predict what will be the useful life of the equipment and determine the depreciated value of the equipment for each year the firm owns the item.

The category for Other Assets includes investments the firm has made in other firms. If the investments are to be held for more than one year, they are listed here. If they are expected to be sold within a year, they are to be listed under Current Assets. The value of copyrights, trademarks, patents, licenses, and similar intangible assets the firm might have are also listed in Other Assets. Of special interest to the design firm is the value placed on copyrighted designs or patents on furnishings the firm may have obtained. These copyrighted designs or patents solely belong to the design firm and cannot be used by others without the permission of the firm. Patents and copyrights are amortized, which is the practice by which the value of the patent or copyright is reduced to record its usage in the firm's earning activities. Amortization is essentially the same as depreciation, except that it applies to intangible assets.

### EQUITIES

*Equities* are claims by outsiders and/or owners against the total assets of the firm. Total Assets must *always* equal Total Equities. The equities side of the balance sheet is made up of two sections, Liabilities and Owner's Equity. *Liabilities* are amounts that the firm owes to others as a result of past transactions or events. Liabilities always have first claim on the firm's assets. The two categories of liabilities are Current and Noncurrent.

Current Liabilities are obligations due within one year or less. Such accounts are considered current liabilities: *Accounts Payable*, claims from suppliers for goods or services ordered (and possibly delivered) but not yet paid for, Notes Payable (short-term loans), and *Accrued Expenses* (expenses owed for the period, but not yet paid). Examples of Accrued Expenses are salaries due, rent, and utility bills not paid. *Deferred Revenues* are revenues received for service or future sale of goods, but the service or goods have not been delivered yet. The most common source of deferred revenues for a design firm would be from retainers or down payments the client has paid to the designer.

Two other current liabilities accounts are Taxes Payable (sometimes called Estimated Taxes), which represent the amount of income tax or other taxes owed to government agencies but not yet paid, and Current Portion of Long-Term Debt, which would show how much of the long-term debt, perhaps resulting from the purchase of a delivery truck by the firm, is to be paid during this next one-year period.

Other Liabilities or noncurrent liabilities are amounts owed that will not be paid during the coming one-year period. The main item listed would be the balance of principal owed on a long-term loan.

The *Owner's Equity* section shows the amount the owners have invested in the firm. For a sole proprietorship, owner's equity would be shown as "Michael Smith, Capital" and the amount Michael Smith invested to start the firm plus any additions he made to the capital of the firm. For a partnership, it is customary to show the amount invested by each partner as a separate line, in much the same way as

*Owner's Equity*

| | |
|---|---:|
| Michael Smith, capital as of January 1, 19X6 | $25,000 |
| Deduct: 19— drawings | (5,500) |
| Michael Smith, capital as of December 31, 19X7 | $19,500 |

FIGURE 11-3
Reporting format of owner's equity for a proprietorship on a balance sheet.

*Owner's Equity*

| | | |
|---|---:|---:|
| Judith Jones, Capital | $10,000 | |
| Alice Smith, Capital | 10,000 | |
| Barbara Rogers, Capital | 7,000 | |
| Total Partnership Equity | | $27,000 |

FIGURE 11-4
Reporting format of owner's equity for a partnership on a balance sheet.

for a proprietorship. A partnership and proprietorship will also show a beginning and ending balance to indicate any withdrawals (or drawings) made by the owners against the assets. Figures 11-3 and 11-4 show owner's equity in these forms of business.

A design firm that is a corporation would show Stockholders' Equity, since the corporation is owned by stockholders. The amount of money obtained to run the corporation is listed as Capital Stock and Paid-in Capital Stock. Par value of issued and outstanding stock is reported to represent the legal minimum claim on assets associated with the stock itself. Paid-in Capital Stock is the excess of par value representing the claims on assets arising purely from the value of stock at the time of its issuance.

Another item in Stockholders' Equity would be Retained Earnings. This represents the claim on assets arising from the cumulative undistributed earnings of the corporation after dividends are paid to stockholders for use in the business. *Retained Earnings* does not refer to cash in and of itself. It may be in some other form, such as a vehicle, equipment, or marketable securities. There is no retained earnings section on the balance sheet of a proprietorship or partnership. Earnings are treated as noted above for these forms of business.

Each general category is added to obtain Total Assets and Total Equities. Total assets must always equal total equities.

## The Income Statement

The *income statement* formally reports all the revenues and expenses of the firm for a stated period of time. The result shows the net income (or loss) for the firm during the period. The income statement is also commonly called a *profit-and-loss statement. Revenues* are the inflows of monies to a company from the sale of goods and services. For an interior design firm, revenues may result from the fees it charges clients or from the amounts received from the sale of goods. For the sale of goods to yield revenue for the firm, the goods must be goods that "pass through" the design firm's hands. What this means is that items that are specified by the designer but sold to the end-user by someone else would not be revenue-producing for the design firm. For example, John Everett specifies tables and chairs for a new restaurant, but the restaurant owner purchases the goods directly from the manufacturer. Since the sale did not pass through Everett's books, he cannot recognize those funds as revenue. The design fee to specify those goods, however, would be revenue for Everett since those funds are billed through Everett's office.

*Expenses* are the outflows of assets used to generate revenue. Since assets must always equal equities, expenses are also decreased in owner's equity. *Net Income* (or Profit) is the eventual difference between revenues and expenses. A loss occurs when expenses are greater than revenues.

The income statement used in the following discussion (see Figure 11-5) is for-

**Income Statement**
**Arizona Interior Designs**
**Period Ending January 31, 19X8**

| | | | |
|---|---:|---:|---:|
| Gross Revenue | | | |
| From Fees | | $18,400 | |
| From Sale of Goods | | | |
| Product | $37,500 | | |
| Freight-in | 2,625 | | |
| Delivery | 3,250 | | |
| | | 43,375 | |
| Total Gross Revenue | | $61,775 | |
| Net Revenue | | | $61,775 |
| | | | |
| Cost of Sales | | | |
| From Products: | | | |
| Cost of Goods | $25,000 | | |
| Freight-in | 2,500 | | |
| Delivery | 3,000 | | |
| From Fees: | | | |
| Direct Labor | 12,750 | | |
| Supplies | 185 | | |
| Reproduction Expense | 95 | | |
| Telephone (Long-Distance) | 105 | | |
| Total Cost of Sales | | 43,635 | |
| Gross Margin | | | $18,140 |
| | | | |
| Operating Expenses | | | |
| Salaries | 9,500 | | |
| Payroll Taxes | 1,400 | | |
| Group Insurance | 95 | | |
| Rent | 850 | | |
| Heat, Power, and Light | 250 | | |
| Telephone | 165 | | |
| Promotion | 105 | | |
| Travel Reimbursements | 175 | | |
| Supplies and Postage | 225 | | |
| Depreciation Expense (Furn.) | 300 | | |
| Depreciation Expense (Auto) | 1,000 | | |
| Insurance | 200 | | |
| Dues and Subscriptions | 57 | | |
| Professional Consultants | 150 | | |
| Printing and Reproduction | 50 | | |
| Interest Expense | 200 | | |
| Total Operating Expenses | | | 14,722 |
| | | | |
| Other Revenue | | | |
| Interest | | | 350 |
| Net Income Before Taxes | | | $ 3,418 |
| Less: Provision for Income Taxes | | | − 627 |
| Net Income | | | $ 3,141 |

**FIGURE 11-5**
Income statement.

matted with the consideration that the firm has instituted a cost accounting system to measure and evaluate costs of doing business against the revenues the firm has generated. In a cost accounting system, certain, if not all, costs directly related to the generation of revenue are costed or charged to the particular revenue-producing activity. For a design firm, this means that all costs related to a particular job are recorded for that job. These costs show up on the income statement under the category of Cost of Sales as either Direct Labor or Direct Expenses. The author believes it is important for a design firm to use this method in order to have an accurate view of the activities of the firm. This point will be discussed further.

The easiest way to understand the parts of an income statement is to start at the top entry and work through the various parts. The income statement in Figure 11-5 shows income generated from fees and goods sold. First note the heading. The date indicates the status of the firm prior to that date.

## GROSS REVENUE TO NET REVENUE

Gross Revenue is all the revenue generated by the firm for the period. For our purposes, we will break this down into Revenue from Fees—the design fees for interior design services—and From Sale of Goods, which are revenues related to the sale of products to clients. We further break down the revenues from Sale of Goods to show (1) Product, the amount the end-user paid the design firm for the goods; (2) Freight-in, which is the freight charges the client paid for goods; and (3) Delivery, which represents the delivery and/or installation charges the design firm billed the client.

Total Gross Revenue is the total amount of revenue generated from all means by the firm for the period. Adjustments that are made for such things as returns and allowances, damages, or any extra discounts the designer offers to clients for prompt payment. These are subtracted from the Total Gross Revenue to obtain Net Revenue.

## COST OF SALES TO GROSS MARGIN

*Cost of Sales* refers to the costs paid in the direct generation of revenues. In retail sales this is called Cost of Goods Sold and relates to changes in inventory. In our example, Cost of Sales is broken down into two parts, as was revenue—from fees and from products. Under the section of Cost of Sales from Products, there are three lines corresponding to those in revenues. The first is Cost of Goods, which shows the change in inventory and any special orders delivered during the period; (2) Freight-in, which shows the charges the firm was billed for goods delivered to the firm; and (3) Delivery and Installation, which shows the cost of delivery and/or installation or products to the company (this could include salaries paid and cost of trucks, equipment, and so on needed to deliver products to the customer).

Under Cost of Sales from Fees are four items. The first, *Direct Labor,* should be the easiest to determine. This is the time the various designers spent directly involved in the generation of the designs under contract where fees for services were charged. The amount of direct labor can easily be determined from the time sheets kept by the staff. This amount can be calculated against the salary paid to the various designers. Direct Labor could also include the time secretarial staff and management staff spend working on the projects under contract. Since this is often harder to keep an accurate account, the time spent on projects by management and support staff is more commonly figured as overhead.

In Figure 11-5, other line items shown are for supplies, reproduction, and long-distance telephone charges. These are legitimate costs against projects done under contract. They are presented to give a truer view of the "profitability" of the firm's activities. Many firms do not show these charges at all, putting them into appropriate categories of Selling and Administrative (or overhead) expenses.

All these adjustments (costs) are totaled and subtracted from Net Revenue. The result is *Gross Margin*, which is sometimes called *gross profit* but which does not represent profit. "Gross margin is the difference between the revenues generated from selling products (goods or services) and the related product costs."[3] Gross margin does show the amount of revenue available to cover selling and administrative (overhead) expenses to keep the firm in business.

### SELLING AND ADMINISTRATIVE EXPENSES

*Selling and Administrative Expenses,* also called Overhead Expenses, are those expenses that are incurred whether the firm produces any revenues or not. They are often thought of as overhead expenses or those expenses needed to keep the doors open. They are reported in as much detail as is needed by the firm and anyone who would be looking at the income statement. Expenses listed in Figure 11-5 represent the various kinds of expense items that are common to an interior design firm.

A few comments about some of these items: The item "Salaries" represents the amount of expense paid out for nonrevenue-generating labor activities (or activities that cannot be easily costed to projects). This usually includes salaries for secretaries, accounting personnel, and management personnel. However, it also would include that portion of the design staff's salaries that cannot be considered direct labor. "Telephone" represents those normal telephone charges and any other charges that the firm cannot, or chooses not to, cost back to specific revenue-generating activities. *Promotion* can be actual promotional expenses such as magazine advertising or the cost of placing the firm's Yellow Pages ad. It can also represent the expense of a business lunch.

As can be seen from the example, a firm can go into quite a bit of detail in order to have an accurate picture of the firm's financial standing. If an interior design firm has invested in a good computer system, the recordkeeping and data entry this much detail requires would be easier. Many management reports that would be helpful in the control of the design firm can then be generated. More detail on this topic will be covered in Chapter 12.

All these expenses are totaled and subtracted from Gross Margin to obtain Net Income. If the design firm is a corporation, this result would be titled "Net Income Before Taxes," since it is necessary for a corporation to show its estimated income taxes on the income statement. Unless the firm has some extraordinary expenses, such as a loss from fire, the next line should show a Provision for Income Tax, which is the estimated tax for the period. This amount is subtracted to determine Net Income. Should the firm receive income from sources other than the operation of the firm, such as interest earned on checking or savings accounts, it would be added before the Net Income Before Taxes result is determined.

This is not true for proprietorships or partnerships, since the income of these types of businesses is personal income and is reported along with any other income made on individual or family tax statements. These forms would not show a provision for income tax. The next line, in these cases, would be Net Income.

*Net Income* represents the amount of income (or loss) that results when all expenses (deductions) are made from revenues. If the result is positive, net income represents the dollar amount of profit the firm made for the period reported. If expenses were greater than revenues, then a loss would be reported for the period.

---

[3]Anthony, Robert N., and James S. Reece, *Accounting Texts and Cases*, 7th ed., Richard Irwin, © 1983, p. 908.

# *The Statement of Cash Flows*

The *Statement of Cash Flows* reports "net cash flows from operating investing and financing activities for a period of time."[4] This information is useful to potential investors and creditors as well as management in their various decisions concerning the firm. The information to prepare the Statement of Cash Flows comes from the balance sheet, the income statement, and, for corporations, from the retained earnings portion of the income statement. Although the report can be useful for those reviewing the financial condition of any business formation, it is primarily prepared by the corporation form of business ownership.

Prior to 1987, this type of financial information was reported as part of the Statement of Changes in Financial Position (sometimes called the Funds Flow Statement). This statement reported the sources and uses of funds during a given period. Because of an increased emphasis of reporting this information on a cash-basis format, the Financial Accounting Standards Board recommended that cash flow information be recorded in the statement of cash flows format. This practice was begun in 1987.[5]

Although the Statement of Cash Flows provides information about cash receipts (inflows) and cash payments (outflows) from all areas of the firm, its primary purpose is to report inflows and outflows for a given time period. Cash, for accounting purposes, is money, checks, or items such as money orders that are accepted by banks. The Statement of Cash Flows also reports the inflows and outflows of cash equivalents. Cash equivalents are very liquid, short term investments, such as money market funds, that can be converted to cash quickly. However, if these kinds of investments are made only for the temporary investment of excess cash, they are not to be considered a part of the data to make up the statement.

The inflows and outflows come from the three areas: operations, investments, and financing. Operations activities are those involved in the normal revenue-generation activities of the firm. Operations flows would come primarily from the payments and receivables from clients and the payments the firm makes to others in the generation of revenues. Depending on the nature of the firm, operations flows might also come from interest earned, if the firm loaned money to someone, and dividend receipts from certain kinds of investments. Investments inflows and outflows result from lending money and receiving payments on those loans; purchasing or selling certain kinds of securities; and the purchase or sale of assets such as property, buildings, or equipment the firm owns. Financing inflows and outflows come from the finances invested in the company by the owners and the subsequent payments to those owners for the investment as well as payments received and returned to creditors, such as banks for mortgages.

The net cash inflows and outflows from operations, investments, and financing are reported in the statement. A firm may use either a direct or an indirect method for reporting operations flows, and can report investments and financing flows either within the body of the operations flow statement or as a separate report to that statement.

## DIRECT METHOD OF OPERATIONS FLOWS

In the direct method, all major categories of inflows and outflows are reported as line items (see Figure 11-6). Subtracting outflows from inflows gives the net cash

---

[4]Imdieke, Leroy, F., and Ralph E. Smith, *Financial Accounting*, John Wiley & Sons, Inc., © 1987, p. 18.
[5]Imdieke and Smith 1987, 646.

**RAINBOW INTERIOR DESIGNS, INC.**
**Statement of Cash Flows**
**For the Year Ended December 31, 19X6**

| | | |
|---|---:|---:|
| Cash Flows from Operating Activities: | | |
| Cash Received from Customers (1) | $58,755 | |
| Dividends Received | 564 | |
| Cash Provided by Operating Activities | | $59,319 |
| Less Cash Paid: | | |
| To Suppliers for Purchases (2) | 17,653 | |
| To Suppliers for Operating Expenses (3) | 27,435 | |
| For Interest and Taxes (4) | 3,576 | |
| Cash Disbursed for Operating Activities | | 48,664 |
| Net Cash Flow from Operating Activities | | 10,655 |
| Cash Flows from Investing Activities: | | |
| Purchases of Property, Plant, and Equipment (5) | −3,550 | |
| Net Cash Flow from Investing Activities | | −3,550 |
| Cash Flows from Financing Activities: | | |
| Net Increase from Customer Retainers | 2,350 | |
| Net Increase from Customer Deposits | 1,775 | |
| Proceeds of Long-term Debt | 8,500 | |
| Payments on Long-term Debt | −1,776 | |
| Dividends Paid | −650 | |
| Net Cash Provided by Financing Activities | | 10,199 |
| Net Increase (Decrease) in Cash and Cash Equivalents | | $17,304 |
| Schedule of Noncash Investing and Financing Activities: | | |
| Notes Payable Given in Exchange for Equipment | | $ 3,550 |
| (1) Accrual Basis Sales | | $60,605 |
| Add: Beginning Accounts Receivable | | 7,900 |
| Less: Ending Accounts Receivable | | −9,750 |
| Cash Received from Clients | | $58,755 |
| (2) Accrual Basis Cost of Goods Sold | | $18,700 |
| Less: Beginning Inventory | | −5,678 |
| Plus: Ending Inventory | | 3,995 |
| Plus: Beginning Accounts Payable | | 5,616 |
| Less: Ending Accounts Payable | | −4,980 |
| Cash Paid to Suppliers for Purchases | | $17,653 |
| (3) Operating Expenses Other Than Depreciation | | $27,920 |
| Less: Beginning Prepaid Expenses | | −1,275 |
| Plus: Ending Prepaid Expenses | | 1,415 |
| Plus: Beginning Accrued Expenses | | 3,325 |
| Less: Ending Accrued Expenses | | −3,950 |
| Cash Paid to Suppliers for Operating Expenses | | $27,435 |
| (4) Interest Expense | | $ 657 |
| Income Tax Expense | | 2,919 |
| Cash Paid for Interest and Taxes | | $ 3,576 |
| (5) Cash Paid for Computer | | $ 3,550 |
| Cash Payments for Building and Equipment | | $ 3,550 |

**FIGURE 11-6**
Statement of cash flows
(direct method).

**RAINBOW INTERIOR DESIGNS, INC.**
**Statement of Cash Flows**
**For the Year Ended December 31, 19X6**

| | | |
|---|---:|---:|
| Net Cash Flow from Operating Activities: | | |
| Net Income | | $10,848 |
| Adjustments to Convert Net Income to Net Cash Flow from Operating Expenses: | | |
| Depreciation Expense | | 1,125 |
| Increase in Accounts Receivable | | −1,850 |
| Decrease in Inventory | | 1,683 |
| Increase in Prepaid Expenses | | −140 |
| Decrease in Accounts Payable | | −1,636 |
| Increase in Accrued Expenses | | 625 |
| Net Cash Flow from Operating Activities | | 10,655 |
| Cash Flows from Investing Activities: | | |
| Purchase of Equipment | −$3,550 | |
| Net Cash Used by Investing Activities | | −3,550 |
| Cash Flows from Financing Activities: | | |
| Proceeds from Customer Retainers | 2,350 | |
| Proceeds from Customer Deposits | 1,775 | |
| Proceeds of Long-term Debt | 8,500 | |
| Payments on Long-term Debt | −1,776 | |
| Cash Dividends Paid | −650 | |
| Net Cash Provided by Financing Activities | | 10,199 |
| Net Increase in Cash | | $17,304 |

**FIGURE 11-7**
Statement of cash flows
(indirect method).

flow from operations. In order to report this, the accountant must convert an accrual basis of accounting to a cash basis of accounting. "The main advantage of the direct method is that it shows the operating cash receipts and payments. Knowledge of where operating cash came from and how cash was used in operations in past periods may be useful in estimating future cash flows."[6]

## INDIRECT METHOD OF OPERATIONS FLOWS

To the nonaccountant, the indirect method is more difficult to understand. Net cash flows from operations are reported by making various adjustments of inflows and outflows from an accrual basis to a cash basis. Adjustments are needed for noncash expenses, revenues, and gains and losses, with further adjustments made to noncash items such as prepaid expenses (see Figure 11-7). "The main advantage of the indirect method is that it focuses attention on the differences between income and cash flow from operating activities. An understanding of the differences may be important to investors, creditors, and others who wish to use assessments of income as an intermediate step in assessing future cash flows."[7]

## CASH FLOWS FROM INVESTMENTS

Cash flows from investments are simply reported as individual line items related to whether they are inflows or outflows (see Figure 11-7). Common inflows are such items as cash generated in the sale of property, buildings or equipment, income from loans made to others, and receipts from the sale of certain securities. Outflows are just the opposite—purchasing equipment, making the loan, or buying the securities.

---

[6]Imdieke and Smith 1987, 649.
[7]Imdieke and Smith 1987, 654.

### CASH FLOWS FROM FINANCING

Cash flows from financing activities are also simply reported as individual line items indicating which were inflows and outflows (see Figure 11-7). Financing inflows represent revenues from the sale of stock, contributions by partners, and loans made by the firm from short- or long-term debts like mortgages. Outflows would be the payments made by the firm to repurchase stock that others hold, stock dividends, and repayments on loans.

The indirect method of reporting cash flows from operations, which utilizes the investments and financing activities as a separate report, is similar in format to the previous cash basis statement of changes in financial condition. A decision as to which format to use should be based on the needs and uses of the statement by the design firm and the recommendation of the firm's accountant.

### NONCASH BASIS REPORTING

Some firms, mainly larger-sized corporations, may have other investments and financing activities that are of a noncash basis. These activities must also be reported, but since they affect a small number of interior design firms, they will not be discussed here.

## Accounting Records and Systems _____

The balance sheet, income statement, and cash flows are summary reports. They are generated from the information maintained in the accounting records.

In accounting terminology, events that affect the financial aspects of a firm, either as revenue-generating or expense-generating, are called transactions. These transactions must be recorded in an organized manner so that the firm can report or review its financial condition.

### ACCOUNTS

Financial organization is established in accounts. Accounts, with various names for clarification, show additions (increases) to the account and subtractions (decreases) to the account. In its simplest form, the account record looks like the letter *T*, hence the name T account (Figures 11-8 and 11-9).

The left-hand side of the T account is called the debit side, whereas the right-hand side is the credit side. *Debit* and *credit* have no other meaning in accounting than left and right respectively. They are not substitutes for the words *increase* or *decrease* since, for some accounts, the increase side of the T account will be on the right and the decrease on the left.

For example, the T account for an asset account, Revenue, would look like the one in Figure 11-8, with increases in revenue entered in the right column (credit) and decreases in the left column (debit). And the T account for an expense account would look like the one in Figure 11-9, with increases being entered in the left column (debit) and decreases entered in the right column (credit). The differences relate to which side of the balance sheet the items of entry belong.

### JOURNAL, LEDGER, AND CHART OF ACCOUNTS

Following a business transaction, entries are made in a journal. A *journal* is a chronological record of all accounting transactions for the firm (see Figure 11-10). Journal entries show the date of occurrence, the name of the account to be debited or credited, the amount of the debit or credit, and a reference to the ledger account

Cost of Sales

| Debit ( + ) | Credit ( − ) |
|---|---|
| $1,900 | |
| 500 | |
| 4,300 | |

FIGURE 11-8
T account for a liabilities account.

Sales Revenues

| Debit ( − ) | Credit ( + ) |
|---|---|
| | $2,500 |
| | 700 |
| | 5,050 |

FIGURE 11-9
T account for an asset account.

| 19X6 | | Accounts | Ledger | Debit | Credit |
|---|---|---|---|---|---|
| | | | | | |
| March | 6 | Cash.......................... | 1 | 2,350 | |
| | | Sales......................... | 26 | | 2,350 |
| | | | | | |
| | 6 | Accounts Receivables.......... | 2 | 678 | |
| | | Design Fees.................. | 3 | | 675 |
| | | | | | |
| | 6 | Inventory..................... | 5 | 5,675 | |
| | | Cash......................... | 1 | | 2,000 |
| | | Accounts Payable............ | 21 | | 3,675 |
| | | | | | |

FIGURE 11-10
Sample journal entries.

to which the entry has been posted. Entries are posted to different ledger accounts from the journal. Posting, therefore, is the transferring of a journal entry to the correct ledger account.

The *ledger,* often called a General Ledger, is a group of accounts. Most people are familiar with the general ledger book, a bound book for all entries. But a ledger does not need to be a bound book. This may work for a small firm, but larger firms will use loose-leaf pages or computers. The general ledger is often supplemented by various subsidiary ledgers. These provide detailed information to support the general ledger. For an interior design firm, an important subsidiary ledger would be the accounts receivable ledger. This ledger would have separate accounts for each client who purchases on credit from the designer.

A Chart of Accounts is a list of all the accounts the firm is using. A list of such accounts is based on management's (and others') desires about what things need to be accounted for; it is a kind of statement about how the firm will categorize the events it seeks to control. The list is numbered in some logical order. These code numbers are the ones used to cross-reference journal entries to posting entries. The chart of accounts should be set up so that it can increase in complexity as the firm grows, with appropriate accounts added as needed. A useful starting place would be the accounts that relate to the information needed to prepare the balance sheet and the income statement. Accounts would be set up for Cash, Accounts Receivables, Fixed Assets, Accounts Payable, Payroll, Telephone, Rent, Sales Revenue from Fees, and so on.

### TRIAL BALANCE

Remember that assets equal liabilities and debits must equal credits. This does not mean debits and credits will be equal within each account, but when all accounts are considered, they will be equal. A test to see if accounts are balanced and that lists all the account balances with the debit and credit side totaled separately is called a trial balance.

There are two purposes of a trial balance. One is to check the accuracy of the posting entries to see if total debits equal total credits. The other is to establish summary balances in all accounts in order to prepare the balance sheet, income statement, and changes in financial condition. A trial balance can be done whenever the accounts are up to date.

## Cash Management _____

For interior design firms to stay in business, a constant inflow of cash that equals or exceeds the outflows of cash is needed to pay the expenses for the same period. The statement of cash flows discussed earlier reports to those outside the firm the sources and uses of funds for a period. In this section, we will briefly discuss a simple cash flow statement that is easily prepared by a manager and used in cash management.

For design firms that do not sell merchandise, the cash flow cycle will be relatively short. Firms that sell merchandise have a constant cash flow problem related to receiving enough cash from some source to pay for the merchandise that is on order. Whatever the case, there must always be enough cash available to pay current bills. Employees will expect to be paid within seven to fourteen days of when work was completed. Suppliers generally have a thirty-day payment period before penalties are charged. The faster the firm can collect on its receivables, the more efficient its cash flow cycle will be. However, it is not uncommon for a firm to have a significant percentage of its receivables out over 120 days.

Good basic business practices will aid in keeping cash flow efficiently operating. Many of those business practices will be discussed in later chapters and in this section. Among them are understanding and following good pricing policies for both fees and products, obtaining credit reports on clients with whom the firm is unfamiliar, preparing design contracts to help protect the designer from possible stoppages or losses of revenue, and instituting policies requiring substantial retainers and deposits before work is begun or products are ordered. Careful timekeeping, scheduling, and project management including constant monitoring of outstanding orders and receivables all will aid the firm in protecting narrow margins of profit. Thorough monitoring of budgeted versus actual time estimates, fee estimates, and gross profit expectations can eliminate errors from happening more than once.

**Cash Flow Statement**
**19X7**

| | Actual January | Projected February | Projected March | Projected April |
|---|---|---|---|---|
| Beginning Cash Balance | $ 9,000 | $13,600 | $13,200 | |
| Projected Revenues | 22,000 | 18,000 | 23,000 | 26,000 |
| Projected Gross Revenues | 31,000 | 31,600 | 36,200 | |
| Operations Expenses | 17,000 | 18,000 | 20,000 | 23,000 |
| Purchase of Computer | | | 6,000 | |
| Line of Credit Debt | 400 | 400 | 400 | 400 |
| Ending Cash Balance | $13,600 | $13,200 | $ 9,800 | |

FIGURE 11-11
Simple cash flow report.

The best situations in cash management require substantial retainers and deposits as well as the prompt receipt of receivables. However, as already pointed out, aged accounts (those older than thirty days) are all too common in the interior design profession. When the firm needs cash, however, the owners can go to the firm's bank for short-term loans. Keeping the banker informed of the financial situation at the design firm will aid in the loan-approval process, as will a good history of prompt repayment of those loans. But going to the bank every time the firm is short of cash to pay bills is not the best solution. Good management of the firm and the firm's cash flow is the answer.

Figure 11-11 shows a simple cash flow forecast. The cash flow statement begins with the current known cash balance. If the entire cash flow statement is for projected cash flow, then the beginning cash balance for each month can be estimated. In order to show how the cash flow statement works, however, the beginning cash balance is the actual balance (as determined by revenue minus expenses). The next line shows the known and projected revenues for the months being reviewed. This projected revenue combines the known work in progress amounts for each period with forecasts of additional work in each month. Adding the beginning cash balance to the projected revenue provides a projected gross revenue amount.

Operating expenses are the projected combined expenses for each month. These would include salaries, fringe benefits, rent, utilities expenses, and other costs of doing business. The next line shows each month's responsibility for a bank line of credit that was obtained in a previous month. This amount is the amount of principal and interest due each month. Note that in March the firm expects a one-time expense of $6000 for a computer. The last line shows the ending cash balance for each month. This balance is carried up to the beginning cash balance line in the forecast months. The reader may wish to fill in April's figures to obtain the ending balance for the month (and to see how well the firm is doing!).

## Summary

This chapter, by no means, fully explains financial accounting. Although interior designers rightly utilize the services of accountants to prepare the formal accounting statements needed periodically, too many leave the day-to-day bookkeeping chores to accountants or others who better understand these financial matters, never bothering to have more than a cursory knowledge of the firm's financial condition. It is important to understand the financial aspects of the interior design business and to be conversant with the terminology and concepts of financial accounting.

In this chapter we have looked at the basic concepts, definitions, and parts of the balance sheet, income statement, and statement of change in financial condition. We have also looked briefly at the concepts related to accounting records and systems.

In the next chapter we will be looking at managerial accounting and some brief concepts concerning management control systems. These relate to reporting methods, generated from the financial statements, created to help owners and/or management plan, organize, and control the design firm.

# Chapter 12

# FINANCIAL MANAGEMENT CONTROL

*Financial management control,* or managerial accounting, is concerned with the planning and analysis of all the financial aspects of the firm. Financial management control reports are prepared to help individuals in the company manage and control the performance of the firm.

Financial management control goes beyond financial accounting. You will recall from the preceding chapter that financial accounting is concerned with the day-to-day and periodic measurement and reporting of resources that would be of interest to external individuals. A financial management control report, on the other hand, would be one that analyzes any kind of financial or numerical information that would be of interest to the owners and/or the managers of the firm. Control reports can show many things. One simple example would be a report that summarizes how much of all possible work time for each designer is billable to clients as opposed to house or nonbillable time.

Financial management control is performed by those in the firm entrusted to plan, organize, and control the organization: owners, business managers, design directors, and so on. In most small firms financial management control is almost always the responsibility of the owner who receives assistance from the firm's accountant in developing reports. In medium- and large-sized firms, the reports are usually generated and analyzed by the managerial element.

As a whole, interior design businesses have been slow to accept this part of business management. However, regardless of the size of the firm, financial management control should be a part of operations. The planning and control aspects of financial management and managerial accounting can assist all sizes of firms in preparing for success and handling problems. As the interior design firm grows, this function becomes more important.

## The Management Function

Financial management control is primarily a function of the management role. As such, it would be helpful to briefly describe managerial activities as they relate to financial management. Management is a very complex activity with many different meanings. For our purposes here, management is the effective direction of staff members and financial resources under a manager's control toward the goals and objectives that the owners of the firm have established.

**119**

There are two broad extremes of management style. One is very autocratic, in which planning and decision-making come down from the manager to the staff. Very little staff input is requested or even tolerated. This autocratic style of management is often apparent in very small firms where the owner also performs all the management functions. The other is more democratic or facilitative. In this style of management, staff input is desired and responsibility is often given to staff members to accomplish certain managerial tasks. Although this style of management is more likely to exist in larger firms, it can appear in any size firm, just as the autocratic style of management may show up in any size firm.

Managers perform four broad, generally accepted functions:

1. Planning.
2. Organizing and directing.
3. Decision-making.
4. Controlling.

In planning, managers help chart the future direction of the firm. Planning involves research of staff capabilities and resources of the firm in its various segments. With this knowledge, managers prepare goals, objectives, and strategies. These goals, objectives, and strategies involve every aspect of the firm: operations, including personnel and production; marketing; and financial planning. The preparation of the annual business plan is an example of this function.

The organizing and directing function occurs as the manager determines how best to use the resources at his or her disposal to perform the work activities of the firm. For example, if the firm is large enough so that a division of the labor for completing projects is desired, the manager determines who will perform which tasks and how these tasks will interrelate.

*Decision-making* is the activity of making reasonable choices between the alternatives available. It is a part of all the other management functions and seems to occur almost all the time in the manager's day. For example, in firms where new projects are generated through a manager, salesperson, or marketing individual, the manager must decide which designer will be responsible for completing the project.

The control function requires the manager to monitor the activities of the interior design department and take any necessary steps to ensure that the plans, policies, and decisions of the manager and the firm are being carried out. This is done in part by reviewing the kinds of reports that will be discussed in this chapter. It also occurs when the manager makes adjustments or develops new evaluative mechanisms to help the firm achieve its goals and objectives.

Although each of these functions is discussed separately, they are continually intermixed. Managers find themselves engaged in all these functions every day. This reality is part of the stress and excitement of the management role.

Various parts of this book discuss more specific activities of the management process. Chapters 8 and 9 looked at personnel management; Chapters 13 and 14 look at the components related to determining pricing and fee structures; and Chapter 19 looks at time management and project control. Other chapters also deal with the whole picture of managing an interior design practice.

There are many fine general books on management in the libraries and bookstores. The reader may wish to review one or more of these books or even take a course in management to gain a more complete understanding of the management function.

# *Goals and Objectives*

Establishing goals and objectives is an important facet of financial management control. An organization's *goals* are broad statements, without regard to any time limit, of what the firm wishes to achieve. One of the goals for an interior design firm might be "to become the premier residential design firm in the city." *Objectives* are more specific statements combined with time limits aimed toward accomplishing the firm's goals. Some objectives for the example goal might be: "During the next year, we will seek to obtain a product mix that will provide the very highest quality merchandise." Also, "In order to gain recognition as a quality residential design firm, we will seek to get at least one project per year published in one of the trade or shelter magazines."

To further ensure successful accomplishment of these goals and objectives, more specific strategies must be established. These *strategies* are highly specific actions that have definite time limits within the year of the plan. To continue with the example, a strategy might be "During the next six months, we will negotiate to be the only design firm in this city to sell Baker Furniture products."

All the goals, objectives, and strategies of the annual business plan must relate back to the firm's mission statement. This *mission statement* is almost always a philosophical statement of what the firm sees as its role in the professional area. Figure 12-1 is an example of a company mission statement.

# *The Annual Business Plan*

The purpose of the *annual business plan* is to bring together all the planning elements of the firm into one plan. This annual plan is a systematic investigation of what the firm can do, what the client base of the firm demands, and what the firm then decides to try to do for the year. Similar in many ways to the originating business plan, it is the ongoing plan for the business. The plan should contain information related to all areas of the business: administration, personnel management, marketing, facilities, and finances.

In many situations, the business plan comes down from the owner to the employees without input from the employees. This is called top-down planning. Employees feel that they are not part of the process or the organization when the plan is handed down to them to accomplish without their input. Since they have no responsibility in establishing the goals, employees feel no particular responsibility in accomplishing them either. In this situation, it is not uncommon for the goals and objectives of the firm and the employees to be in conflict. What the firm wishes to accomplish may not be what the employees feel they are able to accomplish. Top-down planning sets the stage for potential failure of the plan.

It is important for planning to start with the employees and for their input to be considered. Planning should begin with a general discussion of what the owners and managers wish to accomplish for the coming year. Employees, within their work groups, should discuss how they see themselves and their group affecting these general goals. The work groups, with their managers, determine goals and objectives for the group. The managers further review these goals and objectives and present to the group and the owners what they feel are in the best interests of the company and the group. Management then considers all the goals and objectives of the various work groups and proposes the final annual plan.

*The Business Purpose
And Goals Of Goodmans*

## BUSINESS PURPOSE

Goodmans is a furniture-based, problem-solving company in the office products industry. Our mission is to serve our customers with services and products that create more productive, efficient and aesthetic environments. We are committed to maintaining a climate in which our people have an opportunity for personal growth and creativity while being part of a team that delivers total customer satisfaction.

## GOALS

### To Be More Important To The Customer

To identify from the customers' perspective, their needs and values, and to provide solutions through outstanding services, products, and follow-up.

### To Be Better To Ourselves

Communicate and experience the "Goodmans' Culture" at all locations, to continually train for individual skills and provide an opportunity for personal growth and encourage everyone's participation in "The Good Plan." To achieve this in an atmosphere of freedom, excitement and comfort.

### To Be Financially Strong

To financially strengthen the company in order to continue sound growth by meeting and/or exceeding our key financial and performance goals.

**FIGURE 12-1**
**An example of a company mission statement.**
*(Reproduced with permission, Goodmans Design-Interiors, Phoenix, Az.)*

An annual business plan should cover

1. *Goals and objectives.* Goals and objectives should be developed in two parts: first, the overall goals and objectives with appropriate strategies of the whole firm, and second, the goals and objectives of the various responsibility groups. Individual goals and objectives should not be part of the annual business plan since the plan may be shown to external individuals.
2. *Administration.* The administration portion will outline support staff requirements for the projected year. This section will include the goals and objectives of such areas as management, secretarial, bookkeeping, and warehouse, in other words, areas not directly related to the generation of income.
3. *General planning and policy development.* Goals and objectives related to any changes in planning procedures, policy development, and general operational matters would be covered in this section. It may also cover how project boards are to look, what changes to expense policies may occur, and general personnel policies such as vacations and sick leave.
4. *Personnel management.* This section of the plan will deal directly with how staff members will be hired, job descriptions, salary and benefits, training, and performance evaluations.
5. *Facilities and equipment.* The facilities section will cover topics directly related to space utilization, construction, and equipment.

6. *Marketing plan.* The marketing plan must identify what the firm intends to do to generate new business. It does this by clearly identifying in which segments of the marketplace the firm is currently involved and what segments the firm may wish to enter in the coming year. The marketing plan will seek to identify who will be responsible for bringing in new business, how these new markets will be approached, and so on.

7. *Financial plan.* The financial plan outlines all the profit, revenue, and expense levels required to achieve the goals and objectives of the firm. Part of this planning will contain statements regarding such things as billable hours, expected administrative salaries and expenses, and cash flow projections. Budgets from each department will be presented and combined into a projected income statement for the year.

8. *Budgeting.* Budgeting, a function of all the parts of the business plan, will primarily involve financial information related to revenues and expenses. However, such things as time budgeting for various expected projects as well as for house and administrative activities, space utilization budgeting for the housing of offices and support spaces such as the warehouse, and other plans for the current or near future should be included.

Inherent in all of these portions of the plan will be the means of measuring performance. Having goals and objectives with no way of determining success will result in a meaningless expenditure of energy in the planning and writing process. Performance evaluation is not just part of the individual staff employee's productivity results, but relates to all other planning and budgeting analysis. Such things as whether the job descriptions were actually written and were adhered to in hiring, whether the newly purchased truck was cost-effective, and whether projects were obtained from the hospital market or not are all part of performance evaluation of the planning process.

The annual business plan helps a firm know where it is going for the coming year. It also aids a design firm in planning for the long range. At some point, after the firm has had a measure of success, it becomes important for the owners and managers to be looking beyond the immediate day-to-day, year-by-year goals. Long-range planning takes those firms toward greater possibilities. Instead of by accident, firms move ahead by careful planning.

# *Budgeting*

*Budgeting,* a part of the management planning function, involves annual managerial goals expressed in specific quantitative terms, usually monetary terms. Too often, interior design firms budget by taking figures from the previous year and adding a modest percentage of increase for the coming year. This informal method of budgeting can work satisfactorily during normal economic conditions. However, when economic conditions become slow or very volatile, the design firm has a difficult time meeting goals or perhaps even maintaining the practice.

Budgeting encourages the manager to plan for rather than react to the various events affecting the firm. It forces the manager to formally plan his or her coming efforts, and it allows for easier analysis of success and problems. Formal budgeting also permits the discovery of potential problem areas and provides the opportunity to determine a course of action prior to their occurring. In addition, budgeting focuses the efforts of the whole organization by coordinating all the various individual and group efforts toward the firm's annual goals.

Although budgeting generally focuses on profits, it is also important to look at expected expenses and gross revenues. By reviewing last year's figures, managers can begin to forecast what will likely happen in the coming year. With further analysis, budgeting for what the company will actually attempt to accomplish becomes more realistic.

The simplest and most common method of budgeting in many firms is still to look at last year's figures and then, by applying various percentages of increase or decrease, come up with the new budget. As pointed out earlier, this can work fairly well in normal circumstances, but there is greater success if budgeting is done more formally and in sufficient detail to provide a more accurate picture of what the firm needs to do. The past is always a good starting point, but it should be used in conjunction with good research and planning. (See Figure 12-2.)

The common budgeting method of adding percentages of expected growth looks at what can be accomplished based on economic outlooks, built-in prejudices, and conservative forecasting of managers. In small firms where the realization budget may be relatively easy to prepare in relation to the time expended, it might be good to prepare both budgets and compare the two. This comparison may show some potential weak spots in productivity, cost control, or revenue generation.

One well-known budget concept is zero-based budgeting, which received attention during the Carter Administration. Zero-based budgeting assumes that each year the managers of the firm start with a zero budget level and must justify all costs as if the department or activity were starting new. This means that no costs

**Design Department Proposed Budget**
**Arizona Interior Designs**
**19X7**

|  | 19X6 Actual | 19X7 Proposed |
|---|---|---|
| Revenue: | | |
| From Fees | $320,800 | $401,000 |
| Cost of Sales: | | |
| Direct Labor | 217,500 | 271,875 |
| Supplies | 3,580 | 4,475 |
| Reproduction Expense | 2,540 | 3,175 |
| Telephone (Long-Distance) | 1,588 | 1,985 |
| Total Cost of Sales | 225,208 | 281,510 |
| Gross Margin | $ 95,592 | $119,490 |
| Operating Expenses: (Those Directly Costed to Design Department) | | |
| Salaries | 53,590 | 66,987 |
| Payroll Taxes | 15,005 | 18,756 |
| Group Insurance | 650 | 800 |
| Promotion | 1,400 | 1,750 |
| Travel Reimbursements | 3,500 | 4,375 |
| Supplies and Postage | 5,750 | 7,190 |
| Professional Dues | 3,500 | 4,000 |
| Printing and Reproduction | 6,680 | 8,350 |
| Total Operating Expenses | $ 90,075 | $112,208 |
| Net Income | $ 5,517 | $ 7,282 |
| Profit to Sales | 2% | 2% |

**FIGURE 12-2**
A simple budget report.

are considered as ongoing from year to year. Zero-based budgeting is rather complex for a small firm and is generally more adaptable to larger, multidimensional design firms. Very few firms utilize zero-based budgeting anymore.

## *Reporting Performance*

Two important types of reports used by management to determine if the firm's plans are being accomplished are information reports and performance reports. Information reports are generally not made up of financial or other numeric data. They are prepared in a narrative form used to provide management with various kinds of information needed in the operation of the organization. A summary of an article related to general economic forecasts for the geographic area of the design firm, which also discusses how these forecasts may affect the design firm, is an example of an informational report.

The second, and more important to our discussion here, are performance reports. Performance reports consist primarily of financial or other numeric kinds of information. By sifting through financial and other numeric information, such as time records, many detailed performance reports are possible.

For a reporting system to be useful to a manager it must be credible. According to Getz and Stasiowski, a reporting system has credibility when it abides by the following guidelines.

1. It is accurate. This does not mean that the numbers must just add up, but rather that any mistakes in the system must be corrected in the next reporting cycle. . . .
2. The reports must be timely for them to be useful. How timely the reports are depends on how the firm is organized and how much it is willing to spend in the financial area. . . . The typical architectural or engineering firm should not have to wait longer than two weeks after the close of the accounting period to receive financial statements. . . .
3. The reports should be fair. By fair it is meant that cost allocations to the various profit centers should be made on an equitable basis. . . . Generally, direct labor is the basis for distributing overhead costs but this may not always be the best way. . . .
4. The reports should be clear, which means they must be quickly and easily understood. The reports should not require further analysis or additional calculations on the reader's part.[1]

Control reports are most effective when reviewed in terms of variance analysis. *Variance analysis* looks at financial and numerical data in relation to the differences between planned (or budgeted amounts) and actual amounts (see Figure 12-3). However, a manager must not only look at the quantitative differences. For the data to be truly meaningful, he or she must also ask questions as to why the variances occur. This analysis quite often begins with informal meetings with the individuals involved. The manager's judgment is then used to make decisions related to the variances.

Variance analysis of data related to finances is looked at in terms of the variance's effect on net income. "An unfavorable variance is one whose effect is to make actual net income lower than budgeted net income."[2] In this use, the words *favorable* and *unfavorable* do not relate to positive and negative nor should they relate by themselves to managerial performance. They are only to be interpreted as algebraic impacts on the variance of net income.

---

[1]Getz, Lowell, and Frank Stasiowski, *Financial Management for the Design Professional,* Watson-Guptill Publications, 1984, p. 138. Copyright © 1984 Whitney Library of Design, an imprint of Watson-Guptill Publications. Used by permission of publisher.

[2]Anthony and Reece 1983, 908.

**Expense Report ($)**
**April 19X6**

| Expense | Actual | Budget | Variance |
|---|---|---|---|
| Salaries | 12,000 | 10,500 | −1,500 |
| Payroll Taxes | 1,575 | 1,200 | −375 |
| Group Insurance | 250 | 250 | |
| Rent | 1,200 | 1,200 | |
| Heat, Power, and Light | 450 | 375 | −75 |
| Telephone | 275 | 300 | 25 |
| Promotion | 350 | 425 | 75 |
| Travel Reimbursements | 657 | 500 | −157 |
| Supplies and Postage | 550 | 600 | 50 |
| Depreciation Expense | 900 | 900 | |
| Insurance | 750 | 750 | |
| Dues and Subscriptions | 150 | 50 | −100 |
| Professional Consultants | 1,000 | 750 | −250 |
| Printing and Reproduction | 560 | 350 | −210 |
| Interest Expense | 805 | 805 | |
| Total Expenses | 21,472 | 18,955 | 2,517 |

FIGURE 12-3
Performance report—
variance analysis for the
expense report.

**ABC Interior Design, Ltd.**
**Projected Revenue by Client Type**
**19X6, 19X7 (Est.), 19X8 (Est.)**

| | 19X6 | 19X7 | 19X8 |
|---|---|---|---|
| Open Office Planning: | | | |
| Under 10,000 Sq. Ft. | $ 33,550 | $ 45,000 | $ 55,000 |
| 10,000–20,000 Sq. Ft. | 22,575 | 36,000 | 40,000 |
| Over 20,000 Sq. Ft. | 10,800 | 17,000 | 25,000 |
| Subtotal | $ 66,925 | $ 98,000 | $120,000 |
| Medical Facilities: | | | |
| Physician's Suites | 22,575 | 28,000 | 32,000 |
| HMOs | 15,700 | 25,000 | 35,000 |
| Hospitals | 35,600 | 40,000 | 25,000 |
| Subtotal | $ 73,875 | $ 93,000 | $ 92,000 |
| Banking Facilities: | | | |
| Branch Offices | 17,550 | 22,500 | 28,000 |
| Corporate Offices | 5,500 | 10,000 | 10,000 |
| Subtotal | $ 23,050 | $ 32,500 | $ 38,000 |
| Professional Offices: | | | |
| Attorneys | 8,750 | 12,000 | 15,000 |
| Accountants | 3,650 | 5,000 | 7,500 |
| Insurance Co. | 5,400 | 6,500 | 8,000 |
| Corporate | 15,900 | 35,000 | 30,000 |
| Real Estate | 4,750 | 7,500 | 10,000 |
| Others | 4,890 | 8,000 | 7,500 |
| Subtotal | $ 43,340 | $ 74,000 | $ 78,000 |
| Government Agencies: | | | |
| Federal | 5,500 | 7,500 | 9,000 |
| State | 8,500 | 9,000 | 12,000 |
| City | 2,500 | 5,000 | 7,500 |
| Subtotal | $ 16,500 | $ 21,500 | $ 28,500 |
| Grand Total | $223,690 | $319,000 | $356,500 |

FIGURE 12-4
Performance report—
projected revenue by
client type.

It is important for firms to look at certain blocks of information to determine if goals and objectives are being met. Reports related to revenue generation, expenses, and profits are the most important (see Figures 12-3 and 12-4). To have the most use, summary reports should be prepared on a monthly basis.

Some examples of specific reports that can be useful, depending on the size and complexity of the interior design firm, are as follows. Figures 12-5 and 12-6 are examples of some of these reports.

1. Revenues from sources—fees and sales of goods.
2. Work-in-process and aged receivables.
3. Deferred income.
4. Employee utilization and productivity.
5. Comparisons of fees earned to budgeted estimates.
6. Revenues by client type (or size of project).
7. Month-by-month profit-and-loss statements (with variances).

How often should reports be prepared? This would largely be determined by the firm's ability to produce the required reports. If, as is the case for many small- to medium-sized firms, the design director is preparing these reports, getting them

### JLP Design Consultants, Inc.
### Work in Process/Age Analysis
### As of June 1986

| Client | Total | Work in Process | Current | Accounts Receivables | | | |
| | | | | 30 Days | 60 Days | 90 Days | 120 Days and Over |
|---|---|---|---|---|---|---|---|
| Oceansview Real Estate | $ 1,067 | $ 567 | | $ 500 | | | |
| Lands Development Co. | 3,500 | 1,000 | $ 2,500 | | | | |
| A. J. Business Park | 7,500 | 3,000 | 2,500 | | $2,000 | | |
| City Schools | 9,500 | 5,750 | 3,750 | | | | |
| Phoenix Corporation | 15,500 | 6,000 | | 5,500 | 2,000 | | $2,000 |
| Bethany Bank | 8,500 | 5,000 | 3,000 | 500 | | | |
| Meadows Development Co. | 12,500 | 5,500 | 3,000 | | 2,500 | $1,500 | |
| Technical Center Inc. | 25,000 | 15,500 | 6,000 | 2,000 | | | 1,500 |
| S.D.C. Associates | 6,500 | 2,000 | 1,500 | 1,500 | | 1,500 | |
| TOTALS | $89,567 | $44,317 | $22,250 | $10,000 | $6,500 | $3,000 | $3,500 |

FIGURE 12-5
Performance report—work in process/age analysis.

### EMPLOYEE UTILIZATION REPORT
### WEEK ENDING AUGUST 29, 19X6

| WEEK END | # of EMP. | TOTAL HOURS | BILL-ABLE | % BILL | HOUSE | MTG/ ADM. | MISC. |
|---|---|---|---|---|---|---|---|
| 7/18 | 10 | 450 | 256 | 57% | 95 | 15 | 27 |
| 7/25 | 10 | 476 | 325 | 68% | 48 | 12 | 91 |
| 8/1 | 10 | 395 | 185 | 47% | 65 | 15 | 130* |
| 8/8 | 10 | 423 | 356 | 84% | 26 | 13 | 13 |
| 8/15 | 11 | 469 | 278 | 59% | 86 | 21 | 84 |
| 8/22 | 11 | 475 | 322 | 68% | 55 | 15 | 83 |
| 8/29 | 11 | 455 | 312 | 69% | 44 | 25 | 74 |

*Includes one person on paid week vacation.

FIGURE 12-6
Performance report— employee productivity.

done on a monthly basis is a laborious task. In very small firms where the owner must either prepare these reports personally or pay an accountant to do them, they may appear every three to six months—if done at all. Ideally, most kinds of reports would be prepared on a monthly basis where the previous month's data would be available within the first ten days of the month.

This kind of reporting is difficult to handle if it is done manually. Computer systems that can link accounting and other numeric data to generate tabled reports would be a relatively easy solution to the problem. If the software is also available for the computer to prepare charts and graphs from the numeric data, an additional analysis aid would be given to the manager.

## Summary

Financial managerial reports provide important information to the owner and manager of an interior design firm. These reports help the owner and manager make decisions related to many financial, personnel, and operational issues of the practice.

Interior design firms utilizing computers for accounting and data management can quickly produce these and many other useful financial managerial reports. However, the variety and complexity of these reports must aid the managerial function—not burden it with preparation and analysis of useless reports.

A key to the planning and ongoing success of the firm can be found in the annual plan. Managerial reports provide a great deal of the information necessary to prepare the annual plan. The combination of the financial managerial reports and the preparation of the annual business plan will not guarantee overwhelming success for the firm, but it will provide an important basis for proper decision-making in the present and the future.

In the next two chapters we will discuss how the firm may price the goods and services it wishes to provide. Chapter 15 will then cover what makes a legal contract and what should go into an interior design contract.

# Chapter 13

## PRICING CONSIDERATIONS

*E*stablishing the price for goods or product-related services sold by the design firm is critical to whether or not the firm makes a profit. The *price* is, of course, what something sells for. There are many factors involved in determining the price of a product or service. And, unfortunately for the individual new to the interior design profession, there are many different prices with which one has to deal.

In order to understand how prices are established, it would be best to explain the different kinds of "prices." This chapter will deal with the terminology and methodology of preparing prices on the tangible goods sold to the client as a result of the interior design service.

## Price Terms

In the interior design field, there are many terms related to price. Some are terms quoted to the client by the designer and different price terms quoted between a supplier and the designer. To add to the possible confusion, some of these price terms often mean the same thing.

There are three different terms that are used to represent the price the designer must pay to the supplier for the goods: net price, wholesale price, and cost price. *Net price* and *wholesale price* generally mean the same thing and represent a 50 percent reduction (or discount) from the suggested retail price (or list price). Wholesale price can also be defined as a special price to a designer from a supplier at a value lower than what the good would cost the consumer. *Cost price,* however, is not always the same as net or wholesale. Not all designers will have the privilege to purchase goods at the 50 percent discount from all suppliers. Because of the lack of quantity purchasing agreements, some designers receive a discount from the suggested retail that is less than 50 percent. Pricing from manufacturers to designers is governed by federal law. This will be discussed a little later in the chapter.

There are four different price terms designers use to quote prices to clients. These are suggested retail price, list price, selling price, and retail price. The first two generally mean the same thing. *Suggested retail price* is the price suggested by the manufacturer for use by all sellers. The price term *list price* is generally accepted to be the same as suggested retail price. *Selling price* is a term many designers use to refer to the actual price at which they sell goods to the client. Since some designers sell goods at a discount (a price lower than suggested retail) and others may occasionally sell goods at a higher price than suggested retail, selling price is not always the same thing as the first two terms.

It should be pointed out that designers may sell merchandise to the end-user at any price they wish. They are not obligated to sell goods at suggested retail price. In fact, federal laws prohibit manufacturers from requiring merchants to sell goods to the end-user at a set price.

*Retail price* is a term commonly used in retailing. Retailing involves businesses that sells goods to the consumer or end-user, such as department stores and specialty stores. In retailing, retail price generally is not a price suggested by the manufacturer but rather a price determined by the retailer.

In our discussions in this chapter, we will use the term *selling price* to mean the price quoted to the client and *cost price* to mean the price the designer must pay for the goods.

### CATALOG PRICING

When a designer requests a catalog from a supplier, the catalog will often come with a "price list." Many manufacturers send a price list for suggested retail or list prices. When this occurs, the designer must then negotiate with the manufacturer's representative for the discount percentage the design firm may expect. This may be as small as 10 percent or as much as 50 percent. The manufacturer may offer variable discounts to different design firms as long as these decisions are soundly based. Such things as the amount of goods purchased over some specific time and whether or not the designer will inventory goods are two such reasons. The cost price to the designer will result from determining the price after the discount percentage is subtracted from the suggested retail or list price.

Some manufacturers send net price lists with their catalogs. A net price list means the designer can purchase the goods at the price in the catalog. This net price list, of course, is the designer's cost price.

It is common for suppliers to send price lists of list price rather than net price since many suppliers offer varying discounts based on volume of purchases. However, enough firms utilize the net price list, so the designer must be very careful in understanding what price list he or she is reading. A selling price determined by quoting or discounting a net price list means that the designer has sold the goods to the client for the same price that the designer has purchased the goods from the supplier. When the firm receives a price list that is not clearly marked with "suggested retail," "list," "retail," "net," or "wholesale," it should contact the representative or the factory to determine what the price list represents.

## *Discounts*

A *discount* is a reduction, usually stated as a percentage, from the suggested retail price. A designer receives a discount from a supplier for ordering goods. Some designers give clients discounts when the client purchases goods.

The full discount price given by most manufacturers is 50 percent from the suggested retail. Remember that this is also called net price. Some manufacturers use the code word *keystone* to mean a 50 percent discount. This is done to protect designers should clients try to contact suppliers directly to determine the profit margins of the designer. However, not all designers receive the full discount of 50 percent. A manufacturer may determine that a 50 percent discount will only be given to those companies that are "stocking dealers" or that purchase a certain minimal quantity of goods in a given time period. A stocking dealer is a vendor that stocks a certain inventory level of goods at all times. A designer who does not have a retail store but has consistently purchased a similar quantity of goods may be given the same discount as a stocking dealer.

It is simple to determine the cost amount by use of the discount percentage from the suggested retail. For example, if a design firm receives a 50 percent discount for purchases made from Sherry Jones Wallcoverings, then wallpaper with a suggested retail of $35 per yard would cost the designer $17.50 per yard.

The following formulas might help:

$$\text{Discount in dollars} = \text{suggested retail} \times \text{discount percentage is}$$
$$= \$35 \times 0.50 = \$17.50$$

$$\begin{aligned}\text{Cost} &= \text{suggested retail price} - \text{discount}\\ &= \$35 - \$17.50\\ &= \$17.50\end{aligned}$$

These same formulas are used whenever calculating discounts to determine cost.

## QUANTITY DISCOUNT

A *quantity discount* is a discount greater than the normal 50 percent discount allowed because a large quantity of merchandise is purchased at one time. For example, if a designer purchases one chair, the discount would probably be 50 percent if that is the firm's normal discount. If the firm ordered 500 chairs, the manufacturer would most likely give a larger discount—perhaps 55 percent. Remember that quantity discounts given by manufacturers to designers are regulated by federal law to prevent price discrimination.

## MULTIPLE DISCOUNTS

*Multiple discounts* are a series of discounts from the suggested retail price. Multiple discounts are usually only given by manufacturers to designers for very large orders. Occasionally, the design firm may offer a multiple discount to the client— again, because of a very large order. The written notation for such a discount is given as 50/5 or 50/5/2. This does not mean that the designer takes 55 percent off the retail price in the first example or 57 percent off in the second. Rather, each discount is taken separately. For example, if the manufacturer offers a 50/5/2 discount on a large purchase of $500,000 of seating, the cost to the designer would be figured as

| | |
|---|---|
| Total retail price | $500,000 |
| Less 50 percent | −$250,000 |
| | $250,000 |
| Less 5 percent | −$12,500 |
| | $237,500 |
| Less 2 percent | −$4,750 |
| Cost | $232,750 |

## TRADE DISCOUNTS

*Trade discounts* are discounts given as a courtesy by some vendors to designers and others in the trade. These are usually a small percentage off retail, though they can be up to a 50 percent discount. Many retail stores that deal with specialized residential or commercial furnishings products offer trade discounts to the local design community. For example, if Foot Candle Lighting, a retail lighting fixture store, offered designers a 15 percent discount for fixtures purchased from their store for resale, they would be offering a trade discount. To calculate what the cost price to the designer would be, use the previous formula.

$$\text{Discount in dollars} = \$150 \times 0.15$$
$$= \$22.50$$

$$\text{Cost} = \text{suggested retail price} - \text{discount in dollars}$$
$$= \$150 - \$22.50$$
$$= \$127.50$$

## CASH DISCOUNT

Another discount term familiar to design firms that sell merchandise is a cash discount. More commonly used in accounting, *cash discounts* are given by manufacturers and suppliers to those customers who pay their bills promptly. A notation like "2/10, net 30" must appear on the invoice if a cash discount is allowed. The notation translates into an additional 2 percent deduction from the cost price if the invoice is paid within ten days of receipt of the invoice. If it is not paid within ten days, then the cost price is as stated and is due within thirty days. The cash discount is taken after all other discounts are taken. For example, the cost to the firm for an order of goods is $3000. The invoice offered a cash discount of 2/10, net 30. If the firm paid the invoice within ten days, it would only pay $2940.

$$\text{Cash discount} = \text{cost} \times \text{percentage}$$
$$= \$3000 \times 0.02$$
$$= \$60$$

$$\text{Amount due} = \$3000 - \$60$$
$$= \$2940$$

# Selling Prices

Most design firms operating retail showrooms sell merchandise to clients at the suggested retail price. However, since the designer can sell the merchandise at whatever price he or she determines, some firms mark up or add a dollar amount to their cost at a rate so that the resulting price is higher than suggested retail. This is a practice one might find in either residential or commercial retail sales. In commercial design, it is more acceptable to use a selling price other than retail since the client commonly purchases at a price lower than retail for all the company's other needs.

The two methods of determining a selling price, other than using retail, are discounting from retail and markup from cost. Both of these methods are used in commercial design. Residential designers who operate their own studios, but who do not inventory furniture, also may use one of these methods rather than the retail method.

## DISCOUNT FROM RETAIL

The designer can offer to the client any discount he or she wishes. The selling price based on a discount from retail is calculated in the same way the discount is calculated to find cost. For example, the designer has prepared a specification of products with a total retail price of $4500. The designer has decided to offer the goods to the client at a 25 percent discount. The selling price would be $3375. That figure is determined in this way:

$$\text{Discount in dollars} = \text{retail price} \times \text{discount percentage}$$
$$= \$4500 \times 0.25$$
$$= \$1125$$

$$\text{Selling price} = \text{retail price} - \text{discount in dollars}$$
$$= \$4500 - \$1125$$
$$= \$3375$$

## MARKUP FROM COST

Although many in the design community use the discount from retail as the way for finding the selling price, some use an approach that utilizes a markup from cost to arrive at the selling price. A markup is a percentage amount added to the cost of goods to get the selling price. Suggested retail is usually a 100 percent markup from net price. Selling price, however, can be any markup percentage or dollar amount added to the cost price by the designer.

When the cost of the goods is known, it is necessary to multiply the cost by the percentage of markup. For example, an end table costs the designer $100. With a 100 percent markup the selling price would be $200.

$$\text{Markup in dollars} = \text{cost price} \times \text{markup percentage}$$
$$= \$100 \times 1.0$$
$$= \$100$$

$$\text{Selling price} = \text{cost} + \text{markup in dollars}$$
$$= \$100 + \$100$$
$$= \$200$$

If the same table was to be sold at only a 50 percent markup, the selling price would be $150.

$$\text{Markup in dollars} = 100 \times .50$$
$$= \$50$$

$$\text{Selling price} = \$100 + \$50$$
$$= \$150$$

There are two ways to find the markup percentage. One is to find the markup percentage based on the retail price of the product. The other is to find the markup percentage based on the cost price of the product. For example, the retail price of a table lamp is $200, the cost price is $100 and the markup in dollars is $100. To find the markup percentage based on retail price, use the following formula:

$$\text{Markup percentage based on retail} = \text{markup in dollars} \div \text{retail price}$$
$$= \$100 \div \$200$$
$$= 50\%$$

The formula for the markup percentage based on cost price is as follows:

$$\begin{aligned}
\text{Markup percentage based on cost} &= \text{markup in dollars} \div \text{cost price} \\
&= \$100 \div \$100 \\
&= 100\%
\end{aligned}$$

In practice, most retailers use the markup percentage based on retail method of determining the markup percentage, whereas most interior designers use the markup percentage based on cost for determining markup percentage.

### GROSS MARGIN

As you will recall from Chapter 11 on financial accounting, the gross margin is the difference between revenue and cost. In relation to pricing, gross margin is the difference between selling price and cost. Many design firms use the gross margin or gross margin percentage to determine commission on sales. In the preceding example, the gross margin is $875 if we assume a net price for the designer's cost. The gross margin percentage would be 26 percent assuming a cost of $2500.

To calculate the gross margin dollars for the example:

$$\begin{aligned}
\text{Gross margin dollars} &= \text{selling price} - \text{cost price} \\
&= \$3375 - \$2500 \\
&= \$875
\end{aligned}$$

To calculate the gross margin percentage:

$$\begin{aligned}
\text{Gross margin percentage} &= \text{gross margin in dollars} \div \text{selling price} \\
&= \$875 \div \$3375 \\
&= 26 \text{ percent}
\end{aligned}$$

### MARKDOWN FROM RETAIL

A term used in retail when discounts are taken for promotional sales of one kind or another is *markdown*. A markdown is calculated in the same way as a regular discount. Interior designers do not usually refer to the discount from suggested retail to get their cost or the discount they give to their clients as a markdown. They may, however, refer to a discount as a markdown if they "mark down" inventory during a clearance sale.

### PRICING REVIEW

The cost price to the interior designer could be retail, retail less a trade discount, or retail less a full discount, which equals the net price or wholesale price. It can also be retail less a less-than-full discount given by the supplier, a cash discount after the cost amount is determined, or an amount after quantity discounts are taken from the retail price. The selling price to the client could be retail, suggested retail, list price, retail less a discount, or cost plus a markup.

## *Federal Laws and Pricing Practices* _____

The Federal Trade Commission was established by the federal government to prevent unfair or deceptive competition or practices between businesses. One of the most important pieces of legislation that the commission enforces is the Robinson-Patman Act. This legislation makes it illegal for a merchant to charge other merchants different prices for the same goods. "If goods of similar grade and quality were sold at different prices, and these differences could not be justified by differences in production and distribution costs, the practice would violate the Robinson-Patman Act."[1] For example, if a manufacturer were selling the same quantity of product to two different design firms, it would have to offer the goods at the same price to both. However, if one firm had a record of purchasing a larger quantity of goods or stocking a quantity of goods, then the manufacturer could sell the goods at different prices to each designer. However, price discrimination only affects sales between merchants. A merchant has the legal right to sell to the consumer at any price he or she determines. If Wendy Jones Interiors decides to sell a Knoll chair to Mrs. Smith for $1000 and the same chair to Mr. Peters for $750, the designer would not be in violation of any laws as long as Mrs. Smith and Mr. Peters are the end-users.

Another important enforcement duty of the Federal Trade Commission is related to those practices by businesses that limit competition. The Sherman Act prohibits practices where businesses make agreements in restraint of trade or engage in price-fixing. An example of restraint of trade would be when two or more businesses have agreed not to sell in each other's territory or to each other's customers. This agreement is limiting the consumer's options. Price-fixing occurs when two or more businesses agree to sell the same good to the consumer at the same price. This relates directly back to the concept of suggested retail. At one time, certain consumer goods were sold at the same price no matter where someone went to purchase them. These prices were dictated by the manufacturers. Some people even referred to these goods as "fair trade goods." However, enforcement of the Sherman Act negated these "fair trade" pricing policies. Today, all goods sold to the consumer are sold at whatever price any merchant that carries the goods determines to sell them. This means that a suggested retail price by the manufacturer is just that—suggested. The designer can sell the goods at any price he or she determines—higher or lower than the suggested retail. If the manufacturer insists that the designer sell the goods to the consumer at a particular price, then the manufacturer is in violation of the Sherman Act.

There are several other pieces of legislation affecting businesses in order to prevent unlawful business practices related to such things as monopolies, mergers, and labor relations. The ones already discussed, however, have the most relevance to the interior design practice.

## *Freight Matters and Costs*

Freight, also called shipping, is the cost and process involved in the delivery of goods from the manufacturer to the interior designer. Most frequently, freight is handled by trucking companies that are working as a transportation source for the manufacturer. Many of the manufacturers have their own trucks to handle the freighting of products from the factory to the interior designer's warehouse, but many use independent companies—especially for small orders. Goods are sometimes shipped by train, but this is generally done only for very large loads or when the manufacturer sends one of their trucks "piggy-back."[2]

The notation FOB is often found within the price list. *FOB*, according to the

---

[1]Jentz 1987, 778. Copyright West Publishing Company.

[2]*Piggy-back* means that the truck's trailer is loaded on a train flatcar and shipped by train to the general destination. Then the trailer is removed from the train and driven to the warehouse or client's final destination.

Uniform Commercial Code (UCC), means "free on board," and there is usually a second notation such as "factory" or "destination" following it. Some people are more familiar with definition of FOB to mean "freight on board." Both interpretations mean the same thing. We will use "free on board," since that is the definition used by the UCC.

Free on board means that the manufacturer is responsible for the costs of loading the goods onto the truck or train. The costs of transporting the goods to the delivery destination are covered in the second part of the notation. This second notation is the indication as to which party is responsible for the freight charges and when ownership of the goods changes hands. If a manufacturer's catalog says *FOB Factory,* this means the buyer assumes ownership or *title* of the goods when they are loaded on the truck at the factory. In this case, the interior designer pays all transportation costs and assumes all risks during transit. If the catalog has the notation *FOB Destination,* then the manufacturer retains ownership of the goods until they reach the delivery destination. The costs of transportation would also be paid by the manufacturer in this case.

Some manufacturers, as a means of reducing their own liability and as a convenience to their customers, may want to pass ownership of the goods to the buyer as it leaves the factory loading dock, but will pay the freight charges. In this case, the notation in the catalog will read something like "FOB Factory—Freight Prepaid." What this means is that the interior designer has ownership and responsibility for damages during transit, but the manufacturer will pay the transportation charges to the destination.

It is very important for the design firm to understand what the shipping policies are for the various manufacturers and suppliers. Shipping charges can be quite costly for the interior designer if the firm is located a great distance from the manufacturer's factory.

These charges are also legitimate charges that the client should have to pay if the goods are not sent prepaid by the supplier. Most interior designers charge clients "actual freight," which means that the designer will bill the client whatever the interior design firm was billed for the transportation of the goods to the designer's warehouse. Some firms add a small service charge to the actual freight charges to cover handling the payment and the necessity of dealing with the freight companies over damages in transit.

Occasionally, firms will determine a "freight factor." This factor is obtained by finding the average and usual freight charges for all kinds of goods and quantities of goods received FOB Destination. This factor is added to the selling or cost price (as determined by the policies of the firm) of any goods ordered for the client that are shipped to the designer's warehouse. There are a few other terms related to the freight process, but these will be discussed in Chapter 23 and 24.

## *Delivery and Installation Charges*

Most firms also charge clients for the cost of delivering the merchandise to the client's home or office. Many retail stores will not charge for delivery if the client's location is within a limited geographic area of the store's warehouse. Delivery charges can be either a flat rate determined by how far away the client is from the warehouse or an hourly charge door-to-door. *Door-to-door* means that the client is charged from the time the delivery truck leaves the warehouse loading dock to the time it leaves the client's site location.

Some items also require installation. Although wallpaper and carpet need to be installed, we are also including some furniture items. A wall-hung bookcase unit in a home or open office systems furniture in an office need to be installed by a trained installer, just as carpet and wallpaper must be installed by trained personnel. These installation charges are again something that should be absorbed by the client and not the design firm.

## *Sales Tax*

It is very important for the interior designer and the design firm to fully understand the laws relating to the charging of sales tax on the goods and services they provide. Sales taxes not collected from the client will be collected by the state or city from the interior design firm.

In order to sell merchandise to clients, the design firm must obtain resale tax certificates from the appropriate agencies.[3] The resale tax certificate exempts the designer from paying the sales tax at the time he or she orders the merchandise for the client. It is then the designer's responsibility to collect the sales tax from the client.

There is much differentiation in the tax laws from state to state regarding when sales tax must be collected. It is therefore very important for the firm to understand all the laws of the state in which they are doing business. What might be taxable for a design firm working out of an office in Manhattan and selling to a client in New York City might not be taxable in New Jersey. Generally, the following guidelines would be applicable anywhere, but in no way are they to be construed as absolutely true for all practice areas.

In general, design fees, such as hourly fees which do not relate to specific purchases of goods, are exempt from sales taxes. If, however, the design fee is added as part of the selling price of some goods, then the total price would be taxable. For example, if the designer added a 25 percent charge for design services to the selling price of $5000 worth of office furniture, the taxable amount would be $6250—the $5000 of tangible goods and the $1250 of design fee. If the design fee were a separate line item, then sales tax would be charged only on the tangible goods.

As a rule, all items considered tangible personal property would be taxable. Tangible personal property is any property that is movable, can be touched, or has physical existence. Some examples of personal property are sofas, desks, chairs, and draperies. Some processes such as labor, installation, delivery, and freight have various kinds of interpretations as to when sales tax must be collected and when they are exempt. A case in point is draperies. In many states the labor to make the drapery and hang the finished product in the home is taxable since it is considered a vital part of completing the item. But the charges a drapery store might ask just to rehang a drapery after it was cleaned would not be taxable since the labor of hanging the drapery is now considered a service.

Items such as wall-to-wall carpet, wall coverings, and installed mirrors, although they are in essence personal property (they are moved from the factory to the job site), are legally considered fixtures or sometimes capital improvements. A fixture is legally defined as "a thing which was once personal property, but has become attached to real property in such a way that it takes on the characteristics of real property and becomes a part of that real property."[4] Sales tax must be charged if the installation of this product becomes part of the building or becomes perma-

---

[3]The means for obtaining this license were discussed in Chapter 6.

[4]Clarkson 1983, 1203. Copyright West Publishing Company.

nently affixed to the structure in such a way as to make it difficult or impossible to remove without damage to the structure. Depending on the answer to this analysis and the state laws that prevail, tax may or may not have to be charged. In many instances, sales tax would be charged on the material and supplies needed to manufacturer the finished goods, but not the labor. In some states, as in the drapery example, if the labor to manufacture and install the capital good is necessary to make "finished goods," then sales tax would also be charged on the labor.

Certain circumstances (e.g., if the freight and delivery charge can be considered part of making the finished good) will require sales tax to be charged on these activities. However, in most cases, these charges are either considered a service and generally not taxable or are considered part of doing business and are calculated into the price of the goods. When freight and delivery charges are calculated into the price of the goods, sales tax might technically be calculated, but it is not paid to the state or city revenue office. It is important, as with all sales tax collection policies, for the design firm to obtain information from the firm's accountant or the state and city revenue departments as to the requirements for charging sales tax in this situation.

When a designer provides goods or services to clients in a state other than the one in which they are recognized as doing business, they must be sure they understand which state will require the collection of sales tax.

## *Summary*

It is very important for interior designers to understand the many ways they can price the goods and services they sell to their clients. The pricing terminology discussed in this chapter covers the more commonly used terms for the sale and cost price of the goods the designer might sell. It also covered the terminology related to the shipping, delivery, and installation charges of getting those goods to the client.

Along with the information presented in Chapter 14 on determining design fees, we are now ready to look at what goes into a design contract. The design contract will be the main source of information finalizing the pricing for the interior designer's services and the way in which he or she will price any goods sold to the client.

# Chapter 14

## DETERMINING DESIGN FEES

$F$or many interior design firms, the only source of income for the firm results from the fees charged to the client for services. These fees must cover the cost of the designer's time or salary expense and overhead expenses such as electricity, cost of drafting paper, and telephone calls, and provide a margin of profit.

There are a number of different methods that can be used to charge for design services. Although all can be applied to either residential or commercial practice, some are more commonly used in residential and others are more appropriate in commercial practice. Exactly which method or methods should be used for a particular firm and type of practice must be carefully determined by the owner in consultation with the firm's accountant. There is no one way to satisfy all situations and all types of practice.

Although some of these methods require the sale of goods, this chapter focuses on compensation methods for providing required services. Pricing methods for the sale of goods were covered in the preceding chapter.

## Billing Rates

In all cases, the method of charging a fee to the client is related to the *billing rate* of the firm. For some methods, especially the hourly, flat fee and square footage method, the billing rate is primary to the determination of the fee. In other methods, such as cost plus or percentage off retail, it has an indirect bearing on the fee itself.

The simplest method for determining the billing rate is to multiply the *direct personnel expenses (DPE)* by a factor—commonly 3.0. The DPE is a number that includes not only the salary rate of the employee, but also any costs of benefits—such as unemployment taxes, workers' compensation, medical and/or life insurance, FICA, sick leave, pension plans, and paid holidays. Figure 14-1 shows typical direct personnel expenses. The word *direct* in the DPE represents those personnel expenses related to billable time; that is, any time a designer works on a project, that time is billed in some manner to the client. Remember that it is rare for the design firm to bill 100 percent of all the designer's time on the job.

Many firms make the mistake of determining the billing rate only on the salary rate per hour of the employees. When this is done, the firm is reducing the amount of money left to provide for overhead expense coverage and profit. Many firms are

| |
|---|
| 1. Paid holidays |
| 2. Paid vacations |
| 3. Paid sick leave |
| 4. Health insurance |
| 5. Group life insurance |
| 6. Pension or profit-sharing programs |
| 7. Dental insurance |
| 8. Employee discounts |
| 9. Educational expense allowances |
| 10. Professional dues reimbursements |
| 11. Unemployment taxes |
| 12. Social security insurance |
| 13. Workers' compensation insurance |

**FIGURE 14-1**
Typical direct personnel expense items.

also under the impression that the three times factor allows for a profit margin of 33 percent. This is expected since many people believe the three times factor represents first, the salary rate of, say, $10 per hour, then an additional $10 per hour to cover overhead expenses, and the third $10 per hour to represent profit—thus a 33% profit. Many new interior design firm owners have been very surprised to find a net profit of only 2 to 4 percent—if they had any net profit at all.

Billing rates can also be used to help determine if the flat fee and the percentage rate methods are sufficient. The fee divided by the billing rate multiple will give the amount of salary dollars that can be used by that project at the profit margin the firm normally maintains. This method helps determine if the amount of salary dollars available is sufficient to cover the expenses and desired profit for the project. If it is determined that the project cannot be done for that amount, then the firm can either reject the project or try a different fee method or combination of methods to assure proper compensation.

## *Methods of Charging*

There are some differences between residential and commercial interior design that can affect the choice of fee method. In commercial practice, the projects are almost always more complicated than a residential project and, therefore, are handled over a longer time period. Because of the greater complexity and duration, there is more of a chance for something to go wrong. Because of the larger size and complexity of projects, fees for a commercial project are always larger than for residential projects. All these factors also point out the necessity for greater time management, timekeeping, and scheduling.

There are also certain factors that affect the residential project and which must be considered in determining a fee method. In residential projects, it is common for the client to take longer to make up his or her mind concerning the decisions that client is asked to make. Because of this, the designer often finds himself or herself required to do more "shopping" for the products that go into the project. Since many more custom-manufactured items are specified in residences, the delivery and completion time of the project can often take longer than many commercial projects. The designer must sometimes be ready to go back to the client long after they have "mentally" finished with the project. Residential clients are less inclined to pay for design services when the designer is also selling the client the products. They are used to the "free" design services offered by the retail establishments and often argue about being charged twice.

No matter what the configuration of the practice, the client's reluctance to pay a fee for service as well as pay the designer for furniture is a common problem. When the firm is a design/specify practice, the client only pays the firm for interior design services. When the firm is a retail showroom or studio, it is less common for the firm to charge a fee in addition to the cost of the merchandise. However, when the firm both charges for the interior design service and then attempts to sell the merchandise to the client, the firm often runs into difficult negotiations with the client concerning being charged twice. As competition continues to increase in the major markets, more and more firms that in the past confined themselves to selling services are now also becoming suppliers to their clients. This may dramatically change the way firms charge for services in the future.

### HOURLY FEES

The *hourly fee* is commonly charged based on the firm's DPE, as discussed in the first section of this chapter. It is a very satisfactory way of ensuring that the firm is compensated for all the work it does for the client. The hourly fee is a customary method of charging by firms that do not intend to sell merchandise to the client. And it can be used by those in residential or commercial practice.

Many clients, however, are reluctant to agree to the hourly fee since the "meter is always running." The longer the designer works on the project, the greater the charges. The client is often afraid to allow the designer this much freedom in setting the time schedule. They are often afraid that the designer will take extra time in order to increase the fee. Many firms get around this objection by setting a "not to exceed" limit on the contract. What this means is that the designer must estimate the actual amount of time he or she will spend on the project and quote a fee that will cover all the expected work. The client cannot be charged more than that maximum. The designer must be careful in estimating time. He or she should also be sure that a clause is included in the contract to allow additional charges if the cause for delays or extra work is due to the client.

The hourly fee is often used

1. For initial or specific consultations on small-scale projects.
2. To cover travel time to the client's job site, to markets, or for other travel time.
3. When the project involves a great deal of consultation time with architects, contractors, and subcontractors.
4. When it is necessary to prepare working drawings and specification documents.
5. When the designer perceives that the client will have difficulty in making up his or her mind.
6. Whenever it is difficult to estimate the total amount of time needed to complete a job as a result of the design circumstances. An example might be a law office in which each partner wishes to have his or her office designed in a very individual manner.

It is difficult to charge "creative" time on an hourly basis since creative time comes in spurts and unusual moments. The solution to a tricky floor plan or a product specification may occur to the designer in the car on the way to another client. It is not easy to charge a client for this bit of creative time.

Firms use the hourly rate in different ways. One is to use the rate based primarily on a professional level so that, depending on who is doing the work, a different hourly rate is charged. This means that the principal will charge a very high rate for his or her time as compared to the design assistant. A principal could charge $50 to $200 per hour. A senior or project designer might charge $45 to $175 per hour. Midlevel designers might charge $40 to $150 per hour, and design assistants and draftspeople might charge $25 to about $75 per hour.

Other firms find averaging all the rates of the levels of designer and charging one rate no matter who is doing the work to be a satisfactory solution. The danger here is that if the principal or senior designer is largely involved in the project, his or her time will not be generating adequate income. When entry-level designers are involved in the project, they often take longer than experienced designers. The averaging method can result in undercharging or overcharging the client.

A third method of charging the hourly fee is by charging by the kind of service rather than the personnel. In this case, the firm determines three or more levels of service and sets a fee amount to charge for each level of service. Three levels might be design (or creative) service (the highest level of service); documentation and drafting (those activities involved in the preparation of final drafting of floor plans and other drawings, preparation of texture boards or documents, and bid documents); and supervision and/or miscellaneous (which would involve such things as travel time within the city, meetings with architects and contractors, meetings with the client, site visits, and so on). This method has the same problems as the averaging method.

The hourly fee method provides a way of charging the client for all (or almost all) the time put into the solution to the client's project. However, clients often object to the open-endedness of the fee. This method can be used successfully by many designers without the "not to exceed" clause if the client trusts the designer's ability to manage the project.

### FLAT FEE

The *flat fee method* is similar to the hourly method with a not-to-exceed figure. With the flat fee method, however, the estimated fee is usually charged to the client whether the amount of time estimated is correct or not. This means, if the firm has estimated badly and the time involved exceeds the estimated fee, then the firm cannot be compensated for the extra time. If the firm has estimated too high, and the project does not require the full amount of the estimated time, the firm is not obligated to refund any of the fee to the client. The flat fee would include charges for all services and expenses other than those that the firm charges as reimbursable expenses.

In order to use this method, it is important for the designer to know the salary and overhead costs of the company completely and to have a thorough understanding of the services which must be performed. He or she must also have a feeling for the decision-making ability of the client to predict if the client will be difficult or easy to work with and be able to determine if the client understands the time element so that all phases of the project can be satisfactorily accomplished. It is also important for the designer to have job-time histories for similar projects to aid in estimating. And, of course, he or she should have a very good idea of the client's budget.

The designer must be very comfortable in his or her ability to estimate time for various kinds of projects when using the flat-fee method. The firm that has built up a history of working on various kinds of projects and that has a written record of the time element of those projects is in the best position to use the flat-fee method. It is rare that clients will allow the designer to charge more for work than was estimated as part of the original fee. It is, however, a fee method that can be used by both the residential and commercial practice. Because of the greater amount of custom work, the more personalized service involved, greater amount of shopping for products, and generally heavier use of time, it is more difficult to use this fee method in the residential field.

The flat fee method is a satisfactory method of charging fees

1. When goods are not being purchased from the designer. This allows the designer to utilize goods that he or she might not normally use since the designer is not selling the goods. For the client, this may mean that the goods specified are at a lower cost than those the designer is trying to sell.

2. When the amount of goods to be purchased is so small as to result in an insignificant amount in comparison to the time involved. The design firm will put the time into the project knowing that it will be fully compensated rather than depending on the profit on the small amount of goods.

3. Whenever a large amount of like items are to be purchased. This is often the case for projects such as restaurants and office complexes that standardize on products and require little additional time after the final product selections are made.

4. When it is easy to determine the time and requirements of the project.

## RETAIL METHOD

The retail method is the most common method of obtaining fees when the firm actually sells merchandise to the client. In the retail method, the design firm charges the client the retail price suggested by the manufacturer or supplier. If the manufacturer does not provide a suggested retail price, then the design firm marks up the merchandise from the net or cost price. Since both the suggested retail price and the common markup percentage used are 100 percent, the retail method provides a high gross profit margin for the firm.

It is more commonly used by residential firms than those primarily involved in commercial design. And it is commonly used by firms that perceive the amount of time needed on any given project or client to be small in relation to the budget for the merchandise. If it is estimated that a great deal of planning, custom design, drafting, specification writing, or supervision work is required, the retail method would not be a suitable fee method. Should these kinds of activities be the major part of the project, then another fee method should be used, or the retail method in conjunction with another method might be used.

## PERCENTAGE OFF RETAIL

In order to gain a competitive edge, some firms offer merchandise at a percentage off retail (or at a discount). It is a method, common for commercial firms, that has gained slow acceptance from the residential design community. In this method, the design firm reduces the selling price of the merchandise by some percentage off the suggested retail price. Care must be taken in determining what that discount will be since the resulting difference between selling price and the net price is the gross margin needed to cover profit and overhead costs. Firms often use a large discount percentage off retail to induce the client to purchase the goods. However, the larger the discount, the smaller the gross profit margin and the less the potential to pay off expenses and maintain profits.

## COST PLUS PERCENTAGE MARKUP

The cost plus percentage markup method allows the design firm to add a specific percentage to the net cost of the merchandise being purchased by the client. The percentage determined must be sufficient to cover the design firm's costs and profit margin desired if it is the only compensation method used. It is often used in commercial design and is also commonly used in the residential market. It can be the least remunerative method if a very small markup is added to the net price. It can be used as the exclusive fee method if the amount of goods to be purchased from the firm is sufficient to compensate for the time the designer must put into the project.

Many designers/specifiers who do not actually sell the merchandise to the client use this fee method. It works well for these firms and others as long as

1. The budget is not cut at the last moment.
2. The client does not use a lot of existing furniture in the new project.
3. The client does not decide to hold off purchasing any of the merchandise to a later time, thereby reducing the amount of fees the firm may collect.

Another segment of the design community that uses the cost plus percentage method are those firms that are just getting started. Many new design firms offer this method of compensation as a way of competing with the larger, more established firms that can operate at the full retail basis method. If a firm decides to commonly use this method of obtaining fees, it must be sure it is covering the costs of its design practice. Without careful calculation of costs, the designer may not be fully compensated for his or her design talents. Any firm considering the use of this method should use it in conjunction with some other fee to be sure the firm receives a reasonable gross margin to cover costs and obtain a profit.

### PERCENTAGE OF MERCHANDISE AND PRODUCT SERVICES

Akin to the architect's percentage of construction cost method, the design firm can determine and negotiate some percentage of the cost of the goods and installation that will be involved in the project. This might include the furniture, wall coverings, floor covering, ceiling and window treatments, lighting fixtures, accessories, built-in cabinets, and even general construction costs. The percentage of merchandise and product services is used by the commercial design field rather exclusively.

Very similar in concept to the cost plus percentage method, this method is utilized by firms that will not sell any of the merchandise to the client. This method has all the pitfalls of the cost plus method plus an additional one. Since the fee is based on a percentage of the selling price to the client by vendors that the design firm cannot control, the firm could lose a considerable amount of money if the project is bid and won by a firm trying to "buy" a project at a very low price. This method should be used cautiously and only in combination with another method that will ensure fair compensation for design time and services.

### SQUARE FOOTAGE METHOD

In this method, the fee is determined by some rate per square foot times the amount of square footage of the project to be designed. Commonly used in commercial design and rarely used in residential practice, the square footage method can be a profitable way of determining the design fee. Whenever firms have sufficient experience in specific kinds of jobs so that they can be comfortable with a fee rate, the square footage method is an excellent compensation method.

With the square footage method, the firm must determine what will be the percentage for the various phases of the project. As mentioned in the discussion of the hourly fee method, the project could be broken down into at least three phases: design, documentation/drafting, and supervision. Each firm must determine if these phases sufficiently describe a project for themselves. If the firm normally charges a different rate for each of these phases, then the firm must determine what that fee rate would be correlated to on a square footage fee.

For a firm that has never used a square footage fee, it might come up with an average by gathering data on several projects that are very similar to those being considered for square footage factoring. The actual design fee charged divided by the square footage of the project will provide the firm with a historical view of the square footage cost of doing design work.

According to the 1987 "100 Giants" survey conducted by *Interior Design* magazine[1] the average fee in dollars per rentable square footage was a little more than $3. This varied from a low of $2.50 to a high of $5.50 depending on the actual kind of project. Each firm must look at its fee per square foot in relation to the national average and determine if its fee is in line with the national average and what is appropriate in the firm's geographic location. Charging a higher fee than what the local "traffic will bear" will bring frustration and a loss of work.

## COMBINATION METHOD

In many cases, using only one of the described fee methods will not provide sufficient compensation to cover all the expenses and desired profit margin for the firm. It is often necessary for almost all commercial firms and many residential firms that are not primarily retail showrooms to use more than one method of obtaining design fees.

Since projects involve a variety of activities, it is defensible for the firm to charge the client a variety of fees. For example, let us consider a project that involves a lot of time in meetings with the client, contractors, and the architect as a result of the designer's responsibility in specifying interior finish materials, but not a large dollar volume of actual materials to be purchased. The designer may find that an hourly charge for meetings, travel, and on-site supervision in combination with either a cost plus percentage or percentage discount from retail for the merchandise sold would adequately compensate the designer in this situation.

In another case, the project may require a large amount of time in drafting along with the preparation of specifications for rooms that are basically multiples, but the goods would be purchased from a vendor. This might occur for a hotel project or major office complex. Here the designer may charge an hourly fee for the drafting and a flat fee or a percentage of the selling price for the design and preparation of specifications for the areas that are basically the same. Properly considered for the project requirements, a combination of design fee methods can provide excellent compensation to the designer at a fair price to the client.

# *Indirect Job Cost Factors*

In this chapter, we have looked at several common methods of determining fees for the generation of income for the interior design firm. No matter how carefully considered, it is possible for the firm to lose a certain amount of profit because of the unexpected. Although some of these indirect job cost factors can be calculated into the design fee, they more commonly happen once the project has begun as a result of the project process rather than as a planned-for occurrence.

One of the most common indirect job cost factors for firms that are doing strict cost accounting would be overtime. No matter how carefully a project has been estimated, if the design firm must pay overtime salary to any of its staff, the gross

---

[1]Loebelson, *Interior Design*, January 1987, 168.

margin of the project and potential profitability will decline. A career in interior design is rarely a 9:00 to 5:00 job. However, careful supervision of projects by the design director or project designers will help to hold down the amount of overtime needed for projects. Some firms control overtime costs by not paying designers on an hourly basis but rather on a salary basis, as discussed in Chapter 8. This does help on the direct salary expense, but not from the overhead expenses that are still incurred when the office is working past normal business hours.

A second indirect job cost factor that occurs rather often is the indecisive client. This is the person who just can't seem to make up his or her mind about any number of things—colors, furniture styles, patterns, the furniture or space arrangement, and so on. Experienced interior designers learn to recognize the indecisive client during the initial interviews. But often even the most experienced designer gets a client who just can't seem to make up his or her mind. If the fee method is the hourly method, this would have little impact on the final outcome since the designer continues to charge for all the changes and extra meetings. But when a fee method has been established that limits the amount of fee that can be charged, the designer must diplomatically find ways to get the client to make up his or her mind and move on with the project.

An added cost that occurs whenever a designer has ventured into a project that he or she has never done before is the need for technical or professional consultation that was not expected. Often times designers may be asked to do projects requiring construction documents. Most cities have strict regulations as to whom may prepare construction documents. Designers may suddenly discover that they must obtain an architect's or other professional consultant's stamp on drawings even though the drawings were prepared by the interior designer. This unexpected fee will reduce the expected profit margin.

Unusual job site and delivery costs can also add to the cost of a project. In open office systems work, it is common that thermostats, light switches, air-conditioning vents, and the like always seem to end up right where the interior designer planned to hang a wall strip to attach a divider panel. In residential design, it is common for the client to have made some kind of change at the site without telling the interior designer. Sometimes a designer may specify a very large piece of furniture, which may be very difficult to deliver. The most common occurrence is the very large conference table that cannot be delivered up the elevator but must be placed on the top of the elevator cab or hoisted up on cranes from the exterior of the building.

Unless careful project management occurs, furniture may be ready for delivery to the job site, but the job site may not be ready to receive the merchandise. In situations where the design firm does not have a warehouse ready to hold merchandise, an extra cost will be involved in storing and later delivering to the job site. In many cases, this extra cost will be borne by the design firm even though the delay was not caused by the design firm, since the management of the project is all considered to be part of the normal and expected services of the firm.

## *Summary*

All interior design firms are in business to make a reasonable profit while providing quality services to clients. The owners and managers of interior design firms must understand their particular firms and each one's operations and the kinds of clients that each wishes to obtain as well as the general market that the firm is in so that the firm will stay in operation.

The income the firm generates, whether from fees for services only, from the sale of goods, or a combination of both, must be sufficient to cover the costs of the firm and provide a net profit to sustain the firm. In this chapter, we have looked at the different ways the firm can generate this income by several fee methods. No fee method is perfect for all circumstances for all firms. Each firm must determine for its own type of business which situations warrant a particular fee method.

Once the fee method for the particular project situation is determined, the next step is to prepare a design contract or proposal. In our next chapter, we will look at the preparation of such a contract.

# Chapter 15

# PREPARING DESIGN CONTRACTS

*I*nterior designers enter into contracts of one sort or another every day. The most common occurrence of a contractual relationship occurs when a designer offers to provide some service or product to a client and the client agrees to purchase that service or product. In these contractual relationships, it is the interior designer's responsibility to fulfill the agreement. In many cases, designers and clients enter into contracts and they do not know they have done so, or they should have entered into a contract, but did not.

Designers and clients also breach or break those contracts. Sometimes this is done knowingly and willingly (hoping the other party does not sue), sometimes by accident, and sometimes by mutual consent (which is not really a breach at all). Interior designers are also sometimes faced with the threat of "I'm going to sue for breach of contract," or "I'm going to sue because we had a contract." Yet the designer may not even know he or she has breached in the first place or had a contract in the second.

In this chapter we will review the basic ingredients of a contract and contract law as it deals with a contract for services or a combination of services and goods. Then we will look at the kinds of concerns and examples of contracts that can be used by the interior designer. The counsel of an attorney is strongly recommended for a complete explanation of the legal considerations of contracts.

Although a contract for a service and a contract for the sale of goods are similar in many ways, there are several considerations that create important differences. These differences will be discussed in Chapter 22 on the Uniform Commercial Code.

## *Definition and Basic Elements of a Contract*———

Basically, a *contract* is a promise or agreement between two or more parties to perform or not perform some act. The performance or lack of performance of this act can be enforced by the courts. Not all promises or agreements are legal contracts, however.

A legally enforceable contract must have certain elements or it may not be enforceable. The basic requirements of a contract are

1. *Agreement.* This must include an offer by one of the parties and acceptance of the offer by the other party.
2. *Consideration.* This must be legally sufficient enough for a court to take it seriously.
3. *Contractual capacity.* This must exist by both parties involved in the contract.
4. *Legality.* The contract must exist only to support the performance of some legal act.
5. *Reality of assent.* It must be shown that both parties' consent to enter into the contract was genuine.
6. *Form.* The contract must be in a legally appropriate form which most commonly means "in writing."

## AGREEMENT

To be a valid contract, the first element that must exist is that there must be agreement to the contract by the parties involved. For this to happen, one of the parties must make an offer and the other party must agree exactly to the terms of that offer. If either of these elements is missing, there is no contract.

The contract must also include the following categories of information: (1) identification of the parties, (2) identification of the subject matter with which the contract is concerned, (3) what consideration is to be paid, and (4) duration of the contract.[1]

### Offer

For an offer to be binding, there must be serious intention by the offeror (the party who makes the offer to the other party, who is called the offeree). Merely expressing an opinion is not a form of valid intention. For example, if John Doe says to his client that "the project can probably be completed in five days," his client could not sue if it actually takes him ten days, since the five days was an opinion, not a promise. Also, if Doe's client says to him, "I plan to hire your firm exclusively to design all my restaurants," Doe could not sue his client, since the client was only expressing intention, not making a promise.

Interior designers are often invited to bid on design projects or sales of goods. An *invitation to bid* or negotiate is not an offer but merely shows a willingness on the part of the client to enter into discussions with the designer about a potential contract.

An offer must also be given in terms definite enough for a court to determine if the contract was fulfilled or not. For an interior designer to put in the contract the statement "select all finishes" could leave the firm responsible for selecting interior and exterior finishes, when the firm only considered selecting interior finishes.

The third element of a legal offer is that the offer be communicated to the offeree so that the offeree knows of the existence of the offer. Unless the client knows that out-of-town travel expenses are over and above the design fees, the client would not be expected to pay these charges.

The last element in a legal offer is the ability to terminate the offer or the acceptance of the offer. If the designer's proposal states that the price for the services is good for ten days and the client responds on the fifteenth day, the designer is not obligated to still provide the services at the stated price. It should be noted that the time period of the offer begins when the offeree receives the offer, not when it is prepared or mailed by the offeror. Should there not be a time limit stated in the

---

[1]Clarkson 1983, 109.

offer, the time limit terminates at the end of a reasonable period of time considering the circumstances of the offer.

An offer can also be terminated by the occurrence of the offeror (most commonly the designer) withdrawing the offer before the offeree (the client) accepts the offer. It is, of course, important that the offer be withdrawn prior to the offer being accepted. For example, if an interior designer discovers that he or she has miscalculated his or her bid to the city of Chicago but has already turned in the bid, he or she must revoke his or her offer prior to the closing date and time of acceptance of bids. If all bids are due by Friday at 5:00 P.M., and the designer discovers the error on Friday at 5:30 P.M., it is too late to revoke the bid.

Another way to terminate the offer is for the offeree to reject the offer. Should this happen, there is no obligation of either side to fulfill the contract. Should the client later wish to accept the offer, the designer can refuse, accept, or modify the original offer. This is because the client's refusal of the offer terminated the original offer. But if the client says something like, "Is this the best price you can give me on the sofa?" that does not represent a rejection of the offer.

The last method of terminating an offer is for the client to make a counter offer. If Ms. Jones says, "Your design fee is out of the question. I am prepared to only pay $5000 for these services," the offer of $5000 is now a counter offer to the designer which the designer is now in the position of accepting or rejecting.

### Acceptance

The second part of an agreement has to be acceptance by the offeree that shows agreement to the terms of the offer. "In order to exercise the power of acceptance effectively, the offeree must accept unequivocally. If the acceptance is subject to new conditions, or if the terms of the acceptance change the original offer, the acceptance may be considered a counter offer that implicitly rejects the original offer."[2] Should a designer have a contract with a client to design the client's home for a fee of $5000, but the terms of the contract do not ask for a retainer, the designer cannot ask the client to pay a retainer, since that was not part of the original offer.

Generally, acceptance cannot be construed if there is "silence" or no response from the client, unless it can be shown that the client, by his or her silence, has received a benefit from the goods or services the designer has provided. For example, if a designer decides to proceed with the space planning of an office for a client even though the client has not yet accepted the terms of the contract, the client would not be obligated to pay the design fee for the services provided unless the client took ownership (benefit) of the space plans somehow.

Finally, acceptance must be made within the time limit set in the terms of the offer. If no definite terms are stated, acceptance must be made within a reasonable time, considering the conditions of the offer and the subject of the offer.

## CONSIDERATION

*Consideration* is the "price" the offeree "pays" to the offeror for the offeror's fulfilling the promise. Generally, in an interior design contract, the consideration will be the design fees that the client pays to the designer for providing the services agreed to by the client. The consideration must be adequate enough to be fair.

A promise to give consideration for something that has already occurred or that the designer is already obligated to do is not binding. If the client says, "Because you did such a great job on finishing the office installation on time, I will give you

---

[2]Clarkson 1983, 129. Copyright West Publishing Company.

a $500 bonus," the client is not legally obligated to pay the bonus since it is consideration for something that has happened in the past. Considerations are negotiated for actions that take place in the future or in the present, not in the past. Similarly, if the design contract says the designer will provide a water-color rendering of the living room, and later the designer tells the client that he or she must pay the designer an additional $500 for that rendering, the client is not obligated to pay since the firm is already legally obligated to supply that rendering for the consideration outlined in the contract.

## CONTRACTUAL CAPACITY

Both parties to a contract must have legal capacity to make a contract. Contractual capacity relates to the full legal competence of the parties. It is very important for the designer to be sure that the person agreeing to and signing a contract has the legal capacity to enter into the contract. In residential design, the interior designer would normally be dealing with a legally competent adult, either head-of-household or spouse. In commercial interior design, the designer often deals with people other than the actual owner of the business or the chairperson of the board of the corporation. Rarely does a minor (under the age of eighteen) have contractual capacity.

In a commercial project, the interior designer must be sure that the person signing the contract has the authority to bind the corporation or business to that contract. Not all employees, even with fancy job titles, have that authority.

## LEGALITY

Contracts must describe legal acts in order for the courts to have the authority to enforce them. An illegal contract would be any contract that, if performed, would constitute an act against legal statute, break tort law, or in any other way be opposed to the public good. The main way the concept of legality would affect a contract into which an interior designer might enter would be relating to contracts in restraint of trade.

Contracts in restraint of trade are made to be detrimental to the public good and generally have an effect on the potential for fair competition in a given market. If two or more interior design firms in a market area, where they basically were the only sources for furniture, got together and agreed to sell merchandise at the same markup, they would be guilty of collusion, and their agreement would be in restraint of trade—illegal. If one subsequently lowered prices and the other sued saying they had an agreement, the suit would be thrown out—and both firms would likely be charged with a crime.

Some contracts in restraint of trade are actually legal, however. Certain clauses in employment contracts that restrain the activities of former employees can be legal if the restrictions relating to noncompetition are reasonable.

## REALITY OF ASSENT

Sometimes a contract that is made by two parties who have the full legal ability to make a valid contract may not be enforced because the reality of assent of one or another of the parties is questioned.

This might occur because of (1) a mistake (this must relate to a mistake by one or another of the parties in the facts of the terms of the contract, not an error of judgment or quality), (2) fraudulent misrepresentation (the terms of the agreement were presented with information intentionally incorrect in an attempt to deceive the other party), (3) undue influence (when one party exerts so much influence on the other that the party being taken advantage of virtually does not exercise his or her own free will), and (4) duress (this would negate a contract if the offeree was forced under certain kinds of threats to agree to the contract).

## FORM

In many cases, an oral contract would be binding on both parties. But a series of statutes called the *Statute of Frauds* requires that some contracts be in writing in order for them to be enforceable. The three most important considerations as they relate to the interior designer would be (1) contracts for the sale of goods that amount to more than $500, (2) contracts that cannot be completed within one year of their origination, and (3) contracts for the sale of real estate.

### For the Sale of Goods

Interior designers often take orders for furniture and furnishings without any written agreement from the client. "I wouldn't think of asking Mrs. Smith for a contract to order a sofa." Yet many of these same designers later find themselves owning all kinds of furniture and furnishings their clients later refuse to accept.

The Statute of Frauds and the Uniform Commercial Code require a written contract to be in existence for the sale of any goods of an amount over $500. This "contract" need not be any kind of formal contract, but merely a written document that states quantity, description, and terms of the agreement; and it must be signed by the party or parties involved. This aspect of a contract for the sale of goods will be discussed in detail in Chapter 22.

### Contracts Whose Performance Will Take More Than One Year

Interior designers often are involved in contracts that will take more than one year to complete. If the terms of the contract are such that the project or requirements of the contract cannot be completed in one year, the Statute of Frauds will require the contract to be in writing for the contract to be binding. If the terms of the contract indicate that the project will be completed within one year, it would not be necessary for the contract to be in writing. The time limit begins one day after the contract is agreed to by both parties.

### The Sale of Real Estate

A contract for the sale of real estate, which is any land and buildings, plants, trees, or anything else affixed to the land, must always be in writing. Any oral contract for this kind of transaction would not be binding on either party.

## *The Form of the Contract*

Whether or not it is legally required that a contract for interior design services or even the sale of goods be in writing, it is safer for the design firm to establish a policy that all sales of services and goods be accompanied by a written contract. Not all agreements have to have the same form. Just as there is no such thing as an ideal way to charge, there is no ideal contract. To protect the design firm from the potential loss of income, an appropriate variety of contracts should be developed with the assistance of the firm's attorney. These different agreements should focus on the various kinds of business in which the design firm engages.

"The Statute of Frauds and the UCC require either a written contract or a written memorandum signed by the party against [whom] enforcement is sought. In other words, any confirmation, invoice, sales slip check or telegram can constitute a writing sufficient to satisfy the Statute of Frauds."[3] The only signature required is that of the party being charged.

Clearly, it is not necessary for the interior designer to have a long formal contract for every sale or service agreement. Sometimes these long agreements actually are detrimental to the negotiation. The client may be reluctant to sign a formal-looking contract for goods or services. In general, however, the contract must be detailed enough for the designer and the client to understand what is at issue, what services or goods are to be provided by the interior designer, what is the charge, what is the time limit of the agreement, what are the terms of payment, and any other kinds of matters that seem appropriate to the particular agreement. What must be covered in a contract for the sale of goods will be covered in Chapter 22. For now, let us look at a contract for services.

## *Interior Design Contracts: Content and Form*

What the final form of a design contract will be is determined from the information obtained in the meetings with the client, the designer's knowledge and experience with similar projects, and the thorough knowledge of the abilities of the design staff of the firm. All three play an important part in what clauses go into the contract and even if a contract is prepared for the client.

Earlier we discussed the minimal form requirements for a contract to be enforceable. Whether the contract is for a residential project or a commercial project, there are certain specific items that should be in the contract to protect both designer and client.

1. Client's name and address
2. Detailed description of project areas
3. Detailed scope of services to be provided
4. Detailed purchasing arrangements
5. Method and payment of compensation
6. Reimbursements for out-of-pocket expenses
7. Charges for extra services
8. Designer responsibility disclaimer
9. Charges and responsibilities of third parties
10. Photographic and publishing rights
11. Termination of contract
12. Responsibilities of the client
13. Ownership of documents
14. Time frame of contract
15. Matters of arbitration
16. Conditions and amount of retainer
17. Signatures

**FIGURE 15-1**
Checklist of typical clauses in design contracts.

Contracts in residential design projects are often short—only two or three pages—written more as a letter than filled with legalese. Although these rarely have the length and detail in comparison to a contract for a commercial project, both have the same basic parts. Figure 15-1 shows a checklist of what should be in the contract. The first five items will be in almost all contracts regardless of size and type of project. The next six items generally should be covered in a residential contract and certainly in a commercial project contract. Items 12–14 are more specific to commercial projects. The last two items should be in any contract for fees. Each item is thoroughly discussed as it relates to residential and commercial proj-

[3]Clarkson 1983, 215. Copyright West Publishing Company.

ects, noting any differences. These items are discussed in the typical order they would appear in the contract. Refer to Figures 15-2 and 15-3 for sample contracts.

1. *Client's name and address.* It is very important for the names of the clients obligated to the contract to be clearly stated at the beginning of the contract. In residential design, it is important for the husband's and wife's names to be on the contract and that both sign the contract. This obligates each in the event of divorce, separation, or death of either of the spouses.

   In commercial design the name of the person having the authority to contract for the business should be listed, and the contract should be signed by that person. The address of the home office is usually listed here when the business has several locations.

2. *Detailed description of project areas involved.* To avoid confusion and arguments over extra charges or threats of breach, it is important for the project areas involved to be detailed at the beginning of the contract. In a residential project, this may mean as broad as "your residence at 1234 Hummingbird Lane," which means the designer is responsible for the scope of services to be defined in the contract for the entire house. If the services relate to only the living room, the contract should say that.

---

Mr. and Mrs. John Reed
1551 West Willow Street
Seattle, Washington

Dear Mr. and Mrs. Reed:

Thank you for meeting with me concerning the redesign of your home. This letter shall serve as a proposal of the professional services we will provide for remodeling the kitchen and family room at your residence on 1551 West Willow Street.

We will provide the following services:
1. Plan the space, furniture, and equipment based on our meeting of June 12.
2. Prepare detailed ¼-inch scale furniture floor plans of the two rooms as they exist.
3. Prepare detailed ¼-inch scale preliminary space and furniture floor plans for the remodeling.
4. Develop preliminary selections of materials and furniture.
5. Review the preliminary plans and selections with you.
6. After approval by you of floor plans and selections, prepare detailed ¼-inch scale floor plans, working drawings, and written specifications necessary for construction of the spaces.
7. Review the revised plans and selections with you.
8. Provide counsel and guidance in the selection of necessary contractors to perform the required work.
9. Periodic inspections at your home during the construction to be sure all work is done according to professional standards and the specifications.

The fee for the services described will be _____. Any work requested but not described in this proposal or was required after your approval has been given, will be over and above the stated fee and will be charged at _____ per hour.

**FIGURE 15-2**
**Sample design contract for a residential project.**

Billing for services shall be in the following manner:

10% upon signing the contract (retainer)
20% at the end of the preliminary review meeting
50% at the completion of the preparation of drawings and specifications
10% when construction and furniture orders are placed
10% upon completion of the project

All payments are due ten days after receipt of invoice.

Three sets of drawings and specifications will be provided as part of the base charge. Should you require additional sets of the drawings and specifications, they will be provided at our cost plus 10 percent.

The above base fee does not include client-approved expenses for long-distance telephone calls, out-of-town travel to shop for resources, and special renderings. These charges, if required, will be billed separately at our actual cost plus 10 percent.

As we discussed at our June 12 meeting, we will not be providing any of the furniture or materials required.

We will perform the services described in good faith, but cannot be responsible for the performance, quality, or timely completion of work by others. Further, we shall not be responsible for any changes to the project the client or contractor(s) make without informing the designer.

You are expected to grant reasonable access to the premises for the designer and the designer's agents as well as contractors required to perform the agreed-on work. By signing this proposal, you understand that the peace and privacy of your home may be disrupted for the time required to perform the work.

This proposal may be terminated for any reason by either the client or the designer provided ten days written notice is given. In the event of termination by the client, the client will pay the designer for all work done and expenses due up to the date of termination.

It will be our pleasure to begin your project as soon as we have received a copy of this proposal signed by both of you and a check for the retainer. We appreciate your selection of our firm for your interiors project and look forward to working with you.

Sincerely yours,

(Interiors Firm Name)

_____
(Design Director)

_____
(Date)

_____
John Reed

_____
(Date)

_____
Betty Reed

_____
(Date)

**FIGURE 15-2**
**Sample design contract for a residential project.**
*(Continued)*

Mid-west Insurance Corp.
5555 North Avenue
Plains, Nebraska

Dear Mr. Graves:

We are pleased to submit the following proposal of professional interior design services for the space planning and interior design of your branch office in Lincoln, Nebraska at _____ .

SCOPE OF SERVICES

A.  Design Development
1.  Meet with you and/or selected members of your staff to determine all requirements that will affect the space planning and interior design of your project.
2.  Obtain floor plans from the architect.
3.  Inventory existing equipment that might be used in the new space plan.
4.  Determine preliminary programming and project objectives as well as budget considerations.
5.  Review all informational findings with the client.
6.  Prepare preliminary schematic layouts.
7.  Develop preliminary furniture, color, and materials selections.
8.  Review schematic layouts, selections, and sketches with the client.

B.  Design Finalization
1.  Finalize space plans showing locations of walls, furniture, and built-in equipment.
2.  Finalize selections of all materials, finishes, and treatment for furniture, walls, flooring, windows, and ceilings.
3.  Finalize lighting specifications.
4.  Prepare a budget of all interior furnishings.
5.  Prepare presentation boards with representational photos and finish samples.
6.  Present plans, specifications, and presentation boards for your approval.
7.  After final approval of all space plans, furniture layouts, and product selections, prepare appropriate working drawings and documents for the construction of the space and installation of the interiors. This will include dimensioned floor plans, furniture plans, electrical location plans, reflected ceiling plans, and cabinet shop drawings as needed.
8.  Prepare architectural specifications, as required.

C.  Bidding and Construction Phases
1.  Prepare bid specifications for furniture and other moveable equipment.
2.  Provide information for the preparation of bid specifications for floors, walls, windows, ceilings, and lighting fixture materials or products (bid specification to be written by others).
3.  Assist you in obtaining competitive bids for furnishings and equipment.
4.  Assist you in coordinating the schedule for delivery and installation of the work.
5.  Make periodic visits to the job site to ensure that the work is progressing according to the specifications in the bid documents.
6.  Supervise installation of furniture and moveable equipment covered in the bid documents.

**FIGURE 15-3**
Sample design contract for a commercial office project.

D. Project Completion
  1. Upon completion of the installation, the designer shall prepare a punch list of items needing attention by the designer or vendors. This will be reviewed with you prior to transmittal to appropriate parties.

TERMS OF COMPENSATION

For the interior design and consultation services outlined above, you will be billed an hourly fee basis of _____ per hour for Senior Designers, _____ per hour for Designers, _____ per hour for Design Assistants, _____ per hour for Draftspersons, and _____ per hour for secretarial workers.

We estimate the total fee for the project as outlined will not exceed _____ . You will be invoiced monthly for actual hours worked. Payment is due within ten (10) days of receipt of invoice. A late payment charge of 1¼% per month (15% per annum) will be added to invoices thirty days past due.

The total fee is based on a maximum of two revisions after each client review. Work required or requested beyond the two revisions will be charged at the described hourly fees, but will be in addition to the maximum estimate.

Additional services not outlined in this proposal but requested by you or required after your approval that result in changes in the project will be billed separately at an hourly rate of _____ .

Fees include provision of three sets of documents for your use and six (6) sets of contract documents. Additional sets of contract documents shall be provided at a cost of _____ per set.

REIMBURSABLE EXPENSES

Reimbursable expenses are in addition to the charges detailed above. Such expenses as out-of-town travel and living expenses, long-distance telephone charges, special renderings, mock-ups, and reproduction costs other than those detailed shall be billed at actual cost to the designer.

Out-of-town travel in the interest of the project shall only be made with proper notification and approval of the client. At this time, it is estimated that a minimum of three site visits will be necessary during the progress of the project.

GENERAL CONDITIONS

  1. The designer shall not be responsible for the quality, workmanship, or appearance of products should you purchase products other than those specified.
  2. The designer is not responsible if you, the architect, or contractor(s) make changes to the project without notification to the designer.
  3. The designer or representatives of the designer reserve the right to photograph the project upon completion.
  4. This proposal may be terminated by either party upon seven (7) days written notice. In the event of termination by you, you shall pay the designer for all services performed and reimbursable expenses due up to the date of termination.
  5. Drawings, specifications, and sample boards, as instruments of service, are the property of the designer. The designer reserves the exclusive copyright to these items and provides them to you for your use on this

**FIGURE 15-3**
**Sample design contract for a commercial office project.** *(Continued)*

project only. Any reproduction or reuse of the drawings, specifications, and sample boards without the prior written consent of the designer is not permitted.

6. The timely completion of this project and the fees quoted are based on the signed return of this proposal to the designer within ten (10) calendar days.

7. Any controversy or claims arising out of or relating to this project or breach thereof shall be subject to review and settled by arbitration. Arbitration shall be in accordance with the rules of the American Arbitration Association. The decisions of the arbitrator shall be final and binding on both parties.

Approval of this proposal is signified by your signature in the space below. Work will begin on your project when the designer receives a signed copy of this proposal along with a check for a retainer of _____ .

We would like to thank you for the opportunity to submit this proposal for professional interior design services. We look forward to a set of challenges which we pledge to meet with our best professional efforts and attention.

Sincerely,

Authorized:

West Interior Design, Inc.

_____
(Company)

_____
(Design Director)

_____
(By)

_____
(Date)

_____
(Title)

_____
(Date)

**FIGURE 15-3**
Sample design contract for a commercial office project. *(Continued)*

A contract for a commercial project needs to be even more specific. If the address of the project is different from the home office, it should be listed. It may be necessary to list the specific area by department or room and even amount of square footage. "The main dining room, foyer and meeting rooms, but excluding the kitchen of your restaurant at the Harbor Hotel, San Diego," is a clear definition of what rooms in what building will be done on this contract. To say, "your restaurant at the Harbor Hotel," leaves the designer open to a lot of unplanned additional design. Should the client want additional areas to be included or added, a secondary contract may be prepared to cover these areas and the services they require.

3. *Detailed scope of services to be provided.* Services required for a project vary greatly from project to project. So that there is little room for disagreements about doing or not doing something, it is important for the scope of services to be considered thoroughly and spelled out in specific detail. It is best for these services to be outlined in the general order in which they take place and, whenever possible (based on the type of project and in consideration of the fee method), in the phases in which they will take place. Figure 15-4 shows a large range of services that might be required of either a residential

or commercial project. Figure 15-5 shows some additional services more common to commercial projects. Only those services the designer understands are to be performed should be listed in the contract.

One service that should be discussed before going on is on-site supervision requirements. This one service causes considerable misunderstandings between designer and client. To the designer, on-site supervision generally means occasional trips to the job site to be sure that all furniture and furnishings are being installed properly and that all construction is going along as designed. Certain phases of the project will require the designer to be on the job site for substantial periods of time. Other phases will require a short visit once a day or every few days. The client, however, often feels that on-site supervision means that the designer will be on the site all day, every day, seeing to every detail of the construction and installation. For most projects this is, of course, impossible and impractical. How much supervision and what kind—even who in the office or who representing the office—should be clearly spelled out in the scope of services.

Designers must also be careful of using words such as "supervise" or "manage" in relation to the installation of interior finish materials. Today,

---

1. Interview client
2. Inventory existing furniture
3. Measure job site
4. Obtain architectural plans of job site
5. Consult with architects, contractors, engineers, or others
6. Prepare preliminary space plans
7. Prepare preliminary furniture layouts
8. Prepare preliminary color selections
9. Prepare preliminary furniture and finishes selections
10. Prepare preliminary cost estimates
11. Design custom cabinets or other custom items
12. Prepare preliminary specifications
13. Select accessories and graphics
14. Receive client's preliminary approval
15. Review final furniture layouts
16. Prepare working drawings—partitions
17. Prepare working drawings—mechanical drawings
18. Prepare working drawings—custom designs
19. Prepare texture/sample boards
20. Prepare renderings
21. Receive client approval of final documents
22. Purchase goods
23. Observe trades for construction and installation
24. Supervise furniture installation
25. Complete final walk-through and punch-out

**FIGURE 15-4**
Checklist of basic design services.

---

1. Prepare feasibility studies
2. Interview employees via questionnaires
3. Interview employees (one-on-one)
4. Sign design and specification
5. Prepare bid documents

**FIGURE 15-5**
Additional design services typical in commercial projects.

some states are requiring that this work be done only by licensed contractors.

4. *Detailed purchasing arrangements.* This clause should inform the client of the conditions under which the design firm will be selling any products to the client. If the design service is provided by designers on staff of a retail store, the purchasing arrangements will be outlined by store policy.[4] The minimal information that should be covered in this clause is how the client will be charged for furniture and furnishings, the terms of payment, penalties for cancellation of orders, the design firm's responsibilities toward warranties of goods sold, charges for installation, freight, sales tax, delivery costs, and whether or not there is a late payment penalty on the sale of goods.

   The clause should also have specific language regarding what happens if the client purchases the goods specified from someone other than the designer. In some cases, the only way the designer is receiving compensation for services is by the sale of goods. If goods are purchased from someone else, the designer would not receive compensation unless this was covered in the contract.

   It is also common for all these considerations to be spelled out on the contract for the sale of goods and only a reference to these conditions made in the contract for services. Since many commercial designers and some residential designers specify products only and do not sell the goods to the client, this clause may not even be in the contract.

5. *Method and payment of compensation.* This section details how the designer will be paid for his or her services. It should begin by describing how the design fees will be charged. Remember, there are many different ways of charging. For example, "For the above services, an hourly fee of $50 per hour for project designers, $40 per hour for designers, and $30 per hour for assistants will be charged based on actual hours worked per month." This tells the client exactly how they will be charged. This section should also detail how the client will be billed and whether or not there are any penalties for late payment. Moreover, the section might continue, "You will be billed monthly, based on actual hours worked. Payment is due ten days after receipt of invoice. Late penalties of 1½ percent per month on the unpaid balance will be charged for any invoices thirty days or more overdue."

6. *Reimbursements for out-of-pocket expenses. Reimbursable expenses* are those costs that are not part of the design contract but that are made in the interest of completing the project. The most costly reimbursable expenses that might be incurred are for out-of-town travel and living expenses or per diem in connection with the project. *Per diem* is a term that means a dollar amount that is allowed to cover hotel, meals, and transportation costs. These expenses are something that the client should pay for, but they should not be part of the design fee. Other typical reimbursable expenses are long-distance telephone calls, postage, blueprinting, data processing, and overtime. Some firms include the cost of renderings, models, and mock-ups as reimbursable expenses.

   Most firms charge reimbursable expenses at actual cost. Some, however, add a service charge to the expense. If a service charge is added, this should be clearly stated in the contract.

   Many firms only put a clause concerning reimbursable expenses in the contract when they anticipate out-of-town travel, the need for renderings

---

[4]A signed authorization should be part of this policy so that nothing is ordered or given to the client without his or her signature. Confirmation proposals are discussed in detail in Chapter 23.

or models, or inordinate amounts of the other kinds of expenses listed. Expenses such as blueprinting, telephone calls, and data processing are often considered costs of doing business and are not charged to the client.

7. *Charges for extra services.* A clause concerning charges for extra services is provided to deal with the situation where the client may request more areas to be done or more kinds of services to be performed than were outlined in the scope of services. It protects the designer so that he or she will not be required to perform design services for free. It also informs the client as to how additional work can be added to the contract or done at the same time and how the client will be charged.

   This section would also spell out what the situation will be when changes are made by the client to the project after certain phases of work have been completed. If the designer has already received approval for certain phases of the project, and changes are then made by the client, the designer should be compensated for the additional work. For instance, after the space planning was approved by the client and the designer began final drawings, the client decided to add three more offices that had not been originally planned. The designer should be compensated by some reasonable means for the time it will take him or her to redo the space plan and the final drawings. This kind of clause would allow that to happen.

8. *Designer responsibility disclaimer.* This section would specifically describe any portions of the project for which the designer would not claim responsibility. If the designer were not required to plan the lighting for an interior, he or she should state that the firm claimed no responsibility for the lighting in the finished interior. There are also some kinds of activities that can only be done by licensed professionals. If the law requires that exterior landscaping be planned by a licensed landscape architect, the interior designer should disclaim any responsibility for the design of the exterior landscaping.

   Another factor that might be in this section would be the designer's disclaimer if the client purchases products other than those specified. This would protect the designer from potential negligence or product liability suits if the products the client does purchase are not the same as those specified.

   A third situation that might be covered under this section involves the designer's not being responsible for changes made by the owner, architect, or contractor without the designer's consent. Should the client or the contractor change the length of an alcove that is to receive a custom-made piece of furniture, the designer should not be responsible for the furniture not fitting if he or she was not informed of the change.

9. *Charges and responsibilities of third parties.* After meeting with the client, the designer should have an idea of whether or not the project will require the consultation of any third parties such as architects, contractors, or landlords. Although it is possible to calculate these charges into the design contract when they involve short meetings, it is usually safer to make this a separate charge. When a project requires extensive architectural services, the third-party service may be better dealt with as a separate contract between the client and the third party. However, the designer should still charge for the time he or she must spend with the third-party professional. As with item 8, this section might appear in a contract for either a residential or commercial project.

10. *Photographic and publishing rights.* It is unlikely that the designer will wish to photograph or use every project in one of the firm's publications. It should be standard practice, however, to include a clause obtaining permission for

all projects. Clients should know up front the designer's intention to use the projects for photography and publication. Some clients may object to having this kind of intrusion. In some commercial installations, it may be against company policy because of security. Often, when clients object to photographing their living or working quarters, the designer may be able to get permission by not publishing the name of the client. Remember that releases must also be obtained from any recognizable people in the photographs, even if the owner of the space has given permission to photograph the interior.

11. *Termination of contract.* As a means of protection for the designer, a termination clause should be included. This clause is to ensure compensation for services rendered in the event that the project ends for some reason other than by the designer's wishes. If the client runs out of money, cannot take the space, and must end the project, it is important for the designer to be paid for design work that has been prepared. Without this kind of clause, it would be more difficult for the designer to collect. Something like, "In the event the project is terminated through no fault of the designer, the designer will be compensated for all work actually performed." Something more clearly defined, depending on the kind of fee arrangements or exact nature of the project, may be necessary.

12. *Responsibilities of the client.* In many commercial projects there are certain provisions that are important for the client to perform in order for the project to proceed successfully or to be completed with few headaches. These should be outlined in this section. Responsibilities of the client might include providing a place to receive, unpack, and store products prior to installation on the job site; provide reasonable access to the job site; designate an employee to be liaison between the designer and the owner; and provide approvals expeditiously. Some of these conditions, such as having access to the job site, may also be important for residential projects.

13. *Ownership of documents.* Many interior designers and other design professionals wish to protect their design ideas from being copied or imitated without fair compensation. It is necessary to put a provision in the contract that warns the client that he or she may not reuse the design ideas without compensating the designer. The designer must copyright his or her design documents as an added protection. Copyright is the legal means of protecting the drawings or plans and specifications that interior designers produce. Something to the effect of, "Documents and specifications are provided for the fair use by the client in completing the project as listed within this contract. Documents and specifications remain the property of the designer and cannot be used or reused without permission of the designer," will clarify the issue. If the designer needs or wishes to use this clause, it would serve him or her to become somewhat familiar with the copyright law so that he or she can answer the questions of the client. Refer back to Chapter 6 for more information on copyright.

14. *Time frame of the contract.* As we saw in the beginning discussion of contracts, the time frame or time limits of a contract is an important part of the offer. Many interior design projects, whether residential or commercial, must work around some time-ending date, usually the move-in date.

    A second important date is the time limit that the designer can wait before he or she receives the signed contract in order to complete the project by the move-in date. An example of clause is, "In order to complete the project as specified in the scope of services, the signed contract must be received by the designer no later than June 20, 19——." This should help the client in making up his or her mind quickly as to whether or not he or she will engage the designer.

Another time-frame clause that will appear in many commercial contracts relates to renegotiation of the contract when the contract is expected to last over a long period of time. This is not for the project that extends over more than one year, since this should be taken into consideration when the contract is drawn up. Rather, it concerns those relationships between designer and client where the designer is on a retainer for an extended period of time. In this relationship, design work may be scattered over time and it may be necessary for the design firm to renegotiate a fair increase in its fee every so often.

15. *Matters of arbitration.* In any project where the possibility of disagreement might occur, a clause concerning arbitration should be included. This clause would spell out what would happen in the event that there was disagreement between the parties that could not be resolved. Rather than going to court, an arbitrator (a disinterested third party) would be called in to listen to the arguments of both sides and then render an opinion of what must be done. Both client and designer must agree beforehand to abide by the decision of the arbitrator.

16. *Conditions and amount of retainer.* A *retainer* is an amount of money paid by the client to the designer for work that will be done. The retainer is applied by the designer to the total fee of the project as work progresses. In some ways, the retainer acts as "earnest money" from the client showing his or her good faith in proceeding with the project. The retainer provides to the designer operating funds to purchase the needed production goods and services to begin the design project. A *deposit* is a similar concept, but it is usually applied towards the purchase of furniture and furnishings.

If a retainer is expected, the amount and when it is due must be spelled out. It is a good idea also to briefly explain how it will be applied to the total fee. Typically, the retainer clause is at the end of the contract.

17. *Signatures.* Room should be provided for both parties to sign. To enforce the contract, only the client must sign. The client, on the other hand, will want the designer to sign as a token of the designer's good faith.

Each contract, whether for residential or commercial projects, must be developed to suit the individual project. A form or standard contract can be developed to cover almost all contingencies, and then parts can be "cut and pasted" to make the final contract. A word processor makes this very easy.

Standardized contracts can be obtained from both ASID and IBD. These organizations have prepared contracts that meet the conditions of many normal projects. Space is provided to type in standard information, such as the designer's name and address, and some can be imprinted with the design firm's name. Whatever the final form of the contract, it should be periodically reviewed by the firm's attorney to be sure that the contract meets the conditions of the firm's individual practice.

Now let us look at what constitutes legal performance and termination of a contract.

## *Performance*

A contract terminates when both parties perform the acts or activities promised in the terms of the agreement. Sometimes there is disagreement as to whether or not the terms have been performed. This is especially true when the contract insufficiently specifies the required services. In contract law there are three types of performance: (1) complete, (2) substantial, and (3) performance far below reasonable, resulting in material breach.

For complete performance to be considered, the terms expressed in the agreement must be fully accomplished in the manner in which they are specified in the contract. If a design contract has as one of its terms the provision that "the designer provide a water-color rendering of the lobby and dining room," the contract would not be complete if either of these renderings were not provided to the client or if they were not done in water color. This would be true even if all other terms in the contract were completed. In this case, the client would have grounds to sue for breach of contract if he or she so chooses.

Since it is sometimes impossible to satisfy a party's idea of complete performance, the courts hold that performance is complete if it is done so as to be "substantially complete." Substantial completion means that the performance cannot vary greatly from what was spelled out in the contract. If, in the preceding example, the designer provides a rendering of the spaces in the contract but uses markers as the media, the court might rule that the term was substantially performed and that the client must pay the designer for the services performed. Note that the substitution of a different media than was called for does technically constitute a breach of contract.

Performance that is inferior to that which is called for by the terms of the agreement would cause a material breach of contract and would excuse the nonbreaching party from fulfilling his or her obligations in relation to the contract. In our example, should the designer provide only pencil or ink sketches of the areas rather than the water-color renderings, something has been provided but it is inferior to what was agreed to; a material breach would have occurred. The nonbreaching party would not have to pay agreed-to fees and would be entitled to damages.

The phrase *breach of contract* has been used several times in this section. A breach of contract occurs when one of the parties of the contract does not perform his or her duties as spelled out in the terms of the agreement. If the breach is minor (as when the designer does the renderings in marker rather than water color), the client would not be excused from his or her obligation to the designer, but the client would not have to pay until the designer provided the renderings in water color or until some other agreement was worked out. This takes place when only minor discrepancies from the terms of the contract occur allowing the remainder of the contract to be completed. If the breach is material (as when the designer only provides pencil sketches rather than water-color renderings), the client is excused from the contractual agreements and may also be entitled to damages. Major breaches may terminate the agreement.

A breach of a contract can occur easily, especially if the designer has not been careful in the preparation of the terms of the agreement. And, in fact, it is generally easier for the interior designer to breach the contract than it is for the client. It is extremely important for the designer to understand the scope of the project and what the terms of the agreement are so that the designer does not leave himself or herself open to a breach.

## *Termination by Agreement*

Contracts can be terminated by agreement. We saw in the preceding section, where we discussed the termination-of-contract clause, how the designer seeks to protect himself or herself if something occurs which is not the fault of the designer. It is not necessary for there to be such a clause in the contract for the contract to be terminated by agreement.

It is possible at any time for the contract to be terminated if both sides agree to the termination. If a clause does not exist in the original contract, it would be necessary for a second contract dealing with the terms of the termination to be written as a protection to both parties. An oral agreement to terminate the contract is not advisable.

## *Summary*

The major portion of what the interior designer does for clients can be covered by contracts of one sort or another. Too often, designers have let themselves be "stuck" with a loss of fees as a result of their failure to understand what constitutes a contract, to prepare one properly, or to have one at all. The professional designer must realize that in order to protect himself or herself, he or she must insist on the preparation of contracts. The designer must also get the contract signed by the client before beginning design work.

This chapter has described in a general sense what legally constitutes a contract and a contractual relationship. It then covered the kinds of clauses commonly found in an interior design contract. The chapter may not answer all the questions or special needs; therefore, the designer should discuss the matter and form of contracts with an attorney. More information on contracts and contract law can be found in the references in the bibliography. A course in business law that emphasizes contracts would also provide additional material for study.

## DESCRIPTION OF SERVICES

### DESIGN CONSULTATION

The analysis of a building design as it relates to the Client's
needs for present and future concerns.
■ The analysis of lease conditions and terms on the Client's
behalf.
■ The analysis of the physical building forms as they relate
to the specific functional needs of the Client.

### PROGRAMMING

The objective analysis of space requirements and their
interrelationships.
■ The collection, analysis and review, with the Client, of all
pertinent data concerning operations.

### SPACE PLANNING

The physical interaction of programmed spaces in plan and
volume form.
■ The allocation of space to determine functional interrelationships and circulation patterns.
■ The allocation of space for
and furnish

## PDO
### PHOENIX DESIGN ONE

INTERIOR ARCHITECTURE
GRAPHIC DESIGN

# Part 4

## Marketing and Business Development

## Chapter 16

# MARKETING INTERIOR DESIGN SERVICES

*A*lthough many interior designers are fortunate enough to obtain prospects or commissions from referrals and previous clients, more and more design firms are looking to market design services. An important reason for this increasing interest in marketing is the expanding competition design firms now face. Many designers previously working for someone have opened new offices in new market areas. Architects and furniture dealers—especially office furniture dealers—have also started interior design departments or created subsidiary companies. There are also many designers moving into attractive markets, like the southwestern states.

With all the increased competition for design business, firms must look beyond traditional methods of obtaining commissions. Sitting behind a desk at the studio waiting for the phone to ring is still done—by far too many designers. Design professionals committed to the expansion of their businesses, however, must always be thinking past the current project and beyond what former clients might be able to provide. In commercial design, this is especially true since contacts may be promoted, change companies, transfer to other cities, retire, or lose responsibility related to the interior designer's interests. In this chapter we will look at the basic ideas of marketing analysis and the development of the marketing plan.

## *Definitions*

Many designers do not like to think about marketing because they are too busy with other work. Others think marketing means selling and refuse to consider themselves "salespeople." Everytime he or she makes a presentation, the designer is engaging in selling. And selling is a part of marketing. But selling is not marketing, and marketing is not selling. A few definitions might help.

There are many definitions of *marketing*. Most include the concept of moving goods and services from producers to consumers. A definition that relates to how interior designers might look at marketing is "the performance of activities which seek to accomplish an organization's objectives by anticipating customer or client needs and directing a flow of need-satisfying goods and services from producer to customer or client."[1] The well-known management consultant, Peter Drucker,

---

[1]McCarthy 1981, 8.

wrote, "the aim of marketing is to know and understand the customer so well that the product or service sells itself."[2]

*Selling,* on the other hand, "is the personal, oral presentation of products or services to prospective customers for the purpose of making sales . . . . the salesman ideally does more than make the customer desire the product; he tries to win the customer's regard for the company which sells the product (and) tries to extend the confidence and regard of the customer to himself."[3]

The "personal selling" done by the designer to obtain a commission or finalize a project presentation is a part of the marketing process. We will look at personal selling techniques in Chapter 18. Some of the many promotional activities involved in the process of marketing interior design services will be explored in the next chapter.

## Marketing Analysis

*Marketing analysis* involves gathering and analyzing data concerning such things as the abilities and interests of the staff, potential clients, the economy, and the competition. This analysis will allow the firm to make better plans and decisions about the direction of the firm's business efforts. The goal of marketing analysis is to find out what the client wants and then provide it.

Marketing analysis can be done by consulting firms that specialize in this kind of work. Sometimes advertising agencies will do marketing analysis. Small firms and designers just beginning their practices often try to do their own marketing analysis. Although this can meet with success, it is a time-consuming and detailed process. Firms determined to do this work internally should be prepared for a revenue-generating designer being away from client work.

### INTERNAL ANALYSIS

It is important for a design firm to market to the right clients. But before the firm can begin to market to those target clients, the firm must know all about itself and what it can do.

Marketing analysis must start with understanding all about the firm. One of the techniques used by corporations is called *SWOT,* which stands for strengths, weaknesses, opportunities, and threats. SWOT analysis can be used by managers and employees to plot the perceived strengths, weaknesses, opportunities, and threats of the firm. It should be pointed out that this analysis method is sometimes criticized because responses can be either too harsh or too meaningless to have validity. However, SWOT analysis taken seriously and constructively can result in useful planning information.

SWOT analysis is done by preparing statements that relate to positive (strengths) and negative (weaknesses) conditions within the firm and external conditions that affect the firm. An example of a strength might be "average monthly billable hours over 75 percent for all design staff." A weakness would be "high turnover at junior designer and designer levels."

Opportunities and threats are often harder to determine. This is because firms that are busy keeping up with current day-to-day practice often miss seeing potential opportunities for the practice or threats to the practice. An opportunity might

---

[2]Drucker, Peter F., *Management: Tasks, Responsibilities, Practices,* Harper & Row, Publishers, Inc., 1973, p. 64.

[3]*Colliers Encyclopedia,* 1975, vol. 15, 422. Copyright © 1975 Macmillan Educational Corporation.

be a contact with the real estate brokerage company helping a corporation locate housing for headquarter's personnel moving into the design firm's city. Another opportunity might be getting a design project published in a trade magazine. A definite threat would be new legislation limiting aspects of traditional interior design practice, such as requiring contractors' licenses for supervision of materials installation.

This kind of formal internal analysis helps the design firm to understand what it can do, what it wants to do, and what it must work on to improve present services so that the firm will be in a position to offer additional services. It also helps define outside influences on the firm that affect the mix and ability to offer services to clients.

A part of this internal analysis involves determining what the firm's philosophy or mission is. It is not enough for management to say that the firm will provide "the best interior design service in town" unless the owner and everyone associated with the organization understand what being the best means to that particular firm. What does being the best mean? Returning phone calls promptly? Being sure service and delivery people treat the client as the designer would? Satisfying the client "no matter what it takes"?

How might the firm plan its philosophy? If a business plan was done originally, many aspects of this philosophy should have already been developed. If not, the owner needs to do some thinking about what he or she perceives the firm is all about. He or she should also talk to former clients—good and bad—about the performance of the firm and their satisfaction with the firm. Employees should be encouraged to openly provide their comments about what the firm is all about to them. From this discussion and examination, a philosophy of the firm that can be incorporated into the marketing plan as the company mission statement will emerge. The mission statement is a philosophical statement of what the firm sees as its role in the profession. It contains broad statements of what the company wishes to achieve during no specific time period. Refer to Figure 12-1 in Chapter 12 for an example of a mission statement.

SWOT analysis will help the firm know what it can do. This can also be done by simply reviewing the skills and interests of the owner and all the staff. A firm cannot seek open office planning projects if no one has experience in that kind of project. As part of this review, the owner/manager should ask each staff member to provide an up-to-date résumé. In addition, each person should prepare a detailed personal analysis of his or her own skills and interests. For the design staff, additional information concerning key projects done for the present employer as well as past employers might also provide important information. In this case, the designer should discuss his or her role on the project and his or her personal evaluation of the success of the project. All this data will help define what the firm can do.

## EXTERNAL ANALYSIS

External analysis involves research into the marketplace, the consumer, and the competition. The purpose of this analysis is to find out what the consumer needs and wants; if any other design firm is providing for those needs and wants; if so, how they are providing those services; and how much of this kind of service is going to be needed in the future. This information, along with the previous information, helps the design firm find its place in the market and aids in the development of the marketing plan.

External analysis involves the use of primary and secondary sources of information. The easiest sources of information to obtain are from secondary sources.

Secondary sources are generally those sources of information that are already in existence or produced by others. These include such things as government, trade association, and general business publications such as the *Wall Street Journal.* Local business reports in newspapers, chamber of commerce publications, and reporting services such as the McGraw-Hill Dodge Reports are other secondary sources of information.

These publications will give the design firm various forms of information from general economic trends and the announcements of new firms opening in the local area. Local glossy magazines and chamber of commerce reports present economic outlooks and forecasts, show growth of or losses in population, and provide business and demographic information. All this gives valuable hints as to potential clients for the residential and commercial interior designer.

Primary sources are sources of information that provide specifics from people who may have direct knowledge about the information sought. Scientific research methods used to gather primary data sometimes through the use of surveys or questionnaires are observation and interviews—either casual or structured. The most common method of primary data gathering used by design firms would be casual interviews—or more precisely, casual conversation.

Some means of obtaining information through the use of casual conversation include "picking the brains" of past clients, meeting with design professionals at conferences and seminars, and talking with professionals such as architects, contractors, and developers. In addition, contacts with government agency employees, manufacturers' representatives, vendors and subcontractors, and even employees of the firm will provide information that can be used in developing a marketing plan.

Another relatively easy form of primary research—observation—can be done whenever anyone working for the firm is driving around town. Everyone should keep his or her eyes open for new construction, remodeling, or work in progress related to the interior design firm's practice. This kind of observation may not bring an immediate lead, but could result in a contract at a later time.

An expensive form of primary marketing analysis is formal questionnaires or surveys. Surveys may be conducted by mail, telephone, or in person. The decision as to the exact survey to use would involve size of audience, length of survey, and immediacy of response. Although surveys can be helpful to the design firm for some specific kinds of research information, the cost and time involved usually limits its use to large practices.

What the design firm must be looking for in its market analysis are answers to such questions as

1. What are the trends in the profession, and how will these trends affect the firm's potential business?
2. Are there sufficient potential clients for the firm's services within a reasonable distance?
3. How might new technologies or legal considerations (codes, licensing) affect the business?
4. How are the services to be offered put forth in the community now? By whom? Are fees charged or not?
5. Is anyone else offering the services in the way the firm plans to? If no one else is providing the service, it may indicate no need.
6. What can the competition do that the firm cannot?
7. What can the firm do better than the competition?
8. Will the firm be able to get the products and services from suppliers and subcontractors to meet the needs of the potential clients?

The internal and external analysis should provide a body of knowledge about the firm's practice and staff, the kind and amount of clients available, general economic and legal trends or restrictions prevalent in the area, and the competition. This information will allow the design firm to set about preparing a definite plan to achieve the desired results first stated in the company mission statement.

Marketing analysis should not be a one-time endeavor. This is an activity that must be continued by the firm throughout its existence. Part of the business plan should include consideration as to how, by whom, and when market analysis is done on a continuing basis.

## The Marketing Plan

Marketing plans should be developed for a particular length of time—usually one year. Yet consideration for short-term and long-term goals, objectives, and strategies must also be incorporated into the yearly plan. Goals, you will recall from Chapter 12, are broad statements, without regard to any time limit, of what the firm wishes to achieve. Objectives are more specific statements combined with time limits aimed toward accomplishing the firm's goals. Strategies are highly specific actions that have definite time limits within the year of the plan.

Short-term goals, objectives, and strategies would usually be those that can be accomplished in less than one year, whereas long-term goals and objectives are those which are expected to take from three to five years or more to accomplish. Long-term goals and objectives must be accomplished based on short-term goals and objectives. A goal for a small design firm might be "to become well known in Boston for residential restoration work." An objective to meet this goal might be "to have one or more projects published in the local press." A strategy then might be "to invite local columnists and editors to tour previous projects and keep them informed of new assignments."

Just as there is no perfect business plan, it is difficult to offer one outline for a marketing plan for all interior design firms. Some firms will want to have a very formal plan with a table of contents, references, and budgeting information. If the plan is to be used internally so that the owners, managers, and staff know what is going on, a more informal format can be presented.

Figure 16-1 shows a portion of a sample marketing plan. Some of the items the plan should cover would include

1. *An introduction.* Statements based on what information was used to prepare the plan as well as the use and purpose of the plan.
2. *Goals statement(s).* A revised statement of general business goals based on the information gathered in the analysis.
3. *Capabilities.* A discussion of the firm's abilities related to the kinds of clients who previously hired the firm.
4. *Services.* A listing of the services the firm can and is going to offer. Subsequent sections should discuss who will be responsible for them and how they will be done.
5. *Clientele.* Quantitative information as to potential numbers, market share, and possible growth in each client category. Both existing and new client objectives should be stated.
6. *Policy decisions.* A discussion of such things as how the firm will charge services to clients, how the firm will charge for consultants, whether or not the firm will bill reimbursable expenses, whether or not the firm will sell mer-

II. Client base
   A. Current year
   1. Our current client base is primarily from the Midland area. Current clients within the city limits represent 80 percent of total sales. The remaining 20 percent are from clients outside the city limits but within a 30-mile radius.
   2. The majority of current work is residential. Eighty-five percent of clients purchase merchandise and services for homes. Fifteen percent of clients purchase merchandise and services for offices or other commercial facilities.
   3. Services vs. merchandise.
      a. Of residential sales, 70 percent of all revenues are merchandise sales. Twenty percent are from design fees, and 10 percent represent other services such as repairs not needing additional merchandise.
      b. Of commercial sales, 90 percent of all revenues are merchandise sales. Design fees represent only 10 percent of revenues from commercial projects.
   4. Type of purchaser.
      a. Sixty-five percent of residential customers purchase goods or services for their existing homes.
         (1) Sixty percent of purchases are for only a few replacement items in one or two rooms.
         (2) Thirty percent of purchases are for new floor coverings, window coverings, and/or wall coverings.
         (3) Ten percent of purchases are for many items in two or more rooms.
      b. Twenty percent of residential customers purchase goods or services for a new house.
         (1) Forty-five percent of purchases are for new floor coverings, window coverings, and/or wall coverings.
         (2) Thirty-five percent of purchases are for only a few replacement items in one or two rooms.
         (3) Twenty percent of purchases are for many items in two or more rooms.
      c. Fifteen percent of residential customers purchase goods or services for a second (vacation or rental) house.
         (1) Fifty-five percent of purchases are for only a few replacement items in one or two rooms.

**FIGURE 16-1**
A page from a sample yearly marketing plan.

chandise, what policies there will be related to purchasing of products for resale.

7. *Marketing organization.* A statement of who will be responsible for ongoing marketing analysis.

8. *Marketing effort.* Answers to such questions as: In what ways will the firm accomplish its goals? How will it use advertising and public relations? How will results be monitored to see whether or not they are successful? How much financially will be committed to marketing?

9. *Evaluation.* A discussion of how the goals will be measured so as to indicate success of the marketing plan.

10. *Forecasts.* Amount of sales, profit, number of new clients, additions to personnel. These should be stated as both quantitative and qualitative measures.

It is wise to involve the entire staff in the analysis and the planning for the yearly marketing plan. Final decisions, of course, should be made by management. It is almost always true that when plans are passed down by management without staff input, the staff feel resentful of not being taken into the planning process. If the staff do not believe in the plan, it will not be very successful.

## *Summary*

Many designers determine that the way to get more business is to go out and make a few more calls or run another sale on some excess inventory. Although these methods certainly bring in a small amount of business, they are not the kinds of activities that sustain a design practice. If the firm is not calling on or attracting the right clients or running sales on the products clients might want to buy, the efforts will be wasted.

In this chapter we have discussed how the firm can develop a marketing effort by presenting the kinds of analysis that must be obtained and by offering a suggested outline for a marketing plan. In the next chapter we will look at the concept of promotion and many of the promotional tools that can be used to aid in the marketing effort.

# Chapter 17

## PROMOTING THE INTERIOR DESIGN PRACTICE

*P*romotion is the method used to get the designer's message—even existence—before the client. To be more precise, promotion is "communicating information between seller and buyer—to influence attitudes and behavior."[1]

Many use the term *promotion* to mean public relations, but promotion is much more than public relations. Promotion also includes publicity, publishing, advertising, and direct selling. Today, promotional activities are important for the healthy growth of any interior design business.

Competition forces design firms to consider many promotional activities. Should the firm attempt to get a project published in one of the trade magazines? Is it proper for the firm to advertise in local magazines? Can the firm afford to publish a brochure? These questions and many more are being asked in design firms everyday as a part of the continual search for new clients, new markets, and greater recognition.

In this chapter, we will explore many of the ways the interior designer can get his or her message across to prospective clients. And then, in Chapter 18, we will consider selling techniques that are utilized by the interior designer.

## *Public Relations*

*Public relations* refers to all the efforts of the firm to create an image in order to affect the public's opinion of the firm. Getting an article about the firm's involvement in a major project published, producing a brochure, helping coordinate an in-office seminar for the public or other professionals, making contributions to professional organization fund-raisers, and even placing an advertisement in the annual "designers" issue of a local magazine are all examples of public relations activities.

A public relations professional will review and evaluate what the design firm does. He or she will then provide suggestions as to how these services are viewed by the type of clients with whom the firm deals. The firm can then direct its future

---

[1]McCarthy 1981, 761.

promotional efforts to obtain additional clients. A public relations professional can do such things as

- Research public opinion about the firm.
- Write newsletters, brochures, and other general mailings.
- Produce special events and programs like seminars, open houses, and the company holiday party for clients.
- Design a new company logo and graphics identity package.
- Write and place news releases in local newspapers or national trade publications.
- Produce audiovisual presentations.

Through the firm's research about itself and the public, a picture of the activities needed within public relations, publicity, and general promotional activities will emerge. The public relations professional makes suggestions as to which activities are going to lead to the most promise of success—that is, more client contacts and potential sales. He or she may suggest a new company image be started by redesigning the company logo and graphics—or maybe news releases about recent successes. Perhaps a brochure or newsletter mailing to former and prospective clients is appropriate. Whatever the strategy, the result is to gain positive recognition for the design firm in the public's mind. And this recognition will eventually lead to future business and greater revenues.

## *Publicity*

A direct form of promotion is publicity. *Publicity* is "any unpaid form of nonpersonal presentation of ideas, goods or services."[2] This is the kind of promotional communication that design firms strive to achieve as much as possible. Traditionally, this was the accepted form of promoting professional services.

Publicity takes many forms. It can be planned or accidental. Unfortunately, most accidental publicity is bad publicity. Bad publicity—such as being named in the papers after a personal injury suit—is not something a design firm seeks. Design firms seek to create planned publicity that will help potential clients view the firm in a good light and seek them out for design contracts. An example of good publicity would be the mentioning of the interior design firm in an article about the grand opening of a new hotel or corporate center. This article is not something that the design firm pays for, but the information alone would create public awareness and potentially new client leads.

A good activity resulting in publicity is charitable and community service work related to interior design. Helping the community theater with props and set designs might be an example. Volunteering services on restoration projects is another. Many chapters of ASID get chapter members involved in designing rooms in model houses or display houses. These are often tied to a charitable group with proceeds of public tours going to the charitable organization.

Larger firms may, with the cooperation of manufacturers, be able to put on exhibits or seminars. Renting a meeting room in a hotel and filling it with a well-designed product display or providing a good educational seminar for the end-user and other professionals who might help the firm are excellent forms of publicity.

---

[2]McCarthy 1981, 749.

# *Publication Opportunities* _____

The most sought-after kind of planned publicity is publication of projects in trade and shelter magazines. Although this form of publicity often has a limited audience consisting of primarily professional peers, reprints can be obtained and mailed or given to prospective and former clients. ASID has prepared a pamphlet called *How To Get Design Work Published*. This publication lists general guidelines for preparing publication material for most of the trade and shelter magazines. The pamphlet also provides information concerning the type of projects and kinds of materials each of the magazines might be interested in publishing.

Many large cities have local magazines that are used for promoting the good qualities of the city or state. These magazines often have articles on residences or commercial properties, giving designers an outlet to the consuming market. Some of these magazines even have special issues focusing on the local design community.

It is also possible to submit appropriate projects to the professional publications of clients. Such magazines as *Today's Office* and *Corporate Design* run articles and photos of executive offices. *Ayer's Directory of Publications*, published by Ayer's Press, lists information on all the magazines published annually in the United States and is available at most public libraries.

Manufacturers of many kinds of products use photographs of installations with their products in paid advertising. Designers should seek to negotiate for the project designer's and the firm's name to receive a byline in the ad.

Another outlet for publicity is entering and winning one of the various trade competitions. ASID and IBD provide to its members a yearly list of major competitions. Others are announced in the trade magazines or sent to designers through mailings from the sponsoring group. Winning projects of major competitions get published in one of the trade magazines, thus providing to the design firm and designer valuable public recognition. This can also lead to feature articles in the local newspaper or other media resulting in additional public exposure for the firm.

## PRESS RELEASES

A press release is an effective, inexpensive way for any size design firm to achieve increased public awareness. Almost any kind of news or announcement can be prepared as a press release. However, newspapers and magazines, having limited space, will likely only use those items they feel are about significant, newsworthy events. Examples would include announcements for large or unusual projects, sponsorship of a seminar or workshop, the winning of a design award, the opening of the firm, or the relocation of the design firm (see Figure 17-1). In most cities, announcements about promotions and new hires are relegated to a minimal statement in a business briefs column.

Public relations professionals have experience in preparing press releases; they also have many contacts with local and national print, radio, and television media. These contacts can be utilized to obtain the best coverage for the press release. If good journalistic techniques are used, however, an in-house individual can prepare a press release.

The text of the release should be prepared in concise journalistic style, using the five *W*'s and an *H*: who, what, when, where, why, and how. The most significant information should be presented in the first paragraph, with additional details presented in subsequent paragraphs. Text should be typed double spaced with wide side margins for editorial comments. Long releases of three or more pages are less likely of being picked up. One- or two-page press releases have the best chance of

L. Green Design Associates
Interior Design Consultants
9876 West Third Street
Phoenix, Arizona 85001

**For Immediate Release**

For further information contact
Joanna Hughes
Telephone: 602-555-3451

**L. GREEN DESIGN ASSOCIATES AWARDED MILLS INC. DESIGN CONTRACT**

L. Green Design Associates has been awarded the interior design contract for the new Mills Incorporated corporate offices.

Mills Incorporated, a research and development company in the computer industry, will be moving corporate offices consisting of 350 employees to Phoenix from the Midwest.

Linda Green, President of L. Green Design Associates, will lead a team of the firm's designers in the space planning and interior design of the new offices. "It is our intention," said Ms. Green, "that the interior design will integrate employee needs for flexibility and creativity with the company's need to show clients that Mills Incorporated is a contemporary, innovative, yet stable company that can solve the problems of the computer industry."

L. Green Design Associates specializes in the space planning and interior design of professional, corporate, and multiemployee general business offices. The firm has completed projects throughout Arizona, New Mexico, Colorado, and California.

**FIGURE 17-1**
A sample news release.

reaching the media. When the editor or news director reads a press release, he or she may have additional questions. The name, address, and telephone number of the individual responsible for writing the release should be placed at the top of the first page so that media personnel know who they should contact.

It is also necessary to indicate at the top of the release when it can be used. Often, press releases are prepared for immediate release. "Immediate release" indicates that all the information in the text is timely and ready for publication. If the information concerns an event in the near future—for example, a seminar to be held next week—the date of preferred release should be clearly indicated.

Supplemental materials, such as line drawings or photographs, provide information that the text cannot easily explain. They also may make an otherwise routine story more interesting. Magazines will prefer color transparencies rather than color photographic prints. If a black and white photograph is sent, it should be a glossy print. Newspapers will readily use black and white glossy prints, but rarely are able to use colored photographic work at all. When line drawings, such as floor plans, are submitted, these should be PMTs or high-quality mylar reductions. PMT is a Kodak trade name for a diffusion transfer process (sometimes called a STAT) that results in a direct positive reproduction of line copy or artwork.

If people are in the pictures, names and titles and signed model releases should be provided. Not having a model release with the photograph could prevent the photograph from being published.

It should be pointed out that even providing the best-written, concise, informative press release about a truly significant event does not guarantee that print media will pick it up. Being selective, especially at a local level, as to who receives the release may help get it noticed and published or even broadcasted. All areas of the media like to "scoop" their colleagues. Knowing that the design firm has attempted to provide that scoop just may help to get the release noticed.

## *Promotional Tools*

Promotional tools are the many printed mechanisms that are used by the interior design firm to get its story before the public. Although there are any number of tools that can be used, we will look specifically at the company logo and the general graphic image, brochures, photo portfolios, newsletters, and the audio-visual presentation.

Public relations professionals talk about these items as indirect promotional tools. Indirect promotional tools are those printed or visual tools that are directed at nonspecific general audiences. What they are, what goes into them, and how they are delivered to the prospective client all play a role in furthering the image desired by the firm.

### THE GRAPHIC IMAGE

By graphic image, we are referring to the total package of materials used by the designer to communicate written materials and presentations. This includes the company logo, business cards, letterhead and other stationery, business forms, and drawing paper identification.

A *logo,* which is a symbolic image of the company, can be a strong identification mark for the firm. It can be used on all the written communication media mentioned as well as on many other items related to the business. If the firm has delivery trucks, the trucks should be painted the same design and colors as the logo. The logo, in essence, should be the same design and color on all materials related to the company. This consistency will help the client identify the logo with the firm and help bring about client awareness and identification (see Figures 17-2 and 17-3). The rest of the design of the business card, stationery, and so forth must be compatible with the logo.

Firms should be careful in the color selection used for stock and ink, type size, typeface, and size of finished format. Oversized or special-sized cards may be very creative but will be difficult for the client to keep on file. Standard type fonts, such as Microgramma, Helvetica, and Futura, make very clean, easy-to-read business cards and stationery.

### BROCHURES

A brochure can be a helpful tool for the firm. The image the brochure relates should mirror the rest of the firm's image. A few excellent photographs of very good installations will be far superior to a lot of inferior shots and wordy copy. The graphic identification should be carried through from the other graphics. Copy must be well written and brief, since clients do not have a lot of time to read the lengthy history and philosophy a designer may wish to express.

The brochure gives the interior design firm the opportunity to show selections of its best work and tells something about the firm (see Figures 17-4 and 17-5). The content of the brochure gives a taste of what the firm is about, but it does not tell the client everything. Thus, the brochure does what it is intended to do—get an invitation from the client for the designer to tell a more complete and personal story.

The brochure does not need to be a four-color glossy extravaganza, but it should be very well done and have high-quality photography. Care must be taken that the photographs chosen do not date the brochure. Featuring photos of the design staff is a complement to the designer, but when that person leaves, his or her photograph in the brochure can date or even negate the brochure.

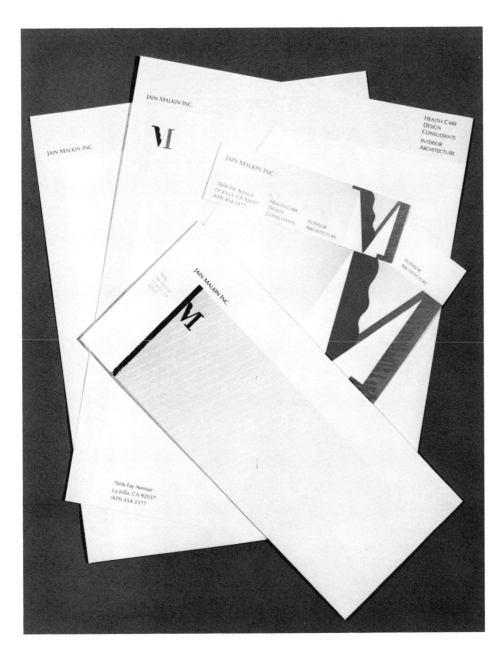

**FIGURE 17-2**
**Design firm logo on letterhead and related materials.** *(Reproduced with permission, Jain Malkin, Inc., LaJolla, Ca.; graphic designer: Miriello Grafico; photo: Eugene Balzer)*

Copy should be short, just enough to tell whom the brochure is from, identify the photos, and tell something about the company. Clients want to get some idea of what the design firm can do for them. The copy should set the stage for further discussions.

The brochure does take expertise in graphics, composition, photography, and copywriting skills. Although the firm may wish to prepare the conceptual content of the brochure, it is recommended that the actual production be left to public relations professionals or professional graphic designers.

## PHOTO PORTFOLIO

Another useful promotional tool is the photo *portfolio*. This is a selection of project photos taken by a professional architectural photographer. If shot in transparency

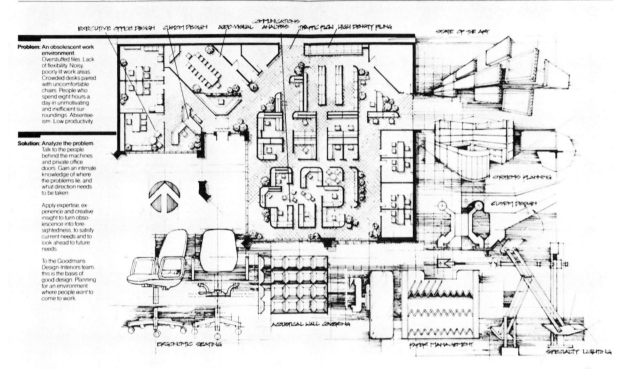

**FIGURE 17-5**
Centerfold of the brochure used by Design-Interiors highlights the final design solution.
*(Reproduced with permission of Design-Interiors, Phoenix, Az.; photo: Christopher C. Everett)*

or negative format, these photos can be used for several purposes. Transparencies can be used for audiovisual presentations. This media is also preferred by magazines for color reproduction. Enlargements from negatives or transparencies can be framed and hung in the office or lobby as a display for the waiting client. A book filled with prints of installations can be shown to the client during the marketing stage of a design project.

It is important to get the permission of the client and have anyone in the photo sign a release—especially if it will be published. This is to protect the designer from being sued for invasion of privacy. It is also a good idea to have a clause in the design contract giving permission to photograph and submit for publication all work, whether the firm expects to do this or not. The photographer will have the release forms should there be people in any of the photos.

## NEWSLETTERS AND CASE STUDIES

Newsletters have long been popular with architects, but rarely developed by interior designers. These are not the in-house communication of firms to tell everyone whose birthday it is; rather, they inform clients and perhaps peers of projects received or completed, new staff hired or promoted, and so on (see Figure 17-6). The newsletter can be inserted in the brochure or sent at a separate mailing.

A case study of a particularly interesting or challenging project can be a separate publication. A case study tells what the design program was, some unique features

**Perkins&Will**

Chicago, New York, Washington
Architects, Engineers, Planners, Interior & Graphic Designers

# PROGRESS

## Facilities Management: Controlling Physical Assets

Reduction in demand for basic and consumer goods and services, slow receivables, lay-offs, and changing capital markets are phenomena almost all sectors of the economy have faced to some degree during the early 80's. The result has been commitment to tighter management of an organization's assets. Asset management includes people, equipment, and facilities. It is no surprise, then, that a full service architecture, engineering and interior design firm like Perkins & Will has experienced increased interest from its clientele in a specialized section of this process—Facilities Management.

In its most comprehensive sense, facilities management is the process of inventorying and evaluating the location, condition, function, and economic value of an organiza-

tion's physical assets. In other times we called this systematic effort Master Planning. While the terminology has changed, the intent has not. Whatever it is called, the objective is to make the best economic use of the real estate owned and/or occupied by an institution. The required activities fall into two categories.

• Identification in an organized and retrievable manner of all pertinent data related to real estate and property assets.

• Analysis of this data to determine the most appropriate means of using and managing the asset.

These analyses take on many different forms depending on an organization's specific objectives. They can deal with land, build-

ings, improvements, interior space, or furnishings. They can address immediate needs for space or cash, or they can position the company to respond intelligently to future conditions.

**Furnishings**

Beginning with the most tangible facilities, companies are looking at their furnishings, carpeting and other moveable equipment to determine whether they are functional, for how long, and what they are worth. When one real estate investment trust recently acquired two neighboring, but dissimilar office buildings, it decided to market the buildings as one unit. To achieve this, the public had to view the two buildings as related even though the architecture, bay

*continued on page 2*

**HARTFORD PLAZA**
**Chicago, Illinois**

Two downtown Chicago high-rises were the focus of efforts to unify the buildings visually through new signage programs and renovation of main floors and public areas. Tenant standards were developed

for various interior design elements; the overall conceptual scheme was designed to allow for phased implementation so the buildings could remain open while renovation proceeded.

April 1983 1

**FIGURE 17-6**
**A newsletter providing information about projects that the design firm has recently been involved with.** *(Reprinted with permission, Perkins & Will, Chicago, Ill.; photo: Eugene Balzer)*

of the project, and may have before-and-after photographs. It can also discuss the solution and ideally has some quotes regarding the quality of the project from the client. Case studies can be developed for a variety of projects. They also can be inserted into the brochure to show a special expertise by the firm (see Figure 17-7).

Neither the newsletter nor the case study needs to be in color, but each should be well done. Both can be accomplished in one or two pages and might include black-and-white photos or line drawings.

**FIGURE 17-7**
Perkins & Will utilizes one-page case studies inserted in a folder for promotional presentations. *(Reprinted with permission, Perkins & Will, Chicago, Ill.; photo: Eugene Balzer)*

### AUDIOVISUAL PRESENTATION

The audiovisual presentation can be an effective way for the design firm to quickly, and very visually, tell its story to the client. This is often a simple presentation prepared especially for the client from the firm's slide collection and narrated by the designer. Many professionals think the simple tailor-made presentation is successful since it is tailored to the specific client and project. They also appreciate its low cost. Today, many firms are using videotape presentations rather than multimedia slide presentations.

Who should be responsible for producing these presentations is an important question. The simple tailor-made presentation should be put together by the designer making the presentation and run through until he or she is familiar with the slides and verbal comments. References on how to prepare slide presentations are listed in the bibliography. The multimedia presentation and videotape presentation, on the other hand, are complex, time-consuming events to create and produce. One source of mailing lists of potential clients could come from professional organizations.

## *Direct Mailing*

Direct mail can be just about anything—from a letter to any number of the items already listed. Since printing and postage are ongoing expenses, the key is to get the mailed item to the right person. To do that, the firm must have a good mailing list. Mailing lists can be purchased from professional organizations.

Many people, however, still think it is wrong or unethical to send out mailings to people the firm does not know. All of us receive "junk" mail from unsolicited sources. Most of that ends up in the wastebasket. Often, unsolicited mail sent to clients ends up the same way. It is best if the list includes only former clients and contacts. The firm can then develop referrals from these names. Even the best prepared mailing may receive only a 2 to 6 percent return when mailed to previously unknown contacts.[3]

Mailings must have some impact and should be designed to catch the eye of the receiver. They need to be well designed and creatively thought out. A good graphics designer or market specialist might be the answer for the design of the mailing. Direct mailings used by interior designers are usually cover letters accompanied by a brochure or newsletter. But direct mailings might also be announcements of sales, holiday promotions, and seminar invitations. Ideally, direct mailings should be followed up by a personal call. It gives the firm a chance to see how the receiver reacted to the mailing and to make an appointment to further discuss its contents or answer questions the receiver may have.

## *Advertising*

Advertising is still a rather controversial way for professionals to promote their services. It was not until 1978 that the AIA gave its approval to some forms of advertising.[4] The IBD Code of Ethics, approved in 1981, states, "Members may purchase dignified advertisements and listings in newspapers, periodicals, directories, or other publications."[5]

---

[3]Kliment 1977, 58.

[4]Jones 1983, 150.

[5]Reprinted with permission from the Institute of Business Designers, 1980, p. 3.

**FIGURE 17-8**
**Magazine advertisement placed by a design firm.** *(Reproduced with permission, Office Designs, Phoenix, Az.)*

*Advertising* is defined as any kind of paid communication in media such as newspapers, magazines, television, or radio. If the firm pays the newspaper to run an announcement of some kind about the firm, it is advertising. If the newspaper runs an announcement or article about the firm and the firm does not pay for it, it is publicity (see Figure 17-8 on the previous page).

There has always been, and still is, a reluctance by the professions to engage in advertising of services. Few interior design firms who earn their revenues from service fees rather than from selling products have utilized the opportunity to advertise. However, as competition gets tougher, design firms will begin to advertise, just as the lawyers and dentists have begun to do.

About the only form of direct advertising all designers use are yellow-page ads in the phone book. Many rely on ads in which the firm's name, address, and telephone number are printed very small. Firms that sell furniture out of retail showrooms or small studios often take out larger-size ads. The firms that make more or most of their money from sales of goods often use advertising related to product promotions or sales. Not only do they use the phone book, but many regularly run ads in magazines, newspapers, and even billboards, and buy radio or television spots.

## *Summary*

Today's highly competitive market makes it very risky for interior designers to expect that all their business will come in on the basis of referrals. Design firms must recognize that promotional activities must be undertaken to ensure a steady supply of clients. It is important to exploit the exposure that publicity brings to a firm. It is also important to be sensitive to the possibility of using other promotional devices as mentioned in this chapter.

The promotional concepts discussed in this chapter suggest many tools the firm may utilize to promote itself to potential clients. These include publicity, news releases, and publication opportunities in trade magazines. It also discussed several mechanisms for communicating information about the design firm to the client via the firm's graphic image, brochures, newsletters, and photographic media. In the next chapter, we will discuss an additional aspect of the whole concept of promotion—that of direct, personal selling.

## Chapter 18

# SALES TECHNIQUES FOR INTERIOR DESIGNERS

*T*he best design idea ever will not become a reality if the designer and design firm cannot convince the client to buy. Interior designers are involved in many different selling situations. In one kind of selling, the designer must make presentations to clients to obtain a design contract. Designers must also sell their design ideas—the color concepts and floor plans of the overall design concept. A third selling situation for many designers requires the selling of products. These may be products that are part of the project concept or individual items the client is looking to buy. Finally, the designer must sell himself or herself; the client must have confidence in the designer before allowing him or her to proceed with the project.

In this chapter, we will first discuss various selling techniques used by designers in these four selling situations. Then we will discuss the formal design-selling presentation. The chapter will conclude with various topics related to developing the selling "image" of the designer.

## *What Is Selling?*

Selling, like marketing, is finding out what the client wants and providing it. Selling, however, is personal, often one-on-one communications. Some people do not like selling or salespeople because they believe sales involves manipulating people to buy what they do not want. This kind of selling is practiced by many so-called salespeople. But that is not the kind of selling we wish to talk about in this chapter.

Interior design professionals, as salespeople, do their utmost to find out what the client really wants in the way of design services and products and then tries to provide those services and products. Satisfying the client and obtaining the sale makes both individuals or groups winners. It is not necessary to try to sell clients what they do not want. If fact, it is bad business to do so.

## *Selling Techniques*

Discovering techniques to help the designer sell his or her services and products is a very personal business. What will work for one designer could lead to frustration and failure for another. Although interior designers use many techniques to help them sell, two important characteristics have always been present in the presentation methods used by successful designers. Those characteristics are enthusiasm for what they are doing and interest in the needs of the client. Successful professionals must have genuine interest in their clients and the needs of the clients.

Clients come to interior designers for help in solving the client's problems in making the home or business attractive and functional. Clients also come to designers to get help in making decisions because many have a hard time making decisions or are reluctant to do so. This is because they are afraid they will get blamed if they make the wrong decisions. Interior designers are hired to help in both of these cases.

### PROBING

*Probing* is a technique for asking different kinds of questions in order to uncover the needs of the clients. Probing is accomplished by asking questions that will either elicit a closed response, such as a yes or no answer, or a response where the client is encouraged to talk. This second kind of probing question is called an open probe.

Questions posed using closed probing techniques are questions geared toward finding out specific information. They are also used when the client is not particularly responsive to other kinds of questions. For example, a designer might ask this short series of questions:

Designer: *Do you have a preferred color scheme?*
Client: *Not really.*
Designer: *Do you prefer warmer colors like oranges, rusts, and yellows?*
Client: *No.*
Designer: *Do you prefer cool colors like blue and green?*
Client: *Yes.*
Designer: *Would a color scheme combining blues and greens together be satisfactory to you?*
Client: *I think I would like that.*

Questions stated as open probes, on the other hand, are attempts by the designer to get the client talking freely about some topic. They are also used to try to get the client to expand on previously mentioned information or to talk in broader concepts.

By the careful combination of open and closed probes, the designer obtains the information required to discover the actual needs of the client. Discovering the needs of the client allows the designer to use a selling technique of describing features and benefits of products and services related to those needs.

### FEATURES AND BENEFITS

An important selling technique, whether selling products or services, is a technique of describing features and benefits. *Features* describe specific aspects or characteristics of a product or service. For example, a plastic laminate top on a desk is a feature of many desks. *Benefits* relate to features of a product or service that directly relate to a client's needs about that product or service. A benefit of the plastic laminate desktop might relate to the ease of maintenance (it will not mar as easily as a wood top).

Once the designer knows the needs of the client, it is relatively easy for him or her to point out the various features and benefits of the services or products being discussed as they relate to those needs. If the services and products meet the needs of the client, obtaining confirmation and closing the sale is much easier and quicker.

## CLOSING TECHNIQUES

*Closing* is the art of knowing when to ask for the sale. If you are lucky enough for the client to say, "I'll hire you," or "I'll take it," without having to ask first, you probably do not even need to read this chapter at all. Most designers, however, do not know how to ask for the sale, whether they are selling their services or selling the products during a presentation. Far too many designers wait for the client to conclude the sales presentation. And the client often does—by not signing the agreement.

Closing techniques involve words and actions that the designer uses to ask for the sale. Asking for the sale assumes that agreement has been reached on the issues being discussed. The sooner the designer asks, the sooner the client signs the agreement, and the sooner the designer can move on to another job.

There are many techniques recommended by numerous how-to-sell books on the market today. Some of those books are listed in the bibliography. The following will recount some of the techniques other professionals use with great success.

One related to the technique of using features and benefits is that of supporting needs with the features and benefits of the product and/or service, and then using a trial close when at least two needs have been supported with features and benefits. Supporting needs with features and benefits shows the client that the designer is really trying to solve his or her needs and provide him or her with only what is needed—not what the designer wants to sell. Remember, trying to close the sale means that agreement has been reached on needs.

> Designer: *You said that you are looking for a sofa bed for the guest room that is comfortable and that will have a fabric which will be easy to maintain. Is that correct, Ms. Smith?*
> Smith: *Yes it is.*
> Designer: *I have already shown you that this sofa bed, made by company X, has been rated by an independent testing company to have the most comfortable mattress on the market. This nylon basket-weave fabric, which you liked, will be easy to maintain. Why don't I work up the final price with the fabric and see when we can deliver it to your home?*

Assuming the price is not an issue, if the client says that will be fine, the designer is finished with the sale, and only needs to finish writing up the paperwork. However, if the client says no, the designer must assume that something has not yet been agreed to and must probe to ask more questions, support needs by discussing other features and benefits, and then try again to close the sale.

Another frequently used closing technique is to close when the designer obtains client agreement to a secondary issue concerning the sale. In the preceding example, when the designer obtained agreement about the fabric choice, he or she would follow with questions related to color of the fabric. When these two issues are agreed to, then the designer is ready to ask for the sale.

Many designers use third-party testimonials or third-party stories to help in the close. "After an extensive product review, IBM accepted this chair group for the company's standard office desk chair." Recalling how a previous client was satisfied by the service or products often helps to alleviate fears in the decision-making process.

A closing technique that many designers use, though perhaps reluctantly, is related to a forthcoming event. For example, a client who may be hesitant to close the sale today may be encouraged if he or she knew that the price on the goods was going up in a few weeks. "I can only guarantee this price for the next ten days, since we have already been informed of a price increase on January 1," the designer would say. This technique is perfectly legitimate and, when related to price increases, is actually a benefit to clients. It should, however, only be used in complete honesty. Telling a client that the price of the goods is going to go up when it will not is not a professional sales technique.

Another useful though unpopular technique is the utilization of some kind of physical action that encourages the client to close the sale. A common physical action is to begin writing up the sales order for the client to sign. Another is to place a pen, in a position for the client to pick up and use immediately, on top of the design contract or confirmation. If the client does not object to the activity or pull back, the designer knows that the sale is about to be closed.

All these techniques help the designer conclude the sales presentation for services or products. Waiting for the client to say "I'll take it" usually leads to frustration and low revenues. There are other techniques described in the books listed in the bibliography. The ones discussed here are those commonly used by many design professionals.

## Concept Selling

*Concept selling* means explaining and obtaining approval from the client of the overall design idea. Concept selling is difficult since it involves selling intangibles. How the living room will really look or how the restaurant will look is difficult for clients to understand. Most have a hard time visualizing the colors and fabrics on the pieces being recommended. Clients also are not used to reading floor plans, making it difficult for them to visualize the interior space plans. The designer must use all of his or her technical training to explain how the space will look before it is complete. This is, of course, why floor plans, color boards, sketches, and even renderings are used to communicate the design concepts in the designer's head to the client.

In concept selling, the designer must gain the client's confidence. Many designers believe that if you are unsure about anything related to the project, you will lose the client. After all, the designer is in the client's home or business learning how the client lives and works. The designer must display total confidence in what he or she suggests the client do to and purchase for his or her home or business.

In many ways, this means becoming the client's "friend," although not in a normal sense. To become too close or too personal a friend with people for whom the designer is working can create difficult situations for both sides. Slow payment, no payments, errors by the designer—all lead to tense moments when the two parties are no longer friends. Becoming friends can make conducting business more difficult. Yet, the designer must show concern, thoughtfulness, and empathy for the client's interiors problems. Being totally businesslike certainly has its place, but so does having a sense of humor and knowing when it is alright to relax and be somewhat casual.

Successfully selling the design concept is the culmination of the design selling responsibilities of the interior design professional. Obtaining agreement, and being able to proceed with the order not only brings financial success to the designer, but also personal satisfaction in seeing tangible completion of the project.

# *Selling Presentations*

It is often necessary to make a presentation to the client in order to obtain a signed design contract. This occurs when the client is either interviewing more than one designer or design firm or is unfamiliar with the designer or firm. Although a formal selling presentation would be more common in commercial design, it is not uncommon for the independent residential designer to also have to make this kind of presentation. In residential retail studios, the formal presentation is more likely an informal meeting of the client and designer. The remainder of this section will discuss the formal selling presentation.

## PREPARATION

There are many questions the designer must ask while preparing to make a major selling presentation.

1. What are the prospective project requirements?
2. To whom will the presentation be made?
3. How many people will attend the meeting?
4. Where will the presentation take place?
5. Who from the design firm should be involved in the presentation?
6. What is it about the design firm that the client will want to know?

The answers to all of these questions will have an influence on the content and format of the presentation itself.

The initial contact by phone or face-to-face visit should be used to gain as much information as possible about the project requirements. This preliminary information sets the stage for the formal presentation. It happens all too often that the designer prepares a full-blown comprehensive presentation for the client when the project only requires a small amount of specification work.

In most cases, the presentation is made to the person who will make the decisions regarding hiring the designer and approving the floor plans and specifications. In residential design, the designer rarely consults with anyone but the owner of the home. Yet, in commercial design, it is not uncommon for the design firm to be contacted by purchasing agents or other representatives of the company rather than the ultimate decision maker. In these cases, it is often necessary to make presentations to these representatives during the beginning stages of the negotiation of the contract and a second presentation to the decision maker. Thus, it is necessary for the designer to be sure he or she knows who will be present for the design presentation and what each person's role is in the decision-making process.

Presenting to one or two people over a conference table or a dining table is not particularly difficult. There are times when the designer must present before a larger group, perhaps five or six people. Occasionally for some commercial projects, it might be necessary to present to a very large group. It is necessary to know how many people will attend the presentation in order to adjust the materials to the proper size audience. For a few people, a photo portfolio of previous projects would work quite well. But for a larger group, it would be more effective to use slides.

Many professionals feel that where the presentation takes place makes a big difference in the success or failure of the effort. Ideally, the presentation should take place in the designer's place of business. This allows the interior designer to control the presentation situation completely. No phone calls, doorbells, children, or co-workers distract the client, which permits the designer to have the client's undivided attention. A conference room at the design studio or office is preferable. The client should be positioned directly across from the designer or at right angles (see Figures 18-1 and 18-2). This allows the designer to easily see and evaluate the client's eyes and body language, which is important for evaluating whether the presentation is going well or whether the client's interest has been lost.

**FIGURE 18-1**
This sketch shows the presentation arrangement where the client and designer sit across the conference table from one another. *(Drawing: Clayton E. Peterson)*

**FIGURE 18-2**
This sketch shows the presentation arrangement where the client and designer sit at right angles to one another at the conference table.
*(Drawing: Clayton E. Peterson)*

When it is necessary to go to the client's "territory," the designer should ask that a conference room be made available. Getting the client out of his or her office moves the presentation to a neutral area and allows for some control of the presentation situation by the designer. A presentation held in an office over the client's desk is not only an awkward situation, but it also allows the client to be distracted by phones, people dropping in, and other interruptions.

In the home, if at all possible, the presentation should be made in the dining room rather than the living room. For most families, the living room is the formal room, the room they can easily say no in. The dining room allows the designer to sit directly across from or at right angles to the client, which is considered a more satisfactory situation.

For most residential projects, the designer who made the initial contact with the client will be making the presentation. In commercial firms, it is common for the contact to be made by the design director or marketing manager. In this case, the presentation could be made by the designer assigned to the project, but more often it is the responsibility of the design director or project manager. The designer(s) who will be responsible for actually doing the project would, however, participate in the presentation.

Anyone from the design firm that comes to the presentation must participate in the presentation or he or she should not be there. Commercial design firms commonly overwhelm clients with great groups of people at the selling presentation with the mistaken belief that the client "wants to see the whole team"; the client walks into the office and is outnumbered by staff members. The presentation is the time for the client to meet the design manager, the project designer, and maybe one or two other individuals who will be directly working on the project.

## CONTENT

It is very important for the content of the presentation to contain the information the client wants to know. Of course, the client wants to know how long it will take and how much it will cost. These are items that the designer may not be prepared to reveal at the formal presentation. Clients also want to know how the designer is going to solve their problem, so it will be necessary to tell the client how the project will be approached. The client may also be interested in seeing how other design problems similar to theirs have been solved. Slides or photographs, especially before-and-after pictures or plans, graphically communicate how the firm solves interior design problems. The professional must anticipate all the questions the client may ask about time frames, charges, who will work on the project, and so on. Not having a legitimate answer to any of these will turn the client to another design firm.

## THE PRESENTATION

A key to a successful presentation is knowing what you are going to say before you say it. Far too many designers try to "wing it" through a presentation, making it up as they go along. They say they do this to be sure they are reacting to the client's questions. And that is what they are doing—reacting. A sales presentation must be a planned communication concerning what the client wants to know and what the designer wants to tell him or her. Winging it may make the presentation look fresh, but it also generally looks unprofessional and disorganized. A prepared presentation may sound the same to the designer since he or she has made it or heard it many times before, but it always sounds fresh to the client since he or she has never heard it before.

An agenda or outline for the meeting should be prepared with the role determined for each participating member of the firm. For an individual presenter, the outline also helps make sure that what is necessary to be said will be said.

The outline should take on the basic form of the strategy in any report or presentation:

1. Tell them what you are going to tell them.
2. Tell them.
3. Tell them what you told them.
4. Ask for the sale.

Visual aids for the meeting need to be organized and checked to be sure they are of a quality presentable to the client. Slides have an uncanny habit of going into the tray upside down. Boards or drawings need to be clean and neat. The proper number of brochures or other handouts must be prepared. Extra sets of handouts should be available in case additional members of the client's party arrive.

During the presentation, the designer should be aware of his or her own body language and the body language of the client. If you must stand, stand relaxed, but with good posture. When sitting, lean forward showing interest in what you are saying and what the client says in response to your statements. If the client folds his or her arms across his or her chest, it might mean that the client does not like what is being said. Watch for the client either pushing back or leaning forward over the conference table. If he or she leans or pushes away from the table, he or she is possibly losing interest in what is being said. If he or she leans forward, this kind of body language indicates interest. There are many other body language indicators that help the designer interpret whether or not the message he or she is sending to the client is being received favorably. More information on body language can be found in some of the books listed in the bibliography.

Use good eye contact. This does not mean staring down the client to make him or her uncomfortable. It does mean to look the client in the eye from time to time. Many perceive eye contact to mean honesty and trustworthiness. Others interpret eye contact or the lack of eye contact to be related to either confidence or disinterest. Maintaining eye contact with an individual for about five seconds, looking away for awhile, and then returning to eye contact so that eye contact is maintained about 50 percent of the time is a beneficial use of the technique.

How you say what you say is also important in communicating a favorable message. Beware of using fillers like *er, well, okay, you see,* and *umm.* These words are indicators of powerless language. To the astute client, these fillers also show lack of preparation and lack of confidence in what the presenter is trying to say and sell. Instead of fillers, a controlled pause to create dramatic effect should be used. And the use of qualifiers in presentations should be eliminated. Qualifiers are words such as *but* or *however* used at the beginning of a sentence. A statement such as "this is the best chair to use in your secretarial pool. However, there are others that have better fabrics available" dilutes the confidence the client needs in the decision-making process. "Such hedges tend to be spoken with nonassertive body language (such as downcast eyes, slumped posture or a nervous smile) and in a timid, uncertain voice."[1]

Many designers and consultants believe that handouts should not be distributed until the verbal portion of the presentation is completed. When handouts are given

---

[1]Elsea, Janet G., *The Four-Minute Sell,* Simon & Schuster, 1984, p. 83.

to the client as the presentation continues, it is almost a certainty that he or she will look through the brochure, newsletters, contract, or whatever was handed out rather than listen to the presentation. The client often misses important points and questions about what was said, which will mean lost time later. This could result in the designer's not being able to present everything he or she wanted to present because information has to be repeated. Enough time should be allowed at the end of the presentation for distributing and going over any handouts prepared for the client.

When the presentation is concluded, the designer should be sure to thank the client for his or her time, shake hands, and use the last few minutes for small talk about continued interest in the project—be friendly, and continue to show confidence in obtaining and completing the project.

### FOLLOW-UP

It is important after the presentation for the designer not to wait for the client to call. The designer should follow up on the presentation with a letter and/or a phone call. The follow-up contact should cover such things as thanking the client for his or her time, restating important points of the presentation, and emphasizing continued interest in working with the client. This courtesy may be all the client needs when deciding between two or more designers or design firms.

Any documentation, site visits, third-party testimonials, or other actions that were promised during the presentation must be taken care of as promptly as possible. Delays also hurt the designer's chances of closing the sale.

## *Image*

You never get a second chance to make a good first impression. The image and reputation of the design firm or the designer are as important in obtaining design contracts and selling concepts as the actual ability of the firm to do the work. The image of the firm is presented in the promotional tools that the firm will use to get itself known to the public. Image is also projected by the people and location of the firm. This section will briefly discuss these aspects of the company's image.

### WARDROBE

The style and formality of the wardrobe must be considered in the overall image. Although interior design is a creative, glamorous profession, serious designers should generally stick to conservative, stylish attire. Of course, the actual client mix will determine how conservative or how trendy the wardrobe of the professional can be.

Who the firm's clients are will have a large influence on the style of wardrobe used by the firm's employees. In commercial design, what the designer wears when the client is a bank president or other conservative businessperson will be different from his or her attire when meeting with the owner of a new restaurant. "Appearance has a direct impact on your credibility because so much information is conveyed. . . . Appearance influences other people's perceptions and may determine their attitudes. . . . That's also why people whose appearance suggests high status are treated measurably better than people whose appearance suggests low status."[2]

---

[2]Elsea 1984, 32–33.

To assist business people in wardrobe selection and grooming, books such as John T. Molloy's *Dress for Success* and others available in bookstores should be investigated.

## LOCATION

Interior design is one of those professions that many think fits nicely into a home environment. In fact, a great number of designers begin their practice by working out of a spare bedroom or a converted garage. Although this is economically attractive, the designer should strive to locate in an office as soon as possible. The designer may be a very talented, creative person, but oftentimes, the home office is a jumble of catalogs, samples, and files—not very attractive to a prospective client. The contract client, particularly, is more concerned about the location and the appearance of the office. After all, if the office does not appear businesslike and successful, the client may be reluctant to award the designer with a large contract.

Cities commonly have zoning restrictions against using a residential location for commercial purposes. Neighbors may complain about traffic, parking, or even delivery trucks around the home office. The home office should be cautiously considered as a location for the interior design practice.

A business office located in a commercially zoned part of town gives the impression of professionalism. The exact location of the business office will be determined, in part, by the nature of the business. If the practice is primarily commercial and seeks the office suite and corporate client, a location in the downtown business district would be the most suitable. Should the practice be specialized for a particular kind of business, such as hotels or restaurants, a location near the main hotel district or a downtown location again must be best. Residential design studios are often located near other suppliers like carpet, wallpaper, or lighting retail stores in suburban locations. This relationship could bring a client to the designer when he or she visits another establishment.

The interior design of the studio, office, or retail store must be of the highest quality to reflect the image the firm tries to achieve. Neat reception areas that give the client an impression that the firm and its employees are professionals is important in attracting the commercial client. Retail stores with well-displayed furniture and furnishings that are cleaned, dusted, and attractively arranged are another important part of projecting the right image to residential and commercial clients. Some owners and managers say that the studio, office, or store that has merchandise, samples, and documents spread out gives the facility the appearance of casualness. More likely it gives the impression of disorganization. Casualness and disorganization are two different things, and it is important for the owner of the studio or office to understand whether the kind of client he or she wishes to attract will be turned off by the sloppy appearance of the facility.

## *Summary*

Throughout this book, we have seen how there is more to interior design than being able to put colors, fabrics, and furniture together into a workable floor plan. One of the most important nondesign activities of the interior designer is selling. Without being able to quickly determine what the client needs and then have the ability to convince the client that the design ideas and products the designer establishes are what is needed, the designer cannot stay in business.

In this chapter we have reviewed some of the many techniques that are used by the designer to sell services and products. We have looked at selling techniques, the formal sales presentation, defined concept selling, and briefly surveyed establishing the personal image of the firm. This concludes the discussion on marketing of design services and business development. In the next chapters we will cover the various activities related to managing the project.

# Part 5

## Project Management

## Chapter 19

# TIME MANAGEMENT AND PROJECT CONTROL

$T$o an interior designer, one of the absolute truths is that time equals money. Whether the designer is paid by the hour or receives compensation in some other way, the efficient, productive use of time has direct bearing on yearly income. It is therefore very important for the interior designer to make the best use of his or her time while on the job.

It is also very important for the designer to control the project instead of letting the project control the designer. Since very few designers ever work on only one project at a time, designers must utilize efficient methods of keeping track of the different projects they are working on. Finding a scheduling method that helps the designer and design manager keep track of every activity for each project and when each phase needs to be completed is an important factor in project control.

## Time Management

As professionals in all fields find they have more to do, theories of time management and organization have evolved. Time management theories were not developed to make the user a slave to his or her job, but rather to help him or her organize time to be as productive as possible on the job. Books discussing time management techniques abound; all are based on similar concepts of creating to-do lists, prioritizing those lists, handling papers once, and keeping a calendar and reminder notebook handy.

Time management has to do with control, decision-making, and planning. It does not suggest that a person controls his or her time so rigidly that there is no room for flexibility to meet emergencies. Nor is it so loose as to prohibit anything of value getting done. In his book *How to Get Control of Your Time and Your Life* Alan Lakin, a renowned time management consultant, discussed the 80/20 rule. As it relates to time management, the *80/20 rule* maintains that when activities are arranged in order of importance, 80 percent of a person's time will be spent performing 20 percent of the activities. What this means is that, in a list of ten items, if a person accomplishes the two most important items, he or she achieved 80 percent of the total value of time spent. Most companies can look at sales records and see that approximately 80 percent of the sales were generated by 20 percent of the sales staff. The main thrust of the 80/20 rule is to concentrate efforts on the few items with the highest priority to generate the greatest value or return.

Determining which activity has the highest priority is done by generating a daily to-do list and prioritizing that list (see Figure 19-1). Early in the morning or very near the end of the day, a person should prepare a list of what has to be done for that or the following day. Items on this list come from previous lists, calendars, schedules, memos, and so on. Decisions are made with regard to what needs to be done for the day—or at least attempted. This can be "complete floor plan revisions for Jones's house," "select carpet for the Andrews living room," and even "pick up cleaning on the way home."

Items on the list should also be planned for expected time use. How long will it take to complete the floor plan revisions, and so on? Because interruptions and emergencies occur, it is wise to plan for one less hour of work per day (for example, plan for a seven-hour work day rather than a full eight-hour day). The one hour of padding allows for phone calls, drop-in visitors, emergency projects, and so forth.

Some time management systems prioritize the list by categorizing each item as *A* or *B*. *A* items are the more important tasks needing to be done that day. De-

| Activities for April 14, 1986 | |
|---|---|
| ① Meet with Roy for Patrick Corp charges (8:30) | 45 min |
| ② Call Dr Cummings          555-0528 | 30 min |
| ③ Meet with Tom Davis & review plans          (10:30) | 1 hr 30 min |
| ⑤ Work on plans for Southeast Center | 2 hrs |
| ④ Lunch meeting     Steelcase (12:30) | 1 hr |
| ⑥ Call carpet installer – set meeting to go over plans & Dr Cummings | 15 min |
| ⑦ Work on specs for Robertson House | 2 hrs |
| ⑧ Work on fab selections for Ellis | |

| Notes |
|---|
| Pick up cleaning |
| Tennis lesson          7:30 pm |

FIGURE 19-1
A prioritized to-do list showing activities and time estimates for completion.

pending on the item, noncompletion of an *A* task could damage the designer's reputation or the reputation of the company. The completion of *B* tasks is less pressing; *B* tasks could be finished the next day or some other day.

Once items are all listed as *A* or *B*, they should be prioritized further by number. After this has been done, the 20 percent of tasks that will gain the 80 percent of value will be discovered. Work on accomplishing task *A1* first, then move on to *A2*, and so on. If *A2* cannot be done (for example, *A2* was to call a client, but the client was not in), move on to *A3* and plan to go back to *A2* a little later in the day. Record that the call was made but the client could not be reached. (Record also if a message was left for the client.)

Crossing items off the list as they are completed shows accomplishment and allows for a feeling of satisfaction. Those tasks not completed are transferred to the next day's list. If an item continually shows up on the list, but never gets done, the task may need to be labeled *A1* some day! It also may point to a problem (for example, a habit of procrastinating too much on certain kinds of activities) or a need to reassess effective use of time during the day.

A key to the to-do list is to break down big projects into small segments. Any larger-sized task should be broken down into manageable segments with target dates that will lead to the completion date required. This will assure getting the project done on time.

It is important to keep the to-do list handy, along with a daily appointment calendar. There are several kinds of calendars available. One of the best calendars to purchase or develop is the "portable desk," which contains a monthly calendar, a day-by-day calendar divided by hours, pages for the to-do list, and memo paper. The portable desk organizes schedules, appointments, and notes in one notebook.

A final note about time management. The suggested methods for time management do work, but it takes a certain amount of discipline to get into the habit of creating to-do lists and prioritizing them everyday. New habits are difficult to generate and it is necessary to keep after this one in order to obtain results.

## *Time Records*

Since so many designers charge for services by hourly rates, it is crucial for accurate time records to be kept for all professional services. Keeping time records involves documenting, as close as possible, all time spent on projects and other office or company business.

Time records are kept for several reasons:

1. To keep accurate records for billing, particularly if charging by the hour for professional services; some clients wish to see time records before paying their bills.
2. To check on the progress of current jobs in order to determine if too much time is being used. If the project is running over the estimated time, the reasons need to be analyzed: Did the client change his or her mind too often? Is the designer being nonproductive? Was there an error in the requirements or plans? Was enough time budgeted?
3. To relate amount of profit to time spent on the project. A client who needs a lot of selling or time-use for activities like specification writing and drafting may not be profitable unless charged by the hour.
4. To help determine budget and fees for new projects based on recorded histories. If the company has a history that 2000-square-foot residence jobs can be accomplished in *X* amount of hours, it saves time and errors in writing

new contracts or even determining if that kind of project should be taken again.

5. To determine how productive staff members are and to give management an indication of how much time is billable (versus time devoted to nonbillable house time).

A wide variety of management control reports can be generated from time sheets. These were discussed more fully in Chapter 12.

Time records are only as accurate as the employees keep them. How exact the records need to be will be a function of management control. Most companies only expect the designers to record time based on quarter hours. And the designers must record the activities of a normal work day plus any overtime. It is easy for most

TIME RECORD

JOB NO.

CLIENT DESIGNER

ADDRESS MONTH OF 19

CITY STATE ZIP SALESPERSON

| DATE | DESCRIPTION OF WORK DONE | DESIGN | DRAFTING | SUPPORT |
|---|---|---|---|---|
| | | | | |
| | | | | |
| | | | | |
| | | | | |
| | | | | |
| | | | | |
| | | | | |
| | | | | |
| | | | | |
| | | | | |
| | | | | |
| | | | | |
| | | | | |
| | | | | |
| | | | | |
| | | | | |
| | | | | |
| | | | | |
| | TOTAL HOURS FOR MONTH | | | |

COMMENTS

TOTAL ____________ HRS. AT $ ________ = $ ________

MATERIALS ________________________ = $ ________

TOTAL CHARGE $ ________

PAGE OF

**FIGURE 19-2**
**Preprinted form that is used to record time worked on design projects.**
*(Reproduced with permission, Goodmans Design-Interiors, Phoenix, Az.)*

people to keep track of a day's activities on one sheet and then transfer the time related to individual projects and nonbillable time to the appropriate sheet for that project. Records need to be kept on a daily basis and, depending on the needs of the firm, compiled on a weekly or monthly basis. The example shown in Figure 19-2 can be used for the daily report sheet or monthly/weekly report. Each report should contain the client's name or the project's name, the designer's name, a description of the work, and the hours of work per description.

# Job Schedules

Project schedules help the designer maintain control of the project. As mentioned earlier, breaking down a large task into manageable units helps to get the task done on time. In contract work, projects are often large, and it is vital to the designer and the client that it be done in an organized fashion.

Project schedules can take many forms, depending on who is using the information. For the designer responsible, they may be day-by-day or at least week-by-week descriptions of what must be done to reach the target completion date. For the project manager or designer director, a week-by-week or monthly schedule would be needed to aid in accepting, estimating, and assigning new work.

*Milestone charts* may be the easiest method of scheduling. Here the designer outlines the activities required by the project and establishes a target date for completion (see Figure 19-3). Space for who has responsibility for each activity may also be part of the chart. An indication of the date of completion should be noted. This will aid in future estimating.

A reasonably easy, yet more graphic method of scheduling is by use of a bar chart. Figure 19-4 provides an example. This can be done on a daily basis for the designers with responsibility for the project, or it can be a simple monthly chart for the design manager. The bar charts will help in future estimating of time needed for similar kinds of projects.

*Bar charts* consist of a description of tasks required on the left and horizontal bars showing the time in days, weeks, or months required to complete the task on the right. A disadvantage of the bar chart method is that it does not necessarily show how one activity affects another activity nor which is more important to complete the project on time. Analysis of the most important activities can be developed with more careful project analysis and a more complex, color-coded bar chart. For most firms, either of these two methods will work very well.

| Project: Weldone Residence | | | | | | |
| Designer: Maryanne | | | | | | |
| Task Name | Days | Earliest Start | Earliest Finish | Latest Start | Latest Finish | Actual Finish |
|---|---|---|---|---|---|---|
| Interview Client | 3 | 9/23/86 | 9/26/86 | 10/3/86 | 10/8/86 | 9/23/86 |
| Obtain Floor Plan | 1 | 9/24/86 | 9/25/86 | 10/7/86 | 10/8/86 | 9/24/86 |
| Inventory Existing Furniture | 1 | 9/25/86 | 9/25/86 | 10/7/86 | 10/8/86 | 10/5/86 |
| Sketch Preliminary Plan | 7 | 9/26/86 | 10/7/86 | 10/8/86 | 10/17/86 | 10/6/86 |
| Preliminary Selections | 5 | 9/26/86 | 10/3/86 | 10/10/86 | 10/17/86 | 10/7/86 |
| Prepare Preliminary Budget | 2 | 10/6/86 | 10/7/86 | 10/15/86 | 10/20/86 | 10/8/86 |
| Meet With Client | 1 | 10/7/86 | 10/8/86 | 10/17/86 | 10/20/86 | 10/8/86 |
| Revise Preliminary Plan | 5 | 10/8/86 | 10/15/86 | 10/20/86 | 10/27/86 | 10/14/86 |
| Revise Selections | 3 | 10/7/86 | 10/20/86 | 10/27/86 | 10/30/86 | 10/17/86 |
| Prepare Final Budget | 1 | 10/20/86 | 10/20/86 | 10/29/86 | 11/3/86 | 10/23/86 |
| Final Presentation to Client | 2 | 10/20/86 | 10/22/86 | 10/30/86 | 11/3/86 | 10/24/86 |

FIGURE 19-3
A sample milestone chart. The chart indicates the activities to be performed, estimated days for completion, and target dates for starting and stopping each activity.

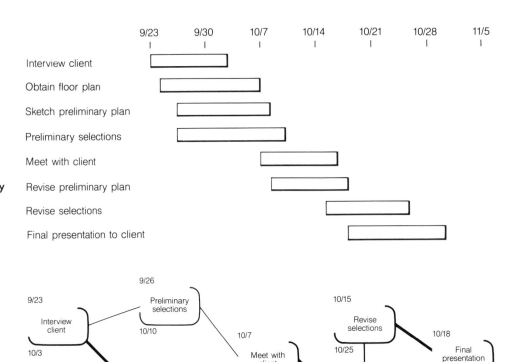

**FIGURE 19-4**
Bar chart that graphically shows the time span required to complete designated project activities.

**FIGURE 19-5**
Critical path method chart. The heavy lines connecting the various boxes indicate the critical path of this project.

For some very complex projects, a third method may be needed. The *critical path method (CPM)* is a scheduling method dependent upon the interrelationships of activities and the detailed tasks of each activity. Any one activity in a sequence cannot be completed unless the previous tasks and related activities have been completed. Primarily used by architects and the construction industry, CPM of scheduling starts by identifying the interrelationships of the tasks to be performed. This analysis shows the project manager which tasks must be done before the next or other tasks can be performed—thus establishing the critical path (see Figure 19-5). For example, a simple critical path in an interior design project would be to obtain needs from the client, prepare floor plans, obtain client approval, order products, and install and/or deliver products. It is clear that it is impossible, as well as unwise, to try to do any of these tasks prior to completing the one directly preceding it.

There are many computer programs that can help the interior designer utilize CPM for scheduling. However, it would be wise for the designer to become more familiar with the concepts of CPM, as detailed in some of the books listed in the bibliography, before investing in any of the available software.

## Control Books or Job Books

Another tool used by many designers to control the project is the project control book or project job book. The *project control book* usually consists of file folders or notebooks in which the designer keeps all the pertinent data and paperwork related to the project in progress. It serves as a complete record of all the designer's efforts to organize a project and can be used to create the installation manual.

Keeping a control book up to date and organized requires discipline—just as time management does. But it is immensely useful to the designer, the design firm, and the client. All the information the designer needs about the project is in one place. As questions arise or changes are made, the designer has a complete reference to use in talking to the client, vendors, or personnel in the design firm. The well-organized control book makes an impressive statement to the client about how the designer and the design firm keep control of projects.

If the designer in charge of the project is absent for any reason, the control book allows other members of the firm to seek out answers to clients' and vendors' questions. Even if the lead designer leaves the firm, another designer should be able to pick up the control book and complete the project successfully.

Having all the information in one place saves valuable time when questions arise. There should be no need to look in separate files for information on ordering, delivery, or color number of the sofa.

The control book will also be invaluable as a future reference. Should the client want to duplicate or be in need of repairs or replacements of items specified, it will be easy to check the control book for exact product information. If legal problems arise during or after the project, the control book will serve as a thorough reference for the firm.

Although projects are all different, many have similar qualities. Control books help the firm with projects that are similar in many ways. For example, control books help determine:

1. Why the design time estimate was or was not accurate.
2. Whether or not products performed as specified and if vendors were a problem.
3. If taking additional work from the same client would be inadvisable—perhaps because an inordinate number of changes were made by the client.

It can also be helpful as a sales tool in marketing efforts. Clients may wish to see how the firm expects to control their project; displaying a well-organized control book, with all its various parts, may be the answer.

In most cases, the control book should have the following kinds of items kept organized chronologically or categorically: meeting notes, correspondence, samples, floor plans, and so on.

## MEETING NOTES

Meeting notes are notes concerning the project taken by the designer or others in the firm. These would be the originals of any notes taken during the various meetings the designer might have with the client, contractors, manufacturers, subcontractors, and architect. Telephone notes to any of these parties would also be kept in this section.

Meeting notes should include the notes taken during the initial interview, which are used to develop the design contract, and all subsequent interview notes or forms obtained concerning client needs. It would be ideal if the notes also contained information such as date and time of the meeting and the names of those in attendance. Many designers send transcribed copies of meeting notes back to the client or other interested parties to be sure there were no misunderstandings during the meeting.

## CORRESPONDENCE TO AND FROM THE CLIENT

Copies of all correspondence sent to or received from the client should be held in the control book. The kinds of correspondence to have handy are any letters or memos, a copy of the letter of agreement, purchase orders from the client, invoices, delivery tickets, and other forms the designer might use to handle the project.

## CORRESPONDENCE TO AND FROM FACTORIES AND REPRESENTATIVES

Correspondence to and from factories and representatives might include letters concerning pricing, special treatments or fabrics, custom work, availability for shipping, freight charges, and so on. Also this would include purchase order copies to the factories, acknowledgments and invoices from the factory to the designer, and freight bills.

## SAMPLES

Fabric samples for all items being specified should be included. These must be accompanied by a full description which would include manufacturer, product name and/or number, color name or number, and a code for determining to what furniture item (for upholstery) or room name/number (for window treatments, wall treatments, and floor finishes) the sample goes.

Samples may be done piece by piece using a control sheet—which has room for other specifications and information the designer would like—or room by room with all samples for one room going on one sheet. The former method works extremely well for contract projects, whereas the latter method would be more appropriate for residential projects. The control sheet, or some variation, would be ideal in setting up an installation manual to make the installation of furniture items go more smoothly.

## FLOOR PLANS

The control book should have a copy of the final floor plan. This may be both the entire project plan or room-by-room plans for very complex projects. If the project is very large, it might be convenient to have the large floor plans reduced to smaller sheets. The copy of the signed, approved floor plans should be in the book.

The design firm should develop a system of coding the plans to the control sheets, as previously discussed, and to the written specifications. This will make it easy to identify specific items on the floor plan and will be a key in the development of installation manuals.

## OTHER ITEMS

Some projects will have additional items in the control book. Depending on the organization and size of the design firm, copies of many forms that normally would be in the bookkeeping area, in the warehouse, or in the hands of the managers might be in the control book. These items might include a copy of the formal bid specification, equipment lists, invoices from manufacturers, time records, and freight information. Follow-up notes, if done by management, concerning profitability, marketing information, problems, or successes may also be kept in the control book.

# letter of
# transmittal

**/567**

| to: | date _____ |
| | job _____ |
| | job no. _____ |
| attention: | location _____ |

gentlemen:     we are sending:     ☐ herewith     ☐ under separate cover

for your:     ☐ use     ☐ information     ☐ approval     ☐ files

the following:
- ☐ prints
- ☐ originals
- ☐ transparencies
- ☐ shop drawings
- ☐ photographs
- ☐ photostats
- ☐ samples
- ☐ catalogs
- ☐ reports
- ☐ specifications
- ☐ see remarks
- ☐ _____

| number of copies | drawing code | latest date | description |
|---|---|---|---|
| | | | |
| | | | |
| | | | |
| | | | |
| | | | |
| | | | |
| | | | |
| | | | |
| | | | |

remarks _____

_____

_____    by _____

**sent via**
- ☐ mail (1st cl.)
- ☐ air mail
- ☐ spec. del.
- ☐ parcel post
- ☐ Environetics messenger
- ☐ air courier
- ☐ u.p.s.
- ☐ receiver's messenger

**Environetics drawings issued for**
- ☐ construction
- ☐ bids
- ☐ other_____

**shop drawings**
- ☐ approved
- ☐ approved as corrected
- ☐ resubmit

**kindly receipt and return to: Environetics International, Inc.**

_____

7/83

**Environetics**

FIGURE 19-6

**A typical transmittal letter. Used by design firms to accompany samples and drawings sent to other designers, vendors, or others involved in the project.** *(Reproduced with permission, Environetics International, Inc., Los Angeles, Ca.)*

## *Project Correspondence*

Many firms design specialized forms for their use in managing a project. Forms for estimating materials, in-house correspondence, and other peculiar control interests of the firm might be designed and utilized. One form used by most design firms is the transmittal letter (see Figure 19-6). The *transmittal letter* is a form letter that can be used for many purposes. It can be used to send information to the client, consulting architects and/or engineers, subcontractors, leasing agents, manufacturers, or anyone else involved with the project.

The transmittal is designed to eliminate the need to write a separate letter or memo in order to transmit or ask for information. It is a handy "fill-in-the-blank" form that should be sent with materials of any kind. It tells the receiver what is being sent and for what purpose. It also give instructions to the receiver for resubmittal or action the sender requires. It is an invaluable aid to speedy correspondence. Usually a two-part form, the original goes with the material being sent and the copy is placed in the job file.

## *Summary*

It is vital for the interior designer to be able to manage his or her time and the time of the firm's employees. It is also important to keep the projects under control. For the individual, that means developing the discipline and skills of time management. For the firm, it is necessary to develop a satisfactory means of scheduling the various projects that come into the office. Control books are used to control the project itself.

In this chapter we have looked at the basic concepts of time management, time records, different scheduling methods, and the values of the control book. All of these materials are presented to help the designer and the firm manage the projects.

## Chapter 20

# WORKING WITH TRADE SOURCES

*T*rade sources are the groups of manufacturers, suppliers, and tradespeople who provide the various goods and services a designer uses to complete a project. Designers work with many kinds of trade sources. The majority would be the manufacturers of different furniture and furnishings products. Others would be the suppliers and tradespeople who supply a custom product or install a product. The designer finds these trade sources in many locations.

Trade sources provide valuable information and assistance to the designer beyond the actual products they offer. It is essential for the designer to find the sources that complement his or her business ideals. In this section we will look at the different kinds of trade sources utilized by the interior designer.

## *Market Centers and Marts*

*Market centers* are concentrations of trade sources in a city. These market centers are generally open only to the trade, although some have policies that allow the public access. *Market* is a term that many interior designers use to mean they are going to visit one of the annual shows held at the marts. A *mart* is a building in which many firms are located; each firm has a separate showroom or shares showroom space. Here, manufacturers and suppliers lease showroom space to display their products. This allows the designer the opportunity to see firsthand samples of the products he or she is specifying. Designers often bring clients to the mart so that the client can see the items to be specified.

Until about fifteen years ago, marts were only located in the major urban areas of cities such as Chicago, New York, Los Angeles, and San Francisco. The Merchandise Mart in Chicago is still the largest single mart in the United States and holds the largest national contract market. Smaller regional contract markets are held in New York, Los Angeles, and San Francisco. More recently, regional marts have opened in various parts of the country. *Contract* magazine, in its December 1985 issue, lists forty-five regional marts.[1] These regional marts are, of course, much smaller than the large marts in Chicago, New York, Los Angeles, and San Francisco.

---

[1]Contract Furniture and Furnishings Mart Directory, *Contract*, Dec. 1985.

All marts have building access policies, and in many cases admittance to the building and its many showrooms is by building pass only. These passes are obtainable by trade members from the mart leasing agent or other mart officials. Showrooms will generally admit those without passes if they have proper credentials identifying them as members of the trade. Student members of ASID and IBD will be able to get into most of the showrooms by showing their student membership cards. Showrooms, however, have their own policies and some may not admit anyone unless he or she has an official building pass. It should be noted that admittance to a showroom does not automatically allow the trade member to purchase products from the manufacturer.

Merchandise, if priced in the showroom, is often tagged with suggested retail prices or price codes. This is done to protect the designer's profit policies as he or she shows clients the products specified for the project. Occasionally, showrooms have display sales where discontinued items or slightly damaged floor samples are sold to the trade at very good prices.

The larger marts have shows where manufacturers introduce their new products. Probably the largest furniture show is held at the Neocon Market in Chicago's Merchandise Mart. In recent years, more than 20,000 interior designers, architects, and related professionals travel to Chicago in June to see the new product introductions. Although contract furniture is highlighted, many residential products as well as floor coverings, wall coverings, lighting, and accessories are shown.

Other large furniture shows are held in other parts of the country. The largest include Designer's Saturday in New York City in October and West Week held in Los Angeles in March. Shows are also held in San Francisco; Dallas; Atlanta; High Point, North Carolina; and other cities throughout the year. Specialty shows are also held at these same marts either just prior to the major market shows or at other times of the year. Most of the smaller regional marts also have shows. These generally attract the local design community.

## *Sales Reps*

*Representatives,* or *reps,* are terms used to refer to the men and women who act as the informational source from the various manufacturers. Reps have authority to quote prices, give product information, make special product presentations, arrange for samples to be sent to the designer, provide the designer with information needed to write specifications, and distribute catalogs to designers and, in some cases, to the end-user.

Manufacturer's sales representatives may also have a role in generating sales independent of a designer or dealer. For products generally used in commercial design, reps are out making calls on potential clients. Leads are generally turned over to dealers or referred to designers. Sometimes, of course, the representatives sell directly to the client, bypassing the designer or vendor.

There are two kind of reps: independent representatives and factory representatives. Independent reps basically work for themselves or a sales representing group. Many handle several manufacturers' products. These products may be related (all are from lighting manufacturers) or, as is more often the case, a combination of furniture and other products. Factory reps work for one particular manufacturer as employees of the company. They represent only that manufacturer's products or possibly only a segment of the manufacturer's product line. Both kinds of representatives are extremely helpful to the interior designer, and most small firms would not survive without their valuable assistance.

# Small Local Showrooms

Although more and more of the larger urban areas have recently seen the emergence of centralized marts, many manufacturers have preferred to remain in free-standing trade showrooms. Most have similar policies for admittance, pricing, and purchasing as showrooms in the marts. These small local showrooms are usually restricted to fabrics, wall coverings, carpet, and flooring materials. However, there are some local showrooms that also display a limited amount of furniture and accessories.

# Specialty Shops

Another trade source for the designer is the specialty shop open to the public and the trade. These are, of course, retail stores selling all the various products an interior designer might use. They are generally not owned or franchised by any of the manufacturers whose products are displayed. Those that are generally serve as retail outlets for the general public of the manufacturer's products and act as open showrooms for the design community. Notable are paint and wallpaper specialists, some carpet and floor coverings stores, and many wall covering shops. These stores often give trade discounts to the interior designer. These trade discounts are reduced prices given to trade members so that designers can then resell the products to his or her clients. The reader may wish to refer back to Chapter 13 for more information on trade discounts.

# Subcontractors and Tradespeople

Subcontractors and tradespeople are individuals who provide goods and services to the design community—and sometimes the general public—such as drapery workrooms, carpet and floor-covering installers, painters, wallpaper hangers, and cabinetmakers, to name a few. Many, like carpet installers, provide only the labor to complete the product construction or installation. Others, such as cabinetmakers, provide materials and labor for the finished goods.

It is important to work with quality craftspeople and subcontractors. New subcontractors, craftspeople, and tradespeople should be investigated by the designer. This investigation should include obtaining references from his or her past clients and inspecting his or her work by visiting previous job sites.

It is also important, when hiring subcontractors such as painters and carpet installers, to determine whether these individuals are licensed contractors. Remember from our earlier discussion that hiring unlicensed contractors in states that require licensing can leave the designer open to law suits and possibly criminal complaints.

# Manufacturer's Dealers and Vendors

Manufacturer's dealers are usually retail furniture stores—as opposed to the specialty shops—that have made special arrangements with one or more manufacturers of furniture. These dealers feature those products in their showroom and frequently stock inventory of considerable size. Many retail furniture showrooms that are manufacturers' dealers also have interior designers available to assist clients. In some cases, these designers compete directly with independent interior designers for design business.

*Vendor* is a term that encompasses all the listed sources and even the interior designer. A vendor is someone who sells products or services either to the end-user or some middle person like the designer. Commercial clients are used to working with vendors, whom they classify as anyone from whom they purchase any product or service. Residential clients, on the other hand, are used to working with salespeople or designers and may not be familiar with the term *vendor.*

## Summary

The sources the design firm uses or maintains information about are many and varied. Those chosen regularly by the design firm should complement the firm's work. Trips to market shows give designers a very good opportunity to review sources and talk to sales representatives or factory salespeople.

Because of the wealth of products available to designers, it is important for them to review catalogs and samples carefully and retain only those that fit into the firm's type of business. It is expensive and space-wasting to hold onto catalogs and samples the firm does not use.

When considering a new product or trade source, the design firm should check the source carefully. Ask for references; look at samples or products before buying for showroom stock or for a client. Find out where in the firm's town the product or service has already been used and investigate installation, product and service quality, and customer satisfaction.

The discussion of trade sources utilized by the interior designer in this chapter provides a brief reference for where to find the products and services the designer will use for his or her clients. The professional must become familiar with the sources available in the geographic areas in which he or she plans to conduct business. The student should investigate the many manufacturers of furniture and furnishings by visiting one of the market shows, looking at catalogs in the school's library, or by visiting local design offices.

Chapter 21

# CONTRACT DOCUMENTS AND SPECIFICATIONS

*T*he products specified for a small project, whether residential or commercial, are usually prepared as a simple "equipment list" of what the client is requested to purchase. But when the amount of the goods to be purchased is large or when construction of interior spaces is part of the project, then a simple list is not sufficient. Documents in both graphic and written form must be prepared in order for more than one contractor or vendor to provide a price to the client.

This chapter deals with the contract documents and specifications used when it is necessary for the client to obtain competitive bids—or prices—for the completion of an interiors project. Since it is not the purpose of this book to discuss the technical design aspects of the profession but rather the business aspects of the profession, this chapter will not describe how to prepare working drawings. The reader should refer to references on architectural drafting for this kind of information. This chapter discusses construction documents, particularly the kinds of written specifications and documents required for an interior design project. It concludes with a brief discussion of the bidding process.

## *Construction Documents*

*Construction documents* are "a set of legal contract documents of drawings and specifications that graphically and verbally describe what is required for a specific construction project."[1] A complete set of construction documents would include architectural drawings, schedules, and specifications.

The drawings portion of construction documents typically consists of all plans, elevations, and details required for building the structure or the interior. For an interior design project, this might include dimensioned partition drawings, section drawings, electrical/telephone location plans, reflected ceiling plans, plumbing plans, HVAC (heating, ventilation, and air-conditioning) plans, other mechanical plans (such as for sprinklers in a commercial building), interior construction elevations, and construction details. Preparation of additional drawings would be by whomever designed the exterior structure.

---

[1]Wakita, Osamu A. and Linde, Richard M. *The Professional Practice of Architectural Detailing*, John Wiley & Sons, Inc., 1984, p. 549. Copyright by John Wiley & Sons, Inc.

Many interior and architectural firms also include equipment plans or furniture plans in the working drawings. Equipment plans show the location of and identify by code the movable equipment in the project. By movable equipment we mean furniture and other equipment, such as refrigerators, that can be easily moved and are not part of the structure. Movable equipment is rarely bid with the construction of the walls. In most projects, these drawings are provided to the general contractor for information only. They are, however, necessary for the furniture bid.

## CONSTRUCTION DRAWINGS

We will only describe how the equipment or furniture plan should be prepared as part of the construction documents and how this plan relates to written specifications.

The equipment plans for bidding purposes must be very clear and understandable. When projects are to be bid, it is a helpful practice for interior designers to prepare a mylar or sepia intermediate of the furniture floor plan and add code information to the intermediate. Codes may be simple numbers or letters accompanied by a furniture schedule describing these items (see Figure 21-1) or more complicated multinumber codes which indicate generic types of furniture and furnishings—not specific product information. These codes then need to be further explained in the specifications. In Figure 21-2, the letter code refers to the kind of furniture piece (*CO* for chair, *SO* for sofa, *TA* for table, and so on); the next one-to-four numbers reference the item to the specification. The numbers after the slash (/) identify the location of the furniture item with the first number indicating the floor of the building and the last two to three numbers identifying the room number.

The exact format and coordination between plans and specifications must be clear enough for the vendor to know what he or she is bidding on and easy enough for the design firm to produce and easily make required changes to the plans. However, formats should be individualized by the design firm.

Trade names and product numbers should not be used on the equipment plans since errors can occur. It is easy to transpose numbers, and if the designer must write product names and numbers many times, it would be easy to make this kind of error resulting in an incorrect bid. Another example would occur when substitutions have to be made. If it becomes necessary to change or substitute a different

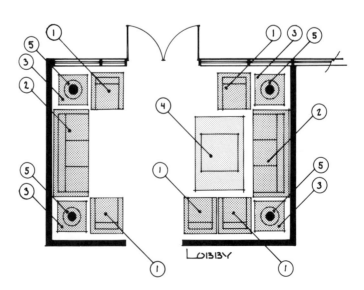

**FIGURE 21-1**
**Simple furniture schedule as used in construction documents.** *(Drawing: Clayton E. Peterson)*

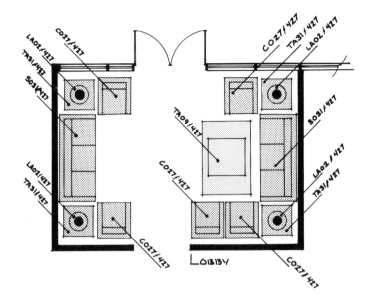

**FIGURE 21-2**
**Coded furniture schedule.**
*(Drawing: Clayton E. Peterson)*

product, forgetting to make the changes in product numbers on the plans can cause incorrect bidding or the wrong product being ordered. Trade names and product numbers, if used, should be limited to the written specifications. All information in schedules or code keys should be generic descriptions.

Although it is better to use generic names for furniture, furnishings, and room names, generic descriptions can lead to misinterpretations if the terms used are not clarified. For example, *Chair* can mean guest chair, arm chair, posture chair, club chair, dining chair, stool, occasional chair, and executive chair. *Table* can mean dining table, coffee table, end table, cocktail table, occasional table, conference table, table desk, and parson's table. And *Rest Room* can mean ladies' room, men's room, powder room, lavatory, bathroom, and lounge.

Many other examples of generic furniture, furnishings, and rooms terminology can be found. Although it is important to use generic terms, it is equally important for terms to be consistent, clear, and defined within the specifications. A key needs to be placed either in the specifications or on one of the sheets of equipment plans to aid in defining all generic terms.

## SCHEDULES

*Schedules* are used to clarify sizes, location finishes, and other information related to certain nonconstruction parts of an interior or structure. Schedules are commonly prepared for doors, windows, and interior room finishes. Interior room finish schedules include information for walls, floor treatments, and ceiling heights and treatments. Schedules for other specific items such as lighting fixtures and furniture are also used by designers.

Most schedules are prepared in tabular form. The format of these schedules varies greatly from office to office. A design firm that has not used schedules before may wish to review examples in architectural drafting texts and then adopt or develop a format that works for the firm.

For the same reasons given for equipment plans, the information provided in the schedules should be generic. Trade or manufacturers' names are to be supplied in the written specifications. For interior design projects that are not very large or complicated, some designers use a materials key with the finished schedule. This materials key does name manufacturers. If it is used, it should be duplicated in the specifications. It would not be appropriate to use a materials key if a performance or descriptive specification is used.

When the project includes unusual designs for doors, windows, or wall treatments, it is necessary to use a graphic schedule or elevation. This graphic schedule will help to clarify those items that do not easily fit into the regular tabular schedules.

## SPECIFICATIONS

The *specifications* portion of the construction documents is the written instructions to the general contractors and vendors as to the materials and methods of construction of the structure or interior and the furniture and other movable equipment that are to be bid on. Specifications are written in technical terms and provide information related to such things as responsibilities of bidders, descriptions of the materials, qualities and workmanship, and installation requirements. It is not uncommon for some designers to also provide quantities of the goods required in the written specifications. Although this is very helpful to the vendors' bidding, it is better and more common to require vendors to be responsible for the quantities.

# *General Conditions* _____

Bid documents for projects involving any kind of construction will include a section of general conditions. These general conditions set forth the various procedures, rights, and duties of each party to the contract. A standardized set of general conditions used by many designers and private business owners is the AIA document A201.[2] It is commonly used since it has stood the test of time and legal interpretation. However, many designers and clients find that the document does not meet their individual needs, so they modify the conditions of the document for their situation. ASID and IBD recommend either using the AIA document or having preprinted forms available that closely follow that document. Figure 21-3 shows but one page of the multipage AIA document.

Items covered in the AIA document include definitions of the contract document, the names of the architect (designer to be substituted) and owner, ownership of documents, and the kinds of activities for which the designer is responsible, the kinds of activities for which the owner is responsible, definitions and responsibilities of contractors and subcontractors, clauses concerning payments, time period of project, claims, insurance, change orders, and other definitions or statements related to the contractual relationship of the parties.

For bids that concern only furniture, AIA document A271, "General Conditions of the Contract for Furniture, Furnishings, and Equipment," can be used. These general conditions are similar in scope to the A201 document but are related to interior furniture and furnishings rather than construction.

Since both of these forms are lengthy legal forms of a generalized nature, it is necessary for the designer to prepare supplemental conditions for the projects. The supplemental conditions spell out any conditions that are more related to the specific project. A supplemental condition that must be stated if the designer uses either of these forms is that *designer* or *interior designer* be substituted wherever the word *architect* is used. The AIA also has a document A571, "Guide for Interiors

---

[2]Meier 1978, 18.

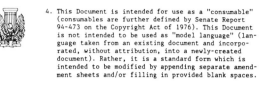
## GENERAL CONDITIONS OF THE CONTRACT FOR CONSTRUCTION

### ARTICLE 1
### GENERAL PROVISIONS

#### 1.1 BASIC DEFINITIONS

#### 1.1.1 THE CONTRACT DOCUMENTS

The Contract Documents consist of the Agreement between Owner and Contractor (hereinafter the Agreement), Conditions of the Contract (General, Supplementary and other Conditions), Drawings, Specifications, addenda issued prior to execution of the Contract, other documents listed in the Agreement and Modifications issued after execution of the Contract. A Modification is (1) a written amendment to the Contract signed by both parties, (2) a Change Order, (3) a Construction Change Directive or (4) a written order for a minor change in the Work issued by the Architect. Unless specifically enumerated in the Agreement, the Contract Documents do not include other documents such as bidding requirements (advertisement or invitation to bid, Instructions to Bidders, sample forms, the Contractor's bid or portions of addenda relating to bidding requirements).

#### 1.1.2 THE CONTRACT

The Contract Documents form the Contract for Construction. The Contract represents the entire and integrated agreement between the parties hereto and supersedes prior negotiations, representations or agreements, either written or oral. The Contract may be amended or modified only by a Modification. The Contract Documents shall not be construed to create a contractual relationship of any kind (1) between the Architect and Contractor, (2) between the Owner and a Subcontractor or Subsubcontractor or (3) between any persons or entities other than the Owner and Contractor. The Architect shall, however, be entitled to performance and enforcement of obligations under the Contract intended to facilitate performance of the Architect's duties.

#### 1.1.3 THE WORK

The term "Work" means the construction and services required by the Contract Documents, whether completed or partially completed, and includes all other labor, materials, equipment and services provided or to be provided by the Contractor to fulfill the Contractor's obligations. The Work may constitute the whole or a part of the Project.

#### 1.1.4 THE PROJECT

The Project is the total construction of which the Work performed under the Contract Documents may be the whole or a part and which may include construction by the Owner or by separate contractors.

#### 1.1.5 THE DRAWINGS

The Drawings are the graphic and pictorial portions of the Contract Documents, wherever located and whenever issued, showing the design, location and dimensions of the Work, generally including plans, elevations, sections, details, schedules and diagrams.

#### 1.1.6 THE SPECIFICATIONS

The Specifications are that portion of the Contract Documents consisting of the written requirements for materials, equipment, construction systems, standards and workmanship for the Work, and performance of related services.

#### 1.1.7 THE PROJECT MANUAL

The Project Manual is the volume usually assembled for the Work which may include the bidding requirements, sample forms, Conditions of the Contract and Specifications.

#### 1.2 EXECUTION, CORRELATION AND INTENT

**1.2.1** The Contract Documents shall be signed by the Owner and Contractor as provided in the Agreement. If either the Owner or Contractor or both do not sign all the Contract Documents, the Architect shall identify such unsigned Documents upon request.

**1.2.2** Execution of the Contract by the Contractor is a representation that the Contractor has visited the site, become familiar with local conditions under which the Work is to be performed and correlated personal observations with requirements of the Contract Documents.

**1.2.3** The intent of the Contract Documents is to include all items necessary for the proper execution and completion of the Work by the Contractor. The Contract Documents are complementary, and what is required by one shall be as binding as if required by all; performance by the Contractor shall be required only to the extent consistent with the Contract Documents and reasonably inferable from them as being necessary to produce the intended results.

**1.2.4** Organization of the Specifications into divisions, sections and articles, and arrangement of Drawings shall not control the Contractor in dividing the Work among Subcontractors or in establishing the extent of Work to be performed by any trade.

**1.2.5** Unless otherwise stated in the Contract Documents, words which have well-known technical or construction industry meanings are used in the Contract Documents in accordance with such recognized meanings.

#### 1.3 OWNERSHIP AND USE OF ARCHITECT'S DRAWINGS, SPECIFICATIONS AND OTHER DOCUMENTS

**1.3.1** The Drawings, Specifications and other documents prepared by the Architect are instruments of the Architect's service through which the Work to be executed by the Contractor is described. The Contractor may retain one contract record set. Neither the Contractor nor any Subcontractor, Subsubcontractor or material or equipment supplier shall own or claim a copyright in the Drawings, Specifications and other documents prepared by the Architect, and unless otherwise indicated the Architect shall be deemed the author of them and will retain all common law, statutory and other reserved rights, in addition to the copyright. All copies of them, except the Contractor's record set, shall be returned or suitably accounted for to the Architect, on request, upon completion of the Work. The Drawings, Specifications and other documents prepared by the Architect, and copies thereof furnished to the Contractor, are for use solely with respect to this Project. They are not to be used by the Contractor or any Subcontractor, Subsubcontractor or material or equipment supplier on other projects or for additions to this Project outside the scope of the

**FIGURE 21-3**
**A page from "General Conditions of the Contract for Construction" (AIA document A201).**
*(Reproduced with permission, American Institute of Architects)*

Supplementary Conditions," available to help the designer prepare the supplemental conditions for the A271 document.

These documents have also been adopted by the ASID and IBD. Since the copyright of these documents belongs to the AIA, it is necessary for the designer to obtain permission from the AIA to make copies or to modify the documents in any way. Should the designer or specifier wish to prepare his or her own set of general conditions, these should be reviewed by the design firm's attorney before being submitted to the client.

# Specifications

Specifications, you will recall, are the written instructions as to what is to be provided by the contractor. They are prepared in a technical fashion and provide information as to what goods or materials are required and workmanship expected. Since it is easier for people to interpret the written word than drawings when there are discrepancies between the two, the courts often base judgments on the specifications. It is therefore important for the designer to prepare the specifications clearly—without any ambiguity, errors, or omissions.

The specifications should complement the drawings, not duplicate them. Specifications should primarily describe the type and quality of materials and goods, quality of workmanship, method of construction and installation, applicable testing methods, provisions for alternates, and requirements for warranties. Drawings should show locations; dimensions; quantities; sizes; generic identification of materials; and interrelationships of space, materials, and equipment. There are four customary kinds of formal specifications: proprietary, descriptive, performance, and reference.

**FIGURE 21-4**
**Proprietary specification.**
*(Reproduced with permission, Knoll International)*

| Reception Area | | | | |
|------|----------|-------------|------|-------|
| *Item* | *Quantity* | *Description* | *Unit* | *Total* |
| 1 | 4 | Knoll 50-125 Wassily Lounge Chair Leather: Black | | |
| 2 | 1 | Knoll 705-1 Mercer Coffee Table Finish: Black Onyx | | |

## PROPRIETARY SPECIFICATION

A *proprietary specification* names the products and materials by manufacturer's name, model number, or part number. With the proprietary specification there is no doubt on what the designer and client wish to have bids (see Figure 21-4). If the specifications allow for no substitutions or do not have an "or equal" clause, then the proprietary bid might be called a *base bid*. "The term base bid means that all people who wish to provide materials for the project must base their bid on the product named in the specification."[3]

The advantages of the proprietary specification are that

1. It is the easiest to write. In many cases, the designer only needs to provide the basic descriptive information of manufacturer, product number, and fin-

---

[3]Reznikoff, S. C., *Specifications for Commercial Interiors*, p. 231. Copyright © 1979 Whitney Library of Design, an imprint of Watson-Guptill Publications. Used by permission of publisher.

ishes/fabrics to complete the specifications. When more detail is needed, manufacturers often provide information to the designer that can be reproduced into the specifications.

2. It is easier to prepare drawings. With known product sizes, drawings are more accurate. The designer does not have to allow in the drawings for possible larger or smaller sizes of product that might be bid.

3. The designer has maximum product control over the project. The carefully worked out design concept will be realized since the products used to develop the design concept will be the ones purchased.

4. The time element from invitation announcement to order entry is faster since alternates do not have to be evaluated by the client. Since everyone is bidding on the exact same products, the competitive bid concept is more fully realized.

There are some disadvantages, however. First, proprietary specification can limit competition if there are not sufficient numbers of bidders that can provide the products. When there are not sufficient numbers of bidders and the proprietary method is used, it is necessary to have an "or equal" clause in the specifications.

The *"or equal"* clause, commonly found in proprietary specifications, allows bidders to substitute what they believe to be products of equal quality to that which was specified. More time must be taken in the evaluation process to determine if equal goods are bid. Design control can be lost as the client may choose products that are similar in appearance but lower in price than the original specification. What is equal in this situation is open to subjective judgment—on the part of the client, the designer, and the bidders.

To protect all the parties concerned when having to deal with an "or equal" clause, definitions of what procedures will be followed concerning the submittal of alternates must be included in the specifications. A common practice recommended by the Construction Specifications Institute is that requests related to substitutions be submitted prior to the close of bid. These requests might include detailed descriptions of the substituted product. In some cases, clients ask that a sample product be submitted prior to close of bid for evaluation.

## DESCRIPTIVE SPECIFICATION

*Descriptive specification* does not use a manufacturer's or trade name for the goods being specified. Rather, it describes, often in elaborate detail, the materials, workmanship, fabrication methods, and installation of the required goods.

There are two advantages of the descriptive specification. First, it allows the designer to prescribe exactly what he or she wishes to specify for the project. When there are many similar products that have subtle differences, such as with floor coverings, a descriptive specification helps to ensure that what is bid is actually equal to what was specified—even if the goods come from different manufacturers. There are also situations when the client wants a certain product for the job, but may have a difficult time obtaining sufficient numbers of competitive bids on that product when using a proprietary specification. A descriptive specification helps to narrow the "or equal" alternates so that the client can get what he or she wants.

A second advantage is that the descriptive specification allows for some performance criteria to be used in the situations for which a complete performance specification would not be appropriate. With floor coverings, many manufacturers have carpets that can meet the simple descriptive specification of such things as fiber, pitch, stitches per inch, and pile height. This may not be enough to be sure that the carpet or carpet quality that is required of the project is bid. Performance criteria related to such factors as static electricity, delamination, and crocking can be included in the specification for these kinds of goods. Other goods, such as furniture, which may not have such stringent requirements, can be written as descriptive specifications (see Figure 21-5).

There are a number of disadvantages to the descriptive specification. First, it requires time to produce and it is also quite lengthy. It also requires more precise description of the products. The specification of an open office system work surface would have to read something like, "a cantilevered hanging work surface, 48 inches wide by 23¾ inches deep by one-inch-thick top with a total height of 8¾ inches. The finished top surface shall be white oak plastic laminate and the edge shall be dark charcoal gray rubber T-molding." The same description in the proprietary specification would read, "Herman Miller, A0 556 FF OLDT DT."

A third disadvantage is that the volume of information needed to prepare a descriptive specification can lead to errors and loopholes allowing for the bidding of products other than what was intended. In the previous example, if the designer did not write in "white oak plastic laminate" but only wrote "plastic laminate" the client would not be getting what was desired—the light oak finish—but would probably get a plain- or neutral-colored finish.

Finally, the descriptive specification, unless written very carefully, can result in a loss of the product and design concept control by the designer. As the example shows, an omission in the specification can result in the wrong finish being specified for the job. It would be within the right of the bidder to ask for additional monies to change the product finish to the intended light oak. The omission and resulting cost to the client could also lead to the client's right to sue the designer.

---

**FIGURE 21-5**
Descriptive specification for open office systems work surfaces.

A. General
    1. Systems products shall have work surface tops and storage units with equivalent hardware to suspend units from architectural walls or freestanding panels. Hanging components shall be removable by hand or with the use of a minimal of tools without disturbing adjacent components.
    2. Vertical support elements (VSE 1–10) shall support hanging components on one-inch intervals and shall easily allow for vertical height adjustments.

B. Work Surface Tops
    1. Work surface tops shall be manufactured of warp-resistant materials and will have radius corners and edges on all sides but the side that shall meet the wall or vertical support element(s).
    2. Work surface tops shall be capable of having various undercounter drawers or storage units suspended below, installed with a minimal use of tools.
    3. Work surface tops shall be finished with high-pressure laminates that are scratch and heat resistant (up to 250°) in a variety of colors, and top shall have a nominal dimension (without support member) of one inch.
    4. Work surface tops shall be available in the following nominal sizes:
        WST-1:   30″ wide by 24″ deep
        WST-2:   36″ wide by 24″ deep
        WST-3:   48″ wide by 24″ deep
        WST-4:   60″ wide by 24″ deep
        WST-5:   72″ wide by 24″ deep
        WST-6:   30″ wide by 30″ deep
        WST-7:   36″ wide by 30″ deep
        WST-8:   48″ wide by 30″ deep
        WST-9:   60″ wide by 30″ deep
        WST-10: 72″ wide by 30″ deep

## PERFORMANCE SPECIFICATION

Another specification, the *performance specification,* is written without trade names. The performance specification establishes the product requirements based on exacting performance criteria. Any product that meets the performance criteria can qualify for use. The performance of the goods is based on the end product of the goods, and thus performance criteria are based on the accomplishment of that end result. For example, a partial performance specification for a divider panel is shown in Figure 21-6.

Performance specifications are based on qualitative or measurable statements. It is common that the specifications require certain tests and methods of testing and that bidders submit test data with their bids. This information is available from the manufacturers both for the use of the designer to write the specification and for the bidders to submit the data to the client.

When data from the manufacturer is not available or appears inconclusive, it may be necessary for the bidder to supply a sample of the product for testing. This is often the case with various textiles. For example, should the designer wish to use a carpet material on the wall, it would be necessary for the designer to specify some kind of performance criteria for that textile in this situation and the manufacturer to either supply data for this use or supply a sample that could be tested.

Advantages are the same as for the descriptive specification: full control when it is not appropriate to use proprietary specifications. Disadvantages are also the same: extra preparation and evaluation time, possible errors, and possible loss of design concept and product control.

---

Performance Specification
Space Dividers

I. General
  A. Two basic types of panels will be required: hard surface and acoustical.
  B. All panels shall meet ASTM E-84 Steiner Tunnel Test.
    1. Maximum flame spread range of 0–25.
    2. Maximum smoke development below 450.
  C. All panels shall have support slots that allow component adjustability on one-inch (1") increments.
  D. All panel connections shall be made with a minimum of hardware and special tools.

II. Acoustical
  A. Shall have a minimum NRC of .85 based on ASTM C-423-66.
  B. Shall have a minimum STC of 13 based on ASTM E-290-81.
  C. Above tests shall be based on the entire panel being tested. Both sides of the panel must be tested.
  D. Fabric covering panel must meet ASTM E-84 Tunnel Test.
    1. Maximum flame spread range of 0–25.
    2. Maximum smoke development below 450.

III. Hard Surface
  A. Panel frames shall be metal with factory-applied baked-on enamel.
  B. Panel face shall be metal with factory-applied baked-on enamel.
  C. Must meet ASTM E-84 Tunnel Test.
    1. Maximum flame spread range of 0–25.
    2. Maximum smoke development below 450.

**FIGURE 21-6**
**Partial performance specification for a divider panel.**

## REFERENCE SPECIFICATION

A *reference specification* utilizes an established standard, such as the standards of the American Society for Testing and Materials (ASTM), rather than writing detailed descriptions or performance criteria for certain products. These established standards generally provide minimal acceptable standards of performance of various kinds of products.

The designer must check these standards to be sure that these minimums are satisfactory for the needs of the project. If the standard is too low, the reference specification cannot be used. It is also necessary for the designer to be fully familiar with the standards since the standards sometimes provide options of materials or workmanship. The designer must be sure he or she is specifying which standard or level of standard is required of the job. If this is not done, the bidder then has the option of using a lower standard than what the designer may have intended.

Although reference specifications are more widely used in construction, they may be utilized by the interior designer for such things as wall and floor products and installation.

The advantages are that there is a great time saving because only the standard must be stated; there is no need for writing a long descriptive or performance specification. Reference specifications can also be used to help explain a complex performance or descriptive specification for specialized products or installations.

The disadvantage is that, if the designer is not fully aware of the complete, up-to-date standard, the designer may allow for products and workmanship that do not meet the desired requirements.

## OPEN AND CLOSED BIDS

When a specification is written so that no other product can be substituted, it is commonly called a *closed bid*. The only closed bid discussed here is the proprietary specification base bid that allows no substitutions. All the other kinds of bids discussed in this section, including the proprietary specification that allows substitutions, are sometimes called *open bids* because they allow the consideration of a multiple number of products for the item being bid.

## ADDENDA

After the contract documents are in the hands of the contractors and vendors, changes or corrections can only be made by the use of addenda. *Addenda* are additions to the contract documents. Each addendum must be in writing and sent to all bidders. Corrections or clarifications should not be made or accepted orally.

According to Rosen, addenda are used to provide any of the following kinds of information to bidders:

1. Correct errors and omissions.
2. Clarify ambiguities.
3. Add to or reduce the scope of the work.
4. Provide additional information that can affect the bid prices.
5. Change the time and place for receipt of bids.
6. Change the quality of the work.
7. Issue additional names of qualified "or equal" products.[4]

---

[4]Rosen, Harold J., *Construction Specifications Writing*, 2d ed., John Wiley & Sons, Inc., 1981, p. 177. Copyright by John Wiley & Sons, Inc.

These clarifications may result from something that the client or designer sees in the documents or from a question from one or more of the bidders. All addenda should be prepared as quickly and as clearly as possible. They should come from the person responsible for creating the documents. If an allied professional or other design team member finds a questionable item, it should be called to the attention of the specification writer, and that person should prepare and send the addendum. When addenda are mailed to bidders, there must be sufficient time for them to react to the addenda prior to the close of bid. Recall that notification begins upon receipt of the notification, not at the time of mailing.

## The Bid Process

*Competitive bidding* is a process whereby the client has the opportunity to obtain comparative prices from a number of contractors and/or vendors for the construction or supply of the project. Competitive bids are almost always required by law for projects involving federal, state, and local agencies as well as public businesses like utilities. Most private businesses also require competitive bids on construction projects and large furniture or equipment orders.

Governmental agencies often use forms called "requests for proposals" or "request for bid or quote." These forms follow different procedures and ask for information in different ways than those discussed in this chapter. Since bidding on government projects can be rather intricate, the reader is referred to Stasiowski or Jones for some introductory information on selling and bidding to governmental agencies. This chapter deals only in a general nature with the bidding process for governmental agencies.

The idea of the bid process is that it allows the client to purchase the products and services of the project at as low a price as possible while maintaining the quality and intentions of the original design concept. This assumption is basically valid as long as the goods or services being bid are either the same or can objectively be compared as equal. That, however, is not always possible. If a client is bidding an open office systems project, it must be possible for the client to objectively evaluate the differences—subtle or otherwise—in the various products bid in order to purchase the goods at the lowest price while maintaining the quality and/or design intentions of the specifications. When there are sufficient bidders of a like product, then competitive bids based on the original idea are possible. When a project is designed and/or specified in such a way that few bidders can supply the same product at a fair price, then the bid process is suspect.

Clients ready to purchase large quantities of product and required to use the bid process often are under pressure to accept the lowest bid. For the designer, this can mean the loss of the original design concept of the project since a different product that does not have the same aesthetic appearance as the original design might be purchased. For the client, it can mean ownership of product that does not meet the performance criteria of the original design.

Competitive bidding is also more expensive than other purchasing methods. There is a greater amount of preparation time of complicated contract documents and specifications for the goods and services. Also, additional documentation related to the bid procedure, general conditions for performance of the bid contract, and other conditions related to the bid and subsequent work must be prepared. When similar but unequal products are bid or products are bid based on performance, the client and designer will be involved in time-consuming evaluations either before bid submittal or before the awarding of contracts. Additionally, there is a potential for claims and suits related to the bid award if one or more bidders feel the award was improper.

Yet, the bid process is likely to continue for most major commercial and governmental projects. The designer who will be involved in these kinds of projects will have to deal with the bid situation.

## INVITATION TO BID

The first step in the bid process is to prepare and conduct an invitation to bidders. Government and public agencies will most likely advertise a bid in newspapers. Some organizations, through careful legal preparation, may have an acceptable "bid list" of potential designers and vendors who will receive the notifications. Private businesses rarely advertise a bid. They most commonly contact several designers or vendors concerning a project or utilize a bid list.

The advantage of a bid list system is that bidders are prequalified by the client so that those bidders who have experience with the particular kind of project, proven personnel, capital to procure the goods, and so on, are the only designers or vendors with whom the client must deal. This also allows the client to maintain a reasonable number of bids rather than a very large number requiring careful evaluation to eliminate unqualified bidders.

The disadvantages are that too few bidders will be used with the potential of a higher price. There is also the probability that less experienced, yet qualified designers and vendors are prohibited from entering the market. Yet, if it is possible to get a sufficient (by the client's estimation) number of qualified bidders through a prequalification bid list system, it is a satisfactory and legal method of obtaining competitive bids.

The invitation to bid provides a summary of the project, the bid process, and other brief pertinent procedures for the project. It informs potential bidders of the project, its scope, and where to obtain further information. The invitation should also state whether a security bond is required, how much it will be, and how long it will be held. The size or length of time the bond will be held may discharge some designers and vendors from bidding.

## INSTRUCTIONS TO BIDDERS

The *instructions to bidders* informs bidders how to prepare bids for submittal so that all submittals are in the same form. This helps to make the various bids easily comparable. Since some designers and vendors offer substitutions to what was specified or do not bid on portions of the project, called exclusions, it is not always easy to start with comparable bids anyway.

Information in the instructions should only relate how to prepare and submit the bids. The following represents what is commonly in the instructions: It will inform the bidders what form and format to use; how, where, and when bids are due; statements related to site visitations and familiarization responsibilities; statements related to how interpretation of discrepancies in the documents will be resolved; how bids can be withdrawn; the procedure for how the award of the bid will be made; conditions for which bids can be rejected; and any other pertinent instructions that may be required by the client (see Figure 21-7).

Important parts of the instructions are the portions of the bid documents usually referred to as the "drawings and specifications." These consist of working drawings and/or equipment plans and the written specifications related to products, materials, and construction methods. The instructions to bidders should only mention

## THE AMERICAN INSTITUTE OF ARCHITECTS

*AIA Document A771*

# Instructions to Interiors Bidders

## 1980 EDITION

Intended for use with the 1977 Edition of AIA Document A271, General Conditions of the Contract for Furniture, Furnishings and Equipment.

SAMPLE

### TABLE OF ARTICLES

1. DEFINITIONS

2. BIDDER'S REPRESENTATIONS

3. BIDDING DOCUMENTS

4. BIDDING PROCEDURES

5. CONSIDERATION OF BIDS

6. POST-BID INFORMATION

7. PERFORMANCE BOND AND LABOR AND MATERIAL PAYMENT BOND

8. FORM OF AGREEMENT BETWEEN OWNER AND CONTRACTOR

9. SUPPLEMENTARY INSTRUCTIONS

A771—1980   1

**FIGURE 21-7**
**"Instructions to Bidders"** (AIA document A771). *(Reproduced with permission, American Institute of Architects)*

## INSTRUCTIONS TO INTERIORS BIDDERS

### ARTICLE 1
### DEFINITIONS

**1.1** Bidding Documents include the Advertisement or Invitation to Bid, Instructions to Interiors Bidders, the bid forms, other sample bidding and contract forms, and the proposed Contract Documents including any Addenda issued prior to receipt of Bids. The Contract Documents proposed for the Work consist of the Owner-Contractor Agreement, the Conditions of the Contract (General, Supplementary and other Conditions), the Drawings, the Schedules and Specifications, all Addenda issued prior to, and all Modifications issued after, execution of the Contract.

**1.2** All definitions set forth in the General Conditions of the Contract for Furniture, Furnishings and Equipment, AIA Document A271, or in the other Contract Documents are applicable to the Bidding Documents.

**1.3** Addenda are written or graphic instruments issued by the Architect prior to the execution of the Contract which modify or interpret the Bidding Documents by additions, deletions, clarifications or corrections.

**1.4** A Bid is a complete and properly signed proposal to do the Work or designated portion thereof for the sums stipulated therein, submitted in accordance with the Bidding Documents.

**1.5** The Base Bid is the sum stated in the Bid for which the Bidder offers to perform the Work described in the Bidding Documents and to which Work may be added or deleted for sums stated in Alternate Bids.

**1.6** An Alternate Bid (or Alternate) is an amount stated in the Bid to be added to or deducted from the amount of the Base Bid if the corresponding change in the Work, as described in the Bidding Documents, is accepted.

**1.7** A Unit Price is an amount stated in the Bid as a price per unit of measurement for materials or services as described in the Bidding Documents or in the proposed Contract Documents.

**1.8** A Bidder is a person or entity who submits a Bid.

**1.9** A Sub-bidder is a person or entity who submits a bid to a Bidder for materials or labor for a portion of the Work.

### ARTICLE 2
### BIDDER'S REPRESENTATIONS

**2.1** Each Bidder by making a Bid represents that:

**2.1.1** The Bidder has read and understands the Bidding Documents and the Bid is made in accordance therewith.

**2.1.2** The Bidder has visited the Project premises, or, if not yet constructed, has reviewed the documents pertaining thereto, has become familiar with the local conditions under which the Work is to be performed, and has correlated personal observations with the requirements of the proposed Contract Documents.

**2.1.3** The Bid is based upon the materials, systems and equipment required by the Bidding Documents, without exception.

### ARTICLE 3
### BIDDING DOCUMENTS

**3.1** COPIES

**3.1.1** Bidders may obtain complete sets of the Bidding Documents from the issuing office designated in the Advertisement or Invitation to Bid in the number and for the deposit sum, if any, stated therein. The deposit will be refunded to Bidders who submit a bona fide Bid and return the Bidding Documents in good condition within ten days after receipt of Bids. The cost of replacing any missing or damaged documents will be deducted from the deposit. A Bidder receiving a Contract award may retain the Bidding Documents and the deposit will be refunded.

**3.1.2** Bidding Documents will not be issued directly to Sub-bidders or others unless specifically offered in the Advertisement or Invitation to Bid.

**3.1.3** Bidders shall use complete sets of Bidding Documents in preparing Bids; neither the Owner nor the Architect assume any responsibility for errors or misinterpretations resulting from the use of incomplete sets of Bidding Documents.

**3.1.4** The Owner, or the Architect, in making copies of the Bidding Documents available on the above terms does so only for the purpose of obtaining Bids on the Work and does not confer a license or grant for any other use.

**3.2** INTERPRETATION OR CORRECTION OF BIDDING DOCUMENTS

**3.2.1** Bidders and Sub-bidders shall promptly notify the Architect of any ambiguity, inconsistency or error which they may discover upon examination of the Bidding Documents or the Project premises and local conditions.

**3.2.2** Bidders and Sub-bidders requiring clarification or interpretation of the Bidding Documents shall make a written request which shall reach the Architect at least seven days prior to the date for receipt of Bids.

**3.2.3** Any interpretation, correction or change of the Bidding Documents will be made by Addendum. Interpretations, corrections or changes of the Bidding Documents made in any other manner will not be binding, and Bidders shall not rely upon such interpretations, corrections or changes.

**3.3** SUBSTITUTIONS

**3.3.1** The materials, products and equipment described in the Bidding Documents establish a standard of required function, dimension, appearance and quality to be met by any proposed substitution.

**3.3.2** No substitution will be considered prior to receipt of Bids unless written request for approval has been received by the Architect at least ten days prior to the date for receipt of Bids. Each such request shall include the name of the material or equipment for which it is to be substituted, including drawings, cuts, performance and test data, and any other information necessary for an evaluation. A statement setting forth any change in materials, equipment or other Work that incorporation of the substitute would require shall be included. The burden of

AIA DOCUMENT A771 • INSTRUCTIONS TO INTERIORS BIDDERS • MAY 1980 EDITION • AIA® • ©1980
THE AMERICAN INSTITUTE OF ARCHITECTS, 1735 NEW YORK AVENUE, N.W., WASHINGTON, D.C. 20006

**FIGURE 21-7**
"Instructions to Bidders" (AIA document A771). *(Continued)*

proof of the merit of the proposed substitute is upon the proposer. The Architect's decision of approval or disapproval of a proposed substitution shall be final.

**3.3.3** If the Architect approves any proposed substitution prior to receipt of Bids, such approval will be set forth in an Addendum. Bidders shall not rely upon approvals made in any other manner.

**3.3.4** No substitutions will be considered after the Contract award unless specifically provided in the Contract Documents.

### 3.4 ADDENDA

**3.4.1** Addenda will be mailed or delivered to all who are known by the Architect to have received a complete set of Bidding Documents.

**3.4.2** Copies of Addenda will be made available for inspection wherever Bidding Documents are on file for that purpose.

**3.4.3** No Addenda will be issued later than four days prior to the date for receipt of Bids except an Addendum withdrawing the request for Bids or one which includes postponement of the date for receipt of Bids.

**3.4.4** Each Bidder shall ascertain, prior to submitting a Bid, that all issued Addenda have been received, and their receipt shall be acknowledged in the Bid.

## ARTICLE 4
## BIDDING PROCEDURE

### 4.1 FORM AND STYLE OF BIDS

**4.1.1** Bids shall be submitted on forms identical to the form included in the Bidding Documents, in the quantity required by Article 9.

**4.1.2** All blanks on the bid form shall be filled in by typewriter or in ink.

**4.1.3** Where so indicated by the makeup of the bid form, sums shall be expressed in both words and figures, and, in case of a discrepancy between the two, the amount written in words shall govern.

**4.1.4** Any interlineation, alteration or erasure must be initialed by the signer of the Bid.

**4.1.5** Where two or more Bids for designated portions of the Work have been requested the Bidder may, without forfeiture of the bid security, state a refusal to accept award of less than the combination of Bids so stipulated. The Bidder shall make no additional stipulations on the bid form or qualify the Bid in any other manner.

**4.1.6** Each copy of the Bid shall include the legal name of the Bidder and a statement that the Bidder is a sole proprietor, partnership, corporation or some other legal entity. Each copy shall be signed by the person or persons legally authorized to bind the Bidder to a contract. A Bid by a corporation shall further give the state of incorporation and have the corporate seal affixed. A Bid submitted by an agent shall have a current power of attorney attached certifying the agent's authority to bind the Bidder.

### 4.2 BID SECURITY

**4.2.1** If so stipulated in the Advertisement or Invitation to Bid, each Bid shall be accompanied by a bid security in the form and amount required by Article 9, pledging that the Bidder will enter into a Contract with the Owner on the terms stated in the Bid and will, if required, furnish bonds as described hereunder in Article 7 covering the faithful performance of the Contract and the payment of all obligations arising under the Contract. Should the Bidder refuse to enter into such Contract, or fail to furnish such bonds if required, the amount of the bid security shall be forfeited to the Owner as liquidated damages, not as a penalty. The amount of the bid security shall not be forfeited to the Owner in the event the Owner fails to comply with Subparagraph 6.2.1.

**4.2.2** If a surety bond is required it shall be written on AIA Document A310, Bid Bond, and the attorney-in-fact who executes the bond on behalf of the surety shall affix to the bond a certified and current copy of the power of attorney authorizing execution of such bond.

**4.2.3** The Owner will have the right to retain the bid security of Bidders to whom an award is being considered until either (a) the Contract has been executed and bonds, if required, have been furnished, (b) the specified time has elapsed so that Bids may be withdrawn, or (c) all Bids have been rejected.

### 4.3 SUBMISSION OF BIDS

**4.3.1** All copies of the Bid, the bid security, if any, and any other documents required to be submitted with the Bid, shall be enclosed in a sealed opaque envelope. The envelope shall be addressed to the party receiving the Bids and shall be identified with the Project name, the Bidder's name and address and, if applicable, the designated portion of the Work for which the Bid is submitted. If the Bid is sent by mail, the sealed envelope shall be enclosed in a separate mailing envelope with the notation "SEALED BID ENCLOSED" on the face thereof.

**4.3.2** Bids shall be deposited at the designated location prior to the time and date for receipt of Bids indicated in the Advertisement or Invitation to Bid or any extension thereof made by Addendum. Bids received after the time and date for receipt of Bids will be returned unopened.

**4.3.3** The Bidder shall assume full responsibility for timely delivery at the location designated for receipt of Bids.

**4.3.4** Oral, telephonic or telegraphic Bids are invalid and will not receive consideration.

### 4.4 MODIFICATION OR WITHDRAWAL OF BIDS

**4.4.1** A Bid may not be modified, withdrawn or canceled by the Bidder during the stipulated time period following the time and date designated for the receipt of Bids, and each Bidder so agrees in submitting a Bid.

**4.4.2** Prior to the time and date designated for receipt of Bids, any Bid submitted may be modified or withdrawn by notice to the party receiving Bids at the place designated for receipt of Bids. Such notice shall be in writing over the signature of the Bidder or by telegram; if by telegram, written confirmation over the signature of the Bidder shall be mailed and postmarked on or before the date and time set for receipt of Bids, and it shall be worded so as not to reveal the amount of the original Bid.

**4.4.3** Withdrawn Bids may be resubmitted up to the time and date designated for the receipt of Bids provided that they are then fully in conformance with these Instructions to Interiors Bidders.

**4.4.4** Bid security, if any is required, shall be in an amount sufficient for the Bid as modified or resubmitted.

**FIGURE 21-7**
**"Instructions to Bidders" (AIA document A771).** *(Continued)*

## ARTICLE 5
## CONSIDERATION OF BIDS

**5.1** **OPENING OF BIDS**

**5.1.1** Unless stated otherwise in the Advertisement or Invitation to Bid, the properly identified Bids received on time will be opened publicly and will be read aloud. An abstract of the Base Bids and Alternate Bids, if any, will be made available to Bidders. When it has been stated that Bids will be opened privately, an abstract of the same information may, at the discretion of the Owner, be made available to the Bidders within a reasonable time.

**5.2** **REJECTION OF BIDS**

**5.2.1** The Owner shall have the right to reject any or all Bids and to reject a Bid not accompanied by any required bid security or by other data required by the Bidding Documents, or to reject a Bid which is in any way incomplete or irregular.

**5.3** **ACCEPTANCE OF BID (AWARD)**

**5.3.1** It is the intent of the Owner to award a Contract to the lowest responsible Bidder provided the Bid has been submitted in accordance with the requirements of the Bidding Documents and does not exceed the funds available. The Owner shall have the right to waive any informality or irregularity in any Bid or Bids received and to accept the Bid or Bids which, in the Owner's judgment, is in the Owner's own best interest.

**5.3.2** The Owner shall have the right to accept Alternates in any order or combination, unless otherwise specifically provided in Article 9, and to determine the low Bidder on the basis of the sum of the Base Bid and the Alternates accepted.

## ARTICLE 6
## POST BID INFORMATION

**6.1** **CONTRACTOR'S QUALIFICATION STATEMENT**

**6.1.1** Bidders under consideration for award of a Contract shall submit to the Architect, upon request, a properly executed Contractor's Qualification Statement, AIA Document A305, unless such a statement has been previously required and submitted as a prerequisite to the issuance of Bidding Documents.

**6.2** **OWNER'S FINANCIAL CAPABILITY**

**6.2.1** The Owner shall, at the request of the Bidder to whom award of a Contract is under consideration, and no later than seven days prior to the expiration of the time for withdrawal of Bids, furnish to the Bidder reasonable evidence that the Owner has made financial arrangements to fulfill the Contract obligations. Unless such reasonable evidence is furnished, the Bidder will not be required to execute the Owner-Contractor Agreement.

**6.3** **SUBMITTALS**

**6.3.1** The Bidder shall, within seven days of notification of selection for the award of a Contract for the Work, submit the following information to the Architect:

.1 the proprietary names and the suppliers of principal items or systems of materials and equipment proposed for the Work;

.2 a list of names of Subcontractors or other persons or entities (including those who are to furnish materials or equipment fabricated to a special design) proposed for the principal portions of the Work.

**6.3.2** The Bidder will be required to establish to the satisfaction of the Architect and the Owner the reliability and responsibility of the persons or entities proposed to furnish and perform the Work described in the Bidding Documents.

**6.3.3** Prior to the award of the Contract, the Architect will notify the Bidder in writing if either the Owner or the Architect, after due investigation, has reasonable objection to any such proposed person or entity. If the Owner or the Architect has reasonable objection to any such proposed person or entity, the Bidder shall have the option to (1) withdraw the Bid, or (2) submit an acceptable substitute person or entity with an adjustment in the Bid price to cover the difference in cost occasioned by such substitution. At the Owner's discretion, the adjusted Bid price may be accepted or the Bidder disqualified. In the event of either withdrawal or disqualification under this Subparagraph, the bid security will not be forfeited, notwithstanding the provisions of Subparagraph 4.4.1.

**6.3.4** Persons and entities proposed by the Bidder, and to whom the Owner and the Architect have made no reasonable objection under the provisions of Subparagraph 6.3.3, must be used on the Work for which they were proposed and shall not be changed except with the written consent of the Owner and the Architect.

## ARTICLE 7
## PERFORMANCE BOND, SUPPLY BOND AND LABOR AND MATERIAL PAYMENT BOND

**7.1** **BOND REQUIREMENTS**

**7.1.1** Prior to execution of the Contract, if required hereinafter in Article 9, the Bidder shall furnish bonds covering the faithful performance of the Contract and the payment of all obligations arising thereunder in such form and amount as the Owner may prescribe. Bonds may be secured through the Bidder's usual sources. If the furnishing of such bonds is stipulated hereinafter in Article 9, the cost shall be included in the Bid.

**7.1.2** If, after receipt of Bids, the Owner requires that bonds be obtained from other than the Bidder's usual source, any change in cost will be adjusted.

**7.1.3** If the Owner has reserved the right to require that bonds be furnished subsequent to the execution of the Contract, the cost shall be adjusted as provided in the Contract Documents.

**7.2** **TIME OF DELIVERY AND FORM OF BONDS**

**7.2.1** The Bidder shall deliver the required bonds to the Owner not later than the date of execution of the Contract or, if the Work is to be commenced prior to that date in response to a letter of intent, the Bidder shall, prior to commencement of the Work, submit evidence satisfactory to the Owner that such bonds will be furnished.

**7.2.2** Unless otherwise required in Article 9, the bonds shall be written on AIA Document A311, Performance Bond and Labor and Material Payment Bond.

**7.2.3** The Bidder shall require the attorney-in-fact who executes the required bonds on behalf of the surety to affix thereto a certified and current copy of the power of attorney authorizing execution of such bonds.

AIA DOCUMENT A771 • INSTRUCTIONS TO INTERIORS BIDDERS • MAY 1980 EDITION • AIA® • ©1980
THE AMERICAN INSTITUTE OF ARCHITECTS, 1735 NEW YORK AVENUE, N.W., WASHINGTON, D.C. 20006

**FIGURE 21-7**
"Instructions to Bidders" (AIA document A771). *(Continued)*

## ARTICLE 8
## FORM OF AGREEMENT BETWEEN OWNER AND CONTRACTOR

**8.1 FORM TO BE USED**

**8.1.1** Unless otherwise required in the Bidding Documents, the Agreement for the Work will be written on AIA Document A171, Standard Form of Agreement Between Owner and Contractor for Furniture, Furnishings and Equipment, where the Basis of Payment is a Stipulated Sum.

## ARTICLE 9
## SUPPLEMENTARY INSTRUCTIONS

**FIGURE 21-7**
"Instructions to Bidders" (AIA document A771). *(Continued)*

where and how these documents can be obtained, how they are to be used by the bidder, and if substitutions or exclusions are allowed and how they are to be submitted. The actual drawings and specifications do not appear at this location in the documents.

## BID FORMS

Bid forms are documents prepared by the designer or the client and provided to the bidders. The bid form is the document that the vendor uses to inform the client of the bid price. The format generally is set up to be a form letter from the bidder to the client. The bid form has blanks in appropriate spaces that are filled in by the bidder. Figure 21-8 is a sample bid form. If no substitutions or exclusions are allowed in the instructions, a statement reinforcing disqualification of a bidder submitting a substitution or exclusion should be provided here.

## BOND FORMS

*Bond forms* are legal documents used to bind the designer or vendor to the contract as assurance that the designer/vendor will perform the requirements of the contract as agreed. There are three bond forms commonly used in the bidding process: bid bond, performance bond, and labor and materials payment bond.

The *bid bond* is required to assure that the designer or vendor awarded the contract will sign the contract. Most companies that submit a bid would expect to go through with the contract. However, some companies submit bids only to find out how the competition is pricing services or products. In another instance, if a company has made an error in its bid, the company may want to withdraw even after the bid is awarded. The bid bond thus acts as "earnest money" to be sure that all who bid are actually interested in going through with the contract. A bid bond in an amount of approximately 5 to 10 percent of the bid price is customary. The bid bond of the successful bidder is usually held by the client for some time after the contract is signed, and other bid securities are obtained. For unsuccessful bidders, the bid bond is returned promptly.

The *performance bond* is required of the winning bidder as a guarantee that the designer or vendor will complete the work as specified and will protect the client from any loss up to the amount of the bond as a result of the failure of the designer or vendor to perform the contract. It is customary for the performance bond to be an amount equal to 100 percent of the value of the bid contract. The designer or vendor, however, pays a surety company a smaller percentage for the bond insurance. This actual amount would vary, based on the actual project conditions and the surety company. The performance bond is returned after completion of the project.

A *labor and materials payment bond* is required by the winning bidder to guarantee that the designer or vendor will be responsible for paying for all the materials and labor that have been contracted for in the event the designer or vendor defaults on the project. This is to prevent the client from being responsible to subcontractors for goods not delivered. This bond is also customarily in an amount equal to 100 percent of the contract price. It also is returned after the completion of the project.

## BID OPENING

Bid proposals are almost always required to be sent to the owner or designer in sealed envelopes. The exact labeling of the envelope, where it is to be delivered, to

BID FORM
FOR
FURNISHINGS CONTRACT

CONTRACT NUMBER: _____

PROJECT: _____

BID OF _____
(name of bidder)
□ a corporation organized under the laws of the State of _____
□ a partnership, with the following individuals as partners:

_____

□ a sole proprietor.

Present Bid To:

_____

$\left(\begin{matrix}\text{Firm Name}\\\text{Firm Address}\end{matrix}\right)$

The Undersigned, acknowledges receipt and review of the Project Documents, consisting of _____ pages of drawings and _____ pages of written specifications, and addenda No. _____ through _____ , and hereby proposes to furnish all materials, labor, and miscellany necessary to provide and install the furniture and furnishings as specified in the aforementioned documents.

The Undersigned further agrees to hold his/her Bid open for thirty (30) days after the receipt of bids. Should the bidder be awarded the contract, he/she shall furnish a Performance Bond and a Labor and Materials Payment Bond in accordance to the General Conditions of the Bid, to the owner within ten days after award of bid.

No substitutions or exclusions to what was specified shall be allowed. Any bidder not bidding on all items as specified shall be disqualified.

###############################################

The undersigned agrees to supply and perform, in accordance with the specifications, all the materials, labor, and miscellany as specified for

_____ Dollars

($ _____ ).

###############################################

The Bid Bond and all other required documentation is attached by the undersigned bidder.

It is understood that the owner reserves the right to reject any or all bids, to withhold the award of bid for any reason, and reserves the right to hold all bids for thirty (30) days after the date of opening.

Date of Bid: _____

Name of Bidder: _____

Address of Bidder: _____

Authorized Officer: _____

**FIGURE 21-8**
**Bid form used to obtain a vendor's price on a bid.**

whom, and by what day and time are stated in the instructions to bidders. Any bid received that does not conform to the instructions can be rejected. It is also customary that bids cannot be withdrawn after the closing date and time for the receipt of bids even if the *bid opening* has not yet taken place.

Bids for governmental agencies or public companies such as utilities are required to have the bid opening at an open public meeting. The place and time will be noted in the invitation to bidders. At that meeting, the client or person charged with administering the bid will announce each bidder and his or her bid price. The client usually does not award the bid at that time. The invitation to bid should have informed bidders about the length of time the client would take to evaluate the bids and make the decision as to the award of the contract. Although most public agencies are most likely going to take the lowest bid, they are not bound to do so if there are legitimate reasons to reject the lowest bid. Care must be taken by the client, therefore, to not announce that company X is the apparent lowest bidder at the bid opening since this announcement could later bind the agency even if they want to reject that bid.

For private companies, the bid opening is not required by law to be open to the public. This means that each bidder might not have the opportunity to know what the competition bid, to know if their own bid was low in comparison to the others, or that it may have been in error. According to Sweet, the courts are beginning to expect the closed bid opening client to act in good faith with the bidders if a bid comes in substantially lower than all other bids and thus not penalize the bidder who makes a legitimate mistake.[5]

### BID AWARD NOTIFICATION

After the bids are evaluated and a decision is made as to the successful bidder, each bidder must be notified of the result. A simple form letter is usually sent to each of the unsuccessful bidders thanking them. It is not legally necessary to inform them as to who the successful bidder was or the amount of the bid. It is often a good idea to include a comment that the bids of the unsuccessful bidders will be held for a period of time as stated in the invitation to bid in the event that the successful bidder does withdraw. This means that the bids of unsuccessful bidders remain valid offers until the date of the holding period.

## *Summary*

It is important for interior designers whose practices involve any structural design work or formal bid specifications to be familiar with the entire contract documents and specifications procedure. It is a common activity for commercial designers, but the residential designers must also understand how to prepare contract documents when they become involved in remodeling projects or custom manufacturing of products.

Floor plans and other working drawings, equipment plans keyed to equipment lists or formal specifications, and various schedules are part of the contract documents. Most familiar to designers are the formal specifications needed when the client requires competitive bids. Four different kinds are discussed in this chapter:

---

[5]Sweet 1985.

proprietary, descriptive, performance, and reference. For designers not commonly associated with the bid process, this chapter also briefly discusses how this important method for client purchasing operates.

Before examining the actual paperwork process of the profession, the next chapter will offer a brief discussion of the Uniform Commercial Code in relation to sale of goods.

# Chapter 22

## THE UNIFORM COMMERCIAL CODE

*T*he sale of goods involves the transfer of title from one party to another. Before this transfer can take place, one party must make an offer to buy or sell the good while another party must accept the offer to buy or sell. This transferring of ownership of goods is covered within a section of law called the law of sales. To guide the relationships between the various levels of buyers and sellers within the law of sales is the *Uniform Commercial Code (UCC)*. The law of sales, as represented by article 2 of the UCC, governs the sale of goods (not services), real property (real estate), and intangible property (such as stocks). The section of the Code that deals with sales is quite extensive.

For the majority of the members of the interior design profession, selling and ordering goods for clients is an everyday occurrence. In speaking to many professional designers during the research for this book, the author has found that although some may have heard of the UCC, few designers know that it is the area of law that regulates the sale of goods.

It is important for those new to the profession as well as for professionals to understand the legal ramifications of selling merchandise. This chapter is not meant to be an in-depth discussion of the Code. We will, however, attempt to provide some basic understanding regarding how the Code affects the daily work of the interior designer who engages in the sale of goods.

## *History*

Most laws related to commercial business activity come from the individual states. During the early years of this country, this often resulted in confusing and conflicting laws. As the nation's commercial business activity became more complex, the problems became more acute.

In the late 1800s, the National Conference of Commissioners on Uniform State Laws was established to create uniform statutes related to business activities. These statutes, revised over the next 55 years, helped to illuminate many of the problems of commercial business. Yet there remained instances when these uniform statutes overlapped. Work was begun in 1945 to revise all the statutes into one uniform document. In 1957, after much work, the Uniform Commercial Code was completed.[1]

---

[1]Stone 1975, 2.

The purpose of the code is to help "state legal relationships of the parties in modern commercial transactions. The Code is designed to help determine the intentions of the parties to a commercial contract and to give force and effect to their agreement."[2]

The code consists of ten articles:

1. General provisions.
2. Sales.
3. Commercial paper.
4. Bank deposits and collections.
5. Letters of credit.
6. Bulk transfers.
7. Documents of title.
8. Investment securities.
9. Secured transactions.
10. Effective date and repealer.

This chapter will be limited to a discussion of sections of article 2.

The UCC has been adopted by all states except Louisiana. This state has only adopted certain sections of the Code. Since 1958, sections of the Code have been revised to meet current needs and to refine the statutes. The following discussion is based on the 1978 revision, which is the last official text of the Code.

# *Definitions*

The interpretation of the statutes stated in article 2 vary, depending on whether the buyer of goods is an end-user (customer) or a merchant. It is therefore necessary to define some common terms as they relate to the Code. Although there are many definitions in the Code, the main ones we wish to look at here are for *goods, sale, seller, merchant, buyer,* and *price.*

A *good* is any item that is tangible—that is, has physical existence—and is movable. Furniture and accessories are tangible goods. The sale of tangible goods is covered by the UCC. Items such as carpet, wall coverings, and window treatments are goods because they do have physical existence, but when these items are permanently attached to a home or building, they are now generally considered real property. Or are they? The sale of the merchandise itself from the supplier to the designer and the designer to the client would be covered by the UCC since the goods do not become real property until they are "permanently" attached to the structure. If the client later wants to remove these goods from his or her home or office and sell them or even sell the building with the merchandise intact, the sale would be governed by real estate law.

A *sale* has occurred when the seller transfers title or ownership of the goods to a buyer and the buyer has provided some consideration to the seller. Whenever the designer agrees in good faith to sell a piece of furniture to a client for some amount of money, and the client takes delivery of the furniture and sends the designer a check for the agreed-on price, a sale has occurred. There are, however, some special considerations with regard to when ownership actually occurs.

A *seller* is anyone who sells goods or agrees to sell goods. The interior designer, selling goods to clients, would be considered a seller. It should be pointed out that

---

[2]Clarkson 1983, 9. Copyright West Publishing Company.

a manufacturer who sells goods to the interior designer could also be considered a seller. However, both the interior designer and the manufacturer are also considered merchants.

A *merchant* is anyone who is involved with the buying and/or selling of the kinds of goods with which he or she is dealing. In other words, "a person is a merchant when that person, acting in a mercantile capacity, possesses or uses an expertise specifically related to the goods being sold."[3] So, although the interior designer who sells a personally owned stereo to a friend is a seller, when he or she sells a chair to that same friend and that sale occurs through the business, the designer is now considered a merchant.

Many interior designers who sell goods never have a showroom, warehouse, or installation crew as employees of the firm. Any interior designer, however, who purchases goods—whether or not through a firm's inventory account—and resells them to a client so that the purchase and resale "pass through" the design firm's books, is a merchant.

A person becomes a *buyer* when he or she contracts to purchase or purchases some good. A buyer also is someone who buys from one who is in the business of selling goods. A client purchasing a sofa from an interior designer is a buyer. Is the interior designer a buyer when he or she purchases the sofa for the client? Yes, and the designer is protected by the same rights as the end-user as long as the purchase is from a seller whose business it is to sell the sofa.

Finally, *price* can be any kind of payment from buyer to seller including money, goods, services, or real property. So it is possible, for example, for a client to offer to trade his or her own professional services as the price of a sofa.

## *The Sales Contract*

For the most part, the statutes related to the sale of goods as covered by the UCC generally follow the principles of contract law. That means that an offer to sell something must be made, an acceptance to buy that good must occur, and proper consideration must be exchanged from buyer to seller. This section will look at how "offer," "acceptance," and "consideration" occur in sales law.

As discussed in Chapter 15 on contracts, the statute of frauds contains a provision that the sale of goods with a value of over $500 must be in writing to be enforceable. This provision is contained within section 2-201(1). Although a written contract for the sale of goods does not mean the designer will force the client to take the goods, it gives the designer the legal right to sue for payment if he or she so chooses.

### OFFER: SECTIONS 2-204, 2-205, 2-206, 2-305, 2-308, AND 2-311

Normally, a contract exists when an offer is followed by an acceptance. In sales law, however, the nature of offers and acceptances renders the point at which a contract exists more inexact. Because offers and acceptances in sales contracts are exchanged verbally, through the mails, and by the conduct of the buyer and seller, it is more difficult to determine exactly when a contract exists. To assist with this problem, the UCC in section 2-204 states that a contract exists when there is sufficient agreement to an offer to consider a contract to be formed. This agreement may be verbal, written, or by the actions of the parties.

---

[3]Jentz 1987, 244. Copyright West Publishing Company.

In contract law, the terms of the offer and acceptance must be clearly stated before the contract can be effective. Because of the unusual circumstances that surround offers and acceptances in sales law, the UCC allows for the offer to be valid even if one or more terms of the agreement are not stated, provided the parties intend to go through with the contract and the courts can agree that a contract was intended and can determine a remedy for breach.

### Open Terms Provisions—An Introduction

There are provisions which allow the contract to be valid even if some of the terms of the contract are indefinite. Terms include quantity, description, part number, delivery location, payment, and price. In general, if the terms are incomplete, it is likely that the contract will still be valid as long as it can be shown that both parties intend to fulfill the contract. However, the more terms left incomplete, the more difficult it will be for the courts to determine if the contract is valid. For example, should a designer order some tables and all the terms needed in the purchase order are present except the finish of the wood, the order would still be valid. However, when the quantity is missing, the order is usually considered invalid as the courts cannot determine the full value of the contract to establish a remedy.

### Open Price Term

If the price is missing, the other party can cancel the offer or determine a reasonable price. For example, should ABC Design Company agree to furnish drapery tiebacks for a client, but forget to provide a price for those tiebacks, the client can either set a reasonable price for the items or cancel the order for the tiebacks.

### Open Payment Term

A third open term related to offers is an open payment term. If it has not been specified when payment for the goods will be due, the UCC stipulates that payment will be due upon delivery to the buyer or at the time of "receipt of goods." The buyer receives the goods when he or she takes physical possession of the goods. Additionally, if payment terms are not specified, the payment must be in cash, check, or agreed-on credit.

For the client, receipt of goods takes place when the goods are delivered to his or her home or office or when the client leaves the designer's place of business with the goods. According to subsections 2-310(b) and (c), receipt of goods shipped from a manufacturer to the designer occurs when the goods are placed in the hands of the carrier. This is the reason that invoices often arrive prior to the goods. However, this means that payment is due before the goods can be inspected. All buyers have the right to inspect the goods before they must make payment. These same subsections provide for that right of inspection, but the inspection must be done promptly. If the goods are not as ordered, the seller must be notified immediately for the buyer not to be bound to payment.

### Open Delivery Term

If the location for the delivery has been omitted, it is customary that delivery be made at the seller's business location. This could be quite costly to the designer in the supplier/designer relationship since it would be the designer's responsibility to pick up the goods from the seller. It is unlikely that major manufacturers of goods would not call to check with the designer as to a delivery location.

Section 2-307 states that delivery and payment are due at one time for all the items being sold unless provisions in the agreement or "circumstances" allow for delivery and payment in lots. The designer should have as a term on his or her purchase order that informs the supplier whether shipment of less than the full order is acceptable. For large-sized projects involving multiple items, it is not unusual for the client to want the goods delivered as soon as they arrive. The designer would like to deliver the goods to the client promptly to keep cash flow operating smoothly. However, in order to receive payments for goods delivered in lots rather than as a whole, a term in the sales contract must be provided to notify the buyer of this fact. Without a written term in the contract, payment would not be required until the entire order is delivered even though several deliveries are made to complete one order.

### The Firm Offer

Normally in contract law, an offer to sell or buy goods has a time limit. That time limit can be set by the offerer. If the offer is not in writing, or not accompanied with payment by the offeree (buyer), the offer can be revoked by the seller at any time before the buyer can accept. However, in sales law, special provisions are made when the seller is a merchant and apply whether the buyer is a merchant or an end-user. If the merchant makes an offer in writing, whether or not consideration has been given by the buyer or a time limit to the offer has been set, the merchant cannot revoke the offer either during the time limit or for a reasonable time. For example, Mary Smith signs a written contract to sell $30,000 of furniture to a client, but the client does not sign the agreement and does not provide any down payment. Ten days later, Mary realizes that she made an error in her calculations. If the client accepts the contract, Mary would lose $2000, since she used a net price list to discount some of the goods. Legally, Mary cannot revoke the offer since it was a "firm offer" in writing and signed by her.

The points in this discussion are important to the interior design practice. They show the value of good paperwork preparation of the specification list, the contract for the client, and purchase orders. Designer omissions can cost time and money. They could even allow for lawsuits against the designer.

## ACCEPTANCE: SECTIONS 2-206 AND 2-207

In most situations, the offerer (the seller) establishes the way that acceptance can be made. If acceptance is not made in the manner specified, the acceptance can be rejected or considered a counteroffer. However, the law generally allows the acceptance to be valid if it is received within the time limit set, even if by a different method of acceptance. Usually the seller would want an oral acceptance followed by a signed acceptance of the sales proposal.

In the designer/end-user relationship, there are usually few problems of questions related to the existence of the contract. This is because, in everyday practice, the designer prepares a confirmation proposal that states who is being charged; lists the quantities, descriptions, and prices of the items being sold; lists the terms of sale such as when payment is due; and then requires the signature of the client on the confirmation. Assuming price is not an issue, rarely does the client make acceptance in any way other than by signing the confirmation. And rarely does the client propose other terms to the sale, thus making a counteroffer.

A key to the agreement between designer and client would be the time limit of the offer and whether or not the client signs the agreement. If the designer's proposal states that the offer is only good for ten days, the client must respond within that ten-day period. If he or she does not, the designer does not legally have to honor the original offer. If there is no time limit, the client has a "reasonable time" to respond. For example, a month after receiving the proposal, the client signs and returns the confirmation. However, the price of the goods to the designer increased during that time. The designer may very well be expected to sell the goods at the quoted price, thus lowering his or her profit margin. Thus, it is important that all offers to sell goods to clients have a time limit for acceptance stated on the confirmation.

The major concerns of acceptance in the UCC relate to the merchant/merchant relationship. Acceptances between merchants become more complicated since offers and acceptances can occur many ways. The most common method for offers to buy and sell merchandise occurs through the mails via the use of purchase orders and acknowledgments. Many designers still insist on telephone orders, although this is not advisable.

In contract law, a contract only exists if all the terms of the offer are exactly matched by the acceptance. Any differences constitute a counteroffer. In sales law, it is not uncommon among merchants for the terms on the purchase order and the terms of the acknowledgment to have some differences. In interior design practice, the quantity, description, and price commonly match. Terms such as ship date and general terms of the sale often vary. The UCC allows for a contract to be formed when the conditions of the purchase order and acknowledgment are different as long as the offeree's response indicates a definite acceptance to the original terms of the offer and there are no conditional terms in the offer or acceptance. For example, designer A sends a purchase order to manufacturer B for some custom-made bedspreads. The purchase order is prepared following the instructions in the catalog. The acknowledgment comes back from B with the statement "on condition that a 50 percent deposit be submitted within ten days of receipt of acknowledgment. No work will be started until deposit is received." If this term is not stated in the catalog, no contract exists unless the buyer agrees since the seller has added a condition to the terms of the offer.

When the differences in terms are minor, and neither party objects to the differences, a contract is formed. If the offer and acceptance are made over the phone, the printed confirmation and acknowledgments are proposals to the oral contract, and again a contract is formed as long as no objections are made and the differences are minor.

What all this means to the designer is that he or she must not only carefully prepare the terms of sale on his or her purchase order, but must also be familiar with terms and conditions of sale from all the suppliers. What is ordered is usually not the problem in interior design orders. The price, ship dates, warranties, and payment terms are more often the issue.

Should the acknowledgment contain discrepancies in quantities, descriptions, and so on, it is important for the designer to make prompt written notification of the errors to the supplier. Failure to do so means acceptance of the acknowledgment, hence a contract, and the designer will "own" the merchandise even if the error is made by the supplier.

If there are material differences between the designer's purchase order terms and a supplier's acknowledgment terms, the designer may be protected by the UCC constraints against material differences. Material differences mean substantial or essential changes to the original. However, to be protected, the designer is encouraged to object in writing to any terms different from his or her own.

## CONSIDERATION

In general, the UCC does not differ with the general contract law precept that consideration must be part of the acceptance. Between designer and client that consideration is primarily a down payment paid on signing the agreement and the belief the client will pay full value at a later time. Between designer and supplier, consideration is generally the good faith credit that the supplier affords to the designer knowing that the designer will pay the supplier after the goods are shipped.

There are strict rules governing consideration when the buyer or seller attempts to modify the contract. For example, after the designer sends the purchase order to the supplier and the supplier acknowledges the order to the designer, but merchandise is not yet shipped, the supplier informs the designer that the price will go up 10 percent as a result of an increase in materials price. The designer subsequently notifies the supplier that he or she accepts the increase. Later, the designer changes his or her mind and says that he or she will only pay the original price. Whether or not the designer accepts the increase orally or in writing, he or she will be bound by the new price. This is true as long as it can be shown by the supplier that the change in price was due to a reason such as a change in availability of materials to manufacture the finished goods causing an increase in price for the finished goods. If the supplier makes a mistake in his or her pricing, the modification of the contract would be invalid.

What this means is that once the terms and conditions are agreed to between the designer and supplier, later modifications agreed to are binding if they are reasonable as a result of something beyond the control of the party asking for the modifications. If the supplier later tells the designer that the price will be higher and the designer does not agree, the contract is revoked. If the original or modified contract must meet the statute of frauds or has a condition that changes must be in writing, these changes must be in writing to be valid.

## *Statute of Frauds*

Although section 2-201 in the Code is very specific about a contract for the sale of goods over $500 being in writing to be valid, there are certain exceptions as stated in subsections of 2-201.

First, between merchants, an oral agreement would be valid if one party sends the other party a signed confirmation outlining the details of the agreement. The receiving merchant has ten days to respond in writing to any conditions or content of the offer to which he or she does not agree. Failure to respond within the ten days forms a valid contract.

Second, an oral contract for the special manufacture of goods which would not be suitable for anyone else, and whose manufacture has substantially been started, forms a contract. For example, Mary Jones Designs places a telephone order to Smith's Drapery Company for the manufacture of ten different-sized, arched miniblinds at a price of over $800. A month later, after production is started but not finished, the client cancels the order so Mary Jones calls to cancel the order. If it is unlikely that the blinds can be sold to another client of Smith's Drapery Company, Mary Jones Designs would be liable. It is for this reason that designers include in the terms of their confirmations a statement that a restocking charge, say at least 25 to 50 percent, is charged for any order the client cancels.

A third case is if one party to the contract admits in court or in legal proceedings that a contract did exist; then an oral contract would be binding for what was admitted. For example, Robert Class placed a telephone order for 50 yards of Wilton weave carpet from an English mill. The value of that carpet was $4000. The mill shipped 500 yards. Class refused the shipment, and the mill sued. Class admits in court that he ordered 50 yards of carpet. Since Class admits that an oral contract did exist, he would be liable to pay for the 50 yards of carpet.

Last, an oral agreement is enforceable up the amount of payment made and accepted or the amount of goods delivered and accepted. For example, if a designer makes a verbal contract to order miniblinds for a client, and the client provides the designer with a deposit, the client is liable to pay for and accept the quantity of blinds the deposit covers. If the designer delivers a portion of the order for the blinds, the client is also liable for the value of the blinds that are delivered.

Far too many designers agree to sell goods to clients and/or order goods for clients without a written contract. The designer placing orders for clients without the client's signing a confirmation may not have legal recourse if the client later refuses delivery. If the designer fails to send a confirming order to the manufacturer, the manufacturer may not be bound to a sale. The designer failing to read an acknowledgment for an oral agreement will be obliged to accept whatever was orally agreed to.

# *Warranties*

*Warranties* place a burden on the seller that the goods he or she sells meet certain standards. Four important kinds of warranties are governed by the UCC:

1. Warranty of title (section 2-312).
2. Express warranty (section 2-313).
3. Implied warranty of merchantability (section 2-314).
4. Implied warranty of fitness for a particular purpose (section 2-315).

When the designer or design firm offers a warranty on the product he or she sells, failure to honor that warranty is a breach of contract duty and gives the client the right to sue.

## WARRANTY OF TITLE

The first aspect of warranty of title is that the seller has title to the goods and can legally sell them to others. Basically this means that the seller, knowingly or not, is not selling stolen goods or goods he or she does not have authorization to sell. If an interior design firm does not have authority to buy and sell Steelcase systems from Steelcase, because of a lack of a dealership agreement, it would not be able to imply to the client that it could purchase the goods from Steelcase and sell the products to the client. Since the designer cannot take title to the goods from Steelcase, he or she cannot pass title to the client.

A second part of warranty of title is that the buyer would be protected from loss if he or she unknowingly buys goods with a lien attached. A lien means that someone other than the person who has ownership or possession of the goods has a security interest in the goods. If the buyer buys the goods knowing that there is a lien, he or she will not be able to collect from the seller.

A third part is warranty concerning infringement. This means that the goods do not have any patent, copyright, or trademark claim by anyone. For example, a designer created a logo whose copyright was registered by the design firm. The client was not shown the design at that time. Six months later, the designer started a design practice and contacted the former client about possible work. The client hired the designer to produce a logo and he or she showed the client the logo the designer designed for the previous employer. The client bought the design and incorporated it into all the letterhead of the firm. The other design firm can sue the client and designer for infringement.

## EXPRESS WARRANTY

Promises, claims, descriptions, or affirmations made about a product's performance, quality, or condition that form the "basis of the bargain" form *express war-*

*ranties.* Interior designers and salespeople, in the course of their discussions with clients about a product's viability, often make statements about what the product can or cannot do. When are these statements covered under express warranty and when are they not?

The seller does not need to use words such as "warranty" or "guarantee" in the sales presentation, nor does he or she even need to intend to make such a warranty. How precise these statements have to be and how strongly they are worded is not clear in the Code.

When statements made by the seller are only the seller's opinion or relate only to the worth of the product, no express warranty is made. For example, Jim Jones says to a client, "This is the best open office system on the market." It is an expression of opinion—not based on statements of fact. This kind of salesmanship, called "puffing," is characterized by statements of opinion, not fact.

However, if the salesperson is believed to be an expert concerning the goods being sold, the statements of opinion are likely to be express warranties. Although the opinions about a manufacturer's product by an interior designer who specifies but does not sell products will probably be considered puffing, the statements of a manufacturer's representative who has worked for that company for many years could be considered warranties. Since the Code does not make it clear as to what is puffing and what is an expression of warranty, it is important to be careful in making statements about the quality and performance of a product. If the statement is reasonable, and a reasonable person believes the statement, a warranty may be created.

## IMPLIED WARRANTY OF MERCHANTABILITY

Implied warranties exist as operations of law and as such do not require that a contractual relationship between the parties be established. The implied warranty of merchantability affects sales made by merchants. In its simplest form, the Code says that the goods must be "fit for the ordinary purposes for which such goods are used."[4] As long as the merchant is a merchant of the kind of goods in consideration, he or she is liable.

Under this section, goods sold must be of fair to average quality and be comparable in quality to other similar goods. They must be fit for the normal purpose of the good. They must be packaged and labeled adequately and must conform to the statements made on the packaging or labels. For example, strippable wallpaper must be strippable; fire-retardant fabric must not ignite or burn within the limits stated on the binder; a solid brass headboard must be solid brass.

This section of the code makes an implied warranty of merchantability applicable to every sale by a merchant. Liability does not disappear even if the merchant is unaware of any defect in the product. The interior designer will likely be liable along with the manufacturer when a product fails or causes some injury to person or property.

## IMPLIED WARRANTY: FITNESS FOR A PARTICULAR PURPOSE

Implied warranty of fitness for a particular purpose affects the goods any seller—merchant or not—sells to another. When the seller knows the intended purpose for the goods and the buyer relies on the seller's knowledge to select or recommend

---

[4]Quinn 1978, 2–143. Reprinted by permission from *Uniform Commercial Code Commentary and Law Digest (1978),* Copyright 1978 Warren, Gorham and Lamont, Inc. 210 South Street, Boston, Mass. All rights reserved.

goods for the purpose, an implied warranty of fitness for a particular purpose would exist.

The seller does not need to know the exact purpose for the purchase. However, if he or she has a general idea of the purpose, and if the buyer has relied on the seller's knowledge or skill in selecting the goods, an implied fitness warranty would also be created.

For example, Mrs. Damon hires John Simmons to redecorate her home. As part of the services offered, Simmons sells to Damon the wall coverings for the kitchen and bathrooms. Damon made it clear to Simmons that the wallpaper in the bathroom would have to withstand a lot of steam and dampness since her husband takes long, hot showers. A few weeks after installation, the wallpaper begins to peel away. Since Simmons knew the purpose of the goods and Damon relied on the professional knowledge of Simmons, a breach of an implied warranty of fitness existed. Of course, the paperhanger, if he or she also knew the purpose of the purchase would be liable for breach.

## MAGNUSON-MOSS WARRANTY ACT

The Federal Trade Commission enforces the Magnuson-Moss Warranty Act. This legislation was enacted to help make it easier for the consumer to understand what was being warranted in any product sold to end-users. Warranties between merchants are regulated by the UCC rules.

The act does not require sellers to provide a written warranty for goods sold to consumers. "But if a seller chooses to make an express written warranty, and the cost of the consumer goods is more than $10, the warranty must be labeled as 'full' or 'limited.' In addition, if the cost of the goods is more than $15 (FTC regulation), the warrantor is required to make certain disclosures fully and conspicuously in a single document in 'readily understood language.'"[5] In this case, who warrants the goods, what is covered, limitations, the legal rights of the consumer, and how enforcement is made must all be spelled out.

Full warranties require repair or replacement at no charge to the buyer should a good be defective. There cannot be a time limit on the replacement. If there is, it is not a full warranty but a limited warranty. Should it not be possible to repair the goods in a reasonable time, the customer has the right to a refund or a replacement.[6] Limited warranties must be clearly stated as to what is warranted and the time limit of the warranty.

## DISCLAIMERS OF WARRANTY

An express warranty can be disclaimed if the manufacturer or seller does not make any express promises or statements of fact relating to or describing the goods. This would be true whether the statements were written or verbal. Saying "we guarantee that this fabric will not show wear for five years" constitutes an express warranty. A disclaimer to that statement might be, "we provide no warranty beyond that of the manufacturer, and their tests under normal use in a home indicate the fabric will show no significant wear for five years."

An implied warranty of fitness disclaimer must be in writing. For example, a designer sold a client a kitchen stool with a cane seat for use at the kitchen counter. The confirmation said something like "ABS Designs provides no warranty of fitness beyond that of the manufacturer's for normal, reasonable use." A few weeks after

---

[5]Jentz 1987, 314 and 316. Copyright West Publishing Company.

[6]Jentz 1987, 316.

purchase, the client uses the stool to stand on, and the cane breaks resulting in injury to the client. The designer would have no liability since the client was using the stool in a manner that was not normal and reasonable for the product; the manufacturer did not design the chair to be used as a ladder.

Disclaimers of fitness are also written with such words as *as is*. It is common to see retailers label used furniture "as is" to protect themselves against claims on used or damaged goods. Even new merchandise, however, is sold "as is" to imply no warranty other than what the manufacturer has provided.

An implied warranty of merchantability can be verbal, but it must be specific as to disclaiming merchantability. For example, Cobb Designs sells Mr. Smith a budget-priced guest chair to be used as a desk chair based on the needs described by Smith. Cobb verbally informs Smith that he does not warrant merchantability of the chair since it is not fit for use as a desk chair. The chair does not hold up, and Smith wants Cobb to replace it. Since it was disclaimed as to merchantability, Cobb would not be liable to replace the chair on those grounds.

Goods that the seller asks the buyer to inspect before the buyer accepts the goods and that the buyer refuses to inspect would have no implied warranty concerning defects. If the seller does not ask the buyer to inspect the goods, and the goods are damaged or defective, the seller would be liable.

## *Products Liability*

When a buyer purchases some good from a seller, the buyer has a right, under common law and sales law, to expect that good to meet certain minimal standards of materials, workmanship, and design for its intended use. If that good fails, certain expressed or implied warranties may have been breached. Manufacturers and sellers of goods may be liable to end-users, bystanders, and other merchants if individuals are physically harmed or if property damage occurs. This is called products liability. Products liability includes tort law related to strict liability and negligence (both of which we discussed in Chapter 7) and contract law related to warranty.

### STRICT LIABILITY

Strict liability means that "people are liable for the results of their acts regardless of their intentions or their exercise of reasonable care."[7] For example, a painter hired to paint the exterior of a home uses reasonable care when using spray painting equipment. However, the next-door neighbor goes out to inspect his house and finds over-spray of the blue paint on the side of his white house. The painter would be liable under strict liability.

Strict liability doctrine can be applied to manufactured products when the purchaser can show that "(1) the product was defective, (2) that the defect made the product unreasonably dangerous and (3) that the defect was the proximate cause of the injury."[8]

For strict liability to be applied to a products liability case, the injured party (plaintiff) must prove several things.

**1.** The good was defective when purchased.
**2.** The defective good is unreasonably dangerous to any user.

[7]Clarkson 1983, 393. Copyright West Publishing Company.

[8]Clarkson 1983, 393.

**3.** Physical injury has occurred to himself or herself or to his or her property.
**4.** At the time of the injury, the good was substantially in the same condition as when purchased.

For example, Mr. Shasta of Shasta Commercial Interiors orders from a textile company fabric described as fire retardant for use on restaurant booths. A few months after installation, a dropped cigarette smolders and ignites the fabric causing extensive damage to the restaurant. A strict liability case would be brought against the textile company and probably the designer if it can be shown that the goods were defective at the time of purchase. Further, it would have to be shown that injury was caused to the premises, that the untreated fabric was dangerous in its use, and that the fabric was in a basically unchanged condition since purchase. Although most of the liability in this case would rest on the manufacturer of goods, there is nothing in tort law or the UCC to prevent the unknowing designer from also being liable.

## PRODUCTS LIABILITY AND NEGLIGENCE

Chapter 7 defined negligence as a failure to use care that is expected of a reasonable person and that this failure to use care results in injury to another person or his or her property. Manufacturers of products must use this same care in the design, materials selection, production, and testing of their products so that they are safe when used as intended.

The plaintiff must show that the manufacturer did not use due care and that the defective product caused the injury. The plaintiff must also show that he or she used the product as designed and knew the risk of using the product incorrectly.

Designers must take time to be sure they are specifying products suitable for the client's use and that the client is carefully warned if the designer feels the client is demanding a product that is unsuitable for the client's use. Written disclaimers indicating that warnings were given and that the designer accepts no responsibility for misuse should be given to the client with a copy kept on file. These may not eliminate all liability, but would show the court a conscientious effort to warn the client.

## WARRANTY LAW AND PRODUCTS LIABILITY

Warranty law and products liability are the only portion of products liability related to the UCC. Warranty responsibility and products liability are based on the areas of warranties discussed in the previous sections. They are mentioned here in relation to an injury to a third party.

In contract law, the only parties that have redress for injuries are the parties to the contract. However, much of what is governed by the UCC easily affects third parties not a part of the original contract. The Code provides regulations that make the manufacturers and/or sellers liable for injuries to parties not a part of the original contract. For example, Mrs. Johnson hires an interior design company to redecorate her home. Through this company, she has some wall-hung shelves installed in the living room. One day, a bracket pulls out of the wall so that a shelf strikes a guest of Johnson. The guest sustains a head injury. If it were not for UCC section 2-318, the guest would not be able to sue the installer for an implied warranty of merchantability—only Mrs. Johnson could.

However, the Code is not clear on how responsible sellers and manufacturers are. It has been written with three alternatives giving different amounts of responsibility. Alternative "A" is limited to household members and their guests who use or are injured by the good. Alternative "B" is broader, not limiting injury to family members or guests, and alternative "C" is the broadest, protecting anyone who is injured by the defective product.

## *Title*

In the selling of goods, ownership or title must change hands. For a sale to take place, goods must exist and be identified in the contract.

Title passes in several ways. The most common is at the time and place the physical delivery of the goods is performed by the seller to the buyer. When the designer buys from a manufacturer, title often passes by use of a shipment contract. In this case, title passes to the buyer at the time the seller turns over the goods to some shipper. A third way title passes is by a destination contract. A destination contract states that the manufacturer turns over the goods to a shipper but the title does not pass to buyer until the goods arrive at the buyer's destination.

## *Risk*

It is very common between merchants that title passes through either a shipping or a destination contract. Title passes to the client when the goods are physically delivered to his or her home or business location. Since title can change at differing times, the Code must address who is liable for the risk of loss during the movement of the goods. Shipping of goods is governed by the UCC in sections 2-319 through 2-323.

*FOB* (free on board)[9] is a term used in conjunction with a destination to indicate where title passes and who has the risk of loss should the goods be damaged in transit. In a shipment contract (FOB factory warehouse), the risk for loss is transferred to the buyer when goods are passed to the carrier. If the goods are damaged before arriving at the buyer's location, it is the buyer's responsibility to recover damages from the carrier. In destination contracts (FOB destination) the risk for loss is transferred to the buyer at the buyer's destination. If the goods are damaged in transit, it is the seller's responsibility to recover the damages from the carrier.

## *Sales on Approval*

A common special sale situation in the interior design profession is the sale on approval. Simply, the client is not sure about a product and takes it to his or her home or business location to see if it is appropriate. If the client subsequently keeps the product, he or she pays for it. If the client does not, the product is returned. There is a normal condition to the sale on approval regulated by the UCC which is explained by the following example. Mrs. Miller finds a sofa on a showroom floor, but just is not sure it will go with her decor. She asks if she could try it "on approval." The store allows her five days to decide. If she calls and says she will keep the sofa before the five days are up, or fails to call before the five days and makes no attempt to return the sofa, the store will consider the sofa as sold and send her a bill. Should Miller damage the sofa before the five days, and before she approves of the sale, the loss would be Miller's. If it were damaged in transit or somehow, but not at the fault of Miller, the loss would be the seller's (sections 2-326 and 2-327).

---

[9]As noted in Chapter 13, *FOB* can also mean "freight on board."

## *Summary*

Selling goods to clients is often a profitable way of producing revenues for the interior design practice. But the buying and selling of goods also has many legal considerations and constraints. Although it is easy, in fact, to pick up the phone and order a dozen chairs or write a purchase order for those same chairs, there are many regulations that govern how that order can be placed legally, how ownership of the goods changes hands, and what responsibility the seller has to the buyer concerning defects or injury that might be caused by the goods.

In this chapter we have tried to explain the basic concepts of what the law of sales, as regulated by the Uniform Commercial Code (UCC), contains. We have defined basic terms related to sales and selling, discussed how a sales contract is made, and noted how a sales contract is different from a normal contract. We have also briefly discussed the statute of frauds, defined warranties, noted the responsibility of the seller and buyer in product liability, and explained when title and risk pass from the seller to the buyer.

Although the UCC standardizes most of the laws related to the sale of goods, the designer must still check with the firm's attorney to know which part of the Code is valid in his or her state and if there are any state or city regulations that supersede the UCC.

With an understanding of what constitutes a sale, the next two chapters discuss the paperwork involved in ordering the goods for the client and carrying through with the completion of the project.

# Chapter 23

## ORDER PROCESSING

*T*he client's acceptance of the equipment specification is the beginning of the next phase of the design project—paperwork management. The interior design firm or vendor responsible for purchasing and delivering merchandise will be required to order, track, and deliver perhaps several hundred—even thousands—of pieces of furniture and furnishings.

The ideal situation is to have an expediter—an individual familiar with the company's paperwork system and the requirements of the many manufacturers and extremely satisfied with working with details and pressures—be responsible for this order-processing function. However, in most firms, this function is the responsibility of the designer in charge of the project. In retail stores, some of this detail will be taken care of by others. Whatever the case, the designer should have a working knowledge of the paperwork system and terminology related to paperwork in the interior design office. This chapter will cover the kinds of forms generally used, including the purchase order, acknowledgment, and invoice.

## *Credit Application*

Many interior designers specify and sell thousands of dollars worth of products to their residential and/or commercial clients. Unfortunately, some of these clients turn out to be bad credit risks. Management should establish a policy related to investigating the creditworthiness of clients before the special order of merchandise or extensive design services begin. Firms that display many items on a showroom floor or in inventory may find it impractical to require a credit check for all purchases. Management may determine, with the advice of the firm's accountant, that special order purchases or design fees over some specific dollar amount require a credit application to be completed by the prospective client.

The form (see Figure 23-1) should be easy for the client to fill out. After it is completed, the form should be turned over to a financial institution or credit agency for review and recommendation. Although the opinion of the financial institution or credit agency should be taken very seriously, the final decision as to extending credit to the potential client should be that of the owner or appropriate manager.

A credit application will never provide 100 percent assurance as to the creditworthiness or good intentions of a client. However, the procedure allows the design

# NEW ACCOUNT CREDIT INFORMATION
ALL INFORMATION MUST BE FILLED OUT COMPLETELY TO AVOID UNNECESSARY DELAY IN SHIPMENT.

### PLEASE **PRINT** OR **TYPE**

Inital Order:

Purchase ☐

Lease ☐

Rent ☐

Salesperson: _____

Amount of credit requested $ _____

**BUSINESS INFORMATION**

NAME _____
(Give complete name as you are registered to do business)

ADDRESS _____ PHONE (____) _____

CITY _____ STATE _____ ZIP _____

PAYING OFFICE

NAME _____ PHONE (____) _____

ADDRESS _____ CONTACT PERSON _____

CITY _____ STATE _____ ZIP _____

Established: Mo. _____ Year _____
At present location: Mo. _____ Year _____
Present Ownership: Mo. _____ Year _____

☐ Sole Proprietor
☐ Partnership
☐ Corporation
☐ Other _____

Incorporation:
Date _____ State _____

Type of business: _____

**PRINCIPLES**

| NAME | TITLE | ADDRESS | CITY STATE | ZIP | DATE OF BIRTH | SOC. SEC. NO. |
|------|-------|---------|------------|-----|---------------|---------------|
| | | | | | | |
| | | | | | | |
| | | | | | | |

**BANKING**

BANK NAME _____

ACCOUNT OFFICER _____

BRANCH _____ PHONE (____) _____

CITY _____ STATE _____ ZIP _____

CHECKING ACCT. # _____   SAVINGS ACCT # _____   LOAN ACCT # _____

Purchase orders required _____

Authorized _____

Purchasers _____

**TRADE REFERENCES (SUPPLIERS)**

| (1) | (2) | (3) |
|-----|-----|-----|
| NAME: | NAME: | NAME: |
| STREET: | STREET: | STREET: |
| CITY STATE, ZIP: | CITY STATE, ZIP: | CITY, STATE, ZIP: |
| PHONE: | PHONE: | PHONE: |
| CONTACT NAME: | CONTACT: | CONTACT: |

I hereby certify that I hold valid sales tax permit # _____ issued persuant to the sales and use tax laws of the state of _____ Type of permit _____

I hereby authorize Goodmans or its agents to make whatever investigative inquiries it deems necessary. In connection with my application or in the course of review and/or collection of any payments due. I further authorize all references and creditors, including banks, to release to Goodmans, or its agents, any and all information pertaining to my account(s).

I hereby agree to pay all invoices for purchases net 10 days subject to 2% per month service charge (Apr. 24%) on past due invoices. I further agree to pay all reasonable collection costs, attorney's fees, and court costs necessary to collect my account whether or not a suit is commenced. Goodman's Inc. retains and I grant a Purchase Money Security Interest in all goods purchased by me until paid.

I certify that the information contained herein is completed and correct, and given for the purpose of obtaining credit.

SIGNED _____   PRINT NAME _____   TITLE _____   DATE _____

### PERSONAL GUARANTY

The undersigned, jointly and severally, unconditionally guaranty the payment when due of all present and future indebtedness of Customer to Goodmans, Inc. including but not limited to interest and attorney's fees.

PRINCIPLE'S SIGNATURE _____   DATE _____   SPOUSE'S SIGNATURE _____   DATE _____

**FIGURE 23-1**
Credit application used to obtain information about credit worthiness of clients.
(Reproduced with permission, Goodmans Design-Interiors, Phoenix, Az.)

firm a greater opportunity in dealing with clients who will honor their financial obligations.

## Confirmation of Purchase/Purchase Agreement_____

Many firms will proceed with ordering merchandise on the basis of verbal agreement by the client. As the reader will recall from the preceding chapter, a verbal "contract" for the sale of goods whose value is over $500 is not legally binding on the client. For this reason, many firms require a *confirmation of purchase*—also called a sales agreement, purchase agreement, or contract proposal—to be completed and signed by the client. This form legally binds the client to fulfilling his or her financial responsibility to the designer. Company policy should be clear that no furniture or furnishings be ordered or begun until a signed purchase agreement has been obtained from the client.

A two-or-more-page form (see Figure 23-2), the confirmation, when signed by the client, becomes a legal contract for selling the described merchandise. The designer must sell the described merchandise at the prices quoted, and the client must pay for that same merchandise.

It is impractical for a firm to type a series of these forms for a large volume of items. In those cases a statement such as "the undersigned agrees to purchase the items described per the attached list" will suffice.

The terms and conditions of the sale must be stated on the proposal agreement, and the client must be made aware of the terms (see Figure 23-3). Terms and conditions might relate to partial deliveries, changes in the job site, warehousing when the client is not ready to accept delivery, and warranties. These terms and conditions should be prepared with the advice of the firm's attorney.

## Purchase Orders_____

One of the most important forms of paperwork is the *purchase order.* The interior designer uses the purchase order to initiate orders for merchandise and services from factories, trades and craftspeople, and other vendors. Additionally, many businesses use purchase orders of their own to initiate orders from the interior designer.

The purchase order must be designed so that all the information that the receiving party needs to complete the order quickly and correctly is easily found. Considering the scope of projects and the number of different clients the design firm may deal with at any one time, it becomes apparent that the format must be standardized and complement the recording methods of the remaining paperwork and accounting systems used by the firm.

All firms, regardless of size, should have a policy prohibiting anything to be ordered without a written purchase order. Many manufacturers do not honor telephoned orders until the written order is received anyway. Telephone orders for any kind of product or service can lead to a duplication of orders and leave the design firm responsible for paying for two pink sofas with orange spots instead of the one requested by a client.

Purchase orders play more than one role for the design firm. The first, of course, is the means of obtaining the needed goods and services in the client's interests. A second important role of the purchase order is to act as a record of all outstanding orders. This role plays a part in the financial accounting of the firm for income tax and loan application purposes. A third function of the purchase order is to act as a

# SALES AGREEMENT

Date of Order_____19____ Delivery Date_____19____

Purchaser_____ Phone_____

Address_____
                Street                        City                State      Zip

Install at: Name_____ Phone_____

Address_____
                Street                        City                State      Zip

SPECIAL INSTRUCTIONS:_____

_____

_____

| MATERIALS AND SPECIFICATIONS | Price Each | TOTAL |
|---|---|---|
| | | |
| | | |
| | | |
| | | |
| | | |
| | | |
| | | |
| | | |
| | | |
| | | |
| | | |
| | | |
| | | |
| | | |
| | | |
| | | |
| | | |

☐ Subject to final measurements

Read the back of this page before signing. The provisions on the back side of this page are part of this agreement.

Installer_____

Sales Representative_____

Purchaser_____

Satifactorily completed _____ Date _____

TOTAL MATERIALS $_____

Labor     _____

Sub Total     _____

Tax     _____

Total     _____

Deposit     _____

Balance Due $_____

FIGURE 23-2
The sales agreement (or confirmation of purchase) is used as the contract for the sale of merchandise. *(Reproduced with permission, Cunninghams Interiors, Flagstaff, Az.)*

# TERMS AND CONDITIONS

**TERMS**

Terms of sale for all discounted items are Net 10 (ten) days from date of invoice. A monthly service charge of 1½% per month (18% per annum) will apply to all delinquent payments and will be added to the balance outstanding. Deliveries are to be paid for upon presentation of invoices covering each delivery. A deposit of 33% is required with all orders unless other terms have previously been established.

If for any reason the customer is unable to accept the merchandise as of the manufacturer's acknowledged shipping date, the customer (with Ball Stalker's assistance) will arrange for and pay for storage and handling. In this event, the Buyer hereby agrees to pay 90% of the invoice price for the merchandise within 10 days of the invoice date and pay the remaining 10% upon substantial completion of the installation. The final payment for all systems and furnishings is due upon substantial completion of installation. Substantial completion is the date when the work covered by this agreement is sufficiently complete so that the buyer can occupy or utilize the project work area or designated portion thereof for the use it is intended.

The security of all merchandise delivered to the project site is the responsibility of the buyer. The Owner shall be responsible for providing security against loss or damage for the materials, furniture, furnishings and equipment stored at the project premises between the dates of delivery and final acceptance by the Owner. Arrangements for such security shall be satisfactory to the Contractor.

This contract shall be governed by and construed in accordance with the laws of the State of Georgia.

This contract contains all the terms, provisions, conditions and warranties of the Sales Agreement and no extension, modification or amendment hereof shall be valid unless it is in writing signed by an Authorized Buyer and Seller.

**CUSTOMER ORDER**

A customer order is considered bonafide and Ball Stalker is obligated to perform to the order specifications when the customer confirms the order in writing by (1) issuing a purchase order, (2) authorizing letter, (3) signs and returns the Ball Stalker acknowledgment, or (4) signs a Ball Stalker Customer Agreement referencing a specific proposal or quotation.

It is incumbent upon the customer to confirm the order in one of the above mentioned methods within 10 calendar days from the date of the Ball Stalker order acknowledgment. The preceding conditions do not apply to QUICK SHIP orders.

**CHANGES AND CANCELLATIONS**

Changes by the customer cannot be accepted after 10 calendar days from the Ball Stalker acknowledgment date. The preceding conditions do not apply to QUICK SHIP orders. Changes in quantity or specification are subject to approval by Ball Stalker and manufacturer. Resultant charges from manufacturer would be paid by the customer. All requests for changes in quantity or specifications shall be delivered to Ball Stalker in writing.

Cancellation by the customer must be in writing and cannot be accepted after 10 calendar days from the Ball Stalker acknowledgment date. A restocking charge of 25% may be imposed for all approved cancellations at Ball Stalker's discretion. Changes at the job site must also be requested in writing and may be subject to additional charges.

**MEANS OF SHIPMENT**

The Ball Stalker responsibility regarding delivery, damage and freight inquiries and claims, etc. is conditioned upon the means of shipment specified in the original order. The following paragraphs identify the five means of shipment and the extent of Ball Stalker responsibility:

1. **LW-Delivered and Installed**—Ball Stalker will bear the full responsibility of delivering the merchandise in acceptable condition, obtaining written customer acceptance, and handling any difficulties regarding damage and freight inquiries and claims.

2. **DI-Direct**—The merchandise is shipped directly to the customer, but Ball Stalker personnel will meet the shipment and assume the full responsibility of "delivered and installed" terms.

3. **LD or DD-Delivery Only**—The merchandise is delivered to the customer's dock. Ball Stalker assumes the responsibility of damage and freight inquiry and claims but does not install the merchandise.

4. **DS-Drop Ship**—The merchandise is shipped and invoiced F.O.B. factory. The customer assumes all responsibility regarding damage and freight inquiries and claims.

5. **I/M-Inter-Market**—The goods are installed by another dealer as instructed by the manufacturer and the other "inter-market" dealer assumes full responsibility for delivery, damage and freight inquiries and claims.

**TRANSPORTATION AND SPECIAL HANDLING CHARGES**

Any transportation costs incurred in shipment of goods from the factory will be paid by the customer. Special handling charges, including special cartoning and crating, imposed by the manufacturer will be paid by the customer.

**DELIVERY AND INSTALLATION**

In the event that delivery and/or installation is required as a part of the proposal, the following provisions shall apply:

1. **Condition of Job Site**—The job site shall be clean, clear and free of debris prior to installation.

2. **Job Site Services**—Electric current, heat, hoisting and/or elevator service will be furnished without charge to Ball Stalker. Adequate facilities for off-loading, staging, moving and handling of merchandise shall be provided.

3. **Delivery During Normal Business Hours**—Delivery and installation will be made during normal working hours. Additional labor costs resulting from overtime work performed at the customer's request will be passed on to the customer.

4. **Installation and Assembly**—Ball Stalker's ability to install or assemble furniture shipped, knocked down or to permanently attach, affix, or bolt in place movable furniture is dependent on jurisdictional agreements between trade unions at the job site. If trade regulations enforced at the time of installation require on-site union tradesmen to complete the installation, the cost will be additional. Delivery of unusual items requiring special handling such as insulated files, marble, glass, etc., shall be charged to customer at applicable commercial rates for such handling.

5. **Delivered Goods**—Goods delivered and brought onto the job site as scheduled shall be inspected by the customer or his agent for damage and count verification. After delivery of merchandise by Seller to Buyer and acceptance of delivery by Buyer, pursuant to the provisions of the Georgia Uniform Commercial Code, all risk of loss or damage shall pass to Buyer, including, but not limited to, any loss or damage by weather, other trades such as painting or plastering, telephone installation, fire or other elements and Buyer agrees to hold Seller harmless from loss from such reasons.

6. **Receiving Documents**—Ball Stalker provides customer copies of receiving documents at the delivery point for all orders other than drop-shipments. It is the customer's obligation to process its internal receiving documents in such a way as to meet Ball Stalker's payment terms.

**STATE AND LOCAL TAXES**

The customer shall pay all taxes, levied or based upon the furniture and services invoiced by Ball Stalker, including state and local sales and use taxes. Customers who are exempt from the above taxes shall provide Ball Stalker with copies of exemption certificate upon confirmation of the order.

**WARRANTY**

All merchandise sold under this agreement is warranted by Ball Stalker Co. to be free from defects in materials or workmanship to the same extent as warranted by the merchandise manufacturers. Ball Stalker agrees to repair or replace at Ball Stalker's discretion defective merchandise covered by the above referenced warranty. This warranty agreement is contingent upon the Buyers promptly notifying Ball Stalker in writing of any claim with respect to the merchandise, and affording Ball Stalker a reasonable opportunity to examine the merchandise and investigate the claimed defect. Ball Stalker IN NO EVENT SHALL BE LIABLE FOR DAMAGES BEYOND THE PRICE PAID BY BUYER FOR SUCH DEFECTIVE MERCHANDISE. This warranty is in lieu of all other warranties express or implied, and it is agreed that there is no oral or implied additional warranties made in connection with the sale of the merchandise sold hereunder.

**GENERAL LIABILITY**

No liability will accrue against Ball Stalker as a result of any breach of these terms and conditions resulting from any work stoppage, accident, fire, civil disobedience, riots, rebellions, and Acts of God beyond Ball Stalker's control.

**FIGURE 23-3**

**Typical terms and conditions on the back side of a confirmation of purchase.** *(Reproduced with permission, Ball Stalker Co., Atlanta, Ga.)*

control mechanism for billings to clients. Many small firms with a very simple paperwork system will use the purchase order as a delivery ticket as well. What is shown as delivered on these forms will key the bookkeeper to send the necessary billing to clients. A fourth function can be for checking for correct pricing by the various suppliers. If the supplier acknowledges a price different from that on the purchase order, the designer should immediately find out what causes the discrepancy.

What the exact content and format of the purchase order is should be established by the needs of the individual firm and its accounting practices. Figure 23-4 is an example of a typical purchase order. The following information should be part of the purchase order either as preprinted information or blank spaces:

1. *Preprinted sequenced numbers.* Using numerically sequenced purchase orders allows the firm to keep track of each purchase order—whether used or thrown out.
2. *The firm's name and billing address.* Preprinted forms look more professional, negate mailing or shipping errors resulting from illegible handwriting, and save time.
3. *Space for the supplier's/vendor's name and address.*
4. *Space for the "ship to" location.* This is very important when the design firm is not having the merchandise shipped to the design firm's office location.
5. *Preprinted boxes or space for additional shipping instructions.* These instructions relate to expected ship date, preferred freight company, and collected or prepaid charges.
6. *Space for the "tag for" information.* The *tag for* information can be at the bottom or the top of the form. The client's name is usually written in this space as a further means of identifying for whom this merchandise or service was ordered. Some firms also put other brief instructions to help the receiving party clearly identify for whom and how the materials are to be used or where the items are to be located on the job.

The body of the purchase order should have space for the following information:

1. *Quantity.* This is not only needed by the supplier, but it is required by the UCC to form a sales contract.
2. *Catalog number.* This should exactly reflect the sequence of numbers and/or letters that the supplier uses to call out the products from his or her catalog. Reversing one number can lead to the wrong product being shipped.
3. *Description.* A complete full description. Again, maintaining the method the supplier uses in the catalog helps prevent having the wrong item shipped. Remember, however, that many suppliers process orders by the catalog number on the purchase order, not the description. The description acts as a check against the catalog number. There is no guarantee that the supplier's order input desk will read the description.
4. *Net price.* Putting the expected net price on the purchase order works as a good pricing check. Net pricing on the purchase order can also help the firm attempting to utilize a cost accounting method for managerial control.

At the bottom of the form should be space for the authorizing signature. Additional information about which the individual design firm wishes the supplier to be aware can be added in appropriate places. An example would be instructions asking the supplier to acknowledge receipt of the purchase order and to provide

## PURCHASE ORDER

| | PG | PGS |
|---|---|---|
| | | OF |

DIRECT INQUIRES REGARDING THIS ORDER
TO:
PHONE NUMBER:

VENDOR:                                    SHIP TO:

VENDOR NO.

| DATE | | FREIGHT TO BE PAID BY: | | | | SHIP | COMPLETE ONLY ☐ | PARTIAL ☐ |
|---|---|---|---|---|---|---|---|---|

FREIGHT TO BE PAID BY:
☐ GOODMANS PHOENIX ☐ SHIPPER ☐ CONSIGNEE
SEND BILL OF LADING WITH INVOICE

DELIVER:
☐ ASAP ☐ NOT BEFORE

**NO C.O.D. SHIPMENTS**

SHIP COMPLETE ONLY ☐ PARTIAL ☐

NOTE: IF SHIPMENT IS MARKED ABOVE "COMPLETE ONLY" AND ITEMS ARE SHIPPED PARTIAL, THEN PAYMENT WILL BE WITHHELD UNTIL SHIPMENT IS COMPLETE.

UNLESS PRICES ARE SAME OR LOWER CALL OR MAIL CATALOGS WITH NEW PRICE LISTS ↘

| QUANTITY ORDERED | CATALOG NUMBER | DESCRIPTION | TAG LINE ITEM | NET COST EACH |
|---|---|---|---|---|
| | | | | |

**\*\*PURCHASE ORDER PLEASE ACKNOWLEDGE\*\***

**PLEASE COMPLY WITH INSTRUCTIONS BELOW:**
**IMPORTANT!!**
1. Please mark all packages and papers with our Order No. and Line Item No. and Cust. Name.
2. Acknowledge receipt of this Purchase Order and confirm delivery date.
3. Submit all Invoices in Duplicate.
4. Bill of Lading and name of carrier must be attached to Invoices sent to Goodmans.

**TAG FOR:**
LINE ITEM NUMBERS AND CUSTOMER NAMES MUST APPEAR ON ALL INVOICES AND CARTONS.

P.O.

_____
AUTHORIZED SIGNATURE

VENDOR'S COPY

**FIGURE 23-4**
An example of a purchase order used by a commercial office furnishings dealer.
(Reproduced with permission, Goodmans Design-Interiors, Phoenix, Az.)

258

an expected shipping date. Figure 23-4 shows some of the other kinds of instructions that might be useful.

Each supplier receives a separate purchase order. Multiple items to the same supplier for the same client can, of course, be sent on the same purchase order. If the designer is placing orders for multiple items to the same supplier but for two or more *different* clients, a different purchase order should be prepared for each client.

If two suppliers are involved in the completion of one finished product, such as a COM (customer's own material)[1] sofa, two different purchase orders must be prepared. One purchase order is written to the sofa supplier, referencing (according to the supplier's requirements printed in his or her catalog) the COM fabric. A second purchase order is written to the fabric supplier referencing the information required by the sofa supplier. This information is often written as an expanded tag for a block of information in the body of the purchase order rather than in the normal tag for space. Most furniture manufacturers require that the fabric be shipped prepaid to the factory. The designer must be sure that the fabric supplier does this, and the designer must remember to add that estimated shipping charge to the cost of the sofa.

## NUMBER OF COPIES

For a small firm, a minimum of three copies of the purchase order would be required. To help in visually tracking the various copies, it is best if each sheet is a different color. The first sheet is always white. The other copies may be any color.

- The white or original copy is the copy mailed to the supplier.
- The second copy should go in the open purchase order file.
- The third copy should go in the client's active file to be used for reference.

The open purchase order file is a numerical sequence of all the purchase orders that have been mailed but against which merchandise or services have not yet been received. In a small firm, the bookkeeper may keep track of this file. When acknowledgments are received, they should be checked for accuracy against the information on the purchase order. Discrepancies should be dealt with immediately. When merchandise has been received and delivered, the bookkeeper can send the proper billing to the client. Orders not yet received can be tracked by checking the expected ship date on the order against the current date. If an order appears to be late, the designer responsible should contact the supplier to establish the reason for the delay.

Larger firms may have a use for one or more additional copies of the purchase order. The most common use for an additional copy is to send to a warehouse or warehouse service. This helps the warehousing location to more effectively service the design firm's needs, since it will know in advance the quantity and expected arrival dates of all the merchandise the firm has ordered. On the occasion that the merchandise is shipped to the client's location rather than the warehouse, the warehouse is alerted of a responsibility to unload and inspect the merchandise as it comes off the truck.

---

[1]COM indicates that the designer is not using a fabric available from the chair or sofa manufacturer. The desired fabric will have to be ordered from a different supplier and sent to the chair/sofa manufacturer.

# Acknowledgments

*Acknowledgments* or confirmations are the forms which the supplier sends back to the designer to indicate what the supplier interpreted the designer's order to be (see Figure 23-5). Depending on the supplier, the designer should receive an acknowledgment in about ten days to three weeks.

Although acknowledgments will vary in format to suit the needs of specific suppliers, it is likely that the following kinds of information will be provided:

1. An order number assigned by the supplier.
2. The design firm's purchase order number.
3. Date the acknowledgment was prepared.
4. A scheduled shipping date. The scheduled shipping date indicates that sometime within the week the date appears is the time that merchandise will be shipped—not necessarily on that day.
5. What the expected shipping situation will be (for example, "Collect—Roadway" means that the design firm will have to pay the shipping charges and that the merchandise will come from the Roadway shipping company).
6. Notations as to who ordered the merchandise, the billing address, and the shipping address.
7. What the tag for instructions is to be.
8. A restatement of quantity, catalog number, description, and pricing information. Many manufacturers will put the net price on the acknowledgment. However, others still quote retail prices. If the retail price has been quoted, the acknowledgment will often also quote the discount the designer is to receive for that order.
9. Other information related to billing and shipping.

Depending on the size of the firm and the organizational structure, someone must be responsible for checking the acknowledgment information against the purchase order. This could be the expediter (whose responsibilities were discussed in the introduction). Checking the acknowledgment information should be done immediately in order to catch any discrepancies between the two forms. Any discrepancies in quantity, catalog number, description, and price should be checked with the manufacturer. Delays in calling attention to errors often result in the design firm receiving the wrong merchandise. This kind of delay can lead to an angry client and poor customer relations. Discrepancies regarding the expected shipping date or other shipping information should also be checked to see how they may affect project completion.

Speedy review of the acknowledgment against the purchase order is also necessary since there is generally very little time to make changes in the order. Major suppliers often give only ten days and certainly no more than three weeks "from receipt of order" to make any changes in the order. Time is of the essence.

The supplier will only send the firm an original copy of the acknowledgment. Again, depending on the firm's size and paperwork structure, the original will probably be attached to the corresponding purchase order in the open purchase order file. A copy may be added to the active project file for reference.

# Invoices

An *invoice* is simply a bill. The interior design firm sends out invoices to clients for services performed and/or goods purchased in the client's name. Suppliers send

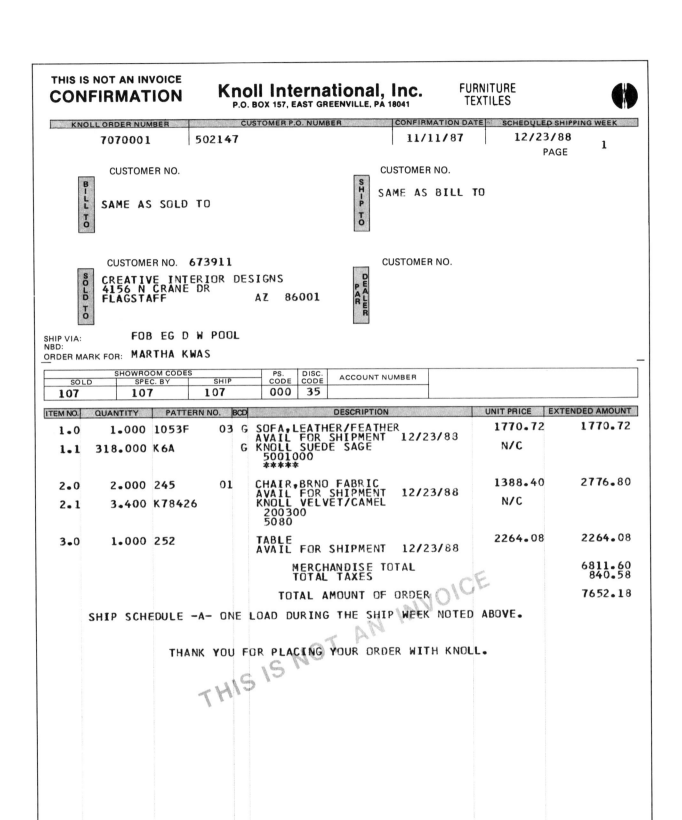

THIS IS NOT AN INVOICE
**CONFIRMATION**

# Knoll International, Inc.
P.O. BOX 157, EAST GREENVILLE, PA 18041

FURNITURE
TEXTILES

| KNOLL ORDER NUMBER | CUSTOMER P.O. NUMBER | CONFIRMATION DATE | SCHEDULED SHIPPING WEEK |
|---|---|---|---|
| 7070001 | 502147 | 11/11/87 | 12/23/88 PAGE 1 |

**BILL TO**    CUSTOMER NO.    SAME AS SOLD TO

**SHIP TO**    CUSTOMER NO.    SAME AS BILL TO

**SOLD TO**    CUSTOMER NO. 673911
CREATIVE INTERIOR DESIGNS
4156 N CRANE DR
FLAGSTAFF    AZ   86001

**DEALER**    CUSTOMER NO.

SHIP VIA:    FOB EG D W POOL
NBD:
ORDER MARK FOR: MARTHA KWAS

| SHOWROOM CODES | | | PS. CODE | DISC. CODE | ACCOUNT NUMBER | |
|---|---|---|---|---|---|---|
| SOLD | SPEC. BY | SHIP | | | | |
| 107 | 107 | 107 | 000 | 35 | | |

| ITEM NO. | QUANTITY | PATTERN NO. | BCD | DESCRIPTION | UNIT PRICE | EXTENDED AMOUNT |
|---|---|---|---|---|---|---|
| 1.0 | 1.000 | 1053F | 03 G | SOFA,LEATHER/FEATHER AVAIL FOR SHIPMENT 12/23/83 | 1770.72 | 1770.72 |
| 1.1 | 318.000 | K6A | G | KNOLL SUEDE SAGE 5001000 ***** | N/C | |
| 2.0 | 2.000 | 245 | 01 | CHAIR,BRNO FABRIC AVAIL FOR SHIPMENT 12/23/88 | 1388.40 | 2776.80 |
| 2.1 | 3.400 | K78426 | | KNOLL VELVET/CAMEL 200300 5080 | N/C | |
| 3.0 | 1.000 | 252 | | TABLE AVAIL FOR SHIPMENT 12/23/88 | 2264.08 | 2264.08 |
| | | | | MERCHANDISE TOTAL | | 6811.60 |
| | | | | TOTAL TAXES | | 840.58 |
| | | | | TOTAL AMOUNT OF ORDER | | 7652.18 |

SHIP SCHEDULE -A- ONE LOAD DURING THE SHIP WEEK NOTED ABOVE.

THANK YOU FOR PLACING YOUR ORDER WITH KNOLL.

K2012  R 7/87        CUSTOMER COPY

**FIGURE 23-5**
The acknowledgment tells the designer what the manufacturer believes to be the
merchandise or service order. *(Reproduced with permission, Knoll International)*

invoices to the designer for the goods or services that the interior design firm has ordered. Figure 23-6 is an invoice from the designer to the client. Figure 23-7 is an invoice from a supplier to a designer.

Invoices from suppliers are commonly sent at the same time that the merchandise is shipped. The invoice generally arrives at the office a few days before the merchandise. Many suppliers have invoices that look very similar to their acknowledgments. The only difference may be the label. Again, someone in the office must be responsible for checking the invoice to be sure that it corresponds to what was ordered. Since it often arrives a few days before the merchandise, it also should be checked against what was received.

It is important for the designer to check the invoice to determine if the manufacturer has extended any special pricing—especially related to prompt payment. The reader will recall the discussion on cash discounts in Chapter 13. These discounts can amount to substantial savings for the firm that can afford to pay the invoice within the specified prompt payment time. Not all suppliers offer this special discount to all designers.

The designer should be sending out invoices to clients for services and/or goods as quickly as possible. Goods should be billed within ten days after the goods are delivered and accepted by the client. Services should be billed when services are completed (for short duration projects), on a monthly basis for larger projects, or on whatever billing basis for services was agreed to in the contract. Delays in billing goods and services causes an increased amount of receivables. This is something that small and large design firms alike cannot afford. Delays in billing can also lead to the few unscrupulous clients into not paying for goods or services at all, unless the design firm can afford to hire an attorney or collection agency to obtain the funds or the goods.

To help in having at least some legal basis for preventing late or no payment, the original contract for services or goods should contain language related to "billing upon delivery" or "payment due ten days after receipt of invoice." Some firms try to use item-by-item billing on large projects. This of course means that if the project has twenty items expected to be delivered, and two arrive, the firm delivers the two and bills for those two. The next time one or more items arrive, those are also delivered and billed. Although this may help somewhat with the firm's cash flow, it can cause many costs and headaches to the firm. It is suggested that whenever possible, deliveries be done in larger quantities of items or as a complete job. This will reduce the delivery costs and the bookkeeping costs of multiple deliveries and billings.

## *Freight Matters*

Chapter 13 contains a discussion of how freight and delivery charges affect the price of the goods, and Chapter 22 reviewed freight concepts as regulated by the UCC. In this chapter we will look at the forms that are related to freight services.

There are various freight matters that result in additional paperwork management for the designer. The first is the bill of lading. The *bill of lading* is the form the supplier provides to the truck driver (see Figure 23-8). The driver carries this form with him or her in the truck; the contents of the truck must match what is on the form. Many times the bill of lading will not be a detailed list but rather a total quantity of items. The designer or the warehouse must check the number of items that are delivered to the firm with the number on the bill of lading. Discrepancies in quantity should be noted on the bill as well as any notations regarding damages to merchandise.

**Ball Stalker Co.**

Office Furniture & Systems

151 Fourteenth Street, N.W.
Atlanta, GA 30318-7801 • (404) 876-8999

# INVOICE

| INVOICE DATE | INVOICE NO. | PAGE |
|---|---|---|
| | | |

CUSTOMER                                    SHIPPED TO

| CUSTOMER ORDER NUMBER | SALESPERSON | BALL STALKER ORDER NUMBER |
|---|---|---|
| | | |

**CASH TERMS**

| ITEM NO. | | QUANTITY | | | DESCRIPTION | UNIT PRICE | TOTAL PRICE |
|---|---|---|---|---|---|---|---|
| OUR | CUST. | ORDERED | DELIVERED | B/O | | | |
| | | | | | | | |

MAIL ALL REMITTANCES TO: 151 FOURTEENTH STREET, N.W.
ATLANTA, GEORGIA 30318-7801

NUMERICAL COPY

**FIGURE 23-6**
**The invoice prepared by the design firm and sent to the client.** *(Reproduced with permission, Ball Stalker Co., Atlanta, Ga.)*

**invoice**

customer | date | invoice number

sold to

ship to

It is the orderer's responsibility to check this document for accuracy, correct fabric selections, etc. Report claims immediately. This order is subject to the terms and conditions on the face and reverse side. Federal employer I.D. 38-0837640.

| order date | your purchase order number | terms | deposit | salesperson | territory | type | order number | ship date |
| contract number | ship to purchase order number | ship from | | | | | bill of lading number | |

| item number | quantity this invoice | quantity remaining | quantity ordered | quantity previously invoiced | product number | product description | unit price | extended price |

ZC21 R 3/87

customer original

•Remit to

**FIGURE 23-7**
An invoice from the manufacturer to the designer. (Reproduced with permission, Herman Miller, Inc.)

UNIFORM STRAIGHT BILL OF LADING — Short Form — Original — Not Negotiable — Domestic

On Collect on Delivery shipments, the letters "COD" must appear before consignee's name or as otherwise provided in item 430, Sec. 1.

RECEIVED, subject to the classifications and tariffs in effect on the date of the issue of this Bill of Lading,

FROM
STREET AND NO.
CITY AND STATE                                    ZIP

CONSIGNED TO
STREET AND NO.
CITY AND STATE                                    ZIP

ROUTING

*If the shipment moves between two ports by a carrier by water, the law requires that the bill of lading shall state whether it is "carrier's or shipper's weight." NOTE—Where the rate is dependent on value, shippers are required to state specifically in writing the agreed or declared value of the property.

SHIPPER NO.                    DATE

C. O. D.    C.O.D.    FEE ☐ CONSIGNEE
           TO BE  ☐
           PAID BY  SHIPPER ☐
$          ADVANCE   C.O.D. FEE   T.L. REV.   C.L. REV.

| NO. PKG. | HM | DESCRIPTION OF ARTICLES, SPECIAL MARKS, AND EXCEPTIONS | *WEIGHT (Sub. to Cor.) | Class or Rate | Check Column |
|---|---|---|---|---|---|
| | | | | | |
| | | | | | |
| | | | | | |
| | | | | | |
| | | | | | |
| | | | | | |

the property described below, in apparent good order, except as noted (contents and condition of contents of packages unknown) marked, consigned, and destined as indicated below, which said carrier (the word carrier being understood throughout this contract as meaning any person or corporation in possession of the property under the contract) agrees to carry to its usual place of delivery at said destination, if on its route, otherwise to deliver to another carrier on the route to said destination. It is mutually agreed, as to each carrier of all or any of said property over all or any portion of said route to destination, and as to each party at any time interested in all or any of said property, that every service to be performed hereunder shall be subject to all the terms and conditions of the Uniform Domestic Straight Bill of Lading set forth (1) in Uniform Freight Classification in effect on the date hereof, if this is a rail or a rail-water shipment, or (2) in the applicable motor carrier classification or tariff if this is a motor carrier shipment.
Shipper hereby certifies that he is familiar with all the terms and conditions of the said bill of lading, including those on the back thereof, set forth in the classification or tariff which governs the transportation of this shipment, and the said terms and conditions are hereby agreed to by the shipper and accepted for himself and his assigns.

Subject to Section 7 of conditions of applicable bill of lading, if this shipment is to be delivered to the consignee without recourse on the consignor, the consignor shall sign the following statement:
The carrier shall not make delivery of this shipment without payment of freight and all other lawful charges.

_____ (Signature of Consignor)

If charges are to be prepaid, write or stamp here, "To be Prepaid."

Received $ _____ to apply in prepayment of the charges on the property described hereon.

_____ Agent or Cashier

Per _____
(The signature here acknowledges only the amount prepaid.)

This is to certify that the above-named materials are properly classified, described, packaged, marked and labeled and are in proper condition for transportation according to the applicable regulations of the Dept. of Transportation.

THE AGREED OR DECLARED VALUE OF THE PROPERTY IS HEREBY SPECIFICALLY STATED BY THE SHIPPER TO BE NOT EXCEEDING _____ PER _____

IT IS HEREBY AGREED THAT THE DECLARED VALUATION ON HOUSEHOLD GOODS OR PERSONAL EFFECTS IS NOT EXCEEDING 10¢ PER POUND PER ARTICLE LOST OR DAMAGED UNLESS A HIGHER VALUE IS DECLARED.

1

_____ SHIPPER

PER _____

Agent, Per _____
(This Bill of Lading is to be signed by the shipper and agent of the carrier issuing same.)

FORM 212-4 (11-77)
(TREAS-146)
ISSUED 9/82

FIGURE 23-8
The bill of lading provides information about the shipper, the receiver, and the merchandise being shipped. (Reproduced with permission, Transcon Lines.)

265

Another form that accompanies the delivery is a packing list. The *packing list* is commonly in a plastic envelope attached to the outside of one of the items being delivered. This list is a detailed list of quantity and description of what is being delivered to the warehouse at a specific time. The packing list should be checked against all items taken from the truck and against the number on the bill of lading. Again, discrepancies should be noted.

The actual freight bill is another use of the invoice. It is usually sent a few days after the shipment leaves the manufacturer. This invoice comes from the shipping company, not the manufacturer, and is the bill for the shipping service.

It is important for the designer or a representative of the design firm (the warehousing service) to inspect all the items as they arrive at the designer's warehouse or job site. Many one-person design firms allow the merchandise to be delivered to the client without the designer being available at the time of delivery for inspection of the goods. This can be very costly when merchandise is damaged. Damaged cartons should be immediately opened and inspected. Whenever practical, all items should be unwrapped or uncartoned to inspect for *concealed damage*—damage that may exist even though the carton or wrapping appears intact. Concealed damage must be reported to the carrier as soon as possible. As the time from acceptance of shipment or the discovery of damages lengthens, successful claims become less probable.

Any damage to cartons, packing, and merchandise should be shown to the driver. Notations as to damaged merchandise must be made on the bill of lading in order to make successful claims. Many firms also use instamatic-type cameras to take pictures of damaged merchandise. This can greatly help in the filing of claims.

Since the filing of freight claims and disposition of the claim is very time-consuming, many firms forgo filing claims on small damage and make repairs themselves. These charges are costed as an overhead expense. Merchandise that has sustained substantial damage in transit should be refused.

Certain items are generally required when filing a freight claim.

1. The bill of lading.
2. The paid freight bill.
3. The manufacturer's invoice for the item.
4. The inspection report prepared by the freight carrier.
5. Documentation of repair costs.
6. Documentation of additional freight costs (if any) resulting from the damage.
7. Other written or photographic documentation that attests to the damage occurring before delivery to the job site or the designer's warehouse.

Since manufacturers will not accept merchandise for return once the design firm has accepted it, the firm must get written permission to return damaged (or incorrectly shipped) merchandise. Each manufacturer has its own policy concerning returns, and these policies must be adhered to in order to receive proper credit.

Someone in the design office must be responsible for checking on shipping progress. Larger firms hire an expediter to track the firm's pending shipments. This activity involves regularly reviewing all pending shipments (via the open purchase order file) and making inquiries related to delayed shipments. The expediting function also involves arranging for faster-than-normal shipments and special shipping conditions. The role of the expediter is discussed in more detail in the following chapter. In some firms, the expediter may also be responsible for filing returns permissions as well as freight claims. A warehousing service should provide the service for filing freight claims.

When the design firm contacts the freight carrier concerning a shipping question, it should have the supplier's name and location, the date of shipment, the description and number of items shipped, and the delivery location. If the information needed is not on the manufacturer's invoice, this information, along with other needed information, can be obtained from the manufacturer.

## *Summary*

In this chapter we have looked at the various kinds of paperwork that must be managed in order to complete a sale of merchandise or the invoice of services. Design firms that function as "designer/specifiers" and do not sell merchandise to the end-user do save themselves a considerable amount of paperwork. Those that wish to sell merchandise as well as perform the design service must be prepared to understand and handle the multitude of paperwork involved.

We have described the credit application, confirmation proposal, purchase order, acknowledgment, and invoice. We have also looked at the paperwork involved in freight or shipping of merchandise to the delivery location and the delivery responsibility. The differences between the paperwork management for residential and commercial projects is very subtle. The forms themselves are the same. The delivery to the job site and other completion stages often require a bit more individualized attention in the residential practice.

Designers who are unable to manage the paperwork should hire someone skilled in that area. Not to do so could result in the firm's having serious or even disastrous cash flow and public relations problems that could lead to the dissolution of the firm.

The next chapter covers the activities involved in the delivery of merchandise to the job site.

# Chapter 24

# POST-ORDERING CONSIDERATIONS

*A*lthough the previous chapter dealt with the different kinds of paperwork involved in the handling of merchandise orders and billings, the project is not complete until all the merchandise is delivered and accepted by the client. In this chapter we will look at the various activities that occur once the orders have been placed and are ready to be delivered to the client. These activities include expediting, delivering and installing, walking through, handling complaints, and following up.

In small design firms these activities are customarily administered by the owner-designer with assistance from others only in the delivery stage. In larger firms, many of these activities are handled by other employees whose specialized job responsibility revolves around the job completion aspects of the project.

Whether administered by the designer himself or herself or as part of the responsibility of others, the project designer always retains ultimate responsibility for the completion of the project. It is an important part of being a professional.

## *Expediting*

As defined in the previous chapter, an *expediter* is an individual familiar with the design firm's paperwork system and the various ordering and shipping requirements of the manufacturers; the expediter is responsible for the speedy processing of orders. In firms large enough to have this specific job function is a person who will constantly monitor all orders *after* the purchase order has been sent and the acknowledgment has been received.

The first activity of the expediter would be to check the acknowledgment from the manufacturers against the purchase order. It is vital to be sure that all the information matches between the two forms to confirm that the correct products and/or services are being supplied. Discrepancies must be taken care of immediately.

Once all the product information has been checked, the expediter will look closely at the expected ship date. He or she must check to be sure that the products are going to ship within the time specified on the purchase order and that they will arrive when they were promised to the client. If the ship date is not when expected, the expediter should inform the designer so that proper actions can be taken. Merchandise shipped earlier than desired may have to be warehoused until the site is ready. If this is the case, the designer must negotiate with the client as to where and who will be responsible for the charges. At the time of order, it is relatively easy for the design firm to request that the merchandise not be shipped until a date beyond the normal shipping schedule. There may be an extra charge if the manufacturer must warehouse the finished goods when the designer requests the shipment to be delayed.

It is not uncommon for the ship date to be later than expected. The designer must contact the client to let him or her know about the delay. Short-term delays may be inconvenient but are seldom critical problems. Delays of three or more weeks may necessitate canceling the original order and finding alternate products.

The expediter would also be responsible for tracking shipments once they have left the manufacturer. He or she should be alerting the delivery people of the impending shipment and where it is to be delivered by the trucking company. If merchandise is to be "drop shipped" to a job site, meaning the merchandise goes to the client's address rather than the firm's warehouse or warehouse service, someone representing the design firm must be on the scene to unload, inspect, and deliver the goods to the client. Truck drivers are not generally responsible for unloading the merchandise from the truck, unpacking it, and delivering it to the client.

Once shipments leave the manufacturer, they are tracked by the bill of lading number, not the purchase order number. The firm receives from the freight company information as to what this number is. This number, along with the name and address of the design firm, the name and address of the delivery site, the name of the shipping company, the name and address of the original shipping location, a description and the number of pieces in the order, and the weight of the order must be available to track delayed shipments.

## Delivery and Installation

*Delivery* includes the activities concerned with moving items such as chairs, case goods, accessories, and other furnishings from the showroom or warehouse to the job site and simply placing them in their correct locations. Delivery involves no special activities of assembly, construction, or physical attachment of the products to the building. *Installation* involves assembly, construction, or physical attachment of products to the building.

### DELIVERY

When merchandise is delivered to the client, it is important for the client to sign documentation to indicate what he or she received. As we discussed in the chapter on the Uniform Commercial Code, this signifies acceptance and transfer of title, thereby requiring the client to pay for what was delivered. If a copy of the purchase order was sent to the warehouse service or the designer's warehouse, the client can sign off on this form. Some firms have a separate delivery ticket that accompanies the merchandise. This ticket is at least a three part form:

1. The top or original copy goes to the client.
2. A second copy is sent to the billing office.
3. The third is retained by the warehouse whenever a back order, which is a partial shipment, occurs.

Any notations of damages or discrepancies between what is delivered and what was ordered should be noted on the delivery paperwork. This helps clarify which damages are the responsibility of the design firm and which damages are the responsibility of the client.

A delivery plan, showing locations for all the furniture and other items for the job, is prepared to let the delivery people know exactly where each piece is to be located. This is an essential aid to the smooth completion of the project. A floor plan keyed to the purchase order number and line item number is one way to do this if the project is small and does not involve many items. For larger projects, and especially in commercial design, other methods are used. Furniture items on the floor plan are keyed to the purchase order to facilitate delivery.

Delivery service should include dusting and vacuuming of the merchandise as well as careful inspection for any scratches or other damage. It may also be the delivery team's responsibility to show the client how to operate certain items, such as adjustable office chairs. However, this is often the responsibility of the designer or the salesperson.

A common responsibility of the delivery service is the removal of all cartoning and packaging materials. No matter how small the job, the empty cartons and paper padding materials should not be left for the client to dispose of.

Clients often expect the designer to be present at all times during the delivery and installation of merchandise. This may seem to be an impractical use of the designer's time, but it can be key for maintaining good public relations. The designer at the job site during this crucial time can reassure the client who is not so sure about the colors or patterns that are being installed in his or her home or office. Color variations and damaged goods may not be noticed until the wall covering or floor covering is about to be installed.

The designer who is present during the delivery and installation of merchandise can speed up the inspection process, assure the client, and, when questions arise, help on the spot. How much time the designer spends at the job site during this time will depend on the client, the contract, the particular complexity of the job, and the designer's availability.

## INSTALLATION

As pointed out earlier, installation is the part of the delivery process that also involves assembly, construction, or physical attachments to the building. Installation would be the attachment of wall coverings, window treatments, carpet and other floorings, wall-hung bookcases or other storage units, mirrors, and the assembly of open office furniture. The installation of such items are usually done by someone other than the supplier of the goods, but not always. Installation service often depends on some other part of the project construction and delivery process being completed, requiring the need for careful scheduling of the construction, delivery, and installation.

Where many items of furniture are to be assembled, specialized sets of drawings are necessary. With open office systems, for example, commercial firms prepare one or more sheets of drawings that aid in the assembly. Plans may be drawn to show panel configurations and finishes, electrical and telephone service, and either plans or elevations for the location of hanging components.

Routine architectural finish schedules, as part of the construction documents, provide the information needed to specify the locations of these finishes. Graphic schedules or interior elevations inform the contractor of the locations of such items as mirrors, complex wall treatments, and various wall-hung units.

Although it does take time to prepare delivery and installation drawings, it is the easiest and simplest way to help assure that all the specified goods are delivered and installed in their proper locations. Success with these documents provides the designer the assurance that he or she is not needed on the job site at all times. Showing the client that these kinds of documents have helped on projects in the past also indicates to the client that the firm can deliver and install the products without the designer being there at all times.

Just as it is important in the delivery function for dusting, vacuuming, and removal of trash, it is also important for all installation people to do the same. Since some companies do not perform such tasks as a routine part of their service, the design firm should be sure that it is included in the contract to the installer. If it is not included, the designer or client will be charged for the extra work.

Flooring and wall covering manufacturers often provide maintenance instructions with their shipments. These should be passed on to the client by the designer. Most furniture manufacturers make this same kind of information available, but may not include it with the shipment. The designer should provide maintenance information for all products specified.

## *Walk-through*

When all the furniture and furnishings have been delivered and installed, it is customary for the designer and client to have a *walk-through*. This is a final inspection of the job to be sure that everything that was ordered is present, and that any omissions or as yet unrepaired damages are noted. Some firms have a special form to record omissions and damages. Most, however, simply record the information on ruled paper and have the information typed. A copy of the typed report can be given to the client and used by the design firm to prepare work orders, repair tickets, and memos to expedite missing goods. For firms charging design fees on a phased basis, the billing of the final part of the fee cannot be made until after the walk-through.

The walk-through is also a good time for the designer to fine-tune the project. Although this can involve some "free" design service, it also can result in some additional specification or sale of merchandise. Commercial clients especially have a hard time budgeting for accessories at the beginning of the project. But when the installation is winding down, they often see the need for wall hangings, desk accessories, plants, and other items that complete the project.

## *Complaints and Repairs*

Complaints and repairs should be taken care of immediately. It is important for unresolved omissions and damages to be taken care of as soon as possible. Regrettably, this is the stage that many designers lose total interest with the job. It is always more difficult to take care of nagging problems with a project than it is to be designing a new project. But unresolved problems cause bad feelings and poor recommendations from clients. Uncollected receivables, because of these small problems, can cause serious problems with the firm's cash flow. The design firm should have highly qualified furniture repair people, experienced with all kinds of wood and metal furniture, available to do repair work.

As much as possible, the firm's aim should be to handle complaints and repairs before the client is even aware of them. A competent warehouse service that inspects and repairs furniture eliminates minor damages before furniture is delivered to the client. Delivery personnel that handle the merchandise as if it were their own also avoid potential problems. The firm should hire only competent, experienced installers. The delivery and installation people must be required to clean up the job site. And delivering all the goods at one time helps to solve a lot of complaints.

## *Follow-up*

It is a good practice for the designer and the design team to do an evaluation of the project as soon after it is completed as possible. This evaluation should cover a time analysis to see if the project was completed within the time estimate. Review of any problems related to the project, the client, the manufacturers and suppliers, the delivery process, and so forth, should be included. The design director may also do a profitability analysis to determine if the project itself was a profit maker or a profit loser. This evaluation helps to evaluate whether or not this kind of project should be sought by the firm in the future.

Within a week of the final delivery, it is important for maintaining good public relations to send a thank-you letter or postcard to the client. Such a note, often a form letter, shows an added measure of concern for the client and appreciation for his or her business. Although the main purpose of the letter is to thank the client for his or her business, it might also request comments on the handling of the project. At this stage, however, it is probably too early to ask about satisfaction with the products.

About a month later, the designer should make an appointment with the client to discuss satisfaction with the products. Although it is hoped that all problems have been resolved long before this, any leftover repairs, omissions, or other problems can be discussed and handled at this time. This follow-up is another excellent public relations effort with the client. A post-project evaluation with the client also helps the design firm to evaluate whether or not to seek this kind of project or client in the future.

On large-sized, complex projects, it is also a good idea to have a second site visit with the client in another thirty to sixty days. It is a standard procedure for firms specifying and selling open office furniture to have these kinds of follow-up visits to help the client make the transition from conventional to open office products.

## *Summary*

Many designers do not enjoy taking care of the paperwork or following up on the orders for the merchandise they specify. Still, this is a very important part of project management.

In this chapter we have looked at what the designer is responsible for after the merchandise has been ordered. We have also looked at some ways of making these final parts of the project easier to accomplish.

This chapter concludes the discussion on project management. The professional designer is constantly dealing with administrative activities and paperwork. These activities, along with the creative processes of the actual design projects, are the heart of the interior design profession.

In the last two chapters we will be looking at other issues of the profession—issues of interest to both the professional and the student of interior design.

# Part 6

## Careers

# Chapter 25

## CAREER OPTIONS

$M$ost people view a career in the interior design profession to mean the designing of spaces and the selling of products related to the home. Some are familiar with the work of interior designers and architects in the design of offices and other public buildings such as hotels, restaurants, medical offices, and so on and recognize this as another way to work in the profession. For the general public and to many potential students, the interior design profession represents selecting colors and fabrics, preparing floor plans, and selling furniture and furnishings such as draperies and carpet. Although these activities are very definitely an important part of the profession, the interior designer does much more.

Many students wonder, "What can someone who majors in interior design do after graduation?" Although most graduating students enter the profession as either a residential or a commercial interior designer, there are other options for the graduate. No discussion of professional practice would be complete without some time spent on what options there are within the profession for either the student or the experienced professional.

In this chapter, we will first look at the two main options in the profession—that of being a residential interior designer or a commercial interior designer. Then we will discuss the various business aspects within those categories. The chapter will also explain other career options that the student or experienced professional may consider.

## *Residential Interior Design*

*Residential interior design* primarily deals with private living spaces, most frequently, of course, the freestanding single-family home. Private living spaces have changed dramatically with fewer people being able to afford the single-family detached house. Residential designers also often design private living space variations such as townhouses, condominiums, and apartments. Although hotels, motels, and dormitories may also be considered private living spaces, they are actually part of commercial or nonresidential design.

Residential designers engage in a practice that frequently calls upon them to do smaller-sized projects than those done by commercial designers. The average single-family detached house today ranges in size from 1000 to 3000 square feet, whereas commercial interior designers may work on projects that can be 5000, 10,000, and even over 100,000 square feet in size.

Once they have gained experience, residential designers are frequently engaged to design the entire house. However, in the early part of his or her career, the residential designer will do more project work with portions of the home, perhaps single rooms within the residence or even consultations regarding individual items within a room.

The extent of the involvement of the designer will vary based, to a large degree, on what kind of firm the designer works for. If the designer is employed by a retail furnishings store, he or she may be more involved with smaller projects than an independent designer would be. Independent designers more frequently are involved in projects involving the entire house.

Another characteristic of residential design is the personal relationship that usually develops between the client and designer. Those engaging in residential design must have the ability to get along with people, be interested in their personal needs, and feel comfortable in becoming the client's "friend." This is due, in large part, to the fact that residential clients are much more particular about what they buy and how it reflects their image when it concerns their home than are those clients who purchase interior concepts and products for their businesses.

The residential designer must develop a sense for questioning the client in such a way as to determine what the client really wants. The designer must also develop an empathy with the client so that expressed desires can be translated into a design concept with which the client can live. And the designer must develop tact and diplomacy in order to show the client the realities of good and bad design ideas.

A major difference between residential and commercial design is that the residential interior designer does far fewer drawings in his or her work. Detailed floor plans, working drawings, shop drawings, sketches, and other graphic presentations are day-to-day realities for the commercial designer. Most projects for private living spaces frequently require simple floor plans and perhaps color boards. Freehand sketches often suffice for even a floor plan. The amount of time "on the boards" preparing technical drawings is significantly less in residential design.

Although the amount of time spent drawing is less, product knowledge—especially with regard to availability of products—is crucial to successful residential designers. It is an unhappy fact that many clients put off redecorating their homes until just before the holidays or a big party. The designer who can quickly put his or her hands on just the right products will enjoy great success.

## *Commercial Interior Design*

*Commercial interior design* involves the design and specification of public spaces such as offices, hotels, hospitals, restaurants, and so on. In this book we have labeled anyone working with these public spaces as a commercial interior designer. In some books, this branch of the profession may be referred to as nonresidential or contract interior design. Nonresidential interior design is self-explanatory. Contract interior design, however, may have two meanings. Some refer to contract design as any kind of interior design for which the client signs a contract for services. In this case, the contract could be for residential or public spaces interior design. The word *contract* can also refer to public space or commercial design and the various kinds of business spaces.

Commercial design, which in this book refers to the design of public spaces, is often a more formal arrangement. This aspect of the profession very commonly, though not always, has a contract for services existing between the designer and the client. In many instances, this contract is for services only. However, part of the designer's responsibility would be to specify the products which are then often purchased by the client from other sources.

Projects are usually larger in size than those of the residential designer. A single office is always a possible project for the commercial interior designer. However, most projects involve greater amounts of space. A small suite of offices could commonly involve 5000 to 10,000 square feet. A large project could easily consist of hundreds of thousands of square feet.

As would be expected, the dollar amount of products specified would also be much greater for commercial projects. A product specification of $100,000 would not be unusual for a medium-sized office complex. Even the specification for a common single office could be $5000 or more.

Because the designer is working with businesspeople, the client expects the designer to be very organized, professional, and knowledgeable about what he or she is doing at all times. These, of course, are qualities that would be expected of today's professional designer, whether in residential or commercial design.

Although residential design deals with primarily satisfying the owners of the home, commercial designers must also consider how individuals other than the owners react to the design. The employees, although they may not be asked for input, must feel that the interior design of their spaces creates a pleasing place to work. The interior must also appeal in some way to the public or clientele of the business. A restaurant interior that pleases the owner but does not attract the public may be a beautifully designed interior, but may be the cause of the business's failure.

Since much of what the commercial designer specifies into projects is special-ordered from catalogs or custom designed, the designer must have broad product knowledge and must be confident of visualizing product size and scale. The designer often does not have products available in stock at his or her company's warehouse. Thus, it is important to have up-to-date information concerning availability and delivery times on a wide range of products.

In general, in comparison to residential design, commercial design requires greater attention to details since there are more details to be concerned with due to the size of products; excellent scheduling and organizational skills; in-depth product knowledge; very good space planning and drafting skills; knowledge of building, safety, and handicapped codes; and knowledge of architectural and mechanical systems and their constraints.

## *Common Employment Options*

In this section, we will look at the places where interior designers commonly obtain employment and what the working environment might be. It is important to understand that the descriptions of employment options are very general in nature. One person's experience in a firm under any one heading might be relatively different from someone else's experience in a different, but similar firm.

### RESIDENTIAL RETAIL FURNITURE STORES

In most residential retail furniture stores, the designer could be working with the client in either the store or the client's home. The working relationship is often a "sales" relationship where the interior designer is attempting to sell the client some selection of products. This selection could be for only one or two items or could involve items for the entire house. The designer is encouraged to sell what the store inventories, but is rarely limited to just those items. Most often, the design service is free to the client. For the business, the expense of the designer's service is covered through the sale of goods at retail (or a high markup), not the service itself. Designers most often are paid on a commission basis with a draw against that commission as a weekly salary. Entry-level individuals are often paid a salary with a small commission. Depending on the philosophy of the store's management, it might take an entry-level person from two to four years to move up to a full designer's position.

## DEPARTMENT STORES

Many large department stores such as Macy's, Marshall Fields, and the May Company have significant interior design departments. Working for a department store is very similar to working for a retail furniture store. A designer could be selling one item or a whole house of products. Often, however, the designer is more limited to selling what the department store carries.

Other department stores such as J.C. Penney and Sears have an interior design studio with a limited range of services. Commonly housed in the drapery department, the designer mostly sells window treatments, floor coverings, and wall treatments. It is less common for the designer to also sell furniture since this is often handled by furniture salespeople.

In both situations, the design service is offered free to the client. The designer is generally paid only commission on sales.

## RETAIL SPECIALTY STORES

A retail specialty store is one in which only a particular product other than furniture is sold (for example, lighting fixture stores, paint and wallpaper stores, floor covering stores). These stores are open to the general public; their goods are almost always sold at retail. Many offer trade discounts to designers and other members of the interiors and construction trades. Design services are most often offered free. These kinds of businesses represent excellent opportunities for the entry-level designer to gain sales experience and product knowledge. Designers are commonly paid a small salary plus a commission.

## OFFICE FURNISHINGS DEALERS

In many ways, the office furnishings dealer is similar to the residential retail showroom. There is a division of work between outside salespeople and the design department; the company has showroom space and an inventory of furniture to back up what is displayed, and the company commonly has its own warehouse and delivery crews. The main difference is that office furnishings dealers rarely sell products at suggested retail. It is more common for them to sell products at a discount from suggested retail or to add a markup onto the cost to the designer.

For the design employee, he or she may work in an in-house design department or in a subsidiary design company owned by the dealership. The designer works with the client either in the store or at the client's facility. Office furnishings dealers primarily design various office complexes. However, some also design other kinds of public spaces such as hospitals and hotels. Designers working in these organizations are often required to have substantial space planning skills and to be good draftspeople.

Depending on the exact nature of the firm, the client might be found by the design department or by a salesperson. Salespeople are usually not required to be designers, although many were at one time, and are often asked not to actually do any interior design. They are to sell the goods to the client while the interior designers space plan and specify the project. Products are often sold to the client through the firm whether the project was originated by the designer or the salesperson.

Many office furnishings dealers have certain exclusive products that they expect the designers to specify most often. Yet the designer can specify almost anything the client's project requires—whether or not it is carried by the firm. Larger dealers create an independent design firm so that they may function as designer-specifiers. In this case, the designers market the firm independent of the dealership and obtain contracts to design projects and prepare bid specifications for many vendors. In-house salespeople must prepare their competitive bids as would any other vendor.

Entry-level people do a wide variety of work for the more experienced designers. It often takes at least two years to advance to a position of project responsibility, although this time estimate may be shorter in smaller firms or in firms with more qualified entry-level designers. The pay is usually a salary for the designers and commission for the salespeople. Designers might be eligible for commission on certain items or for bonuses.

## ARCHITECTURAL OFFICES

More and more architectural offices are starting interior design groups. In the smaller firms, this group may consist of one person doing the interiors work for the architectural projects of the firm. In larger offices, it may be a separate design company that prepares interiors documents for both the building the architectural firm is working on as well as outside design projects. The work may involve residential or commercial projects or both, depending on the nature of the architectural practice.

In larger firms, the designer will often be involved in team projects. In addition, this job opportunity requires the designer to have very good space planning and technical skills and to be more familiar with formal working drawings and formal bid specifications.

In the past, the company was compensated by charging a fee for the interiors service since few architectural firms sold products to clients. Today, firms are discovering that income can be made by the selling of goods, and so the compensation method could be many ways. Designers are most often paid a salary. However, some of the upper-level designers may be paid a commission if their job responsibilities also include marketing.

## INDEPENDENT DESIGN FIRMS

An independent design firm is a company that has no affiliation with a particular product, unlike the residential retail store or the office furnishings dealer. Because these firms are "independent," they may specify any product for their clients that is available in the marketplace. The firm may specialize in residential or commercial work, but usually does a combination of both. It may be a small, one-person studio or a large firm with dozens of employees. Many are design-specify operations that do not sell products to the client. However, as with architectural firms, the independent design firm recognizes the added revenue potential of selling goods, and many are also offering this service.

Unless the firm also sells the goods, income is generated through the fees charged. Salaries, especially in the smaller firms, will generally be lower than in other situations. And often the designers will be paid a salary only.

## SPECIALIZED INDEPENDENT FIRMS

A specialized independent firm is a firm that primarily designs a certain kind of commercial interior. This might be restaurants, hotels, or health care facilities. The firm may deal with restoration work, or it may be very specialized as in the case of lighting designers. These companies require the designer to do extensive traveling since the firm's work would come from all over the country, if not the world. The specialized firm must either market itself very successfully or also engage in some other varieties of work to keep from being adversely affected by economic conditions that could limit its practice.

These companies do not usually sell goods to the client, so they obtain all their revenues from design fees. The designers would only be paid a salary with a possible bonus.

## MANUFACTURER DESIGNERS

An individual may work for a manufacturer in several ways. A designer could work in the manufacturer's showrooms. All the major manufacturers have showrooms in one or more cities. Designers would work with the interior designers and other allied professionals who come to the showroom. Usually, this is a sales position and the designer is paid on a small salary and/or commission.

A second way of working with the manufacturer is as a product designer. Depending on the product, the company may require the designer to have an industrial design background rather than an interior design background. A few manufacturers, notably those that produce open office furniture, have staff designers to aid designers and architects in planning and specifying the company's products. These last job opportunities are generally at a factory location rather than a showroom location.

When working for a manufacturer, there is often the opportunity to travel around the United States and work outside the country. Many of the major manufacturers have showrooms in foreign countries: those doing design layout work with designers and architects also have the opportunity to travel within the United States.

Compensation would depend on the actual job. Showroom sales positions would be commission based, product designer positions might be salary or commission based or paid by special compensation packages, and design layout work would generally be salary based.

## INDUSTRIAL AND CORPORATE FACILITY PLANNING FIRMS

Many large corporations have in-house interior designers or facility planners. These individuals would either be in charge of the direct planning and design of all the spaces of the corporation or work with outside designers in the design of corporate facilities. Responsibility might involve the design of the chief executive officer's office, the layout of a new manufacturing plant, or a collaboration with the architect on a new facility. In some situations, the designers might travel to various company locations. Designers working in this kind of situation would be paid a salary or possibly an hourly wage.

## THE FEDERAL GOVERNMENT

The federal government's General Services Administration (GSA) is responsible for employing interior designers. These designers prepare space plans and systems plans, design office facilities, and participate in other kinds of government agency interior design work. The designer is commonly limited to the products currently on the GSA purchasing schedules, although some projects allow additional flexibility in product specification. The GSA designer will design spaces in a certain geographic area of the country. He or she will be working on projects throughout that area, which may require some travel away from the main office. Salary, based on an individual's "GS" rating, is sometimes a bit higher than entry-level salary in the private sector, and the government, of course, offers excellent benefits.

## STATE AND CITY GOVERNMENTS

Some state and city governments have salaried interior designers and architects. This is rare, however. These professionals function much in the same way as designers for the federal government. Some state agencies, like the university system, have architectural or design personnel to design or coordinate contracted work. Few state and city governments have designers preparing layouts and specifications for the state, since many states have laws forbidding state agencies from performing work that competes with the private sector. Compensation would be salary based. States and cities also have very good benefits packages.

## UNIVERSITIES

Many medium- and large-sized universities have a facilities planning office. This office would work with architects, interior designers, and the university staff to develop new building designs and remodel existing structures. As mentioned earlier, if the institution is part of the state system, the designer would only work to coordinate what is needed by the institution with private sector designers. Compensation would be by salary.

Universities and colleges also hire faculty members with experience in the interior design field. The minimal educational requirements for a faculty position is a master's degree and some professional experience. Most universities expect faculty members to continue their education beyond a master's degree and/or remain active in the design profession. Many universities also hire practicing interior designers as adjunct or visiting instructors to teach during a semester.

# *Alternative Career Options*

The foregoing represents many of the primary ways that interior designers may practice their profession. These typify the kinds of job opportunities that most students and the general public recognize as the career options in the interior design profession. However, there are many other ways that an interior designer with certain specialized skills or experiences may work in the field.

## PROFESSIONAL RENDERER

The professional renderer is very skilled in perspective and various rendering media. He or she might be employed by a large interior design or architectural firm or may be self-employed as a free-lance renderer. If the individual works for a firm, he or she rarely would be expected to perform other interior design functions. The renderer would be compensated by a salary.

Those individuals who are self-employed work for many firms in the trade. They would charge their clients based on the rendering. Size and media use would be important criteria for determining the fee.

## MODEL BUILDERS

Allied to the professional renderer are model builders. These individuals might also be professional renderers or they may only produce architectural and interior models. A few large architectural firms have staff model builders, but this is not particularly common. In this situation, the employee would be compensated by a salary. In the larger cities, there are firms that specialize in model building. Employees for such firms would also be compensated by salary. For the self-employed model builder, compensation would be based on the fee charged to the architect or designer.

Model building requires an excellent sense of scale, knowledge of the kinds of material that can be used to produce a scale model, and a concern for the detail and patience inherent in model building.

## SALES REPRESENTATIVES

Sales representatives could work in residential retail stores, office furnishings dealers, and specialized retail stores. Sales representatives can also work for manufacturers outside the showroom.

The reader will recall the discussion of the sales representative ("rep") in Chapter 20. The independent rep works for himself or herself, representing many products from a variety of manufacturers. The rep visits with all the interior design and architectural firms that might specify the products. The rep is compensated with a commission whenever the product is sold in his or her territory, whether or not the representative has anything directly to do with the sale.

A factory rep works for one manufacturer as an employee. He or she handles all or part of the product line of that manufacturer in a specified territory of the country. Much like the independent rep, the factory representative works with designers and architects who might specify his or her product line. Some factory reps also have specific obligations to dealers in his or her territory. A dealer might have an exclusive right to sell the product in a specific city or area of the country.

The factory representative would be paid a commission on all goods sold in his or her territory whether or not the rep had anything to do with the sale. Both kinds of reps can have large territories, especially in the western states, and must travel extensively. In most cases, individuals must have proven sales experience to obtain a position as a manufacturer's representative.

## ARCHITECTURAL PHOTOGRAPHERS

An architectural photographer could be an interior designer who took several photography classes in college. However, most are photographers by trade. These individuals specialize in the photography of exteriors and interiors and are hired by the interior designer, the architect, or the owner of the building. It is rare that an architectural photographer would be on staff of an architectural or interiors firm. Those working for an architectural photographer would be paid a salary. Those owning the business compensate themselves as any business owner would.

## PRODUCT DESIGNER

The independent designer creates designs for furniture and interior products and then sells the designs to a manufacturer. Today, most product designers are industrial designers by training rather than interior designers. Compensation results from the royalties paid by the firm that buys the design.

## COMPUTER SPECIALISTS

When students think of computers in the design office today, they think of CADD (computer-aided design and drafting). Working as a CADD operator would involve the use of the computer as a design tool in the space planning and production of drawings for interiors and architectural projects. A firm utilizing a CADD system would require the designer to have a general interior design or architectural background with experience with some kind of CADD software.

Interior design firms also use the computer in other ways. One is for specification writing. The computer can speed up the production of complicated formal specification bid packages as well as detailed equipment lists for open office systems projects. This use of the computer may be a specialized job or part of the everyday experience of the interior designer.

Computers are also used for project scheduling, word processing, order entry, and bookkeeping. Except in small firms, project scheduling would be the only use of the computer exclusively for the interior designer. Computers are becoming increasingly important in interior design, yet they are still used by only a minority of firms.[1] See Chapter 10 for a discussion of the computer and its suitability to the interior design profession.

## SPECIFICATION WRITER

The larger firms have specialized individuals on staff to prepare the formal specification bid packages. These staff positions are often filled by trained interior designers or architects, but also by individuals with a general educational background who enjoy the detail of specification writing.

## INSTALLATION SUPERVISOR OR CONTRACT ADMINISTRATOR

Installation supervisors (or contract administrators) are responsible for the on-site and in-office supervision of the installation and/or construction of the project. In an interior design firm, this individual would be out at the job site making sure the building and interior construction was not deviating from that on the original plans. When the furniture and furnishings were ready for installation, he or she would be on the job site ensuring that everything went where it was supposed to go and taking care of the inspection for damages, omissions, and repairs. This vital function releases the designer to generate more design projects with his or her time. The position is not always filled by a trained interior designer. The individual with this responsibility must know how to read blueprints, understand the construction process, be familiar with the ordering process, and understand the installation process of a variety of products. Installation supervisors are most often salaried employees of the design firm, warehouse service, or installation service firm.

## INTERIOR DESIGN MANAGEMENT

A position in interior design management requires extensive experience in the field or experience in general management. Most design directors are former designers who have worked their way up through the ranks. It is important for the design director to have knowledge of interior design and a good general business knowledge or experience related to the management of personnel, marketing, and general business principles. Design management personnel are most often paid on a salary basis with some bonus or commission structure to supplement that salary.

---

[1]McLain-Kark and Tang 1986.

## MUSEUM WORK

Interior designers with experience or additional training in museum, restoration, or curatorial areas can work for the many historic site museums around the country. This can be very rewarding work for those individuals with a keen interest in history and restoration. Most of these job opportunities require advanced degree work in such areas as art history, history, and anthropology.

## JOURNALISM

It is possible for interior designers who are very good writers or who have had training in journalism to obtain employment with a city newspaper or a trade or shelter magazine.

# *Summary*

One of the interesting and exciting aspects of the interior design professional is the variety of ways that one can work in the field. It is not absolutely necessary for everyone to be a great salesperson or a great artist or space planner to find a niche in interior design. This chapter has reviewed many areas of interior design that one might find for an exciting, rewarding opportunity. Although some do require training or experience beyond the undergraduate level or the normal interior design program, many are positions that the trained interior designer can achieve with work experience in the field.

In the final chapter we will be looking at how to prepare for obtaining that first or next job by reviewing portfolios, résumés, and the job interview process.

# Chapter 26

## GETTING THE NEXT—OR FIRST—JOB

$W$hether a designer is an experienced professional looking for more responsibility and different challenges or the beginning professional getting ready to find that first job in interior design, the job search can be a time-consuming and stress-producing period. Going to a bookstore and looking for a guide to aid in the job search can also be frustrating. There are a multitude of "how to write better résumés" and "how to interview" books on the market today.

This chapter will provide the professional and the student with some tips related to finding a job in interior design. All the examples are specifically based on the needs of the professional and beginning interior designer as he or she seeks a professional design position.

## *Portfolios*

A portfolio is a visual presentation of what the individual can do as an interior designer. A person's portfolio is never "finished." It must be constantly updated and refined to meet current or expected needs in the job search process. For the experienced professional, the portfolio must show the complete range of present and past abilities. For the student seeking that all-important first job, the portfolio must exhibit the very best work that the student can do while exhibiting the breadth of the student's abilities so as not to limit the prospective employee from any reasonable opportunity.

Whether the portfolio is for the professional seeking to change jobs or the student in search of the first job, the portfolio must be suited to the kind of job for which the individual is interviewing. One showing multiple examples of water color renderings when the company is looking for drafting skills wastes both the employer's and the job seeker's time. It also shows the prospective employer that the job seeker has not done any homework about the design firm or its needs.

In addition, portfolios should be self-explanatory. Many times it is necessary for the designer to send his or her portfolio to a prospective employer for a review before an interview will be granted. When the designer is not there to explain his or her involvement, the parameters of the project, and how the designer arrived at the solution, the prospective employer will expect the portfolio to be able to answer these questions. If it is not self-explanatory, all that can be reviewed is technical competence in the preparation of drawings and boards.

There is very little difference in what the portfolio will contain or even, to some extent, look like between the needs of the professional and the student. A professional's portfolio will be more extensive than a student's and will probably contain photo prints or slides of completed work. But the basic contents and even format will be very similar. For that reason, the remaining discussion of the portfolio will be a generalized discussion on what to include, the format, the media, and the written materials.

## WHAT TO INCLUDE

It is important for the portfolio to include examples of all the skills of which the individual is capable. For the experienced interior designer it is also necessary to show the breadth of project experiences that have been undertaken during professional practice. Examples of as much of the following kinds of design documents must be included:

1. Freehand sketches.
   a. Perspectives, elevations, and/or isometric drawings.
   b. Sketch problems that show the decision-making process.
2. Furniture floor plans.
3. Color boards.
4. Working drawings.
5. Lettering skills.
6. Technical renderings in any media in which the designer is competent.
7. Slides, photographs, or publication reprints showing completed projects for which the designer was primarily responsible.

Although most of the examples are commonly parts of projects, it is important to show at least one complete project presentation. This complete project would include a verbal explanation of the design problem, floor plans, color boards, renderings, and any other written or graphic documents that were a part of the project requirements. A copy of the individual's résumé should also be included in the portfolio. Having a neat copy of the résumé in the portfolio guarantees being able to present an unfolded copy to the prospective employer.

## FORMAT

A key decision in producing the portfolio is the format. It is important to remember that portfolios must be hand-carried; laid out on conference tables and desks; possibly transported in taxi cabs, passenger cars, and airplanes; and may even be mailed across the country. A common format size for boards and drawings in the profession is 20 inches by 30 inches. Although this size format works well for the preparation of drawings and presentation boards, it makes for a very cumbersome package to carry. Format sizes that are easier to present and transport are 8 inches by 10 inches, 11 inches by 14 inches, 14 inches by 17 inches, and 16 inches by 20 inches. The larger-size formats make it easy to present original work. Smaller formats are easier to handle.

Whatever size format is decided on, it is important for all the examples to be consistently presented in either a vertical or horizontal manner. This helps to show the designer as an organized professional. It also aids in reducing nervousness during the interview by avoiding having to keep flipping the portfolio around. If both horizontal and vertical presentation formats have been used, items may need to be eliminated from the final portfolio. However, if the item is particularly important to the overall story the designer is trying to tell, the item may be included by use of photo reproductions.

The pages of the portfolio will need to take a certain amount of abuse. Items that are not on mat boards might need to be mounted on a mat or other similar backing materials. Sketches, renderings, and plans might also be mounted on colored paper or photographic paper and inserted into plastic notebook sleeves.

The physical binder itself should be of good quality and look very professional. Drawings rolled up in a tube may be convenient for carrying, but they do not communicate the right level of professionalism—neither do cardboard portfolios that many students use during college. It is not, however, necessary to spend a lot of money on leather-bound books. Smaller formats can even be held in many common three-ring binders.

## MEDIA

Many examples of original work are done on paper and/or boards of 18 inches by 24 inches or 20 inches by 30 inches format. If the designer decides to present all original work, it would be necessary to use a large-size portfolio. If it is decided to take advantage of the smaller sizes of formats, many items will need to be redone into other media. There are several different kinds of media that can be used to present the portfolio items.

Color-slide transparencies (35 mm) are a popular portfolio media used by many designers. Slides are easy to transport and are relatively inexpensive to produce. A disadvantage of using slides is the necessity of carrying a slide viewer. The job-seeking designer should not assume the prospective employer will have a slide projector available to show slide-formatted work. Carrying and setting up a slide projector is also an extra headache the prospective employee may not want to add to the interview situation. A hand-held viewer would be better than a projector, but these should be easy to operate and reliable.

Amateur photographers can take slides of flat work themselves with a small amount of equipment. All that is needed is a 35-mm camera, a tripod, and, if daylight film is used, an area where good, consistent, natural light can be available for the lighting of the design works. If natural light cannot be used, the proper combination of film and photoflood lights must be used. Using the camera's flash unit can produce glare, hot spots, and inconsistent results.

Photographic prints are easier to present but are more expensive than slides to produce. Photographic prints, whether color or black and white, should be at least 5 inches by 7 inches. Prints 8 inches by 10 inches are even better, yet each 8 inch by 10 inch print can cost several dollars to have made.

Many firms use the services of professional architectural photographers to take photos of high-quality or unusual projects. Designers involved in these projects should obtain duplicates of the slides or prints from the design firm or client through the photographer for their personal portfolio.

A common medium used by designers is the PMT. You will recall from Chapter 17 that PMT is a trade name held by the Eastman Kodak Company for high-contrast positive prints. This is an exceptionally good medium to use to reduce the size of working drawings and floor plans to a manageable size. Design items to be produced as PMTs must be crisp, black-and-white technical work. Color work cannot be made into PMTs.

## WRITTEN MATERIALS

Each section of the portfolio should be labeled. Pieces that are not self-explanatory should have brief written descriptions of the problem or the piece. Since hand lettering is considered an important skill by many design firms, written materials could be hand-lettered. However, it is also acceptable for written materials to be typed or done with transfer letters. But avoid using a large variety of typefaces and sizes. Different sizes of type will call attention to more important identification items or statements, but too many will be confusing and may give an impression of disorganization.

Remember that the portfolio tells a visual story about the job seeker. If it is neat and well organized and contains design documents that show the range of skills for which the prospective employer is looking, the interviewer will have a favorable impression of the designer. If it is sloppy, has fabric samples falling off, and appears to have been thrown together, it will likely lead to a short interview and a "don't call us, we'll call you" response.

The portfolio must show the job seeker's best work, provide a good impression, and supply an honest presentation of skills and abilities. It is acceptable to get a professional's help to photograph materials. It is not acceptable to use other people's work or have someone else do work on your portfolio submissions.

## *Résumés*

A résumé is simply a summary of a person's qualifications. Yet, a résumé plays a significant part in whether an applicant will obtain an interview for a first or new job. In some companies, a résumé is also important in reviews for promotions. Presented on one or two pages (rarely more), the résumé must instantly communicate vital information related to work experience, education, personal information, special skills or experiences related to the desired position, and career objectives.

### CONTENT

Certain bodies of information will be expected in all résumés. This would include a limited amount of personal information, a career summary, educational accomplishments, and work experiences (see Figures 26-1 through 26-4). Some individuals also include professional memberships and information about community service and outside interests. Except for professional memberships these are optional and should be deleted if they make the résumé too long or if they do not favorably add to the overall impression and qualifications.

The career summary, in a few brief sentences, provides a significant statement concerning the applicant's ability to handle the job for which he or she is applying. For example, "Fifteen years sales experience for office furnishings dealers specializing in Herman Miller and Steelcase open office systems. Exceeded sales goals eleven out of fifteen years" might be a career summary for an individual now seeking a position as a representative with a manufacturer.

Educational accomplishments should begin first with the highest degree earned. Included would be the name of the institution and its location, the kind of degree and the year granted, major, minor, and any academic or career-related activities. Students should list their grade point average only if it was exceptionally high. About a year after graduation, the grade point average should be dropped from the résumé. Employers will not be quite as interested in how well a person did in school as they are in what the designer is currently able to do.

Depending on which format is chosen for the résumé, the work experience portion will be written differently. The work experience section must list the name and location of the company, the years worked for each, and the title of the position held. One or more brief narrative statements as to skills developed or used and responsibilities in each position should also be provided. For example, to describe a job with a small specialty studio, the designer could write "Sales Associate. Sold drapery, wallcoverings and floorcoverings" or, to be more specific, "Sales Associate: Worked with clients in store and in their homes. Responsible for estimating, pricing, and installation supervision of custom window treatments, wallcoverings, and floor coverings. Obtained a 10 to 15 percent increase in sales last three quarters." The second example provides a prospective employer much more information as to what the designer could do at the new design firm.

A few words about personal information: What must be on the résumé are a current address and telephone number. Anything else is purely up to the individual. Applicants feel they must put down marital information, names of children, service records, height, weight, and health conditions. The employer cannot legally ask for any of this information, except within the bounds described in Chapter 9. Volunteering the information could prejudice a decision, and the applicant would not have any grounds for challenging the prejudiced decision.

## FORMAT

There are many formats for résumés. No one format works in all cases. Which of the three basic formats to use should depend on the audience the résumé is for and the purpose for the résumé. The experienced designer attempting to make a career change from "on the boards designer" to salesperson will need a different format than the technician trying to obtain a position of total project responsibility. The three basic formats are chronological, functional, and combination.

### Chronological Résumé

The *chronological résumé* states educational and work experiences exactly when they occurred, in reverse order. It is easy to follow and clearly shows the work history of the individual. Many professionals prefer to read this traditional format for résumés since it is familiar to most people in industry. It is not recommended, however, if the job seeker has a spotty work record, is seeking to make a significant change in his or her career, or has been out of the normal work force for some time (see Figures 26-1 and 26-2).

When using this format, experienced professionals should provide work history in reverse chronological order, followed by educational experience. For the professional, work history is more important than educational experience. Students should place educational experience first since that is the most recent activity.

### Functional Résumé

The *functional résumé* presents information to emphasize qualifications and skills, rather than the order in which they were obtained (see Figure 26-3). Many employers do not like the functional résumé since they are concerned with a prospective employee's work history. If a functional résumé is presented, it would not be uncommon for the prospective employer to ask for a chronological work history to be provided.

### Combination Résumé

A *combination résumé* utilizes qualities of both the chronological and functional résumés and combines them into one. Usually, this results in a résumé where functional skills are described as in the normal functional résumé, followed by a chronological listing of educational and work experiences. A combination résumé highlights skills related to the new job and deemphasizes either a limited or spotty work history. This kind of format can work very well for students whose skills

**DIANE SMITH**
606 W. Overlook
Kent, Ohio 44240
(216) 555-1912

**OBJECTIVE:**

Entry-level design position with office furnishings dealer or commercial interior design firm. Particularly interested in position combining client contact and design skills utilization.

**EDUCATION:**

(May, 1985)

Interior Design major. Marketing minor.
University of Cincinnati, Ohio.
Course work emphasized commercial space planning and design, architectural drafting, presentation techniques including marker rendering, mechanical systems, 2-D CADD and liberal studies courses. GPA 3.8/4.0.

**EXPERIENCE:**

Summer, 1985   **Monroe's Interior Designs, Akron, Ohio.**
<u>Intern.</u>
Student intern for commercial/residential independent design firm.
Was given responsibility for space planning and specification of two small offices. Became familiar with many commercial/residential products through attending presentations by sales representatives, visiting showrooms and product research for senior designers. Assisted senior designers by drafting working drawings and preparation of presentation boards.

Summer, 1984   **DLW Construction Co., Kent, Ohio.**
<u>Draftsperson.</u>
Assisted owner of small construction company in the preparation of various working drawings. Was responsible for completing all required drawings for five home remodeling projects.

Summers,   **J.C.'s Wallpaper, Toledo, Ohio.**
1983 & 84   <u>Salesperson.</u>
Estimated and sold wall coverings, paint and paneling. Developed sales skills and applied design skills in working with residential clients. Learned about the proper installation of wallcoverings by talking with installers and visiting installation sites.

**HONORS/ACTIVITIES**

American Society of Interior Designers
Student Chapter, 1983-1985

Phi Kappa Phi Honor Society

Arts Center, Kent, Ohio. Photography Exhibit
Two photos selected for exhibit, Spring, 1985.

**PORTFOLIO AND REFERENCES AVAILABLE UPON REQUEST**

FIGURE 26-1
Chronological résumé prepared by a student seeking a first job.

John P. Smith
3506 Prairie Drive
Bloomingdale, Illinois
(312) 555-0112

## OBJECTIVE

Design management in progressive commercial interior design office.

## SUMMARY

Eight years experience in commercial interior design. Thorough knowledge of building codes, several open office systems products, and all aspects of office design. Experience in contract negotiation and supervision of other designers for successful completion of projects.

## DESIGN EXPERIENCE

**Interiors Works, Inc.** Chicago, Ill.
Project Designer (1984 to present)
Designer (1981 to 1984)
Space plan and design commercial facilities. As project designer, specialized in open office planning, primarily utilizing Haworth and Herman Miller systems. Also responsible for designing several branch bank facilities and medical office suites. Supervised designers and design assistants in completing assigned projects. Negotiated with clients to obtain design contracts. Responsible for obtaining contracts of over $55,000 in fees in past two years. Negotiated with vendors and tradesmen and supervised installations.

**Professional Interiors.** Chicago, Ill.
Design Assistant (1978-1981)
Space plan and design commercial facilities. Firm specialized in executive office design, law offices and banking facilities. First year assisted senior designers with drafting, product research and specification writing. Later given design responsibility for small to medium sized projects. Continued to assist senior designers on team projects. Assisted in space planning two open office systems projects of over 50,000 square feet each.

**Associated Architects.** Evanston, Ill.
Intern (Summer, 1978)
Student intern at architectural office. Worked in interior design department assisting project designers. Utilized drafting and rendering skills.

## EDUCATION

Purdue University. Purdue, Indiana
1978 Bachelor of Fine Arts. Major: Contract Interior Design

## AFFILIATIONS

Institute of Business Designers, Professional member.
American Institute of Architects, Affiliate member

FIGURE 26-2
Chronological résumé prepared by a professional seeking a change in employment responsibilities.

**JOHN P. SMITH**

---

3506 E. Prairie Drive,  Bloomingdale, Illinois                    (312) 555-0112

---

### SUMMARY

Eight years experience in commercial interior design. Experience in contract negotiation. Supervised other designers for successful completion of assigned projects. Thorough knowledge of building codes, several open office systems products, and all aspects of office design.

### MAJOR WORK EXPERIENCES

#### 1978 to present

Contract Negotiation

Responsible for making client contacts to negotiate design contracts. Provided draft of design contracts to Design Director for approval. Personally responsible for obtaining over $55,000 in fees in past two years (represents 22% of total fees obtained in those two years).

Employee Supervision

Supervised as many as three designers and five design assistants at one time for completion of various projects. Commonly supervised one designer and two design assistants.

Project Responsibilities

Designed projects during last four years of over 750,000 square feet with total design budgets of over 25 million dollars. Specialized in open office planning. Familiar with Haworth, Herman Miller and Knoll systems. Also experienced in designing banking facilities and medical office suites.

Most Recent Projects:
  Midwest Power Systems--25,000 square feet
  MicroChip, Inc.--14,000 square feet
  Sports Medicine Affiliates--35,000 square feet
  Harris Trust--approximately 15,000 square feet
  Chase, Harrigan and O'Neil--executive offices--5,500 square feet

FIGURE 26-3
The same professional's résumé as shown in Figure 26-2, but prepared as a functional résumé.

John P. Smith, Page 2

**EDUCATION**

**Purdue University. Purdue, Indiana**
**1978 Bachelor of Fine Arts. Major: Contract Interior Design**

**AFFILIATIONS**

**Institute of Business Designers, Professional member**
**American Institute of Architects, Affiliate member**

FIGURE 26-3
The same professional's résumé as shown in Figure 26-2, but prepared as a functional résumé. *(Continued)*

Mary Smyth
1223 Karen Drive
Phoenix, Arizona
(602) 555-0350

OBJECTIVE

Position with manufacturer as sales representative or working with architectural/design community.

SUMMARY

Twelve years total experience in commercial and residential interior design and sales. Includes seven years sales experience with office furnishings dealers or as free-lance designer/sales.

SALES SKILLS

Maintained numerous commercial accounts with last employer. Developed many new accounts. Generated over four million dollars in sales last year (second highest total for twelve sales people). Equaled or exceeded sales goals last four years.

SUPERVISION SKILLS

Hired, trained and supervised two sales assistants to help manage my accounts. First sales assistant recently began working as sales representative.

MARKETING SKILLS

Developed successful marketing strategies for three architectural firms, two interior design firms and two contractors. Member of marketing committee for present employer for last year.

DESIGN SKILLS

Experienced in residential and commercial space planning and interior design. Familiar with open office systems products and various qualities of commercial and residential furniture and furnishings products.

EXPERIENCE

Account Representative. Responsible for maintaining existing commercial accounts and obtaining new commercial accounts. Territory is by client rather than geographic limitation. Equaled or exceeded sales goals last four years. Booked over four million dollars in sales last year (second highest of twelve account representatives). Quality Office Furnishings and Products. Phoenix, Arizona., 1982-present.

**FIGURE 26-4**
A combination résumé for a professional seeking new responsibilities in his or her career as a sales representative.

<u>Free-lance Designer</u>. Organized and operated design business. Responsible for obtaining and maintaining clients, writing contracts, doing residential and commercial interior design and marketing consulting. Supervised two part-time employees for office support work. Developed successful marketing programs for seven clients. Smyth Design Consultants, Ltd. Oak Park, Ill. 1980-1982.

<u>Designer/Sales Representative.</u> Responsible for developing commercial and some residential client accounts. Responsible for space planning and design of interior as well as selling products for the project. Equaled or exceeded sales goals all but one quarter. Top sales producer in third year. Assisted in organization of interior design department. Best Interiors. Chicago, Ill. 1977-1980.

<u>Designer</u>. Design residential interiors. Responsible for planning, specifying and selling of concepts and products. Was promoted to outside designer within year and a half (it normally takes three years to be able to sell out of the store). Equaled or exceeded sales goals all but first two quarters. Residential Interiors. Chicago, Ill. 1974-1977.

EDUCATION

Southern Illinois University. 1974. Bachelor of Science. Major: Interior Design. Minor: Marketing.

PROFESSIONAL MEMBERSHIP

American Society of Interior Designers, Professional member since 1978.

**FIGURE 26-4**
A combination résumé for a professional seeking new responsibilities in his or her career as a sales representative. *(Continued)*

learned in school and internships will be of greater interest to a prospective employer than work history in a series of part-time jobs (see Figure 26-4).

### REFERENCES

Many employers check references or call previous employers. If there is any question that a previous employer will give a bad reference, ask that the employer not be contacted. It will be necessary to provide a brief explanation of the circumstances surrounding this request to the prospective employer, however. Remember that it is a common courtesy to ask individuals listed for nonemployment references if they may be used as references.

Students can also use the services of college career placement offices to maintain references. This is a convenience for those who are asked to provide personal references since they only have to write the reference once and then it is kept on file at the placement office. Prospective employers then request a copy of the reference from the placement office.

### APPEARANCE

The appearance of the résumé can, by itself, make a good or bad impression. It must have perfect spelling and use good grammar. Headings should be bold so that they stand out and attract attention. Single-space the résumé with double space between major changes. Do not forget to leave sufficient side margins so that the prospective employer may write notes in the margins. If at all possible, use only one page. However, if this means cramping all the information so that there are barely any margins, use two pages.

The original copy should be typed to produce a dark black image. If a good typewriter is not available, use a typing service. Word-processed résumés are acceptable, but be sure the final copy is printed on either a letter-quality printer or a laser printer. When a quantity of résumés at one time is required, have it offset printed on bond paper, not photocopied.

Interior designers tend to use a creative design or a creative method of printing or folding the résumé. It is rare that odd colors of paper and creative designs on résumés get an interview. The content of the résumé and cover letter are what get the interview. Stick to white, buff, or maybe a light gray paper and minimal, if any, attention-getting designs.

## *Job Search*

Professionals looking for new positions usually hear about openings by word of mouth. Others discreetly put out the word to allied associates that they are looking for a new position. Sometimes it is necessary to start calling around to other firms in town to see if there is any interest in the job-seeking professional.

It is also common for professionals to use general or design trade professional employment agencies. Professional designers often work with executive search companies when they seek management positions. Both of these organizations charge either the employee or the employer for the agency's aid. If the job seeker uses an agency to obtain leads, he or she should understand all the restrictions and fees involved.

Employed professionals looking for another position must be discreet. Understandably, employers do not like their employees looking for another job while still working. Yet, of course, not everyone can afford to quit the current job until a new job is found. And almost all job-search books advise readers to not quit the current job before a new job is obtained.

A few hints for the professional seeking a new job while presently employed: Do not use company time, company telephones, or company supplies for the job search. It is acceptable to schedule appointments over the lunch hour, but it is not acceptable to fake appointments to go on interviews. If it is necessary to take an extended period of time for the interview, use vacation time—do not call in sick. Remember, the employee owes a duty of loyalty to the employer as long as the employee is on the payroll. Abusing the employer by making interview appointments or long-distance phone calls at the present employer's expense is not only unprofessional, but it could be grounds for termination.

For the student, the job search begins long before graduation. The student must evaluate what part of the profession holds the most interest. Is it doing residential or commercial design? Is the student afraid to make presentations and therefore not a salesperson? Are technical working drawings boring, but working with colors exciting? These kinds of questions coupled with questions related to life-style choices, geographic preferences, and many others need to be asked to determine where and what kind of employment to seek. Sometimes using a book such as Richard Nelson Bolles's *What Color Is Your Parachute?* is a help in determining career goals more precisely.

The student should be seeking information about the various aspects of the field and potential employers from many sources. College advisers and career counselors are helpful sources of information regarding different design companies. The student should also be talking to relatives who might have worked with designers. He or she should also be asking for time to talk to working professionals. Who better to tell the student about what it is like to work in residential design than someone actively doing just that kind of work?

University career placement offices will have information about many corporate employers. Unfortunately, most interior design businesses are closed corporations, and information about them will probably not be listed in the resources of the placement office. It is necessary to be more creative in employer research.

Students can review the Yellow Pages ads. This does not always provide the name of the owner or the manager, but it can give some information related to the company. Many firms list in their ads product lines which the company carries. These product listings will help the student determine if the firm is primarily a residential or a commercial firm.

Many of the larger cities now have home and garden magazines. These are filled with advertisements by many different interior designers. Also, some cities have a "promotional" magazine that covers cultural, home, business, and social events. Many design firms also advertise in these magazines.

The Sunday classified section is a likely place to find interior design and trade-related job notifications. These classified ads, however, often only provide the barest amount of information about the position. Sometimes the firm does not even publish its name, but asks the respondents to mail résumés to a box number. The job seeker should respond to anything that sounds remotely possible and interesting. A student should not be discouraged from applying if the ad states that only applicants with *x* years of experience apply.

## *Cover Letters*

A good cover letter allows the job applicant the opportunity to personally introduce himself or herself to the prospective employer. In it, the applicant can point out significant skills that directly relate the employment opportunity and express personal interest in the company. Each letter must sound as if it were written only for that firm, even if it contains primarily "stock" paragraphs used in many letters.

## CONTENT

The cover letter, as with most résumés, should be only one page in length. Longer letters, even from experienced professionals, may not get read by busy design directors or personnel managers. It is important for the letter to get the reader's attention and make him or her want to read your résumé as well as call you for an interview. This is done by using good business writing techniques.

It is generally recommended by business writing consultants and employment counselors that the cover letter contain about four paragraphs, each with a particular purpose.

The first paragraph should attract attention by stating the purpose of the letter in concise words. If the letter is in response to an advertisement, this paragraph should give the name and date of the announcement. If it is a letter of inquiry, this should be clearly stated (see Figure 26-5).

The second and third paragraphs should contain specific information about the applicant's skills and interests in the position in order to keep the reader interested. These paragraphs would describe skills, previous work experience, or educational accomplishments specifically related to the position. Here also would be statements as to personal goals and interests as related to the particular position and company. Although there is no set order in which this information should be presented, it is most frequently presented in the sequence of importance to the position as the applicant understands it. Professionals would not only describe skills but also other accomplishments, such as sales records and management experience (see Figure 26-6). For students, this section would deal primarily with course work, pointing out particularly proficient skills. Students would also want to describe responsibilities during internships or other interior design or trade-related work accomplished while in school.

The last paragraph should seek action by the prospective employer. Ask for an interview, but do not just ask and then wait for the employer to respond. The paragraph should also state that the applicant will be calling the employer concerning a convenient time for an appointment. Many job seekers will be in the city where the letter was sent for only a few days. If this is the case, it should be mentioned in the closing paragraph so that the prospective employer knows when the applicant will be available. The last paragraph should also reference the enclosed résumé as well as the availability of the portfolio for review. It is also a good idea in the last paragraph to thank the reader for taking the time to review the letter and résumé.

## APPEARANCE

The appearance of the cover letter can quite easily attract more attention than the content. The author remembers receiving, in response to a newspaper advertisement for an experienced interior designer and space planner, a hand-written letter on ruled paper. Many interior designers try to make the letter as creative looking as possible, using fancy type styles, funny folds, logo style designs, and pastel colors. These techniques do attract attention, but they also often get in the way of the content and businesslike attitude for which the employer may be looking. The exact job opening and the kind of design firm will dictate whether these creative techniques are a help or a hindrance to the effectiveness of the cover letter.

Sally Jones
215 N. Ford Drive
Chicago, Illinois 60653
(312) 555-1278


August 18, 1986


Mr. Roger Smith, Director of Design
Myer's Interior Design
82 W. Willow Lane
Tucson, AZ.

Dear Mr. Smith:

I am writing in response to the classified advertisement for a position as a designer your company had in the Chicago Tribune of August 17. I would like to point out that I first heard of your firm while enrolled in the interior design program at the University of Arizona. Ms. Jane Johnson of your design department kindly helped me with product information for projects and told me quite a bit about the company. I was quite impressed.

At the University, I specialized in residential interior design. My training was quite complete, covering all phases of design development, production, presentation and business practices. From project evaluations, I can state that I have strong skills in space planning, color coordination, technical drafting, presentation skills and rendering.

My internship was completed at Beverly Miller's Interiors in Chicago. My responsibilities included color coordination, preparation of presentation boards, drafting, rendering and order processing. This experience has taught me the excitement and complexity of residential interior design.

I am anxious to begin my career and would like to meet you personally so as to present my portfolio to you. It is very exciting to me to find your organization has an opening as I have decided to return to the Tucson area permanently. I will be calling your office on August 27 to confirm an interview appointment. I have enclosed my current resume for your review.

Thank you for your time and I look forward to meeting you next month.

Sincerely,


Sally Jones

Enclosure


FIGURE 26-5
Cover letter prepared to respond to a newspaper advertisement for a design position.

Jennifer Woods
4436 Euclid Avenue
Kalamazoo, Michigan 49007
(616) 555-0809


November 15, 1985


Mr. Roger Brown, President
Design Associates, Ltd.
980 State Street
Erie, Pennsylvania

Dear Mr. Brown:

Over a nine year period, I have been promoted from Designer to Senior Project Designer at Environmental Interiors, a highly respected commercial design firm in Kalamazoo. During the last few years I have been personally responsible for obtaining and designing five of the eight largest projects ever undertaken at Environmental Interiors. As Senior Project Designer, I was also responsible for supervising up to six designers at a time on one or more projects.

At this point in my career, I seek an opportunity to apply my design and supervisory skills in a management position.

It is not difficult to hear flattering comments about the quality design work produced at Design Associates. I believe the negotiation and design skills that I have refined at Environmental Interiors will further add to the success of your firm.

As you will see from the enclosed resume, I have broad commercial experience including open office planning for many types of facilities, professional offices, medical suites, banking facilities, university and college facilities and even restaurants.

Over the past four years, I have been preparing myself for management by enrolling in the local community college and the university with an aim of completing a second undergraduate degree in business.

I have considerable talent, enthusiasm and interest to offer as a design manager to Design Associates, Ltd. and would appreciate the opportunity to meet with you personally to discuss such a position. I will call you next week to confirm a convenient time for a personal interview.

Sincerely yours,


Jennifer Woods


Enc.

FIGURE 26-6
Cover letter inquiring about possible positions.

There are some letter-writing techniques that almost all personnel managers and owners will appreciate.

1. *Individualized salutation.* Except when answering a blind ad, part of the research of the job seeker is to find out exactly to whom the letter should be sent and the spelling of his or her name. This indicates to the prospective employer that the job seeker has made a serious effort to find out something about the company.

2. *Perfect typing and absolutely perfect spelling.* Word processing makes these so simple for everyone to achieve, whether a word processor is used or a typing service is hired to produce the letters.

3. *Quality bond paper and business-sized envelopes.* Black ink on white or cream paper is the most businesslike combination.

4. *Standard business letter format.* This means the applicant's name and address are to appear at the top followed by the date. Next would be the company's address and a salutation followed by the body of the letter. The word *Enclosure* or the abbreviation *Enc.* should follow below the signature to indicate that something besides the letter is in the envelope.

Figures 26-5 and 26-6 provide two complete letters of application to show content and format suggestions.

# *Interviews*

Looking for a job is serious work. People spend an average of 1600 or more hours during the year at their jobs. It is important that any job be one that delivers the most fulfillment and rewards. The interview is the door to each job.

## PREPARATION

Once an interview is obtained, it is necessary for some preparation to be done. First, find out with whom you will be interviewing. It is not always the person who responded to your letter. Larger design firms will have a personnel manager who is in charge of interviewing prospective employees prior to the design director. Ask for the names and job titles of each interviewer. If more than one person will conduct the interview, ask if an itinerary will be provided so that you know how much time will be spent with each person.

Double check the day and time of the interview. No matter how much time has passed from when you set up the interview, call the day before to reconfirm the time. If you have any question on how to get to the studio or office, or are not sure where to park, ask for directions at this time. In large cities, it is probably safer to take a cab than it is to drive, but check for suggestions on that also. If there is any reason why you cannot make the interview, call and personally talk to the interviewer to tell him or her.

Most interviews will last from one to two hours. In either case, plan for about twenty minutes to show your portfolio and the rest of the time for questions.

There are many things to do the evening before the interview. Check the outfit you plan to wear. Make sure it is clean, well pressed, and that it does not have loose buttons or threads. Be sure your shoes are shined. Go through your portfolio to familiarize yourself with what you are going to show and confirm in your mind the order in which you wish to show it. Place an extra unfolded copy of your résumé in the portfolio. Also check to be sure that a pen and pencil is in either your portfolio, pocket, or handbag.

It is never permissible to be late unless it is due to something totally beyond your control. If you are held up in traffic, or miss your plane or connection, call the interviewer as soon as you can.

Make a point of arriving at the office or studio at least ten to fifteen minutes early. These few extra minutes give you a cushion in case of traffic jams or difficulty in finding the office. It also gives you a chance to try to relax and collect yourself before going into the interview. Before you check in with the receptionist, go to the restroom to check your overall appearance.

When you check in with the receptionist, be sure to smile and tell him or her who you are, with whom you have an appointment, and the time of that appointment. Most likely you will be told to have a seat. Try to use this time to compose yourself. Read a magazine; don't fiddle with your portfolio, briefcase, or handbag.

## WHAT TO WEAR

What you wear to the job interview is a part of the overall impression you will leave with the interviewer. Many interior design professionals find it acceptable for everyday business apparel to be more trendy and flamboyant. However, most interviewers are expecting far more conservative apparel for the interview. If you have researched the company as well as you can, you will have some idea of what normal business attire is like at the design firm. This will be your guide as to how trendy or how conservative you must dress for the interview.

In general, however, more conservative apparel is the best bet. Business suits with ties for men are standard. Conservative fabrics in solid colors are commonly accepted. Women should also choose conservative suits and dresses with jackets. Sun dresses, sleeveless dresses, or low-cut dresses do not project the kind of impression sought by businesspeople.

Wear apparel that is comfortable. Do not use the job interview to break in a new pair of shoes.

Women should also be careful about what kind of accessories they add to the outfit. Refrain from wearing loud-colored or patterned scarves, dangling, noisy bracelets or oversized earrings—anything that attracts more attention to the accessories than to yourself.

Remember, many people begin forming their opinion within the first fifteen to thirty seconds of the meeting. Although this impression will rarely make or break the interview in and of itself, it is often an important part of the overall decision-making process.

## THE INTERVIEW

The purpose of the interview is for the employer to get to know you personally, ask you questions, and try to evaluate whether you would be a good addition to the firm. The interview is also a time for you to evaluate whether this particular firm is really the kind of firm for which you wish to work. Just because a firm has a good reputation does not mean that everyone will want to work for it.

When the interviewer greets you, be prepared to shake hands. It is not necessary to use a bone-crushing handshake. Just make it sincere. When you arrive at the conference room or office where the interview will be held, wait for some indication from the interviewer as to where to sit. If he or she does not make any indication as to where to sit, choose a chair either directly across from the interviewer or at a ninety-degree angle. These two positions make it easier to show your portfolio and to maintain eye contact.

Try not to use distracting habits. Don't play with a paper clip or a pen, fuss with hair or accessories, and so on. No matter how much you might want a cigarette, don't smoke, even if the interviewer does. Smoking makes it difficult to talk and to show your portfolio.

Let your body language and visual "presentation" communicate the interested complete professional. Be sure to listen to the questions. Do not think of what you want to say and then not hear what is being asked. Think before you speak, and do not interrupt the interviewer. Use eye contact, but do not try to stare the interviewer down. Use body language that is open and receptive to what is being discussed, not defensive. Smile; show interest. If you do not show interest in your work as you describe it, or in the company through the questions that are asked by the interviewer, you are guaranteed to not get an offer.

Stress your qualifications and what you can do for the company. Be enthusiastic with your answers and stress your positive characteristics, but do not exaggerate your experience or abilities. It will not take much time to find out you are not an expert water-color renderer if you are not. And do not try to pass off someone else's work for yours in your portfolio. That too will be found out very quickly and will almost always lead to dismissal.

Graduating students, particularly, need to indicate a willingness to learn. Joe Allen didn't know much about computers, but when the interviewer asked about his computer experience, he was honest and said that he had minimal knowledge but was definitely willing and interested in learning. When no one else expressed that willingness, he obtained the job offer.

Never bring up personal problems, argue, blame others, or beg for the job. Even if you left your previous job under difficult circumstances, do not blame anyone at the other company for the problems. It tags you as a difficult person and will probably influence the interviewer to pass you over. If you are asked if you were ever fired, you do have to be honest, but it is not necessary to go into a long, detailed discussion of what happened. Make some brief comments about what happened and hope the interviewer moves on.

If, during the interview, you determine you are not interested in working for that company, complete the interview, but inform the firm promptly that you are not interested in pursuing the position further. For students, do not even accept an interview if you really have no interest in the company. Some students like to go to interviews to "practice" for the ones they want. This is bad business etiquette that can come back to haunt you later.

Unless the interviewer brings it up, do not ask about salary and benefits until the latter part of the interview. Be prepared with a salary range that you need to have. Employers, of course, want to hire you at as low a salary as is reasonable for the position. But, do not sell yourself short. If the salary offer is way below what you need to live on, or is way below what you understand the competition is paying, say so. Remember that benefits like paid insurance are an important part of the compensation package. One company with an excellent health insurance program, a profit-sharing program, and a generous discount for personal purchases, but which offers a low salary might be a better opportunity than another company with a higher salary but weaker benefits (if all other things are equal). Interior design compensation is notoriously low in comparison to other professions. In 1987, junior designers were paid anywhere from $13,500 to a little over $26,000 depending on the size of the design firm and the location within the country.[1]

---

[1]Loebelson 1987.

For the most part, if you are offered a position, be prepared to either accept or reject at that time. If you are offered a different position than what you expected or are being offered a lower salary than you were expecting, it is acceptable to ask for some time to consider the offer. If you really want the position, say so. If you have another interview that day, do not keep one employer dangling to see if someone else might have a better offer.

Should you not be made an offer, but you have no indication that you are being rejected, ask the interviewer when he or she will be ready with a decision. Ask if the design firm will be interviewing anyone else. Do not leave without knowing when he or she will make a decision and what the salary range is. These are important bits of information you need to make a decision.

The time of the offer or nonoffer is the best clue the interview is over. Watch for other clues like the interviewer stacking the job application, your résumé, and his or her notes together, and the interviewer pushing his or her chair back in preparation for getting up. When the interview is over, get up and leave promptly. If an offer was made and you accepted it, many interviewers will take you on a brief tour of the office or studio and introduce you to some of the other employees. Be sure, at the end of this tour, that you understand what day you are to start, the time, and anything else that needs to be taken care of by you either prior to your first day or on your first day.

### TYPICAL QUESTIONS

There are many kinds of common questions that are asked in interviews. It is important to prepare yourself for these questions in advance. Any that are now considered illegal will be discussed in the following section.

According to the *Catalyst Guide,* the ten most common interview questions are

1. What are your major strengths?
2. What are your major weaknesses?
3. How is your previous experience applicable to the work we do here?
4. Why did you leave your former job?
5. Is there someone we can contact who is familiar with you and your activities?
6. Where do you see yourself in the company ten years from now?
7. What are your interests outside work?
8. Why do you want to work here?
9. Are you applying to other companies?
10. What kind of compensation are you looking for?[2]

In an interior design interview there are some other questions that are commonly asked.

Are you willing to take a design test?

Why did you decide to major in interior design?

Are you willing to travel?

Do you prefer to work alone on projects?

### ILLEGAL QUESTIONS

As discussed in Chapter 9, there are many questions that can no longer be asked in a job interview or appear on a job application. These questions relate to age, sex,

---

[2]Reprinted by permission of the Putnam Publishing Group from *Marketing Yourself: The Catalyst Women's Guide to Successful Resumes and Interviews.* The Catalyst Staff. Copyright © 1980 by the Catalyst Staff.

religion, and ethnic origin. Many questions that do not seem to indicate sexual discrimination actually do. Questions to a woman related to whether she is single or married, what her husband does for a living, or whether or not she plans to have children are all considered illegal. These discriminatory kinds of questions and responses must not form the basis for deciding to offer or not to offer a job to an individual.

There are ways to ask certain "discriminatory" questions so as to make them legal. This is especially true if the question and response has a direct bearing on the ability of the individual to perform the job. Although it is illegal to ask you, "How old are you?" it is legal to ask, "Are you between the ages of 25 and 45?"

When you are asked a question that you believe to be illegal or that you feel uncomfortable in answering, you must be prepared to say something. Many of the job-hunting books suggest that you either answer the question anyway, forget about it, or say something like, "I do not understand what that has to do with the requirements of the job or my qualifications to do the job." Many interviewers may not have hired anyone for some time and may not be aware that some questions cannot be legally asked anymore. Making a big issue of such questions, if you honestly feel the person is asking the question innocently, could mean not getting the job. If the interviewer asks too many of these kinds of questions or ignores your hesitancy to answer, you always have the right to terminate the interview and choose to obtain a job somewhere else.

The whole question of discrimination in hiring decisions is still in its infancy. Although legal cases are being heard, there is still a lot of gray area. You must decide whether or not you want to work at a firm that appears to discriminate.

## *Follow-up*

It is important that as soon after the interview as is practical you make notes to yourself about what transpired. This is true whether you have accepted an offer, rejected an offer, or not even received an offer. Notes related to salary, benefits, expected performance levels, and general impressions of the firm will be important if you have not made a decision about the company or the company has not made a decision about you. If an offer was not made or you were rejected, these notes will help you understand what may have gone wrong so that you can correct the errors for future interviews. These same bits of information are necessary to be sure that agreed-on responsibilities are the responsibilities on which you will later be evaluated.

Good business etiquette also calls for you to send a thank-you letter to the interviewer immediately after the interview (see Figure 26-7). Thank the interviewer for his or her time, restate your interest in the position, if you are still interested, and follow through on any promised information you agreed to supply.

If you were offered a position but asked for time to consider, it is best if you both call the interviewer promptly and follow with a refusal or acceptance letter. In this way, the company knows promptly whether or not you are interested in the position, in the case of a refusal, has a letter for company records.

If you are still interested in a position with the firm when you know that the firm will be interviewing others, it is necessary to keep the design firm interested in you. Be sure to add a short paragraph to summarize your qualifications and how you now see that you can add to the company.

Follow-up is a way of continuing the good impression of yourself to the employer. This short note, which should still be typed using good business letter form,

Judith Jones
5217 Prospect Street
Ft. Collins, Colorado 80525
(303) 555-0142


March 30, 1986


Mr. William Green, Director of Design
Practical Interiors
2300 S. College
Ft. Collins, Colorado 80526

Dear Mr. Green:

Thank you for giving me the opportunity to meet with you yesterday and learn about your design organization.

While you interview the other individuals you are considering, I hope you will take the time to examine my resume and will decide in my favor for the position of Project Designer. I feel confident in my ability to be a productive contributor to the on-going success of your firm.

I would like to review three important facts that show I am the most qualified candidate for the position of Project Designer. First, I have three years experience with a full-service independent design firm where my assignments required the utilization of all the traditional design skills in both residential and commercial design. Second, my proven sales skills affirm my ability to successfully work with clients. Third, my successful completion of the NCIDQ examination so recently after entering the profession confirms my dedication to my professional growth.

Should you need any further information I will be happy to provide it. I look forward to your positive response to my application at the end of the week when you conclude your remaining interviews.

Sincerely,


Judith Jones

FIGURE 26-7
Follow-up thank-you letter after a job interview.

will indicate to the employer that you are a professional. Even if the firm does not have an opening for you now, you will be remembered later.

## *Summary*

Each of us grows in our own way seeking fulfillment in our careers. As the professional gains experience in the field, he or she seeks greater levels of responsibility and challenges in the workplace. Often, it is necessary to seek new responsibility in other firms, even other cities. For the student, the first job is an important first step in a successful and satisfying career in the profession. Obtaining these positions does not come easily to most of us.

At one time or another, preparing portfolios and résumés and embarking on the job search and the stressful interview process will affect all who read this book. It is hoped that the information in this chapter will help each level of professional make the search and achievement of the "right" position possible.

# GLOSSARY

**Accounts payable.** Claims from suppliers for goods or services ordered (and possibly delivered) but not yet paid for.

**Accounts receivable.** The account that shows what others owe to the firm as a result of sales or billings for goods and services.

**Accrual accounting.** An accounting method where revenues and expenses are recognized at the time they are earned (in the case of revenues) or incurred (in the case of expenses) whether the revenue has actually been collected or the expense actually paid.

**Accrued expenses.** Expenses owed to others for the period, but not yet paid. Salary owed during an accounting period but not yet paid is an example.

**Acknowledgments.** The paperwork forms which the supplier sends to the designer to indicate what the supplier interpreted the designer's order to be.

**Addenda.** Corrections or changes are made to the contract documents by the issuance of addenda (*addendum* is the singular form). Addenda are written by the person or firm responsible for the original set of contract documents.

**Advertising.** Any kind of paid communication in media such as newspapers, magazines, television, or radio.

**Agency relationship.** The common law relationship when one person or entity agrees to represent or do business for another person or entity. Today's employer-employee relationship is a reflection of the agency relationship.

**Annual business plan.** A systematic investigation and written report of what the firm can do, what the client base of the firm demands, and what the firm then decides to try to accomplish for the year. The plan should contain information related to all areas of the business.

**Assets.** Any kind of resource—tangible or intangible—that the firm owns or controls and which can be measured in monetary terms.

**Balance sheet.** An accounting form that shows the financial position of a firm as of a particular moment in time with a statement of its assets and equities.

**Bar charts.** A scheduling method consisting of a description of tasks required in the left-hand margin and horizontal bars on the right-hand side showing the time in days, weeks, or months required to complete the task.

**Base bid.** Refers to a proprietary specification that contains an "or equal" substitution allowance. All bidders must base their bids on the goods specified by product name.

**Benefits.** Direct or indirect additional payments to the employee for the work performed. Benefits may include paid vacations, profit-sharing programs, and group health insurance.

**Benefits selling.** A selling technique whereby the seller describes certain features of the product or service that relate to the needs of the client.

**Bid.** An offer for the amount one will pay to provide the specified goods and/or services required.

**Bid bond.** Required of all bidders to assure that the designer-vendor awarded the contract will sign the contract.

**Bid opening.** The time that the owner of the project reveals who has bid on the project. In most situations, the bid opening is private and only the owners and designers responsible for creating the contract documents are present. Governmental agencies and many public utilities are required to have bid openings open to the public. In this case, anyone may attend the bid opening and find out what others have bid for the project.

**Bill of lading.** The form that the supplier provides to the truck driver to show what is being shipped and who has title to the goods.

**Billing rates.** A rate combining salary, benefits, overhead, and profit that is used as the basis for charging clients for services.

**Bond forms.** Legal documents used to oblige the designer-vendor to the contract as assurance that the designer-vendor will perform the requirements of the contract as agreed. Three common bond forms are the bid bond, performance bond, and the labor and materials payment bond.

**Breach of contract.** Breach simply means *to break*. A breach occurs when one of the parties of a contract does not perform his or her duties as spelled out in the terms of the agreement.

**Break-even point.** The point at which revenues equal expenses. At this point, the firm is neither making nor losing money.

**Budgeting.** Involves annual managerial goals expressed in specific quantitative terms, usually monetary terms. Budgeting encourages the manager to plan for the various events affecting the firm rather than reacting to them.

**Business plan.** Provides substantive thought as to what the business is all about and how it is going to operate.

**Buyer.** A person who contracts to purchase or who purchases some good.

**Cash accounting.** The accounting method whereby revenue and expense items are recognized in the period the firm actually receives the cash or actually pays the bills.

**Cash discount.** An accounting term referring to an extra discount for paying the invoice promptly. A notation that commonly looks like "2/10 net 30" appears on the invoice to notify the designer of the cash discount.

**Chain of command.** The organizational structure that helps everyone in the organization understand what the formal communication patterns are.

**Chronological résumé.** States educational and work experiences exactly when they occurred, in reverse chronological order.

**Closed bids.** A specification that is written so that products cannot be substituted for what was specified.

**Closing.** The selling art of knowing when to ask for the sale.

**Codes.** Systematic bodies of law created by federal, state, and local jurisdictions to ensure safety.

**Combination résumé.** Utilizes qualities of both the chronological and functional résumé and combines them into one.

**Commercial interior design.** The branch of interior design concerned with the planning and specifying of interior materials and products used in public spaces such as offices, hotels, airports, and hospitals. It is sometimes called *contract interior design* because of the use of a "contract" for services.

**Commission.** A payment method for an agent acting on behalf of the employer. Commission relates to a percentage amount paid to the agent (interior designer) calculated on the sale of goods and/or services.

**Compensation.** The method of paying the employee for the work performed.

**Competitive bidding.** A process whereby the client has the opportunity to obtain comparative prices from a number of contractors and/or vendors for the construction or supply of the project.

**Concealed damage.** Damage to goods that is not obvious since the original packaging is not damaged. Most often occurs when items are shipped in cartons.

**Concept selling.** Explaining and obtaining approval from the client of the overall design idea. Concept selling is difficult since it involves selling intangibles.

**Confirmation of purchase.** The business form that spells out what goods the designer has agreed to order for or sell to the client. It is also called a *purchase agreement* or *contract proposal.*

**Consideration.** The "price" one pays to another party for fulfilling a contract.

**Construction documents.** Legal documents consisting of working drawings, schedules, and specifications describing what is required for the completion of an architectural and/or interiors project.

**Contract.** A promise or agreement between two or more parties to perform or not perform some act. The performance or lack of performance of this act can be enforced by the courts.

**Control function.** This management function requires the manager to monitor the activities of the firm and take any necessary steps to ensure that the plans, policies, and decisions of the manager and the firm are being carried out.

**Copyright.** The method of legally protecting, for a specified period of time, written materials and graphic designs.

**Copyright notification.** In order to begin the legal protection of written materials and graphic designs, the following must appear in a conspicuous place on the work: (1) "Copyright," "COPR," or ©; (2) year of publication; and (3) the name of the copyright claimant.

**Corporation.** An association of individuals created by statutory requirements creating a legal entity. The corporation has existence independent of its originators or any other member or stockholder. It can sue and be sued by others, can enter into contracts, commit crimes, and be punished. A corporation has powers and duties distinct from any of its members and survives even after the death of any or all of its stockholders.

**Cost of sales.** Refers to the costs paid in the direct generation of revenues. Called *cost of goods sold* in retail; in this case, it refers to changes in inventory.

**Cost price.** The price that the designer must pay for the goods.

**Credit.** In accounting, this term means the right-hand side of an account.

**Crime.** When a person (or business, in the case of a corporation) commits a wrong against society that is regulated by statute.

**Critical path method (CPM).** A scheduling method that begins by identifying the interrelationships of the tasks to be performed. This analysis shows the designer which tasks must be done before the next or other tasks can be performed, thus establishing the critical path.

**Debit.** In accounting, this term means the left-hand side of an account. It has no other accounting meaning.

**Decision-making.** The activity of making reasonable choices between the alternatives available. An important part of the management function.

**Deferred revenues.** Revenues received for services or the future sale of goods, but the service or goods have not yet been delivered.

**Delivery.** Includes the activities concerned with moving tangible items from the showroom or warehouse to the job site and simply placing them in their correct locations.

**Deposit.** A deposit is paid by the client before the designer orders any furniture. It is applied to the final purchase amount.

**Depreciation.** Results from the concept that capital equipment has a limited useful life. It is intended to express the usage of a fixed asset in the firm's pursuit of revenue.

**Descriptive specification.** Describes, often in elaborate detail, the materials, workmanship, fabrication methods, and installation of the required goods.

**Direct labor.** The time the various employees spend directly involved in the generation of the revenues of the firm.

**Direct personnel expense (DPE).** A number that includes not only the salary of the employee but also any cost of benefits such as unemployment taxes, medical insurance, and paid holidays.

**Discount.** A reduction, usually stated as a percentage, from the suggested retail price. A full or normal discount from suggested retail is 50 percent.

**Down payment.** (See *Deposit.*)

**80/20 rule.** A business rule used in many situations. Here, from a list of ten items arranged in the order of importance, if one accomplishes only the two most important items, one achieves 80 percent of the total value of time spent.

**Employment at will.** The doctrine that an employee who is not bound by a written contract, has no written terms of his or her employment spelled out, and has the right to quit his or her job without notice can also be fired by the employer at any time with no explanation.

**Equities.** Claims on a balance sheet by outsiders and/or owners against the total assets of the firm.

**Ethical standards.** Define what is right and wrong in relation to the professional behavior of the members and even the practice of the profession.

**Expediter.** An individual familiar with the design firm's paperwork system and the various ordering and shipping requirements of manufacturers. The expediter is responsible for the speedy processing of orders.

**Expenses.** The amount of outflows of resources of a firm as a consequence of the efforts made by the firm to earn revenues.

**Express warranties.** Promises, claims, descriptions, or affirmations made about a product's performance, quality, or condition that form the "basis of the bargain."

**Features.** Descriptions of specific aspects or characteristics of a service or product. Used during selling.

**Financial accounting.** Concerned with reporting accounting information for use by individuals outside or inside the firm.

**Financial management control.** Concerned with the planning and analysis of all the financial aspects of the firm to help internal individuals manage and control the performance of the firm. Often called *managerial accounting*.

**Flat-fee method.** The designer determines some dollar value to perform all the services required for a project. The client is then charged that amount whether the project takes a time shorter or longer than the estimate.

**FOB (free on board).** The shipper must assume the expense of loading the goods onto the truck as well as the expense and risk for shipping the goods to the FOB destination. Also referred to as *freight on board*.

**FOB destination.** The manufacturer retains ownership of the goods, pays all shipping expenses, and assumes all risks until the goods reach the delivery destination.

**FOB factory.** The buyer assumes ownership or title of the goods when they are loaded on the truck at the factory. The buyer assumes the transportation expenses and all risks.

**Functional résumé.** Presents information to emphasize qualifications and skills, rather than the order in which they were obtained.

**General partnership.** Two or more people joining together for the purpose of forming a business, and these people alone sharing the profits and risks of the business.

**Goals.** Broad statements, without regard to any time limit, of what the firm wishes to achieve.

**Goods.** Tangible items that have physical existence and can be moved.

**Gross margin.** The difference between revenues and cost of sales. Represents the amount of revenue available to cover operational (selling and administrative) expenses.

**Gross profit.** Another term for *gross margin*. Does not represent profit.

**Gross revenue.** All the revenue, prior to any deductions, generated by the firm for the accounting period.

**Hourly fee.** The most commonly charged fee. It is based on the firm's direct personnel expense. For each hour or portion of an hour that the designer works on the project, the client is charged some dollar amount.

**Income statement.** An accounting report that formally reports all the revenues and expenses of the firm for a stated period of time. The result shows the net income (or loss) for the firm during the period.

**Installation.** The specialized part of the delivery process that involves assembly, construction, or physical attachments of products to the building.

**Instructions to bidders.** A document that informs bidders how to prepare bids for submittal so that all submittals are in the same form.

**Invitation to bid.** Provides a summary of the project, the bid process, and other brief, pertinent procedures for the project. It informs potential bidders of the project, its scope, and where to obtain further information.

**Invoice.** A bill that is sent from the manufacturer or supplier to the designer indicating how much the designer must pay. The designer also uses an invoice to bill the client for goods and/or services provided.

**Job descriptions.** Communicates the qualifications, skills, and responsibilities of each job classification within a design firm.

**Joint venture.** A temporary contractual association of two or more persons or firms who agree to share in the responsibilities, losses, and profits of a particular project or business venture.

**Journal.** In accounting, a chronological record of all accounting transactions for the firm.

**Labor and materials payment bond.** Required of the winning bidder to guarantee that, should the designer-vendor default on the project, the designer-vendor will be responsible for paying for all the materials and labor that have been contracted for.

**Ledger.** In accounting, the ledger is a group of accounts. Sometimes called a *general ledger.*

**Liabilities.** In accounting, amounts that the firm owes to others due to past transactions or events. Liabilities always have first claim on the firm's assets.

**Limited partnership.** A business formation created according to statutory requirements. A limited partnership is formed with at least one general partner and one or more partners designated as limited partners.

**List price.** Generally accepted to be the same as *suggested retail price*—a price to the consumer.

**Logo.** A symbolic image of a company or organization.

**Markdown.** A term used in retail to represent discounts taken from the normal selling price.

**Market.** In reference to designer resources, a term that many interior designers use to mean they are going to visit one of the annual shows held at the marts.

**Market centers.** Concentrations of trade sources in one area of a city.

**Marketing.** Includes all the activities of moving goods and services from producers to consumers.

**Marketing analysis.** Involves gathering and analyzing data concerning such things as the abilities and interests of the staff, potential clients, the economy, and the competition in order to make better plans and decisions about the direction of the firm's business efforts.

**Mart.** Where many firms have located in one building.

**Merchant.** Anyone who is involved with the buying and/or selling of the kinds of goods with which he or she is dealing. A person acting in a mercantile capacity.

**Milestone charts.** An easy scheduling method whereby the designer outlines the activities required by the project and establishes a target date for the completion of each task.

**Misrepresentation.** The altering of facts to deceive or use fraud in order to receive personal gain.

**Mission statement.** A philosophical statement of what the firm sees as its role in the profession. It contains broad statements of what the company wishes to achieve during an unspecified time period.

**Multiple discounts.** A series of discounts from the suggested retail price given by manufacturers to designers for very large orders.

**Negligence.** A failure by one party to use due care so that injury is sustained by another person or a person's property.

**Net income (loss).** The amount of income or loss that results when all expenses are subtracted from revenues. If the result is positive, net income represents the dollar amount of profit the firm made for the period. If the result is negative, net loss indicates that expenses exceeded revenues for the period.

**Net price.** A price representing a 50 percent discount from suggested retail.

**Objectives.** Specific statements combined with time limits aimed toward accomplishing the firm's goals.

**Open bid.** A bid specification written in such a way as to allow multiple numbers of products for the item being required.

**"Or equal."** A term in a specification which allows bidders to substitute what they believe to be products of equal quality to that which was specified.

**Owner's equity.** The section on the balance sheet showing the amount the owner has invested in the firm.

**Packing list.** A detailed list of the quantities and descriptions of what is being shipped to the designer from a manufacturer or supplier. It is commonly in a plastic envelope attached to the outside of one of the items.

**Per diem.** A dollar amount that is charged to the client to cover hotel, meals, and transportation costs when it is necessary for the designer to travel out of town in the interests of the project.

**Performance bond.** Required of the winning bidder as a guarantee that the designer-vendor will complete the work as specified and will protect the client from any loss up to the amount of the bond as a result of the failure of the designer-vendor to perform the contract.

**Performance evaluation.** Systematic evaluation of positive and negative work efforts of an employee. It is used to review past performance in relation to agreed-on responsibilities to form the basis of salary increases, promotions, and/or retention.

**Performance specification.** A specification establishing product requirements based on exacting performance criteria. These criteria must be based on qualitative or measurable statements.

**Personal goals.** Concrete ideas representing some kind of end that a person tries to achieve.

**Portfolio.** A visual presentation of what the individual can do as an interior designer.

**Practice acts.** Guidelines established by legislation as to what a person can or cannot do in the practice of a profession in a particular state. Individuals whose profession is guided by practice acts must register with a state board and meet exacting requirements.

**Prepaid expense.** The early payment of expenses in a period prior to their being required. The prepaid expense is an asset since the value of the prepaid expense, not yet due, still has value to the owner.

**Price.** Any kind of payment from buyer to seller including money, goods, services, or real property.

**Private corporation.** A special form of corporation created by persons in many professions. Its formation is regulated by state statutes.

**Probing.** A selling technique for asking questions in order to uncover the needs of the client.

**Profit-and-loss statement.** Another name for the *income statement.*

**Project control book.** File folders or notebooks in which the designer keeps all the pertinent data and paperwork related to the project in progress.

**Promotion.** Providing information about services or products from the seller to the buyer. Includes publicity, publishing, advertising, and direct selling.

**Proprietary specification.** Names the products and materials by manufacturer's name, model number, or part number.

**Publicity.** A direct form of promotion that is unpaid.

**Public relations.** Refers to all the efforts of the firm to create an image in order to affect the public's positive opinion of a firm.

**Purchase order.** The business form that the designer uses to order goods and/or services for the client or to order supplies needed by the design firm.

**Quantity discount.** A discount greater than the normal 50 percent discount allowed because a large quantity of merchandise is purchased at one time.

**Realization budgeting.** A budget method that begins when the manager forecasts the potential revenue generation of each member of the firm.

**Reference specification.** Utilizes an established standard such as the standards of the American Society for Testing and Materials (ASTM) rather than written detailed descriptions or performance criteria for required products.

**Reimbursable expenses.** Those costs that are not part of the design contract but which are made in the interest of completing the project.

**Representatives or "reps."** Refers to the men and women who act as the informational source to the interior designer about the various manufacturer's products. Independent reps work for themselves and are usually responsible for many different manufacturers' products. Factory reps work for only one manufacturer as an employee.

**Residential interior design.** Concerned with the planning and/or specifying of interior materials and products used in private residences.

**Résumé.** A summary of a designer's qualifications.

**Retained earnings.** The claim on the assets arising from the cumulative undistributed earnings of the corporation for use in the business after dividends are paid to stockholders.

**Retainer.** An amount of money paid by the client to the designer for design services to be done. The retainer is customarily paid upon signing the contractual agreement.

**Revenue.** The amount of inflows from the sale of goods or rendering of services during an accounting period.

**Sale.** Occurs when the seller transfers title or ownership of the goods to a buyer and the buyer has provided some consideration to the seller.

**Schedules.** Used to clarify sizes, location, finishes, and other information related to certain nonconstruction parts of an interior or structure. Schedules are commonly prepared for doors, windows, and interior room finishes.

**Seller.** Any person who sells or contracts to sell goods to others.

**Selling.** Finding out what the client wants through the use of personal communication and providing it.

**Selling and administrative expenses.** Those expenses that are incurred whether or not the firm produces any revenues. They are often called overhead expenses and thought of as those expenses needed to keep the doors of the business open.

**Selling price.** Refers to the actual price that is quoted to the client.

**Sole proprietorship.** The simplest and least expensive form of business. The company and individual owner are one and the same.

**Specifications.** The written instructions to the contractors and vendors concerning the materials and methods of construction or the interior products that are to be bid.

**Statement of cash flows.** An accounting statement reporting, for a specific period, the changes in cash flows from operating, investing, and financing activities.

**Statute of frauds.** Statutory requirements that call for written contracts in certain circumstances. For the interior designer these include a contract for the sale of goods having a value of over $500, any contract that will take over one year to complete, and any sale of real estate.

**Strategies.** Specific actions as part of a business or marketing plan that have definite time limits within the year.

**Strict liability.** When a person is held liable for injury to others regardless of fault.

**Subchapter S corporation.** A special form of corporation that may utilize many of the benefits of a corporation, but which pays taxes as a partnership.

**Suggested retail price.** A term related to the price, to be used by the seller and suggested by the manufacturer.

**SWOT.** A marketing analysis technique. *SWOT* stands for strengths, weaknesses, opportunities, and threats.

**Tag for.** Information that the designer requests the manufacturer to affix to the goods and note on the invoice to help the designer deliver the goods to the correct client.

**Title.** In sales law, title refers to the legal ownership of goods. The person who holds title to the goods owns the goods.

**Title acts.** Legislative measures concerned with limiting the use of certain titles to individuals who meet agreed-on qualifications and who have registered with a state board.

**Tort.** When a person commits a wrong against another and causes injury to the harmed party. Torts are civil matters and therefore are not legislated by statute.

**Trade discounts.** Discounts given as a courtesy by some vendors to designers and others in the trade. These are usually a small percentage off retail.

**Trade sources.** The groups of manufacturers, suppliers, and tradespeople who provide the various goods and services a designer uses to complete an interior design project.

**Transaction privilege tax license.** Allows the interior designer to pass on the state sales tax to the consumer. Issued by state and municipal taxing authorities.

**Transmittal letter.** A form letter than can be used to send information to anyone involved with the project or from whom information is requested.

**Uniform Commercial Code (UCC).** The body of law that guides the relationships among the various levels of buyers and sellers in business transactions.

**Variance analysis.** A managerial technique whereby one looks at financial and numerical data in relation to the differences between planned or budgeted amounts and actual amounts.

**Vendor.** Someone who sells products or services either to the end-user or to another merchant, like the designer.

**Vignette.** A display of furniture and furnishings in a store or showroom that is done to simulate an actual room.

**Walk-through.** A final inspection of the job to be sure that everything ordered is present and that any omissions or damaged goods are noted.

**Warranties.** A statement or representation made by a seller concerning the goods. Warranties are related to quality, fitness of purpose, or title.

**Wholesale price.** A special price to a merchant (buyer) from a merchant (buyer) at a value lower than what the good would cost the consumer.

# Appendix

## PROFESSIONAL ORGANIZATIONS AND ASSOCIATIONS

- American Institute of Architects
  1735 New York Ave., N.W.
  Washington, D.C. 20006
  202-626-7300
- American Society of Interior Designers
  1430 Broadway
  New York, NY 10018
  212-944-9220
- Foundation for Interior Design Education Research
  322 Eighth Avenue
  New York, NY 10001
  212-929-8366
- Governing Board for Interior Design Standards
  341 Merchandise Mart
  Chicago, IL 60654
  312-527-0517
- Institute of Business Designers
  341 Merchandise Mart
  Chicago, IL 60654
  312-467-1950
- Interior Design Educators Council
  P. O. Box 8744
  Richmond, VA 23226
  607-255-1811
- International Facility Management Association
  11 Greenway Plaza Suite 1410
  Houston, TX 77046
  713-623-4362
- International Society of Interior Designers
  Design Center Los Angeles
  433 South Spring St., Suite 6-D
  Los Angeles, CA 90013
  213-680-4240

- National Council for Interior Design Qualification
  118 East 25th Street
  New York, NY 10010
  212-473-1188
- National Home Fashions League
  107 World Trade Center
  P. O. Box 58045
  Dallas, TX 75258
  214-747-2406

# CHAPTER BIBLIOGRAPHY

## CHAPTER 1

Abercrombie, Nicholas, Stephen Hill, and Bryan S. Turner. 1984. *The Penguin Dictionary of Sociology.* New York: Allen Lane Publications (Penguin).

American Society of Interior Designers. July 1985. *ASID Membership Information.*

———. September 1987. *Membership Bulletin.*

———. December 1985. Title Registration Declared Top Priority in '86. *Report.*

———. 1986. First Interior Design Practice Act Passed in Nation. *Report.* 12.

———. Spring 1986. ASID/NCIDQ Meetings Resolve Confusion and Controversy. *Report.*

Anscomb, Isabelle. 1984. *A Woman's Touch.* New York: Elisabeth Sifton Books (Viking).

Ball, Victoria. 1982. *Opportunities in Interior Design.* Skokie, Ill.: VGM Career Horizons.

Castleman, Betty. June 1987. How Will Licensing Affect Me? *Designers West.*

Chewning, Richard. 1984. *Business Ethics in a Changing Culture.* Reston, Va.: Reston Publishing Co., Inc.

*Collier's Encyclopedia.* 1984. Vol. 13, New York: Macmillan Educational Co. s.v. "Interior design and decoration."

DeWolfe, Elsie. [1913] 1975. *The House in Good Taste.* Reprint. New York: Arno Press.

Ebstein, Barbara. January–March 1985. Licensing: The Design Concern for the Eighties. American Society of Interior Designers. *Report.*

Friedmann, Arnold, John F. Pile, and Forrest Wilson. 1982. *Interior Design—An Introduction to Architectural Interiors.* 3d ed. New York: Elsevier Science Publishing Co., Inc.

Gueft, Olga. 1980. The Past as Prologue: The First 50 Years. 1931–1981: An Overview. *American Society of Interior Designers Annual Report 1980.* New York: American Society of Interior Designers.

Hughes, Nina. June 1987. Interiors Platform. *Interiors.*

Institute of Business Designers. January 1984. *Membership Information.*

———. Fall 1984. *Perspective.*

———. 1980. *Code of Ethics.* Pamphlet, IBD Practices P105.

———. March 1984. *IBD News.* Arizona Chapter.

———. January 1986. *IBD News.* Arizona Chapter.

Kettler, Kerwin. May 1985. Is There More to Licensing Than a License? *Designer Specifier.*

Pile, John. 1978. *Open Office Planning.* New York: Watson-Guptill Publications.

Russell, Beverly. March 1985. Interiors Business: New Moves Toward Interior Design Licensing. *Interiors.*

Stein, Harry. 1982. *Ethics (and Other Liabilities).* New York: St. Martin's Press.

Sweet, Justin. 1985. *Legal Aspects of Architecture, Engineering, and the Construction Process.* 3d ed. St. Paul, Minn.: West Publishing Co.

Tate, Allen, and C. Ray Smith. 1986. *Interior Design in the 20th Century.* New York: Harper and Row Publishers.

## CHAPTER 2

Bliss, Edwin. 1983. *Doing It Now.* New York: Bantam Books.

Brothers, Joyce. 1978. *How To Get Whatever You Want Out of Life.* New York: Ballantine Books.

Buscaglia, Leo. 1982. *Living, Loving, and Learning.* New York: Charles B. Slack, Inc.

Campbell, David. 1974. *If You Don't Know Where You're Going, You'll Probably End Up Somewhere Else.* Niles, Ill.: Argus Communications.

Freudenberger, Herbert J. 1980. *Burn Out.* Garden City, N.Y.: Anchor Press (Doubleday and Co.).

Friedman, Martha. 1980. *Overcoming the Fear of Success.* New York: Warner Books.

Harragan, Betty Lehan. 1977. *Games Mother Never Taught You.* New York: Warner Books.

————. 1983. *Knowing the Score.* New York: St. Martin's Press.

LeBoeuf, Michael. 1979. *Working Smart.* New York: Warner Books.

Sher, Barbara, with Annie Gottlieb. 1979. *Wishcraft—How to Get What You Really Want.* New York: Ballantine Books.


## CHAPTER 3

Dible, Donald M. 1974. *Up Your Own Organization!* 2d ed. Reston, Va.: Reston Publishing Co., Inc.

Jenkins, Michael D., and Max Perlman. 1986. *Starting and Operating a Business in Arizona.* Milpitas, Calif.: Oasis Press.

Loebelson, Andrew. 1983. *How to Profit in Contract Design.* New York: Interior Design Books, Inc.

Mancuso, Joseph R. 1985. *How to Write a Winning Business Plan.* Englewood Cliffs, N.J.: Prentice-Hall, Inc.

McCaslin, Barbara S., and Patricia P. McNamara. 1980. *Be Your Own Boss.* Englewood Cliffs, N.J.: Prentice-Hall, Inc.


## CHAPTER 4

Anthony, Robert N., and James S. Reece. 1983. *Accounting Text and Cases.* 7th ed. Homewood, Ill.: Richard D. Irwin, Inc.

Dible, Donald M. 1974. *Up Your Own Organization!* 2d ed. Reston, Va.: Reston Publishing Co., Inc.

Knackstedt, Mary. 1980. *Interior Design for Profit.* New York: Kobro Publications, Inc.

Loebelson, Andrew. 1983. *How to Profit in Contract Design.* New York: Interior Design Books.

Siegel, Harry, and Alan M. Siegel. 1982. *A Guide to Business Principles and Practices for Interior Designers.* Revised Edition. New York: Watson-Guptill Publications.

Stitt, Fred. A., ed. 1986. *Design Office Management Handbook.* Santa Monica, Calif.: Arts and Architecture Press.


## CHAPTER 5

Anthony, Robert, and James S. Reece. 1983. *Accounting Text and Cases.* 7th ed. Homewood, Ill.: Richard D. Irwin, Inc.

Barnes, A. James. 1981. *A Guide to Business Law.* Homewood, Ill.: Learning Systems Co.

Clarkson, Kenneth W., Roger LeRoy Miller, and Gaylord A. Jentz. 1983. *West's Business Law, Text and Cases.* 2d ed. St. Paul, Minn.: West Publishing Co.

Jentz, Gaylord A., Kenneth W. Clarkson, and Roger LeRoy Miller. 1987. *West's Business Law—Alternate UCC Comprehensive Edition.* 3d ed. St. Paul, Minn.: West Publishing Co.

Loebelson, Andrew. 1983. *How to Profit in Contract Design.* New York: Interior Design Books.

Prentice-Hall. 1987. *1987 Federal Tax Handbook.* Englewood Cliffs, N.J.: Prentice-Hall, Inc.

Research Institute of America. 1987. *Federal Tax Coordinator,* 2d ed, Vol. 6. New York: Research Institute of America.

Siegel, Harry, and Alan M. Siegel. 1982. *A Guide to Business Principles and Practices for Interior Designers.* Revised Edition. New York: Watson-Guptill Publications.

Sweet, Justin. 1985. *Legal Aspects of Architecture, Engineering, and the Construction Process.* 3d ed. St. Paul, Minn.: West Publishing Co.

## CHAPTER 6

Barrientos, Lawless J. 1983. *Arizona Business Kit for Starting and Existing Businesses.* New York: Simon and Schuster.

Davidson, Marion, and Martha Blue. 1979. *Making It Legal.* New York: McGraw-Hill Book Co.

Jentz, Gaylord A., Kenneth W. Clarkson, and Roger LeRoy Miller. 1987. *West's Business Law—Alternate UCC Comprehensive Edition.* 3d ed. St. Paul, Minn.: West Publishing Co.

Prentice-Hall. 1987. *1987 Federal Tax Handbook.* Englewood Cliffs, N.J.: Prentice-Hall, Inc.

Research Institute of America. 1987. *Federal Tax Coordinator,* 2d ed, Vol. 6. New York: Research Institute of America.

Strong, William S. 1984. *The Copyright Book: A Practical Guide.* 2d ed. Cambridge, Mass.: MIT Press.

Sweet, Justin. 1985. *Legal Aspects of Architecture, Engineering, and the Construction Process.* 3d ed. St. Paul, Minn.: West Publishing Co.

## CHAPTER 7

Barnes, A. James. 1981. *A Guide to Business Law.* Homewood, Ill.: Learning Systems Co.

Clarkson, Kenneth W., Roger LeRoy Miller, Gaylord A. Jentz. 1983. *West's Business Law, Text and Cases.* 2d ed. St. Paul, Minn.: West Publishing Co.

Hopf, Peter S., and John A. Raeber. 1984. *Access for the Handicapped.* New York: Van Nostrand Reinhold Co.

Jentz, Gaylord A., Kenneth W. Clarkson, and Roger LeRoy Miller. 1987. *West's Business Law—Alternate UCC Comprehensive Edition.* 3d ed. St. Paul, Minn.: West Publishing Co.

Reznikoff, S. C. 1979. *Specifications for Commercial Interiors.* New York: Watson-Guptill Publications.

Sweet, Justin. 1985. *Legal Aspects of Architecture, Engineering, and the Construction Process.* 3d ed. St. Paul, Minn.: West Publishing Co.

## CHAPTER 8

Beam, Burton, T., Jr., and John J. McFadden. 1985. *Employee Benefits.* Homewood, Ill.: Richard D. Irwin, Inc.

Block, Judy R. 1981. *Performance Appraisal on the Job.* New York: Executive Enterprises Publications Co., Inc.

Charnov, Bruce H. 1985. *Appraising Employee Performance.* Westbury, N.Y.: Caddylak Publishing.

Coxe, Weld. 1980. *Managing Architectural and Engineering Practice.* New York: John Wiley and Sons.

Finter, Andrea. July 1984. Designer Salary Poll Links Job Tenure and Compensation. *Contract.*

———. June 1985. Senior Designers' Average Pay: $37,300. *Contract.*

Foote, Rosslyn F. 1978. *Running an Office for Fun and Profit.* New York: McGraw-Hill Book Co.

Getz, Lowell. 1986. *Business Management in the Smaller Design Firm.* Newton, Mass.: Practice Management Associates, Ltd.

Gibson, Woody. October 1980. Design Wages Depend on Function. *Contract.*

Shapero, Albert. 1985. *Managing Professional People.* New York: The Free Press (Macmillan, Inc.).

Slavin, Maeve. September 1983. Jobs Are Not What They Used to Be. *Interiors.*

Stern, Natalie. November 1982. Top Contract Furniture Sales People Can Boost Earnings 33% with Timed Move. *Contract.*

Stitt, Fred. A., ed. 1986. *Design Office Management Handbook.* Santa Monica, Calif.: Arts and Architecture Press.

Tobias, Sheila, and Alma Lantz. November 1985. Performance Appraisal. *Working Woman.*

Wagner, Michael. September 1985. Interiors Business. Salaries and Bonuses Are Up for Designers. *Interiors.*

## CHAPTER 9

Bernardo, Stephanie. July/August 1985. Fire Me . . . and I'll Sue! *Success!*

Block, Judy R. 1981. *Performance Appraisal on the Job.* New York: Executive Enterprises Publications Co., Inc.

Charnov, Bruce H. 1985. *Appraising Employee Performance.* Westbury, N.Y.: Caddylak Systems, Inc.

Clarkson, Kenneth W., Roger LeRoy Miller, and Gaylord A. Jentz. 1983. *West's Business Law.* 2d ed. St. Paul, Minn.: West Publishing Co.

Epstein, Lee. 1977. *Legal Forms for the Designer.* New York: N and E Hellman.

Harragan, Betty Lehan. September 1986. Career Advice. *Working Woman.*

Harris, Joan. 1984. *Create Your Employee Handbook Fast and Professionally.* Westbury, N.Y.: Asher-Gallant Press.

Jentz, Gaylord, Kenneth W. Clarkson, and Roger LeRoy Miller. 1987. *West's Business Law— Alternate UCC Comprehensive Edition.* 3d ed. St. Paul, Minn.: West Publishing Co.

Lawson, J. W., II. 1970. *How to Develop a Company Personnel Policy Manual.* 5th ed. Chicago, Ill.: The Dartnell Corporation.

Liddle, Jeffrey L. 1981. Malicious Terminations and Abusive Discharges: The Beginning of the End of Employment at Will. *Employee Termination Handbook.* Englewood Cliffs, N.J.: Executive Enterprises Publications Co., Inc.

Laking, Jon, and Robin Roark. 1975. *Retailing Job Analysis and Job Evaluation.* New York: National Retail Merchants Association.

Sack, Steven Mitchell. 1981. *The Salesperson's Legal Guide.* Englewood Cliffs, N.J.: Prentice-Hall, Inc.

Stitt, Fred A., ed. 1986. *Design Office Management Handbook.* Santa Monica, Calif.: Arts and Architecture Press.

Sweet, Justin. 1985. *Legal Aspects of Architecture, Engineering, and the Construction Process.* 3d ed. St. Paul, Minn.: West Publishing Co.

## CHAPTER 10

Crichton, Michael. 1983. *Electronic Life.* New York: Alfred A. Knopf.

Dietsch, Deborah. February 1985. Low-Cost CAD on Desk-Top Computers. *Interiors.*

Getz, Lowell. 1986. *Business Management in the Smaller Design Firm.* Newton, Mass.: Practice Management Associates, Ltd.

Getz, Lowell, and Frank Stasiowski. 1984. *Financial Management for the Design Professional.* New York: Watson-Guptill Publications.

Gladstone, Daniel. September 1985. Designing with CAD. *Interior Design.*

Henderson, Justin. February 1986. CAD, an Underutilized Design and Marketing Tool, Can Help Large, Medium, *and* Small Firms Operate Efficiently. *Interiors.*

Loebelson, Andrew. 1983. *How to Profit in Contract Design.* New York: Interior Design Books.

———. January 1987. 10th Anniversary Edition of *Interior Design* Magazine's 100 Top Interior Design Firms. *Interior Design.*

———. July 1987. The Second 100 Interior Design Giants of 1987. *Interior Design.*

McLain-Kark, Joan H., and Ruey-Er Tang. Fall 1986. Computer Usage and Attitudes Toward Computers in the Interior Design Field. *Journal of Interior Design Education and Research.* 12: 25–32.

## CHAPTER 11

Anthony, Robert N. 1983. *Essentials of Accounting.* 3d ed. Reading, Mass.: Addison-Wesley Publishing Co.

Anthony, Robert N., and James S. Reece. 1983. *Accounting Texts and Cases,* 7th ed. Homewood, Ill.: Richard D. Irwin, Inc.

Getz, Lowell, 1986. *Business Management in the Smaller Design Firm.* Newton, Mass.: Practice Management Associates, Ltd.

Getz, Lowell, and Frank Stasiowski. 1984. *Financial Management for the Design Professional.* New York: Watson-Guptill Publications.

Horngren, Charles T. 1981. *Introduction to Financial Accounting.* Englewood Cliffs, N.J.: Prentice-Hall, Inc.

Imdieke, Leroy F., and Ralph E. Smith. 1987. *Financial Accounting.* 1st ed. New York: John Wiley and Sons.

Loebelson, Andrew. 1983. *How to Profit in Contract Design.* New York: Interior Design Books.

## CHAPTER 12

Anthony, Robert N., John Dearden, and Norton M. Bedford. 1984. *Management Control Systems.* 5th ed. Homewood, Ill.: Richard D. Irwin, Inc.

Anthony, Robert N., and James S. Reece. 1983. *Accounting Texts and Cases,* 7th ed. Homewood, Ill.: Richard D. Irwin, Inc.

Garrison, Ray H. 1985. *Managerial Accounting.* 4th ed. Plano, Tex.: Business Publications, Inc.

Getz, Lowell. 1986. *Business Management in the Smaller Design Firm.* Newton, Mass.: Practice Management Associates, Ltd.

Getz, Lowell, and Frank Stasiowski. 1984. *Financial Management for the Design Professional.* New York: Watson-Guptill Publications.

Glueck, William F. 1980. *Management.* 2d ed. Hinsdale, Ill.: Dryden Press.

Stitt, Fred A., ed. 1986. *Design Office Management Handbook.* Santa Monica, Calif.: Arts and Architecture Press.

## CHAPTER 13

Clarkson, Kenneth W., Roger LeRoy Miller, Gaylord A. Jentz. 1983. *West's Business Law, Text and Cases.* 2d ed. St. Paul, Minn.: West Publishing Co.

Jentz, Gaylord A., Kenneth W. Clarkson, and Roger LeRoy Miller. 1987. *West's Business Law—Alternate UCC Comprehensive Edition.* 3d ed. St. Paul, Minn.: West Publishing Co.

McCarthy, E. Jerome. 1981. *Basic Marketing.* 7th ed. Homewood, Ill.: Richard D. Irwin, Inc.

Quinn, Thomas M. 1978. *Uniform Commercial Code Commentary and Law Digest.* Boston, Mass.: Warren, Gorham and Lamont.

Siegel, Harry, with Alan M. Siegel. 1982. *A Guide to Business Principles and Practices for Interior Designers.* Revised Edition. New York: Watson-Guptill Publications.

## CHAPTER 14

Foote, Rosslyn. 1978. *Running an Office for Fun and Profit.* New York: McGraw-Hill Book Co.

Getz, Lowell. 1986. *Business Management in the Smaller Design Firm.* Newton, Mass.: Practice Management Associates.

Getz, Lowell, and Frank Stasiowski. 1984. *Financial Management for the Design Professional.* New York: Watson-Guptill Publications.

Loebelson, Andrew. 1983. *How to Profit in Contract Design.* New York: Interior Design Books.

———. January 1987. 10th Anniversary Edition of *Interior Design* Magazine's 100 Top Interior Design Firms. *Interior Design.*

Siegel, Harry, with Alan M. Siegel. 1982. *A Guide to Business Principles and Practices for Interior Designers.* Revised Edition. New York: Watson-Guptill Publications.

Stasiowski, Frank. 1985. *Negotiating Higher Design Fees.* New York: Watson-Guptill Publications.

Stitt, Fred A., ed. 1986. *Design Office Management Handbook.* Santa Monica, Calif.: Arts and Architecture Press.

## CHAPTER 15

Alderman, Robert L. 1982. *How to Make More Money at Interior Design.* New York: Whitney Communications Corporation.

Barnes, A. James. 1981. *A Guide to Business Law.* Homewood, Ill.: Learning Systems Co.

Clarkson, Kenneth W., Roger LeRoy Miller, Gaylord A. Jentz. 1983. *West's Business Law, Text and Cases.* 2d ed. St. Paul, Minn.: West Publishing Co.

Davidson, Marion, and Martha Blue. 1979. *Making It Legal.* New York: McGraw-Hill Book Co.

Jentz, Gaylord A., Kenneth W. Clarkson, and Roger LeRoy Miller. 1987. *West's Business Law—Alternate UCC Comprehensive Edition.* 3d ed. St. Paul, Minn.: West Publishing Co.

Loebelson, Andrew. 1983. *How to Profit in Contract Design.* New York: Interior Design Books.

Neubert, Christopher, and Jack Withiam, Jr. 1980. *How to Handle Your Own Contracts.* Revised Edition. New York: Greenwich House.

Siegel, Harry, and Alan M. Siegel. 1982. *A Guide to Business Principles and Practices for Interior Designers.* Revised Edition. New York: Watson-Guptill Publications.

Stasiowski, Frank. 1985. *Negotiating Higher Design Fees.* New York: Watson-Guptill Publications.

Sweet, Justin. 1985. *Legal Aspects of Architecture, Engineering, and the Construction Process.* 3d ed. St. Paul, Minn.: West Publishing Co.

## CHAPTER 16

Bachner, John Phillip, and Naresh Kumar Khosla. 1971. *Marketing and Promotion for Design Professionals.* New York: Van Nostrand Reinhold Co.

Brannen, William H. 1981. *Practical Marketing for Your Small Retail Business.* New York: Prentice-Hall, Inc.

Clark, Leta W. 1980. *How to Open Your Own Shop or Gallery.* New York: Penguin Books.

*Collier's Encyclopedia.* 1975. Vol. 15, s. v. "Marketing." New York: Macmillan Educational Co.

Coxe, Weld. 1971. *Marketing Architectural and Engineering Services.* New York: Van Nostrand Reinhold Co.

Drucker, Peter F. 1973. *Management: Tasks, Responsibilities, Practices.* New York: Harper and Row Publishers.

Hayes, Rick Stephan, and Gregory Brooks Elmore. 1985. *Marketing for Your Growing Business.* New York: Ronald Press Publication (John Wiley and Sons).

Jones, Gerre. 1983. *How to Market Professional Design Services.* 2d ed. New York: McGraw-Hill Book Co.

Knackstedt, Mary. 1980. *Interior Design for Profit.* New York: Kobro Publications, Inc.

McCarthy, E. Jerome. 1981. *Basic Marketing.* 7th ed. Homewood, Ill.: Richard D. Irwin, Inc.

McCaslin, Barbara, and Patricia P. McNamara. 1980. *Be Your Own Boss.* Englewood Cliffs, N.J.: Prentice-Hall, Inc.

Morgan, Jim. 1984. *Marketing for the Small Design Firm.* New York: Watson-Guptill Publications.

Weitz, Barton A., and Robin Wensley. 1984. *Strategic Marketing.* Boston, Mass.: Kent Publishing Co.

## CHAPTER 17

Austin, Richard L. 1984. *Report Graphics.* New York: Van Nostrand Reinhold Co.

Bachner, John Philip, and Naresh Kumar Khosla. 1977. *Marketing and Promotion for Design Professionals.* New York: Van Nostrand Reinhold Co.

Clark, Leta. 1980. *How to Open Your Own Shop or Gallery.* New York: Penguin Books.

Coxe, Weld. 1971. *Marketing Architectural and Engineering Services.* New York: Van Nostrand Reinhold Co.

Hays, Rick Stephan, and Gregory Brooks Elmore. 1985. *Marketing for Your Growing Business.* New York: Ronald Press Publications (John Wiley and Sons).

Institute of Business Designers. 1980. Code of Ethics (Pamphlet P105). Chicago: Institute of Business Designers.

Jones, Gerre L. 1983. *How to Market Professional Design Services.* 2d ed. New York: McGraw-Hill Book Co.

_____. 1980. *Public Relations for the Design Professional.* New York: McGraw-Hill Book Co.

Kenney, Michael, for Eastman Kodak Company. 1982. *Presenting Yourself.* New York: John Wiley and Sons.

Kliment, Stephen A. 1977. *Creative Communications for a Successful Design Practice.* New York: Watson-Guptill Publications.

Knackstedt, Mary V. 1980. *Interior Design for Profit.* New York: Kobro Publications, Inc.

McCarthy, E. Jerome. 1981. *Basic Marketing.* 7th ed. Homewood, Ill.: Richard D. Irwin, Inc.

McCaslin, Barbara S., and Patricia P. McNamara. 1980. *Be Your Own Boss.* Englewood Cliffs, N.J.: Prentice-Hall, Inc.

Morgan, Jim. 1984. *Marketing for the Small Design Firm.* New York: Watson-Guptill Publications.

## CHAPTER 18

Delmar, Ken. 1984. *Winning Moves—The Body Language of Selling.* New York: Warner Books.

Elsea, Janet G. 1984. *The Four-Minute Sell.* New York: Simon and Schuster.

Fast, Julius. 1970. *Body Language.* New York: Pocket Books (Simon and Schuster).

Fisher, Roger, and William Ury. 1981. *Getting to Yes.* New York: Penguin Books.

Frank, Milo O. 1986. *How to Get Your Point across in 30 Seconds or Less.* New York: Simon and Schuster.

Goodman, Gary S. 1984. *Selling Skills for the Non-Salesperson.* Englewood Cliffs, N.J.: Prentice-Hall, Inc.

Hopkins, Tom. 1982. *How to Master the Art of Selling.* New York: Warner Books.

Johnson, Spencer, and Larry Wilson. 1984. *The One-Minute Sales Person.* New York: William Morrow and Company.

Jones, Gerre. 1983. *How to Market Professional Design Services.* 2d ed. New York: McGraw-Hill Book Co.

Kenney, Michael, for Eastman Kodak Company. 1982. *Presenting Yourself.* New York: John Wiley and Sons.

King, David, and Karen Levine. 1979. *The Best Way in the World for a Woman to Make Money.* New York: Warner Books.

LaBella, Arleen, and Dolores Leach. 1983. *Personal Power.* Boulder, Colo.: New View Press.

Loebelson, Andrew. 1983. *How to Profit in Contract Design.* New York: Interior Design Books.

Molloy, John T. 1975. *Dress for Success.* New York: Warner Books.

_____. 1977. *The Woman's Dress for Success Book.* New York: Warner Books.

_____. 1981. *Molloy's Live for Success.* New York: Perigord Press (William Morrow and Co.).

Nierenberg, Gerard I., and Henry H. Calero. 1971. *How to Read a Person Like a Book.* New York: Pocket Books (Simon and Schuster).

Nierenberg, Juliet, and Irene S. Ross. 1985. *Women and the Art of Negotiating.* New York: Simon and Schuster.

Roth, Charles B. 1970. *Secrets of Closing Sales.* 4th ed. Englewood Cliffs, N.J.: Prentice-Hall, Inc.

Smith, Terry C. 1984. *Making Successful Presentations.* New York: John Wiley and Sons.

Stasiowski, Frank. 1985. *Negotiating Higher Design Fees.* New York: Watson-Guptill Publications.

Thompson, Jacqueline, ed. 1981. *Image Impact.* New York: A and W Publishers, Inc.

Ziglar, Zig. 1982. *Zig Ziglar's Secrets of Closing the Sale.* New York: Berkley Books.

## CHAPTER 19

Bliss, Edwin C. 1984. *Doing It Now.* New York: Bantam Books.

Burstein, David, and Frank Stasiowski. 1982. *Project Management for the Design Professional.* New York: Watson-Guptill Publications.

Lakein, Alan. 1973. *How to Get Control of Your Time and Your Life*. New York: A Signet Book, New American Library.

LeBoeuf, Michael. 1979. *Working Smart*. New York: Warner Books.

_____. 1983. *The Productivity Challenge*. New York: McGraw-Hill Book Co.

Loebelson, Andrew. 1983. *How to Profit in Contract Design*. New York: Interior Design Books.

Siegel, Harry, with Alan M. Siegel. 1982. *A Guide to Business Principles and Practices for Interior Designers*. Revised Edition. New York: Watson-Guptill Publications.

Stitt, Fred A., ed. 1986. *Design Office Management Handbook*. Santa Monica, Calif.: Arts and Architecture Press.

## CHAPTER 20

Contract Furniture and Furnishings Mart Directory. December 1985. *Contract*.

Corlin, Len. December 1985. Mart Fever Is Epidemic. *Contract*.

_____. December 1986. Marts Accelerate Development. *Contract*.

## CHAPTER 21

Clough, Richard H. 1986. *Construction Contracting*. 5th ed. New York: John Wiley and Sons.

Institute of Business Designers. 1981. *Forms and Documents Manual*. Chicago, Ill.: Institute of Business Designers.

Jones, Gerre. 1983. *How to Market Professional Design Services*. 2d ed. New York: McGraw-Hill Book Co.

Meier, Hans W. 1978. *Construction Specifications Handbook*. 2d ed. Englewood Cliffs, N.J.: Prentice-Hall, Inc.

Reznikoff, S. C. 1979. *Specifications for Commercial Interiors*. New York: Watson-Guptill Publications.

Rosen, Harold J. 1981. *Construction Specifications Writing*. 2d ed. New York: John Wiley and Sons.

Simmons, H. Leslie. 1985. *The Specifications Writer's Handbook*. New York: John Wiley and Sons.

Stasiowski, Frank. 1985. *Negotiating Higher Design Fees*. New York: Watson-Guptill Publications.

Sweet, Justin. 1985. *Legal Aspects of Architecture, Engineering, and the Construction Process*. 3d ed. St. Paul, Minn.: West Publishing Co.

Wakita, Osamu A. 1984. *The Professional Practice of Architectural Working Drawings*. New York: John Wiley and Sons.

Wakita, Osamu A., and Richard M. Linde. 1977. *The Professional Practice of Architectural Detailing*. New York: John Wiley and Sons.

## CHAPTER 22

Clarkson, Kenneth W., Roger LeRoy Miller, and Gaylord A. Jentz. 1983. *West's Business Law, Texts and Cases*. 2d ed. St. Paul, Minn.: West Publishing Co.

Jentz, Gaylord A., Kenneth W. Clarkson, and Roger LeRoy Miller. 1987. *West's Business Law—Alternate UCC Comprehensive Edition*. 3d ed. St. Paul, Minn.: West Publishing Co.

Quinn, Thomas M. 1978. *Uniform Commercial Code Commentary and Law Digest*. Boston, Mass.: Warren, Gorham and Lamont.

Reznikoff, S. C. 1979. *Specifications for Commercial Interiors*. New York: Watson-Guptill Publications.

Stone, Bradford. 1975. *Uniform Commercial Code in a Nutshell*. St. Paul, Minn.: West Publishing Co.

Sweet, Justin. 1985. *Legal Aspects of Architecture, Engineering, and the Construction Process*. 3d ed. St. Paul, Minn.: West Publishing Co.

### CHAPTER 23

Getz, Lowell. 1986. *Business Management in the Smaller Design Firm.* Newton, Mass.: Practice Management Associates, Ltd.

Jentz, Gaylord A., Kenneth W. Clarkson, and Roger LeRoy Miller. 1987. *West's Business Law—Alternate UCC Comprehensive Edition.* 3d ed. St. Paul, Minn.: West Publishing Co.

Loebelson, Andrew. 1983. *How to Profit in Contract Design.* New York: Interior Design Books.

Siegel, Harry, with Alan M. Siegel. 1982. *A Guide to Business Principles and Practices for Interior Designers.* Revised Edition. New York: Watson-Guptill Publications.

### CHAPTER 25

Ball, Victoria. 1982. *Opportunities in Interior Design.* Skokie, Ill.: VGM Career Horizons.

Loebelson, Andrew. 1983. *How to Profit in Contract Design.* New York: Interior Design Books.

McLain-Kark, Joan H., and Ruey-Er Tang. Fall 1986. Computer Usage and Attitudes Toward Computers in the Interior Design Field. *Journal of Interior Design Education and Research.* 12: 25–32.

Siegel, Harry, with Alan Siegel. 1982. *A Guide to Business Principles and Practices for Interior Designers.* Revised Edition. New York: Watson-Guptill Publications.

### CHAPTER 26

American Society of Interior Designers. April 1981. Preparing Your Portfolio. *Report.*

Angel, Juvenal L. 1980. *The Complete Résumé Book and Job-Getter's Guide.* New York: Pocket Books.

Bolles, Richard Nelson. 1987. *What Color Is Your Parachute?* 1987 ed. Berkley, Calif.: Ten Speed Press.

Catalyst Publications. 1980. *Marketing Yourself.* New York: Bantam Books.

Josefowitz, Natasha. 1980. *Paths to Power.* Reading, Mass.: Addison-Wesley Publishing Co.

Loebelson, Andrew. July 1987. The Second 100 Interior Design Giants of 1987. *Interior Design.*

Marquand, Ed. 1981. *How to Prepare Your Portfolio.* Revised Edition. New York: Art Direction Book Co.

Stoltenber, John. April 1987. The Eight Laws of the Jungle. *Working Woman.*

Wilson, Robert F., and Adele Lewis. 1983. *Better Résumés for Executives and Professionals.* Woodbury, N.Y.: Barron's Educational Series, Inc.

# INDEX